CONTENTS

For Leigh and Laurent
—and their Julie and Olivia
—and the reaffirmation of an old alliance.

Acknowledgments

I am greatly indebted to many persons who assisted me during the three years of research and writing which went into this book, but most particularly to:

my wife, who endured me, and who also served as an editorial tuning fork of unerring pitch; Richard Squires, for continuing encouragement and sound editorial advice; Charles Lee, Director of the South Carolina Archives, for guidance in pursuing several fresh avenues of approach; the efficient staff of the Library of Congress for sympathetic assistance in directing me to many important sources; North Callahan, Professor of History at New York University, for valuable professional advice; and Mrs. Jean Conaty, who typed the first draft of the manuscript and also proved to be a perceptive editor.

All battle maps included in this book are taken from *Battles of the American Revolution, 1775 - 1781* by Col. Henry B. Carrington, published by A.S. Barnes & Co., New York, 1876.

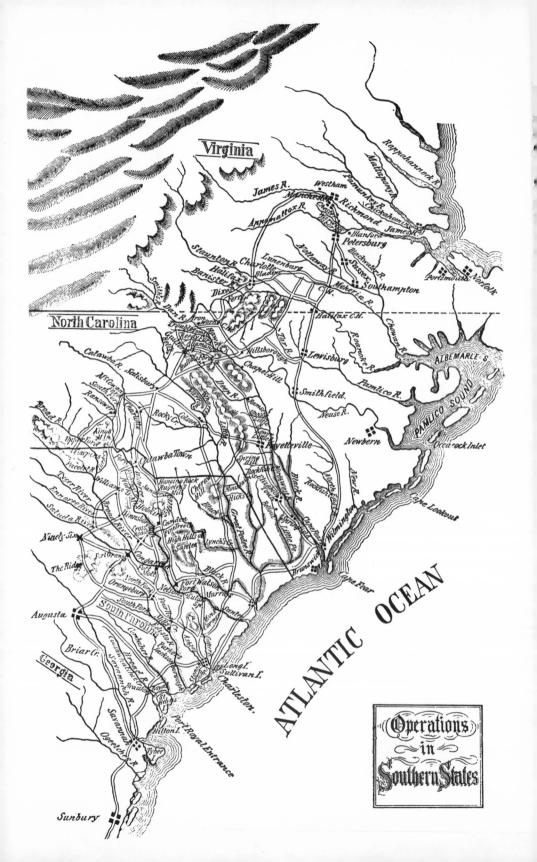

PREFACE

I N THE DRAMA OF THE AMERICAN REVOLUTION, THE FINAL, CRITICAL YEARS of war in the Southern Colonies are often perfunctorily dismissed in favor of the better-known earlier campaigns. Lexington, Bunker Hill, Quebec, White Plains, Trenton, Saratoga and Monmouth are familiar battles to most Americans, while King's Mountain, Cowpens and Eutaw Springs are at best obscure names from a forgotten history text. Most of us are aware that Britain eventually surrendered at Yorktown, Virginia, but how and why Lord Cornwallis went there is regarded as an elusive and not terribly important detail in the struggle for American independence.

This book is an effort to recast the battles and events commencing with the British drive southward in the winter of 1779-80 in simple chronology, and to trace Britain's ill-conceived Southern strategy from the victorious siege of Charleston to the disastrous defeat at Yorktown. How, within a period of 22 months, did British Commander Sir Henry Clinton's predictions of total victory end in total defeat?

In truth, the Revolution was won in the South. This in no way denigrates the bloody and often bigger battles fought elsewhere, but there is no denying the reality that Cornwallis, in trying to fan out from Charleston across the Carolinas and Virginia, was the victim of a phantom policy which led him inexorably, battle by battle, to his doom on a Virginia cape.

Sir Henry himself admitted in later years that the American victories at King's Mountain and Cowpens were "the first link of a chain of events that followed each other in rapid succession until they at last ended in the total loss of America."

In attempting to reconstruct the fighting from among the 137 battles or skirmishes of the Southern Campaign, the author has drawn on the lives and views of four principal protagonists: Lord Cornwallis, who commanded all British troops after Clinton returned to New York; 25-year-old Banastre Tarleton, Cornwallis' favorite cavalry commander; Nathanael Greene, who led the American forces after the defeat of Horatio Gates at Camden; and Daniel Morgan, the rugged Indian fighter who whipped the British in a stunning upset at Cowpens. The lives of these four men are inextricably tied to the culmination of the Revolution, and some knowledge of the character and development in combat of each is vital to the task of putting the major events in perspective.

To understand why Britain picked Charleston as the soft underbelly of Patriot resistance, one must first examine the Crown's grand strategy. All along, Britain's commanders considered the colonists to be vulnerable in three places—Charleston, New York and Philadelphia. There were many Loyalists in the Southern Colonies, and South Carolina particularly was considered potentially friendly territory. The colony had prospered within the Empire and appeared to be a happy, industrious and profitable place for an American to live. Rice and indigo were principal crops and, under the policy of mercantilism, the colony furnished key raw materials to Britain. In exchange, South Carolina was a ready market for Britain's finished products. The rice planters, with their slave labor, sold heavily to London and received premium prices. It was quite natural for Britain to consider South Carolina and its port of Charleston to be the very heart of Loyalism.

Of course, there had been an unpleasant business for the British back in 1776, before the Declaration of Independence, when the Americans drove off a British fleet which attempted to take Charleston. And that incident had been preceded by the unsuccessful uprising of some 1600 Loyalists under General Donald McDonald, who in early February marched with his contingent of North Carolinians against the port city of Wilmington. At Moore's Creek Bridge, on the approaches to the city, the Loyalists were met by about 1000 Patriots under Colonel Alexander Lillington. In a hail of artillery, rifle and shotgun fire, the Loyalists were driven off. In the counterattack by the Patriots which followed, more than half the Loyalists were killed or captured. But by 1779 there were all kinds of rationalizations for these little debacles. Most of all, the British reasoned, what was needed in the South in 1780 was a large army of regulars, ably commanded, as a focus of strength to draw Loyalist volunteers to the Crown's banners.

After all, it was long past time to Americanize the war, and there were more reasonable people in the Southern than in the Northern Colonies. As late as 1775, "good Southerners" had tried hard to negotiate grievances within the Empire. South Carolina's delegates to the Continental Congress voted against independence when it was first proposed. It was only after fighting broke out in Massachusetts that the colony supported the Declaration.

As late as 1778, James Simpson, the Royal Attorney General of South Carolina, had urged Britain to put more reliance on her Southern friends. In a letter to Lord George Sackville Germain, Secretary for the Colonies, he wrote:

> "I am of the opinion whenever the King's troops move to Carolina, they will be assisted by very considerable numbers of the inhabitants, that if the respectable force proposed moves thither early in the fall, the reduction of the country without risk of much opposition, will be the consequence, and I am not without sanguine expectations, that with proper conduct such a concurrence of many of the respectable inhabitants in the lower settlements may be procured that a due submission to His Majesty's Government will be established throughout the country."

It was a beguiling idea—getting the natives to do the fighting —but it is doubtful that the British would have turned southward in 1779-80 if the first two phases of their grand strategy had succeeded.

Phase one, sealing off the Hudson Valley by sending troops down from Canada and up from New York, had proved a costly draw.

Phase two, a drive from New York to capture Philadelphia, brought Britain a meaningless victory. Nothing better illustrated Britain's failure to understand the kind of fight she was in than the mistaken belief that capturing symbolic places and ground would cause the Americans to give up. From the outset, Britain waged a European-type war in a strange land whose people and terrain never had adapted to British-made rules. In Europe, a capital was the seat of government, the beating heart for a host of executive and administrative functions and a center of prestige. Philadelphia was no more vital to the American concept of independence than Hanoi is to Vietnam's. The Continental Congress could sit anywhere—or not at all. Independence for the Colonies was an idea whose time had come. Britain, unfortunately for her, stayed on long past that time, for reasons which appeared as sound in the eighteenth century as those arguments for staying in Vietnam put forward in recent years by four American Presidents.

Phase three, the drive south, was the last leg of a dead-end policy. It was based on the fantasy that King George and things British were truly loved by the majority of Southerners and that, if a big, dependable army were moving serenely through the Carolinas, the faithful would flock to join its ranks.

In the autumn and early winter of 1779, Clinton and Cornwallis mapped their strategy. It was to combine a show of strength with a propaganda-style battle for the minds and hearts of the Southerners. The combination of efficient ground forces and leniency to such wayward sons as had opposed the mother country was expected to bring "due submission" to His Majesty's forces. There is scant evidence that Britain ever gave adequate consideration to the zeal and determination of the Patriots. Conversely, the Crown's officers were late in recognizing that most other Americans were neutral and only wanted the war to go away. That left the Loyalists, whose allegiance often was a fragile thing. Despite all these elusive factors, Britain's top commanders clung stubbornly to the notion that they were never more than one big victory away from winning—if only the wretched Americans would stand up and fight!

As Cornwallis and Tarleton prepared to accompany Sir Henry and his forces by sea to Charleston, the men who would oppose them most determinedly in the South were comparatively idle. Greene, who had become one of Washington's most respected generals, had not been actively involved in any fighting during the early months of 1779. He spent winter quarters in New Jersey but, like a strategic chess piece which Washington held in reserve, was a knight ready for a slashing entry onto the Southern scene.

Greene was no stranger to Cornwallis, having run from him in 1776 at Fort Lee, north of New York. Sooner or later, Greene sensed, the Americans would have to stop running and face Cornwallis. Greene was a general who would do this only if he could choose the time and the terrain. And he was a general who, like Washington, understood that defeat in battle was meaningless as long as he kept intact a fighting core of resistance to the invaders. For all these reasons, Greene was the man to whom General Washington turned for his Southern command when disaster overtook Gates.

Colonel Daniel Morgan, at King's Ferry in Rockland County, New York, was a seething, embittered regimental commander in 1779, destined for early, although brief, retirement. He went home that summer after being passed over for promotion and spent his time sulking and corresponding with military friends.

The war was in Morgan's blood and he found the role of observer to be rankling. When news of the British strike at Charleston reached him, Morgan knew at the instinctive level that he would fight again. The fall of Charleston, Morgan was certain, signalled the reactivation of Britain's Southern strategy. Soon the Redcoats would fan out across the Carolinas and stand poised for a major drive across his beloved Virginia to the sea. That drive, Morgan promised himself, would be consummated only over his old bones.

As Christmas neared, Clinton prepared to leave New York with a force of some 6000 men for the big push on Charleston. This time it would be a massive invasion and, when Charleston fell, Sir Henry would turn the ground fighting over to Britain's ablest field officer, Lieutenant-General the Earl Charles Cornwallis.

The Earl, in the midst of a personal feud with Sir Henry, looked forward to an independent command with enthusiasm. There was even the possibility that he might succeed Clinton, who had offered to resign because he had not received adequate reinforcements. In any case, with the decision of command still hanging in the balance, the British put to sea on the day after Christmas, 1779, supported by Admiral Marriot Arbuthnot's warships. Destination: Charleston.

Much has been written of the severity of life on this voyage: how seven transports broke up in the ice before clearing New York harbor, how this led to uncomfortable and unsanitary crowding on the other ships, and how rough seas and coastal storms harrassed the troops.

No matter how rugged that voyage, however, it was nothing compared to the reception awaiting the British in South Carolina.

I
THE PROTAGONISTS

Cornwallis

DURING THAT MISERABLE VOYAGE SOUTH, GENERAL CORNWALLIS DREW solace from the fact that he was at least a better sailor than Sir Henry Clinton, whose discomfort was extreme. It was, nevertheless, faint consolation for the Earl, whose 41st birthday passed on New Year's Day. It must have been a melancholy one, for he continued to mourn the death of his wife, Jemima, which had come early in 1779. Cornwallis was a reserved man who put much store in personal loyalty, a quality he admired in others and often imputed to himself in letters and conversation. Strangely enough, the record shows he was at constant odds with his commanding officer, Sir Henry, and ultimately was destined to turn against his favorite subordinate and cavalry commander, Banastre Tarleton.

A case can be made that Cornwallis was sinned against in both relationships and hence was less guilty than either of the others. Sir Henry, downright psychotic in his belief that anyone who opposed him was perforce a conniving and potentially traitorous villain, must have been a difficult commander to support. Tarleton, a vain, self-serving bully who believed in pursuing and hacking up unarmed men rather than taking prisoners, was among the less attractive of Britain's field commanders. Yet Cornwallis, who outwardly dedicated his life to the army and made personal loyalty a fetish, was to become involved in outrageous disputes in his chain of command— disputes which continued for many years after the war ended.

The festering quarrel with Clinton stemmed from Cornwallis' support of Sir William Howe, Clinton's predecessor. On one most unloyal occasion, Cornwallis repeated to Howe derogatory remarks made about him by Clinton. This infuriated Clinton, who heard about it indirectly from Howe. Although the dispute was papered over, the subsequent relationship between Clinton and Cornwallis remained at best a wary one. Com-

Charles Cornwallis. From a mezzotint by I. Jones after the portrait by Daniel Gardner, 1793. (New York Public Library.)   **17**

pounding the problem on the voyage south was the uncertainty of London's decision as to who would ultimately command British forces in America. Clinton finessed that question by including Cornwallis, step by minute step, in all the plans for the coming siege of Charleston. If Clinton were to be relieved, he wanted to make certain that Cornwallis shared responsibility for whatever might go wrong. This alone was not an unusual policy for a field commander—then or now—but it was also part of a serious chess game between two master army politicians.

Had not Cornwallis' wife died, it is unlikely that he would have come back to the Colonial campaign at all. Clearly, he wanted no part of being Number Two in America, but his great grief at his wife's death drove him back to find forgetfulness in the consuming details of war. It is not hard to imagine that as the convoy bucked the high waves, His Lordship had ample time to review the brilliant career which now stood at a turning point.

From birth, Cornwallis had a valid claim to impeccable social position and potential wealth. His family could trace its origins back four centuries and the name itself points to Cornwall. No doubt a very distant ancestor set out for Suffolk to carve a new life, but the earliest recorded was a sheriff of London during Edward III's reign named Thomas Cornwallis. He established landed estates at Brome in Suffolk and gave the family its foothold there. Four hundred years later, there were still Cornwallises in Suffolk.

The general's father, Baron Charles Cornwallis, added to the family's standing by acquiring the titles of Viscount Brome and Earl Cornwallis. He also married well—to Elizabeth Townshend, daughter of Lord Townshend and niece of Sir Robert Walpole. A good marriage was a key ingredient in a society totally dominated by the aristocracy. Now, only the vast wealth was lacking and it was to remain for the eldest son of this union, Charles, to combine the longevity, ingenuity and talent which were requisites of material progress in England at the time. At 23, young Cornwallis succeeded his father as the second Earl. In America he would add lustre to the name, and with it would come great wealth.

Portraits show that Cornwallis had a weight problem. He had a large nose, a broad face and a square chin—with just the ripple of a second one curving into his collar. His hooded, rather reserved look was partly the result of an injury in a hockey game on the fabled playing fields of Eton. Cornwallis took a blow on the head from a hockey stick which lent one eye a peculiar cast. He was known to be sensitive about his appearance and to describe himself in later years as "rather corpulent."

Eton left other marks on Cornwallis. In an age when only the chosen few got any education at all, he got the best. At the same time, he was exposed to the stuffy, pervasive class distinction—and the savagery—which Eton fostered. Sons of the nobility brought along their own tutors and were often above the discipline of even the headmaster. They lived in the town, away from the petty tyranny of the campus.

It was expected at Eton that a young man learn to ride, to shoot and to accept or administer a thrashing. Latin was compulsory, not because of its practical value but rather because it set one off from the commoners. Cornwallis excelled in Latin and was an enthusiastic athlete, although there is scant record of his abilities in this latter area. Not even his family was surprised, however, when he decided that the rigorous army life was to be his career.

The army was low on pay and high on prestige, hardly an obvious choice for a well-born but not very wealthy young man; but undaunted, Cornwallis prevailed upon his father to purchase him a commission in the First Grenadier Guards. Many Englishmen of the period would have been content to politick at home and rise serenely in the service without ever hearing gunfire, but not Cornwallis. Instead, he was eager for combat which, happily for him, abounded at the time.

Britain and France were at each other's throats all over the world—in Europe, in India, on the high seas and in the American Colonies—and Cornwallis was eager to join his unit. First, however, he needed to equip himself for whatever ordeals might lie ahead. To Cornwallis that meant acquiring some military knowledge, an idea totally foreign to many aristocrats who bought commissions and learned tactics at the expense of their men.

In 1757, the young man again turned to his father, this time for permission to travel abroad. Accompanied by a traveling companion who had been a professional soldier, Cornwallis settled down at Turin, Italy, where he enrolled in the military academy, considered to be one of Europe's best. At the same time Cornwallis kept one eye, his good one, on the Grenadier Guards who were then at Hanover as part of an Anglo-German force under Prince Ferdinand of Brunswick.

The training was highly informal and Cornwallis' stay was brief, but his curriculum included mathematics and fortifications, techniques of drill, German and, lastly, ballroom dancing; together these made up the bizarre kit of the "professional" officer in eighteenth-century England.

After several months, Cornwallis decided he was ready to fight, but it required Royal permission to get a posting to Hanover. Against his better judgment, the harrassed first Earl once more interceded for his son, this time through a highly placed colleague who pleaded with the King himself. When this elicited a firmly negative response, Cornwallis set out to join his regiment anyway, audaciously disobeying a Royal order and hoping not to get caught.

His military career might have been nipped in the bud had it not been for the kindly assistance of the Marquis of Granby. When Cornwallis reached Hanover, the Grenadier Guards had been committed elsewhere and it remained for the Marquis to take the young man into his own command as an aide-de-camp. Cornwallis, not yet 20, then embarked on a long period of service in the Seven Years' War. He performed with some distinction and learned staff procedures during three years with Granby. By 1761, he was a lieutenant-colonel and regimental commander, and it is widely recorded that he fought and led his troops well, particularly at Kirch Donkern and Grebenstein in a war which made England the world's chief colonial power at the expense of France.

That Cornwallis emerged unhurt from the fighting is perhaps the result of his father's death in the summer of 1762, which brought the young officer home as the second Earl of Cornwallis. He was seated in the House of Lords and quickly began the transition from the problems of soldiering to the even more perplexing problems of peace and the management of his family estate.

Evidence indicates that the first Earl left his son a tidy income of about £3500 a year and a landed estate which badly wanted attention. As the new head of the family, it was Cornwallis' responsibility to look after the welfare of his brothers, arrange marriages for his sisters and furnish direction in all matters pertaining to the acquisition and development of rental lands in the Culford, Eye and Brome areas.

Beset with these problems, which surely seemed petty after the excitement of battle, Cornwallis nonetheless fulfilled his obligations and the estate prospered under his management. What is more, he somehow found the time to court and win his own Countess, Jemima Tullekin Jones, whose portrait by Sir Joshua Reynolds shows her to be a handsome woman with wide-set eyes, a long, graceful neck and a rather introspective look. Jemima was the daughter of a professional army officer, a regimental colonel, which automatically gave her respectability. But it was acknowledged that her social position was inferior to that of Cornwallis. This in no way deterred the Earl, who courted Jemima avidly and made her his wife in 1768. The modest size of Jemina's dowry and the little inheritance she received upon the death of her father both suggest that Cornwallis had no motive other than love in choosing her. They remained a happy and devoted couple during their relatively brief years together.

Curiously, the man who was to lead British troops in their last, frantic campaign in the American Colonies was steadfastly opposed to the war until it became a reality. In 1765 he voted against the Stamp Act, thereby aligning himself with a Parliamentary faction which saw itself as a bulwark against the flaunting of monarchical power. The next year Cornwallis was among the little group of five peers who opposed the Declaratory Act in which Parliament claimed the right to legislate for the Colonies in all matters.

Again Cornwallis' devotion to the principle of personal loyalty dominated his conduct. While he opposed the Crown in Parliament on various issues affecting Colonial policy, he quickly put aside that opposition when the war came. Cornwallis set stern standards for his own conduct and expected others to do the same. No one was surprised, least of all Countess Cornwallis, when the Earl was among the first of the titled leaders to make himself available for action in the New World.

Cornwallis saw plenty of action in the early years and had his first brush with General Nathanael Greene in 1776. After the British captured Fort Washington, Cornwallis was ordered to capture Fort Lee, some 10 miles north of New York City. Greene, already respected by the British as an elusive foe, commanded a garrison of about 4000 men.

The Earl, with about 4500 men, moved north of the fort, crossed the Hudson and then marched south, hoping to catch Greene by surprise. It might have worked had not a deserter warned Greene of the impending attack, giving the Americans a chance to slip from the British grasp. So precipitous was Greene's departure, however, that Cornwallis captured ample stores of materials which the fleeing Americans abandoned. It was to become a dismal and familiar pattern for Britain throughout the war; time and again they maneuvered for a position from which they might expect to administer a crushing defeat, and time and again the enemy melted away. Cornwallis himself was destined to spend much of his time chasing and failing to catch the elusive and not very combat-minded Americans.

At Trenton, the Earl may have lost the biggest single opportunity to end the Revolution with one mortal blow. On New Year's Day, 1777, he was commanding about 8000 British regulars at Princeton and was given the assignment of closing with Washington's troops a few miles away. Leaving covering forces at Princeton and Maidenhead, he proceeded with the main body—about 5000 in all—toward Washington, whose forces were numerically equal. Along the Princeton-Trenton Road, Washington's snipers took some of the fight out of the British while heavy rains turned the road into a bog. Frequently the advance guard had to fan out and take cover to avoid the snipers, who then retreated to new vantage points and waited for the enemy to resume its march. It was a long, tough day for Cornwallis and the British. At nightfall, instead of risking an attack with tired, hungry troops, Cornwallis bivouacked north of the village, deciding to "bag the fox" in the morning.

Washington helped foster the illusion that the fox was waiting to be bagged. He left a detachment of several hundred men to keep the campfires burning while he stealthily moved the main body of his troops around the British right flank. When the British awakened, Washington was enroute to Princeton, where his army fell upon Cornwallis' outmanned covering force and all but wiped it out. Later, Henry Clinton was to refer to this bit of Cornwallis' generalship as "the most consummate ignorance I ever heard of in any officer above a corporal."

Scant wonder, then, that Cornwallis and Clinton, seasick, in abrasively close quarters on the voyage south in 1780 with neither one knowing who was in charge, eyed each other like a pair of highly bred British bulldogs.

Greene

CORNWALLIS' AMERICAN OPPOSITE IN MUCH OF THE FIGHTING OF 1780-81 was to be a Rhode Island Quaker, Nathanael Greene. His upbringing, in contrast to the Earl's, was so drab and spartan that rising above it clearly required massive effort and talent. That he emerged as a great strategist of the Revolution made his accomplishment all the more remarkable.

Greene's family was a relatively old one in Rhode Island. He was born on July 27, 1742, at Potowomut, Rhode Island, to Nathanael and Molly Mott Greene, whose Colonial ancestry reached back four generations. By the stern standards of the day, the elder Nathanael Greene was fairly well-to-do—a thrifty, industrious Quaker preacher. He had a large, if somewhat rocky, farm with grist-, flour- and sawmills, orchards and pastures. Tilling the soil was hard work, something young Nathanael got acquainted with early in life.

By the time he was six, Nathanael learned that the path for Quakers was steep and rugged. He tended sheep, drove cows and cut and hauled wood for fires. Schooling opportunities for the boy were limited and frowned upon, but his pious father prospered. Eventually the elder Greene built an ironworks on his property, giving the family diversification of income—so much so that young Nathanael never wanted for food, clothing and other necessities as he was growing up.

What he thirsted for was intellectual stimulation because his formal education had been meagre. An itinerant tutor taught him to read, write and do simple sums, which, in the view of his Quaker father, was quite enough. Such minimal schooling gave the boy a feeling of inferiority which was reflected later in life when, in tribute to his father's piety, humaneness and industry, he let slip that he had been denied the type of education he had sought.

Nathanael Greene. From an oil portrait by Alonzo Chappel, circa 1784. (New York Public Library.)

Nathanael Greene was not to be denied knowledge, however, even if he were denied the university training which must have been his greatest early aspiration. When he was about 18, he met a voluble Yale student, William Giles. By then, Greene was man-of-all-work at the farm and forge, and still trying to break the shackles of Quaker innocence. He listened raptly to stories of Yale, and it was Giles who convinced Nathanael that he should undertake self-education through wide reading. From that day on, young Greene haunted the neighboring libraries and quickly acquired a reputation as a bookworm.

This quest for knowledge troubled Greene's father, who stuck to his Quaker principles (though he was reported to own a sedan chair and to tipple a bit, both thoroughly un-Quaker eccentricities). When taxed concerning his long hours with books, young Nathanael stood his ground. He was careful never to shirk his jobs at the forge and mill, and the elder Greene could never complain that his work was neglected. In his scant spare time, Nathanael read voraciously. Graduating from Fox's *Instruction for right Spelling and plain Directions for Reading and Writing true English*, Greene advanced to Barclay's *Apology*, Locke's *Essay on Human Understanding*, Jacob's *Law Dictionary* and Blackstone's *Commentaries*. The die was cast. Nathanael Greene's rugged path was to be adorned with learning.

There were other, equally important influences in the young Quaker's intellectual development. One was the Reverend Mr. Ezra Stiles, minister of the Second Congregational Church at Newport. Ezra Stiles was an intellectual, destined to become President of Yale. He took an interest in Nathanael, talked with and advised him, and generally provided him with much-needed inspiration to continue his independent study. There was also the law student, Lindley Murray, younger than Greene but the possessor of a quick mind and a keen ear for the English language. Murray kindled in Greene an interest in the law and a feeling for language and social graces—qualities which were to set Greene apart from many of the homespun American generals whose abilities were confined to the simpler soldierly virtues.

In his 20's, Nathanael may even have raised some doubts in his good father's mind concerning the Quaker age of innocence. He was to write this implicit criticism of his father: "Friends concluded that a Liberal Education was rather prejudicial than beneficial to Society. Not rightly discovering where the Evil lay, they argued from the abuse to the disuse of the thing." No doubt the elder Greene retained some reservations about the propriety of his son's quest for the written word, but there is no evidence to show that he offered any serious opposition.

In appearance, Greene was impressive. Perhaps the combination of hard physical work and his avid desire for an education gave him a maturity beyond his years. He was about five feet, ten inches tall, almost barrel-chested, with sandy hair which later darkened and then turned prematurely grey in his early 30's. His blue-grey eyes could become steel-hard when he was angered. His chin was solid, his complexion ruddy; he smiled easily and his manner was affable.

Like Cornwallis, Greene had a blemished eye, the result of a fever which followed a smallpox inoculation. He also suffered periodically from asthma, and had a slightly stiff right knee, an affliction which may have resulted from an injury at the forge. Apart from the fact that it gave him an unmilitary gait, the knee proved no great hindrance to Greene in the war.

In 1770, when Greene was 28, he was put in charge of his father's new forge at Coventry on the Pawtuxet River near East Greenwich, Rhode Island. There Nathanael built a well appointed, eight-room Georgian house and immediately established himself as a prize catch for the young ladies of the area. The few years before he went off to war were to see Nathanael cast aside his Quaker religion, marry outside the faith and almost literally use the forge to beat plowshares into swords.

His new home was called Spell Hall and frequent visitors included his brothers, his cousins and one David Howell, a tutor at the College of Rhode Island. Howell, who was to become a congressman and a judge, was impressed with Greene, especially when he found the youthful ironmaster bent over books by candlelight before and after others in the house had departed or sought their beds.

Nathanael Greene's stature in the community grew rapidly in these years. The forge employed many of the heads of households in the area and Greene was accepted in the best circles, yet he was still an ironmonger amid bankers and lawyers, a far cry from the rigid social structure in which Charles Cornwallis was reared. In 1770, confirmation of Greene's stature and ability to overcome obstacles came with his election to the Rhode Island General Assembly from Coventry.

For years Greene had been in love with Hannah Ward, the frail daughter of Samuel Ward who headed a loose coalition of southern Rhode Island politicians. Unfortunately for Greene,

Miss Ward was neither amused nor impressed by his ardent courting; she spurned him until she died in 1773 of the period's most pernicious disease, tuberculosis.

While Greene was involved in Colonial politics, he was swept up in one of the events which did much to fire him, as well as Rhode Island, with Revolutionary fervor, the *Gaspée* affair.

The *Gaspée*, a British revenue schooner, preyed on American ships in and around Narragansett Bay. Any ship violating the British Parliament's navigation and revenue laws (and most of them tried it) was summarily seized and escorted to Boston where its captain faced trial before an Admiralty court. The *Gaspée's* commander, one Lieutenant William Dudingston, was particularly offensive to Rhode Islanders because he pursued his quarry ashore, where his authority was at best disputable, to make arrests.

On June 9, 1772, the exploits of the *Gaspée* and Dudingston came to a timely end while New England got an issue which helped bring on the Revolution. The schooner, chasing a Rhode Island vessel, ran aground off Namquit Point, Warwick. A raiding party from the mainland set out after dark, exchanged gunfire with the *Gaspée*, wounded Dudingston, overpowered the crew, took them ashore and burned the hated vessel to the water line.

The British in Boston were burning, too. They offered £100 for information leading to the arrest of the guilty parties. A mulatto servant who had been with the raiders came forward to collect, but his story was negated by the testimony of pillars of the Colonial community (perjurous, no doubt, and protective of either themselves or their friends). As a result, the British were never able to bring the culprits to "justice"—but their bumbling was massively compounded when the Crown's commission, investigating the whole thing, heard an officer of the *Gaspée* name Nathanael Greene as one of the raiders!

Nathanael was as outraged as he was innocent. He had been visiting friends far from the scene and had viewed the smoldering remains of the *Gaspée* only the next day. This commission, Greene thundered, had alarming implications for every lover of liberty in the New World. He was vindicated, but that did not assuage the bitterness with which he viewed Britain's exploitation of the Colonies; very likely the false accusation did much to launch him on his military career and break with his Quaker heritage.

It was a time of turmoil for Greene in every respect. After the death of Hannah Ward, Greene commenced to favor a 19-year-old beauty, Catherine Littlefield, with his attentions. Catherine and Nathanael soon became a constant couple at parties, fairs and dances. Rumors abounded of a coming marriage. At the same time Greene was taking an active part in military drills at Plainfield, already convinced that a showdown with England might be in the offing. In August of 1773, Greene's soldiering, regarded as illicit in many quarters, became an issue at the monthly meeting of the East Greenwich Quakers. Was he or was he not taking part in military drills? The culprit was neither disposed to deny the charges nor to mend his ways. Accordingly, he was read out of the meeting until such time as he chose to return to the path of brotherhood. Nathanael Greene, American first and Quaker second, chose instead the brotherhood of arms and the path of revolution.

Little has been recorded of Greene's courtship, but it came at a troubled time in his life and it is clear that the vivacious Catherine helped restore his sense of humor, normally a delightful one. After a courtship of a few months, wickedly fast for the times, Catherine Littlefield became Mrs. Nathanael Greene at three in the afternoon of July 20, 1774. They were married by a Baptist, Elder John Gorton.

Of Catherine it is written that she was beautiful, high-spirited and fun-loving—and she was thirteen years younger than her husband. Prior to the marriage, Greene had been plagued by problems of the forge, the war and Rhode Island politics. Now he seemed to recapture his own high-spirited nature in his love for Catherine. The problems remained and grew more complicated, but Greene had strength to cope with them.

Although he was to remain devoted to Catherine until he died, he soon found that, like Cornwallis, the time he could spend in his wife's company was destined to be severely limited. Preparations for armed resistance to the British mushroomed with the onset of winter. Greene himself spent much time at the ironworks, where he daringly pigeonholed orders for ship anchors so that Colonial cannon could be forged. Early and late, and on weekends, he drilled with and helped organize the Kentish Guards, Rhode Island's crack fighting unit. Nathanael served the guards as a private, swallowing his hurt pride when the unit decided against making him an officer. This curious affront to a man of his stature has never been adequately explained. It was, however, to be an affront of short duration.

When the Rhode Island Assembly met three days after the Battle of Lexington and Concord, the burning issue was the raising of a force to supplement the hard-pressed Massachusetts troops. The assembly, cognizant of Private Greene's soldierly qualities, leadership potential and enthusiasm for the Patriot cause, designated him Brigadier General in command of the Army of Observation—three regiments with an overall strength of 1500 men.

Nathanael Greene, taking the quick vault from private to general without breaking stride, plunged immediately into the myriad tasks of recruiting, outfitting, provisioning and training his little army. It was here, under extreme pressure and not knowing how much time he had before the British were to move in force against his Massachusetts neighbors, that Greene's genius for organizing and improvising became apparent, not only in Rhode Island but throughout the New England Colonies.

It was Greene, too, who took the lead in voicing the unthinkable thought: that there must soon be a declaration of independence from Great Britain. Well into 1775, many Americans were persuaded that a show of strength might be sufficient to enable the Colonies to negotiate all differences with the mother country, and that concessions on both sides could avoid war. Greene indulged no such illusions. On December 12, 1775, at a dinner party with his close friend, James Varnum, and the prominent Quaker, Moses Brown, Greene spoke his piece. America, he said, must cut all ties with the Crown. The Quaker remonstrated with the young general, saying that every effort should be put forward to preserve unity and peace, but in a firm tone General Greene replied that he had abandoned his "hopes for peace."

Rhode Island was to become a leading colony in severing relations with Great Britain. In May of 1776, the legislature passed an act freeing its citizens from allegiance to the Crown. Greene's reaction was prompt and unswerving. Said he: "Nobly done. God prosper you and crown your endeavors with success."

Revolutionary fervor spread thereafter with stunning speed. In less than a month, the Pennsylvania radicals took over the assembly, forcing it to release its delegates from previous binding instructions to seek a peaceful solution. Richard Henry Lee, implementing the will of the Virginia Convention, gave the Continental Congress the resolution for the freedom and independence of the Colonies. After stormy debate, Thomas Jefferson's Declaration of Independence carried on July 4. There was to be no turning back; David was moving to face Goliath.

It was to be four long years and many grim battles later before Nathanael Greene's path led southward to the showdown with Charles Cornwallis. In the intervening time, Greene was to become one of George Washington's most competent and trusted generals. He fought at Trenton, Germantown, Monmouth and Newport. And he endured the winter trial with Washington at Valley Forge.

In taking command of the Southern armies in 1780, Greene knew he was moving from frying pan to fire—and that he was facing rugged opposition in Cornwallis. He knew, too, that the troops he was to command were tired, sick and ill-equipped. But above all, Nathanael Greene, by this time 38 years old, understood that this campaign must be decisive.

Tarleton

MAJOR BANASTRE TARLETON, JUST 25 WHEN HE SAILED SOUTH WITH Britain's army in the winter of 1779, had already captured the attention of his superiors and most particularly that of Lord Cornwallis. He was outranked by many of his colleagues, but none save Cornwallis himself was to see so much action and become the center of such a storm of contention as Tarleton.

This lusty adventurer was destined to raid in advance of Cornwallis' Southern troops, to be condemned for the cruel slaughter of unarmed men at Waxhaws, to fight brilliantly at Camden, to meet his match at Cowpens and to share with Cornwallis the bitter ending at Yorktown—the more bitter for Tarleton because of the disdain in which he was then held by American officers.

One of the seven children of John and Jane Parker Tarleton, Banastre was born at Liverpool, England, on August 21, 1754. He was the third child in a time before that spot in the sibling pecking order held any onus. On the contrary, Banastre displayed from the outset a sense of security and total self-confidence. John Tarleton, Senior, elected mayor of Liverpool when Banastre was 10, was popularly, even affectionately, known to his constituents as "Great T." Some sense of that greatness clearly permeated the character of young Banastre.

As a son of Mayor Tarleton, Banastre undoubtedly attended school in Liverpool; there is evidence that John Tarleton went to great lengths to provide sound education for his boys. Little, however, is recorded of Banastre's early school life. It is known that he was small for his age, but very solidly built, aggressive and active on the playing fields, intelligent and uncommonly strong. It is likely that he neglected his studies in favor of cricket, at which he gained a reputation as a batsman.

It is generally agreed that John Tarleton's fortune was

Banastre Tarleton. From a mezzotint by J.R. Smith after portrait by Sir Joshua Reynolds, 1782. (New York Public Library.)

amassed in the slave trade. His ships plied back and forth from the Tarleton plantations in Jamaica, Curaçao and several other large islands in the West Indies. He considered himself to be a seafaring man and his only known portrait shows him in the cabin of one of his ships. When he stood for Parliament in 1768, he was defeated and thereafter devoted his time to business and increasing the family's holdings. He purchased estates at Aigsburth and Bolesworth Castle. The latter of these, in the hands of his son John, who was a year younger than Banastre, became the hub of the family's life in later years.

Young Banastre and his older brother, Thomas, went up to Oxford in the autumn of 1771. Banastre, for reasons having little to do with his own inclinations, was pointed in the direction of a law degree at University College. The outstanding faculty there was to find, as did many persons over the years, that he was a difficult individual to motivate.

The young man had neither the ambition nor the temperament to succeed in a rigid program of study. He turned instead to the playing fields where his athletic ability gained him widespread recognition in riding, boxing, tennis and cricket. Others could hit the books; Banastre preferred hitting an adversary or galloping off on a spirited horse. Still, life was jovial, the companionship varied and he always seemed to do just enough academic work to survive.

Even as a very young man, he was not without wit and charm. It is recorded that on one occasion, during an intermission at Drury Lane Theatre, Banastre rose and with complete nonchalance leaned from his box to deliver a whimsical eulogy on a friend seated nearby. Shortly thereafter he departed Oxford, apparently with the consent and perhaps even the advice of the faculty. It was of scant concern to Banastre Tarleton. "Great T." had passed on, leaving him a fortune of some £5000; gay, wicked London beckoned.

He set himself up in his own quarters, ostensibly to read law in the Middle Temple, but as at Oxford he gravely neglected his studies in favor of gambling and wenching. In both of these, he found that the Cocoa Tree in St. James' Street was an admirable base of operations. This gaming club, the height of fashion with London's eighteenth-century elite, became Tarleton's favorite haunt and soon separated him from his fortune.

In gambling, as in the war to come, Tarleton was a plunger. When his money was gone, he took the course of action so often open to the well-born who suddenly became impoverished. As the London Chronicle described it: "Being of a lively disposition and rather involved in his circumstances, he had recourse to the army, as a profession in which, from his natural activity and courage, he would be sure of making his fortune or dying in the pursuit of it."

Young Tarleton took advantage of a rare opportunity for military service which turned up before he was 21. One John Trotter, as was the custom of the period, put up for sale his commission as Cornet in the elite First Regiment of the King's Dragoon Guards. Tarleton saw the commission as a way out of his financial difficulties. Cornet was the lowest of all commissions but purchase of the rank still cost £100 for each shilling of pay per day. Since a cornet's pay was eight shillings a day, Banastre had to come up with £800. In humility, he turned to his mother for the money and on April 20, 1775, the commission was secured. Unbeknown to Banastre, the events of the preceding day in the far-off Colony of Massachusetts were to have profound effects on his life. His name was first published as a commissioned officer in the *London Gazette* of May 2, under "military promotions." It was misspelled "Banestier," a mistake which would often be corrected as his fame burgeoned in the years ahead.

When word of Lexington and Concord reached London, it became clear that Britain would have to commit larger and larger forces to keep control of her rebellious Colonies. An inkling of how great the British effort was to be came with the departure of Major Generals William Howe, Henry Clinton and John Burgoyne for Boston in May of 1775. There were other portents; on June 22, General Charles Lee, who had fought in America under Braddock, created a minor sensation when he resigned from the British army, renounced his pension and joined the Patriots.

On October 17, the 16th Regiment of Light Dragoons was ordered to prepare for the long trip to America. On November 4, five regiments of infantry got their sailing orders. Their commander: Cornwallis. The muster rolls of the First Dragoon Guards for December 24, 1775, showed "absent by King's leave" as the entry after the name of Cornet Banastre Tarleton. In a characteristically impulsive gesture, he had volunteered for overseas duty under Cornwallis.

Banastre was not to go without fanfare. Prior to leaving for the port of embarkation at Portsmouth, the swashbuckling cornet, wearing the stylish uniform of the dragoon guards topped off by the tightly cut scarlet coat, paid a farewell visit to the Cocoa Tree. It is noted that somewhere along the way Tarleton had acquired an enormous sword which bumped along ominously as he strutted about the gaming rooms. At this juncture in his life Tarleton was described, and Sir Joshua Reynolds later confirmed in portrait, as a dark, slender, wire-hard soldier with piercing, deep-set eyes and a hawk-like beak of a nose. He also had the reputation of being a ladies' man, one which he enjoyed and was to embellish in America. This day, Tarleton, great clanking sword much in evidence, discussed the impending war in the Colonies with friends and habitués of the Cocoa Tree. When the conversation turned to the traitor of the year, General Charles Lee, Tarleton sprang to his feet, unleashed his sword and waved it in slashing circles, astonishing everyone within range of his voice with a shrill cry: "With this sword I'll cut off General Lee's head!"

Banastre Tarleton never precisely made good on that threat but he played an important role with the small force of dragoons which captured Lee in December of 1776. An excerpt from his letter to his mother, dated December 18, 1776, tastelessly describes this little skirmish as the "coup de main" which "put an end to the campaign." It was an early example of the exaggeration of his own accomplishments to which Tarleton was to become a hopeless addict during the Southern Campaign.

For a period thereafter, time seemed to drag for Cornet Tarleton. He wrote his mother again from Brunswick, New Jersey, in May of 1777: "Winter quarters in America are stupid and afford no description for the pen."

Nonetheless, subtle changes had begun to take place in the character of the American opposition. General George Washington's ragged army, routed time and again by Howe, had made an unbelievable crossing of the Delaware in a howling blizzard at Christmas of 1776, and smashed a contingent of drunken Hessians at Trenton. Slowly it dawned on the British that the American forces were no longer a joke. There remained, they reasoned, a bit of fighting to be done, and none among them craved action more than Banastre Tarleton.

He fought well at Philadelphia. Then, in an effort to capture Henry Lee who was holed up near Valley Forge in the Spread Eagle Tavern, Tarleton had a close brush with death. Anxious to capture or kill another Lee, Tarleton led the charge of a picked group of cavalry, but Light Horse Harry was more pugnacious than Charles; he returned the fire of the attackers and stood firm. The dragoons were routed and Tarleton was one of a handful who got away alive. His horse suffered three wounds, his helmet was literally shot off his head by one of Harry Lee's sharpshooters and buckshot penetrated his dragoon's jacket. Grimly, Tarleton and his comrades conceded that the hated rebels had begun to learn the soldier's trade.

After the skirmish with Lee, Tarleton's military life became too inactive to suit his tastes. Raids and ambushes were his specialty but the Americans were too elusive to be often engaged by such tactics. Still, life for Tarleton cannot have been as boring as he indicated to his mother. The record of the British army's activities in this period is replete with charges of "extravagant entertainment" and "sensualities" leveled by Loyalists and Patriots alike.

A Philadelphia newspaper in 1778 carried an advertisement placed by two British officers which stated: "Wanted to hire with two single gentlemen, *a young woman*, to act in the capacity of housekeeper, and who can occasionally put her hand to *anything*. Extravagant wages will be given, and no character required. Any young woman who chooses to offer, may be further informed at the bar of the City Tavern."

It was such naked proposals as this which prompted Benjamin Franklin to remark: "General Howe has not taken Philadelphia—Philadelphia has taken General Howe." And indeed the record shows that in six months of dissipation and inactivity, Howe's army grew soft, undisciplined and reluctant to return to the field.

Banastre Tarleton, however, was not a man to advertise for a bed mate or go stale in a barracks atmosphere. Already he was noted for what one historian called "a sanguinary and resentful temper, which made him unmerciful to his enemies." Though details are lacking, he reputedly pursued the ladies with the same avidity as he chased rebels, at the same time artfully angling for his next promotion. More than that, Tarleton had luck—a quality any commander needs to advance in protracted warfare.

When the British embarked for Charleston in 1779, the British Legion, largely a Loyalist cavalry force, was entrusted to the command of the 25-year-old Major Tarleton. It was one decision on which Clinton and Cornwallis apparently agreed.

For Tarleton, the greatest fame, and trials, still lay ahead. In South Carolina he was to acquire his dreaded reputation and ugly name: "Bloody" Tarleton.

Morgan

I T IS TYPICAL OF DANIEL MORGAN THAT HE LEFT NO EARLY TRACKS AS EASY to follow as those which lead the student of history along the life paths of Cornwallis, Greene and Tarleton. For this very reason, there are more unsubstantiated legends about Morgan and his prowess than are attached to the careers of the others.

Even his birthplace is in doubt. Most authorities say he was born in Hunterdon County, New Jersey, but Bucks County, Pennsylvania, also claims him. Neither community, however, offers much in the way of documentation for their contentions.

It is not surprising that no one can vouch for Morgan's exact birth date. At best, it narrows down to the winter of 1736. His parents were James and Eleanor Morgan, who came to America from Wales in 1720 and settled in Bucks County.

Historians report that Morgan's father, like Greene's, was an ironmaster and that he turned out cannon balls, grape and shot for the Patriot forces. Unfortunately, little more is known of Morgan's family life or early days, except that it seems certain he had no formal education.

He was said to have worked for his father splitting logs, clearing land and doing the myriad farm chores of the day. In any case, by 1753, when he was 17 or 18, young Daniel had had enough. Without a word he vanished from the family farm, making his way slowly south through Pennsylvania and supporting himself with odd jobs as he went along.

Spring found him in western Virginia, a burgeoning young giant, six feet, two inches tall, rawboned and ox-strong. He readily found employment clearing farm land, later superintended the operation of a sawmill and finally became a wagoner hauling supplies from Fredericksburg to outlying settlements.

Morgan grew up fast. Although he could barely read, write or do simple arithmetic, his prodigious strength, rugged visage

Daniel Morgan. Drawn by J. Herring from a sketch by John Trumbull, date unknown. (New York Public Library.)

and open manner made him a commanding and acceptable figure on the frontier.

Two shattering experiences in this period helped shape the life and philosophy of Daniel Morgan. The first came in 1755 when Morgan, then an experienced wagoner, signed on with General Edward Braddock's army, enroute to fight the French and Indians at remote Fort Duquesne.

It was an uncertain venture at best, with the Redcoats from England wending their way through strange and hostile terrain, constantly on the alert for attacks by Indians who were intent on removing their scalps. Morgan, carefree and bellicose by nature, brought up the rear of the supply train with his wagonload of British goods. The ambush they finally walked into was set on July 9 near the banks of the Monongahela River. It was a day of carnage—and a lesson not to be lost on Morgan.

In bright sunshine, Braddock's advance force under Lieutenant-Colonel Thomas Gage suddenly drew withering fire from 220 French regulars and Canadians plus about 650 Indians. What dismayed and terrified the British was the fact that not one of those deadly riflemen could be seen. They were all concealed in the forest, behind and in the closely spaced trees, or prone in the waving grass.

Braddock, who had the traditional European contempt for "savages" and guerrilla-type warfare, advanced his troops on line and ordered the fire returned blindly into the trees. The result, of course, was disastrous. The final casualty list showed that of Braddock's force of 1459, some 63 officers and 914 men were killed or wounded. Only the Virginians made a fight of it, seeking cover and returning fire from concealed positions.

That Braddock's proud troops broke and ran, losing more than 2/3 of their total strength, had a profound effect on Morgan. The Old Wagoner, as the British called him, behaved with great coolness and courage, helping to evacuate the wounded and placate the terrors of retreat. Morgan himself heard Braddock, mortally wounded, pronounce his own military benediction when he died on July 13 on the long road back: "We shall know better how to deal with them another time."

George Washington, who took charge of the burial, had the good sense to inter Braddock in ground which would be battened down by the remaining wagons as the retreat continued. It was the only way to disguise Braddock's grave and permit him to rest in peace. The Indians, intent on revenge, would undoubtedly have dug Braddock up and taken his scalp if they could have found him.

It was a solemn ride back across the rough trails for Daniel Morgan. It gave him time to contemplate the marked differences between the Indian and European linear styles of fighting. One can only speculate what must have been turning over in the mind of the Old Wagoner. It is unlikely that at this stage, his own status little better than that of a laborer, he harbored any ambition to command troops. But it is certain that were he ever to be involved again in Indian fighting, he would profit from the melancholy lesson of the Braddock debacle.

1758 turned out to be a landmark year in the French and Indian War. The British had begun to gain the upper hand. It was a trend which they wished to accelerate by augmenting their forces with the best young officers they could find—in some cases native Americans.

Morgan, who had become a renowned Indian fighter after the Braddock campaign, was natural material for a frontier commission. He had much to recommend him. On one earlier occasion, he had killed four Indians in four minutes with his rifle, knife and bare hands. Already he had the reputation of a man the militia would follow.

Several leading men in western Virginia suggested to Governor Robert Dinwiddie that Morgan be made a captain. That was too much for the economy-minded governor, even though it was conceded that Morgan had his own following and could perhaps muster volunteers to the British fold. At last, in compromise, Morgan was offered the commissioned post of ensign, lowest commissioned rank in the British army. He accepted.

It is ironic that Morgan at 22, untutored, unlettered and virtually a "foreigner" in Virginia among the British, became a commissioned officer. For Morgan, this was status. Being an ensign set him apart from the other frontiersmen. Even then Morgan, like Tarleton, began to steer an individualistic course, but his flamboyance was of another kind. The Old Wagoner, tempered by hard work and constant danger, had the common touch: he treated enlisted men as equals, which endeared him to them. His deeds spoke louder than words, for he had already done in his enemies with his bare hands. Banastre Tarleton's style was just the opposite: he preferred sword brandishing and loud declamation. But the two had one thing in common: either was ready to fight at the drop of a slur.

The second incident involving Indians which profoundly affected Morgan's life centered around a dispatch mission from Edward's Fort to the commander of the Colonial troops at Winchester. Morgan was accompanied by two enlisted men.

Enroute, it was necessary to pass a stone formation which projected over the edge of a flashing stream, in the vicinity of a settlement known as Hanging Rock. Morgan very nearly died there.

As the three men rode by in single file, they drew brisk fire from French and Indians who zeroed in on the Americans from covered positions above. The enlisted men were killed instantly. Morgan took a musket ball in the back of his neck. The left side of his neck bone was grazed and the ball emerged through his left cheek, taking a handful of teeth with it. It was a miracle that his jawbone was left intact.

Blood spurting from his face, so weak from shock he could hardly sit his saddle, Morgan grasped the neck of his horse, wheeled around and headed back toward Edward's Fort. An Indian pursued him, as Morgan later recounted it: "running open-mouthed, tomahawk in hand, expecting every moment to see his victim fall. But when the panting savage found the horse was fast leaving him behind, he threw his tomahawk without effect and abandoned his pursuit, with a yell of disappointment." Half-dead and clinging to his horse, Morgan reached the fort.

It was a ghastly wound; there was no way of telling how much blood Morgan had lost. Even with his rugged constitution, his recovery long teetered in the balance. Finally, after six inactive months, he was himself again.

Curiously, the man who went on to fight at Quebec, Saratoga and Cowpens was never to suffer a battle wound. A fraction of an inch in either direction on the part of one Indian's musket ball might have changed the whole course of American history.

This searing injury, which left Morgan's neck and face hideously scarred for life, seemed only an adornment to his physical prowess and mental serenity. He had a high forehead topped with a mass of thick dark hair. His scar was ominous, and one can believe it lent a rather formidable set to his face. Offsetting that scar was a full, almost placid mouth. It was an arresting face, one not often forgotten by friend or foe.

It was during this period that Morgan, proud of his massive frame and convinced that perhaps he led a charmed life, became the frontier brawler historians love to write about. At gambling, fist fighting and drinking, Morgan admitted having no peer. To all these activities he brought a lusty and at times profane enthusiasm.

The historical accounts of Morgan's brawling suggest that he might well have been the match for any heavyweight champion to come along in the next two centuries. He was clearly a young man endowed with excessive energy, a characteristic which kept him in the military service. The trouble at the time was simple enough: there just wasn't enough fighting going on. On Saturday afternoons, this lack of action drove Morgan and other young men of the neighborhood to a tavern operated by one Benjamin Berry, a man whose ideas about good, clean fun closely coincided with Daniel Morgan's.

Located between Winchester and the Shenandoah River, Berry's was a rough-hewn country place where a muttered oath or a fancied slur might at any time precipitate a boxing bout or a wrestling match. The backwoods imbibers invariably gathered around the competing gladiators, made bets and cheered for their favorites. The record is sparse, but it has been said that when peripheral fights broke out among the adherents of one contestant or another, proprietor Berry ducked behind his bar and the rafters shook with roaring brawls.

At this juncture, Morgan's men considered him to be the Berry King, but one powerful adversary remained unconvinced. He was Bill Davis, biggest and toughest of the four Davis brothers, who until Morgan's appearance had managed to dispose of all neighborhood opposition just by walking into the tavern and staring everybody down.

It was inevitable that Morgan should take on Bill Davis and one Saturday afternoon the match was set. Morgan arrived with his friends: so did Davis. After convivial drinks all around, the two young ruffians squared off. Historians have called it "a long and terrible fight." In all probability, after the punching, kneeing, biting and gouging, the two were down on the floor for the type of all-in mayhem common to the times. In any case, Morgan's dexterity won out. Davis was soundly beaten, and Daniel Morgan proclaimed champion of Berry's Tavern.

It was a defeat which festered in the chests of the Davis brothers. Bill Davis, in and out of his cups, swore revenge on Daniel Morgan, but wanted no part of another one-to-one confrontation. Rather he chose to press a visit on Berry's with his brothers and such other young men of a similar persuasion as he could round up. The Davis clan occupied the facilities, denying them to Morgan and his cohorts.

This was not the sort of challenge from which Daniel Morgan could turn away. The next weekend, he got his own fist slingers together and arrived early at Berry's, occupying the entire playground area. When the Davis gang showed up, no time was lost in getting down to the business at hand. It is difficult to conjure up memory of a gang fight in a frontier movie to equal the action which surely took place that Saturday at Berry's.

Morgan was everywhere, pounding, slashing, kicking and gouging. As one biographer put it: "His fist was generally the first and last argument to which he resorted, and if it did not fully convince those upon whom it was used, it had a persuasive power which few were disposed to deny."

Those who denied it that day were demolished, and for a long time thereafter the community around Berry's was known as "Battletown." Morgan deserves credit for giving the frontier outpost its interim name. Today, Battletown is the respectable town of Berryville, Virginia, and a thriving county seat.

In this period, Morgan was a fearsome figure. His face marred by the scar from the musket ball, his reputation as a barroom brawler unsurpassed, he was frequently brought into court on charges of assault and battery or disturbing the peace.

At the same time, his personal fortunes diminished to a new low. Morgan wrote to a Mr. Francis Triplett on May 25, 1769, with regard to a debt apparently owed the latter: "I should have been very glad to have settled it, if it lay in my power, but if it was to save my life, I could not have paid five pounds."

The biggest change in Daniel Morgan's life took place on March 30, 1773, when he married Abigail Curry. Like Morgan, Abigail seems to have had very little formal education, but she is described as a pretty girl with an alert mind. She was ambitious for her husband. Subtly, she drew him away from his roistering, rowdy friends and he somehow managed to buy a large, two-story house on a good piece of farm land which he nostalgically named "Soldier's Rest."

For a time—and if one can believe the record, for the rest of his life—Daniel Morgan was to be a good and industrious husband, totally devoted to Abigail. He cultivated his farm, added some livestock, acquired neighboring tracts of land and began to show considerable business acumen.

Much of the credit for this must go to Mrs. Morgan, who had a strong and wholesome influence on her husband. She helped him with his reading and writing and taught him much that he didn't know about arithmetic. Theirs was a love based on a good and expanding understanding. She bore him two daughters and instilled in him a desire to stay at "Soldier's Rest," even though his old hangout at Battletown was temptingly nearby.

Abigail could keep Daniel away from Berry's Tavern, but there was to be precious little "Soldier's Rest" for him. The handwriting on the wall for Morgan, as for Tarleton, was the fighting at Lexington on April 19, 1775. He was at home that spring with his family and the only violence left in him from the old days at Battletown was verbal. Morgan quietly offered to thrash anyone who had the poor taste and judgment to twit him about his reformation.

That Abigail was deeply religious and managed to pass such inclinations along to Morgan was still another remarkable step in the subtle kind of change he underwent. One can imagine, though, that the crisis at Lexington and the call to arms which it generated may have been received by Morgan with the same sort of exhilaration and relief which many American husbands have experienced in two centuries of going off to war. We know, for example, that Morgan's voice was among the first in Virginia to sound the call to arms when Frederick County officialdom named "Daniel Morgan, Esquire" to command a company of Virginians and lead them northward to the fighting fronts.

As Morgan was to learn from no lesser figure than the President of the Continental Congress himself, it was a highly nebulous assignment. John Hancock wrote him on June 22, 1775: "...You are therefore carefully and diligently to discharge the duty of captain, by doing and performing all manner of things thereunto belonging."

Among the "manner of things" which needed doing, none took a higher priority than mustering this first company of Virginians. It took Morgan just 10 days to assemble his riflemen—96 strong. Like their leader, the Virginians tended to be hardy, lean, tall and rawboned. The men wore buckskin trousers, leggings with fringes and thick, wide belts from which hung tomahawks and scalping knives. Hunting shirts of the time topped off the Virginia soldiers' uniform, and across the breast of each, as he started off for God alone knew where and how long, were the words: "Liberty or Death." These were men who had fought Indians hand to hand, and if the rumor preceded them that they were not averse to the idea of scalping a few of the Crown's own, all this could be regarded as a 1775-brand of psychological warfare.

It was in weaponry and tactics that the Virginians truly excelled. Each man was a rifleman par excellence. Most of them had been shooting since they learned to walk. As youths, they had been reprimanded at home if they brought back less squirrels than the number of bullets expended. They had also been expected to hit the squirrel in the head.

By aping the Indians, by insuring that his unit stood apart from all the others and by establishing an esprit based on pride and daring, Daniel Morgan, consciously or unconsciously, set up one of the American army's first "Special Forces." In just three weeks Morgan's raiders, mounted and spoiling for a fight, reached Cambridge, Massachusetts, a distance of about 600 miles. So well conditioned were they that not a man was lost by sickness or any other cause along the way.

As always, Morgan's crew was a mixed crowd. Besides Virginians, there were Scotch-Irish, Pennsylvania Dutch and other frontiersmen whose lineage was difficult to define or trace. Morgan is said to have been pleased with his "Dutchmen." "As for the fighting," he said, "the men of all races are pretty much alike. They fight as much as they find necessary and no more. But sir, for the grand, essential composition of a good soldier, give me the 'Dutchman'—he starves well."

Before long, the British outposts in the area commenced to feel the presence of Daniel Morgan's Virginians. No Redcoat was safe at 200 yards and British morning reports of the period were dotted with losses of officers, artillerymen and pickets— all knocked off at long range by the men with the long rifles. Soon the Virginians became known in British circles as the "widow-makers."

These events gave rise to towering legends. It was common, one story went, for Virginians to take target practice, shooting at a piece of paper the size of a dollar. One man fired for the center of the target. It was the duty of the second man to hit the same hole without enlarging it. In truth, ammunition was so scarce that the Virginians seldom if ever took target practice, unless the target happened to be the buttons of a British uniform.

The long, brutal march to Quebec, in which Morgan played a key role, is so well known and so detailed in accounting that few comments are needed here. Perhaps no group of American soldiers ever underwent greater exertion or hardship than did the contingents commanded by General Richard Montgomery and Colonel Benedict Arnold. Morgan, subordinate in command to Arnold, accompanied him and they suffered together in the audacious effort to wrest Quebec as a fourteenth colony from General Guy Carleton.

Had not the brave General Montgomery been killed, Morgan's company, which actually entered and fought in the city, might have been relieved. In such a case, Canada might well be part of the United States today.

The record shows that Morgan fought to the bitter end and even refused, despite threats of death, to surrender his sword. When his men pleaded with him to hand over his sword to the superior British force surrounding them and spare his own life, Morgan finessed it. Spotting a cleric in the crowd, he cried: "Are you a priest?"

"I am," responded the man.

"Then I give my sword to you," said Morgan. "No scoundrel of these cowards shall take it out of my hands."

Thus, Morgan, his great frame already beset by ills which the fording of freezing rivers and sleeping on frozen ground had earned him, went into captivity.

It was a time of respite for Morgan and the handful of his surviving Virginians. From the outset, Morgan was treated with the respect which British gentlemen traditionally offered a worthy and admired foe. But his hosts made one mistake. They sent an emissary to offer Morgan, only a captain then, a colonelcy in the British army.

Morgan replied: "I hope, sir, you will never insult me again in my present distressed and unfortunate situation, by making me offers which plainly imply that you think me a scoundrel."

After months of imprisonment, Daniel Morgan interceded with Britain's General Guy Carleton and won "parole" for himself and a number of his men. What this meant, in effect, was that a group of Patriots were released to sail back to the United States on a kind of scout's honor. They agreed not to rejoin the fray unless the British acquiesced, and then generally in exchange for the services of British prisoners of war similarly released. It was all very gentlemanly.

As soon as Morgan reached his native soil in New York, General George Washington, who had followed the Quebec campaign with considerable interest, befriended the Old Wagoner. He recommended that Congress acquiesce in the exchange of Morgan, that Morgan be promoted to the rank of colonel and that he be given command of a Virginia regiment.

Waiting impatiently for this development, which also had been given a salutary push by Benedict Arnold, Morgan returned to Abigail and his daughters at "Soldier's Rest." He hadn't long to wait. Before the end of 1776, Colonel Daniel Morgan was "exchanged" and back in the field, having raised with great difficulty a body of fighting men, once again from Virginia.

It was getting on toward the Battle of Saratoga, another encounter which, because of its fame and the preponderance of accountings, must receive scant attention here. For a timely appraisal of Morgan at this point in his career, one need only turn to Henry Belcher, an appreciative British writer:

"Daniel Morgan, that remarkable bushman and sharp-shooter, had collected and was the leading spirit of a body of marksmen, perhaps at that time without compare in any part of the world. Morgan's huge frame and stature, his handsome features, his rough yet kindly demeanor and the glamor attached to his earlier mysterious adventures on the Indian borders, made of him an ideal scout master in a war of surprises, guerrillas and snipers."

In the bloody fight at Saratoga, the performance of Morgan and his rangers helped carry the day. Even Horatio Gates, the American general in command, embraced him after the battle and said, "If you are not promoted immediately I will not serve another day." Still, when the official report of the battle was made by Gates, the name of Morgan was omitted.

There are differences of opinion among historians as to why Gates turned his back on Morgan at this juncture. Some say Gates approached Morgan, asked that he join in a palace guard revolt against George Washington, and that Morgan, by the bluntness of his refusal, alienated Gates. There is no denying the fact, however, that Saratoga was a critical defeat for Britain in the Colonies. It helped bring France into the war on the American side, an event which in the end tipped the balance at Yorktown.

Few persons more than Daniel Morgan and his sharpshooters deserve credit for the victory at Saratoga. For Gates, it was a final hour of glory—dubiously his. For Morgan, it was like a brilliant second-act curtain of a distinguished career in the long war for independence.

At times in the next two years, it may have seemed to Morgan and others that his military career was ended. After Saratoga, Morgan went through a period of relative inactivity. He was deeply offended that he was not given an infantry command, which went instead to Mad Anthony Wayne, and he confided in a friend: "The infantry are to go out in a day or two. It is said General Wayne is to have the command of it. When I see that confirmed, I face to the right about and start homewards, nor should anything induce me to continue except that my staying would save America from destruction...."

True to his resolve, Morgan drafted his letter of resignation on July 18, 1779. He was senior in age and service to Wayne and, in pique, he wrote: "I must conclude from what has happened that my country has no more occasion for me. I therefore beg leave to retire." In Philadelphia, Morgan handed his resignation to the Continental Congress. It was accepted and he returned to his family in Winchester, Virginia.

• But destiny was to try Morgan by fire yet another time. That final trial was to come on an open slope of a chilly January morning in South Carolina, looking down across the scrub pine and the gnarled oaks and the waving grass at Hannah's Cowpens.

II
THE LATE AFFAIR

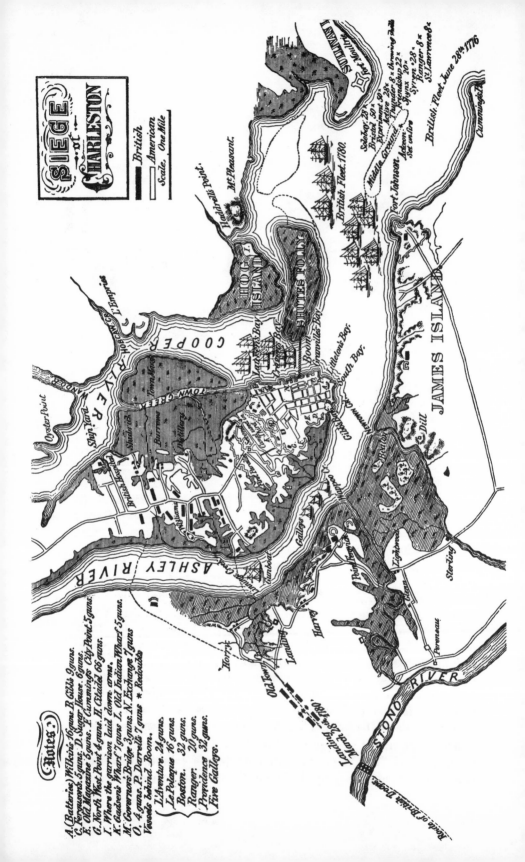

SIEGE of CHARLESTON

British
American
Scale. One Mile

Notes:
A. Batteries; Wilkins 16 guns; B. Gibb's 9 guns.
C. Kempwork 5 guns; D. Sugar House. 6 guns.
E. Old Magazine 5 guns; F. Cumming's City Point. 5 guns.
G. North West Point 4 guns; H. Citadel 66 guns.
I. Where the garrison laid down arms.
K. Gadsen's Wharf 7 guns; L. Old Indian Wharf 5 guns.
M. Governors Bridge 3 guns; N. Exchange 7 guns; * Redoubts
O. 4 guns; P. Darrell's 7 guns; * Redoubts
Vessels behind Boom.

L'Aventure. 24 guns.
Le Polique 16 guns.
Boston. 32 guns.
Ranger. 20 guns.
Providence 33 guns.
Five Galleys.

STONO INLET

Fort Moultrie

SULLIVANS ISLAND

Hadrell's Point.

Mt. Pleasant.

British Fleet. 1780.

HOG ISLAND

JAMES FORRY

Fort Johnson

JAMES ISLAND

COOPER RIVER

HOB CAW G.

L'Empris.

Oyster Point

Ship Yard

ASHLEY RIVER

British Hospital

STONO RIVER

Solebay. 28 x
Bristol. 50 x
Experiment.
Active. 28. 8 x during 32 x
Thunderbomb. 22 x
Acteon. 28 x
Syren. 28. 20 x
Syren. 28. 8 x
St. Lawrence x.
Cummings x.
Middle Ground
Set onfire

British Fleet. June 28th 1776.

Roads, or British Ships.

Charleston

THE ROUGH VOYAGE SOUTH OF MORE THAN A MONTH'S DURATION ENDED in early February, 1781, with the British fleet at rest in the Tybee River below Charleston.

Sir Henry Clinton, always a careful planner, consulted his maps and conferred with his commanders. Charleston, defended by some 5000 men under General Benjamin Lincoln, appeared ripe for the application of a classical European siege. The city lay at the end of a thin neck of land flanked by the Ashley River on the west and the Cooper River on the east. Charleston, Sir Henry reasoned—and Lord Cornwallis agreed— could be pounded to bits or starved out if the British controlled the two rivers and put a substantial force on the neck of land behind the city while the fleet prevented evacuation by sea. The single imponderable in this plan was a counterattack from the sea by a very large enemy fleet, but British intelligence assured Clinton that such relief was highly unlikely. Still, Sir Henry made his moves in cautious good order and determined that this time Charleston would not repel the invaders.

Although Clinton and Britain's naval commander, Admiral Arbuthnot, were something less than congenial, arrangements were made to secure extra guns and gunners from the naval vessels. Clinton then called for reinforcements from New York, the West Indies and Georgia. The admiral balked at the idea of risking his ships of the line by sailing them across the shallow bar outside the harbor, and it was not until March 20 that he allowed smaller vessels, lightened by the removal of guns and stores, to move in close. This put them under potential challenge from the guns of Fort Moultrie on Sullivan's Island, which had dealt the British harsh punishment four years earlier.

While Arbuthnot was getting his ships into position, Clinton's troops, which had been encamped on John's Island since February 14, moved slowly up the North Edisto Inlet toward Charleston. The army next began to use the ships which had crossed the bar to ferry troops across the Ashley River. Methodically, with everything going according to plan, Clinton broke ground for the siege works on April 1.

Until word could come from London, Clinton involved Cornwallis intimately in all of these moves. Not only was Sir Henry meticulous in preparing for siege, he was also concerned not to leave a personal flank exposed. The relationship between the two men remained proper, if a bit strained. By April 3, the first two-mile trench facing the city was complete. Now only the Cooper River remained to be shut, thus sealing Charleston off from the sea. Arbuthnot flatly refused to sail even light vessels up the Cooper. An unknown river, he argued with every right, was no place for the British navy. So Sir Henry detached a force of 1500 men from Cornwallis' own regiment, placed them under the command of Lieutenant-Colonel James Webster and ordered them to secure the upper reaches of the river.

It was Sir Henry's sly way of letting Cornwallis know who was in charge. That issue had been resolved some two weeks earlier when word arrived from Germain confirming Clinton's continued authority as commander-in-chief in the Colonies. It was a platitudinous communication, expressing satisfaction with Clinton's performance and at the same time lauding the abilities of Cornwallis. The unhappy commanders were still, to all appearances, working in tandem.

In actuality, Germain's message altered everything. Cornwallis who had been willing to cooperate in the siege plans when it appeared possible he might soon take command, now curtly withdrew, asking to be consulted no more.

To the hyper-suspicious Clinton, this looked like a revolt against his authority. He denied Cornwallis a separate command, giving it instead to Colonel Webster. He committed Cornwallis to the siege planning, ordering him to concur. He intimated that Cornwallis had agitated against him among the junior officers. Cornwallis heatedly denied all this, and at the same time accused Clinton of failing to enforce a standing order which directed officers with dual commissions in provincial and regular regiments to resign one or the other. Clinton countered by declaring that he had not had time to enforce the order. The situation at the top command became all but impossible.

It grew worse when Clinton was informed that Cornwallis maintained a friendly working relationship with Arbuthnot, while Clinton and the admiral were barely on speaking terms.

Now it appeared to Sir Henry that British forces in their entirety were in seething revolt against his command, including his chief subordinate, the naval commander and all the junior officers!

Clinton turned to his aide for advice on what to do with Cornwallis. The aide, Major John Andre, who probably understood that Clinton was carried away with his own suspicions, made a logical suggestion: send Cornwallis out to take over from Colonel Webster. Charleston could not long survive the siege and, once the city was safely in British hands, was it not Clinton's intention to leave the Earl in charge of ground operations in any case? This way, Cornwallis would already be in position to press the campaign into South Carolina when the city fell.

Suddenly, the idea of putting Cornwallis behind Charleston appealed to Clinton. He was quite sure Lincoln could not break through the siege lines, and even if he did mount a successful attack to the rear and break through Cornwallis, it could in no way rebound against Sir Henry.

Thus when reinforcements arrived from New York, Clinton summoned Cornwallis, gave him additional troops and sent him on his way on April 24. Clinton's instructions to the Earl: shut off the route of escape across the Cooper. Cornwallis left at once and did not return to the city until after it had fallen. This move enabled Clinton to report on the succession of events in the siege without any prominent mention of his subordinate.

Charleston never really had a chance. Cornwallis, although scarcely credited for it by Clinton, helped insure the ultimate success of the siege. He had no more than reached his command post before learning from Arbuthnot that the Americans had placed a heavy cannon on Mount Pleasant below Fort Moultrie and within range of the navy ships. There was a second gun position at Lampries Point, opposite the northern part of Charleston. Arbuthnot wanted both strong points cleared by Clinton before his ships entered the Cooper. Sir Henry replied that the army could not go after the strong points until the navy controlled the river.

In resolving this situation, Cornwallis acted on his own. He personally led a reconnaissance-in-force against Mount Pleasant in the early morning of April 26. The defending troops cut and ran; Cornwallis took the feared gun without even an exchange of fire.

The grateful Arbuthnot decided he could work with Cornwallis. The next night the admiral put 500 marines and sailors ashore at Lampries, which was also abandoned by the Patriot forces with scant opposition. This time the British took five cannon, and Cornwallis jubilantly sent Major Patrick Ferguson to take command. Lincoln was now cut off in Charleston with no communication in any direction by land or by sea, while Cornwallis had a death grip on the neck of land behind the city. His ambitious cavalry officer, Banastre Tarleton, had already routed Brigadier General Isaac Huger's forces at Monck's Corner. On May 2, Ferguson reduced a strong point on a bridge leading from Mount Pleasant to Sullivan's Island.

One last-gasp effort was made to relieve Lincoln's trapped forces. Colonel William Washington, trying to cross the Santee with a cavalry force near Lenud's Ferry, was intercepted by the eager Tarleton and routed on May 6.

Sir Henry prepared to collect his prize. With all escape hatches closed, he ordered a bombardment to begin. On May 9 and 10, Charleston took a frightful pounding from Britain's massed guns. General Lincoln, recognizing that he was powerless to spare the city from havoc and slaughter, surrendered on May 12, with Cornwallis very much in the wings. The Earl had pleaded with Clinton to put him in command of a storming party. Clinton had no intention of utilizing his subordinate and consistently ignored the requests. In the end, the city fell without a fight and Clinton could report that his plans—and his alone—had brought victory.

Blithe and confident, Sir Henry Clinton secured the British occupation of Charleston before returning north. Loyalists were formed into militia units and placed in Ferguson's command. Other detachments were sent out to pacify the back country. The local police were reorganized under new leadership. Cornwallis requested that he be given command of the Carolinas campaign and Sir Henry quickly acquiesced; it had been a foregone conclusion that the Earl would remain to take charge of the ground fighting, once the issue of the top command had been settled. Sir Henry was riding the crest of a popular wave in London and was bedazzled by prospects of early and total victory. He wrote a friend: "I am clear in opinion that the Carolinas have been conquered in Charleston."

Sir Henry had another compelling reason for hurrying back to New York. A widower, he had formed a liaison with his housekeeper, the daughter of an Irish country gentleman. What had begun as a casual romance had quickly become an affair of the heart and, despite the bothersome detail of the lady's husband, Sir Henry had become an ardent lover.

It had not been a matter of physical cohabitation. Mary Baddeley nee O'Callaghan had been carrying her carpenter-husband's child when first she met Sir Henry. After the birth of her child, Mary's sense of propriety had kept her out of Sir Henry's bed, and he was to write: "But though I am persuaded she had a great esteem for me, I never for many months could gain an inch, even though I could easily see her husband seemed rather to wish a certain degree of intimacy between us."

During the winter of 1777, Sir Henry pressed his suit successfully, and with greater luck than he normally found on the field of battle. As he described it in another letter: "Though she admitted me to certain liberties, I never could prevail upon her to grant me the last—until resentment did what opportunity and importunity and a warm attachment could not effect. She detected her husband in an intrigue with a common strumpet. She came to me directly, told him she would, and surrendered."

This was perhaps Sir Henry's finest hour in the Colonies. He was to remain in the company of his housekeeper until he died, a fate which fortuitously was forestalled some 15 years beyond the untimely passing of Mary's husband, who succumbed to a fever in 1780.

Earl Cornwallis was a little less certain than Clinton that all was well. He had, in all, about 4000 fighting men in the line. Later Clinton was to say he left the Earl with a force of 6000, but most authorities agree that this figure seems high, even counting those sick, wounded or otherwise engaged in Charleston. In any case, Clinton received more good news on June 5, 1780, just three days before he set sail for New York: Banastre Tarleton, two months short of being 26 years old, had driven his cavalry more than 100 miles in two days to overtake Colonel Abraham Buford's regiment of 350 Continentals at Waxhaws on May 29.

Buford had evacuated Camden in the face of the British advance and believed himself to be retreating in security toward North Carolina. Tarleton's men, driven mercilessly by their commander, overtook and all but surrounded Buford before he knew he was in danger. As usual, the impetuous Tarleton had left his mounted infantry far behind but he nevertheless immediately demanded of Buford a surrender on the same uncompromising terms the British exacted from General Lincoln at Charleston. Buford's reply was curt: "Sir, I reject your proposal and shall defend myself to the last extremity."

That extremity was not long in coming. Tarleton, who had used the conference period with the Americans to align his assault forces, at once mounted a furious cavalry charge. The

Continentals, still under the impression that their fate was being negotiated, were caught by surprise. The confusion was total as some Americans returned the fire, while others laid down their arms and begged for quarter. They got none from Tarleton. Unarmed men were cut to pieces by Tarleton's cavalry. The dead numbered 130. Another 150 were so severely wounded that they could not be evacuated. The prisoners taken by the Legion were just 53.

Of the attacking force, only five were killed and 15 wounded. The British captured all of Buford's artillery, ammunition and baggage, and Tarleton gained two distinctions: an unchallenged reputation for cruelty in the field and the sobriquet "Bloody," both of which dogged him to the end in America.

Cornwallis, who wasn't there and had only Tarleton's report to go on, assured Sir Henry that it was a glorious victory. Patriot survivors saw it differently, charging that Tarleton's troops had butchered unarmed men who were trying to surrender. In any case, the result contributed to Sir Henry's euphoria and sent him away more convinced than ever that the reduction and occupation of Charleston had for all intents and purposes finished off the Carolinas.

If Cornwallis had his doubts, as most historians seem to think, he was at least pleased and relieved with one development: after four years of serving someone else's plans and strategies, he was now on his own. Sir Henry's instructions to the Earl had made that clear. Cornwallis could attack or defend as he thought best, keep in touch with Clinton and operate independently to subjugate the Carolinas.

But the delusion which plagued the British to the end was still a prime factor in Clinton's plans. Clinton still believed that Cornwallis, moving northward, would be massively reinforced by the Loyalists and that sentiment in the South strongly favored a British victory. Conversely, Clinton also believed that if Cornwallis were to give the Patriots a few thrashings they would quickly defect to Britain's side. In this, Sir Henry—and Cornwallis, too—gravely underestimated the staying power and the will of the Americans who would soon face the Earl in the field.

The Earl's strategy, stated briefly, was to move north, subjugate South Carolina, recruit and enlist, move on into North Carolina, recruit and enlist, then drive across Virginia to the sea. Along the way, it would be necessary to close with and destroy Patriots who had the temerity to oppose the Crown.

Cornwallis, through no fault of his own, was slow in opening his campaign. He went back to Charleston after Sir Henry sailed and devoted himself to problems of supply and communication. Some regulars had to be posted in Charleston and his own second-in-command, Lord Francis Rawdon, an able young officer, needed reinforcing at Camden. Cornwallis also had to send good men to the outlying posts around Charleston in order to provide for the city's security. There were also the logistics of replenishing arms and uniforms for all his forces after the rough winter at sea and the spring siege, making plans for forage and supply and preparing for the drive north. In all, it took the Earl a month to deal with these tasks.

One problem he never solved: what to do with prisoners of war and with civilians devoted to the Patriot cause. He put some prisoners on the British ships outside Charleston where they died fast enough to alienate many other Americans. More were sent to the West Indies, either in British uniform or as deportees, where they would not have to fight their own countrymen. Unfortunately, there was no way to rehabilitate or "brainwash" a civilian to convert him to Loyalism. It was natural that Cornwallis, a military man, concluded that the only way to win the minds and hearts of the Americans was to escalate the war, and show that Britain had a preponderance of power and was willing to use it. This philosophy propelled him inevitably toward the clash with General Horatio Gates and his American forces in the battle for Camden.

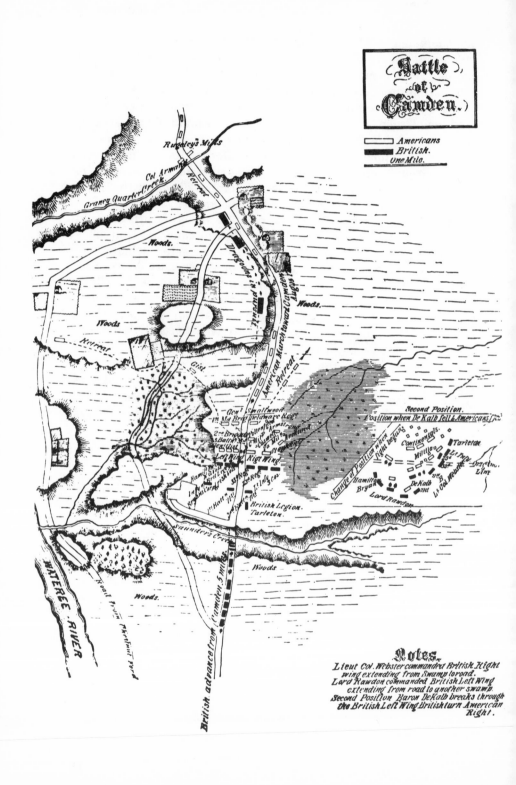

Camden

THE MAN CHOSEN BY THE AMERICAN CONGRESS TO DO SOMETHING about Cornwallis and his drive north from Charleston was British-born Horatio Gates, the "hero of Saratoga"—a title which was strongly disputed by some field-grade American officers in the battle, and has been questioned by historians ever since.

Gates was a hard man to read. His manner was reserved and his appearance intellectual. In 1780 he looked considerably older than his 52 years. From humble origins, he had progressed through the ranks, distinguishing himself more as a political infighter than as a warrior. He had served Britain in Europe, the West Indies and Ireland before retiring to the Virginia countryside in 1772. When Congress rapidly mustered its troops after Lexington and Concord, Gates's credentials looked better than most and he was made adjutant, a job which gave him a good base in the young army. Gates learned where the power levers were and advanced rapidly, sometimes through adroitness and sometimes, his detractors say, through manipulation and intrigue.

At Saratoga, Gates had praised Daniel Morgan and Benedict Arnold, but only to their faces. His enthusiasm for the role of his subordinates was considerably diluted when he faced upward in the chain of command, and as a result it was Horatio Gates alone who was lauded by the grateful Congress. In any case, Saratoga had been a major victory for the Americans and now it was up to Gates to repel the British invaders who were moving north from Charleston.

By August 13, Cornwallis had established himself in Camden, taking up residence, as was his aristocratic custom, in the best house in town, that of Joseph Kershaw, a flaming Patriot and a prominent merchant. His Lordship graciously allowed the wife and children of Kershaw to remain in residence, but Kershaw

59

himself was banished to Bermuda. It was Cornwallis' way of showing the local populace that he meant business.

The terrain around Camden, in Cornwallis' view, was appropriate to the British army's concept of fighting ground. Gone were the flatlands and the mosquito-ridden swamps of Charleston. This was a countryside of towering pines and undulating hills, well suited to Tarleton's cavalry and ideal for infantry maneuvering. The Earl was concerned with reports reaching him from Loyalist spies that Thomas Sumter, operating in his rear, was gaining strength and that a Patriot force under Gates was on its way toward Camden.

Cornwallis feared a trap. He wasn't sure how many men Sumter had and reports varied on Gates's overall strength. Still, the temptation to fight was great: the terrain was favorable, his men were in good spirits. It was a chance for a major engagement which, if successful, very likely would tilt local sentiment in Great Britain's favor. True, there were risks, and Cornwallis weighed them carefully. A defeat now could destroy much or all that had been gained in pacifying the countryside— but so could a retreat. Camden was an important symbol, a thriving city vital to the two contesting forces. Above all, it was to be a test of his own mettle, a battle from which he could not turn; it was to be the first major fight in which he alone would have full responsibility. Thus either defeat or retreat, leaving Camden in the hands of Gates and the Patriots, was unthinkable. Cornwallis would fight.

Serene in his decision, the Earl set out to learn all he could about his adversary and to prepare for the clash which by then was imminent. A Loyalist spy brazenly talked his way into Gates's headquarters at Rugeley's Mills on August 14, pretending to be a Maryland Patriot willing to spy for the Americans. Gates was taken in and while the spy did a nose count for Cornwallis, the hero of Saratoga promised his visitor rich rewards later. This marked the beginning of a series of blunders which, in their totality, served to obliterate Gates's military reputation.

The next day Cornwallis unleashed Tarleton, whose dragoons went far enough forward to capture three Americans. To save their necks they told all: that even then Gates was on the march, heading for Camden, and in his command were perhaps 6000 men.

On the surface, the odds seemed to favor the Americans. Cornwallis had only a third that number fit for duty—about 800 of his troops were hospitalized in Camden—but there again, not abandoning those sick British troops was a good reason for facing Gates. Besides, Cornwallis firmly believed—perhaps rightly —that his 800-plus regulars and similar number of provincials were among the best fighting men in the world. There was to be no turning back.

In truth, Gates had nowhere near 6000 men, nor did he know what his true strength was. He was short on cavalry and long on militia, only some 1400 of whom were Continental regulars—a bad mix to bring against Cornwallis. So haphazard had been his march and control procedures that he blundered into battle without any positive plan and with scant knowledge of either his enemy or the terrain.

Good officers like Baron Johann DeKalb and Adjutant Otho Williams must have been appalled as Gates prepared to take on Cornwallis. The Americans, on the march constantly for more than a month, were weak from undernourishment and disease. Major General DeKalb, a Bavarian-born soldier with titled pretentions, had been in charge until Gates arrived in late July to take command. Under Gates the forced marches became longer and more exhausting. Food, as usual, was scarce and the citizens largely indifferent to the Patriot cause. No matter, Gates was hell-bent for Camden where he hoped to take Lord Rawdon by surprise. He might have moved with less haste had he known that Cornwallis was on the scene with his veterans—waiting.

Williams and DeKalb could not prevail upon Gates to give the troops any rest, however, and as a result they neared Camden and starvation simultaneously in early August. Making matters worse was the presence in the area of the North Carolina militia. Knowing their own countryside, these men made the most of the available forage. As a result, Gates' troops reached Rugeley's Mills on the afternoon of August 15 almost too weak to stand up, let alone fight.

But the worst was yet to come. Gates, still ignorant of Cornwallis' presence, felt he had forces strong enough to whip Rawdon and take Camden. He ordered a night march on the city, preceded by a meal of "bread and fresh beef with a dessert of molasses mixed with mush or dumplings." The effect on the starved troops was disastrous, operating "so cathartically as to disorder very many of the men who were breaking ranks all night, and were certainly much debilitated before the action commenced in the morning."

It can only have been coincidence that Cornwallis left Camden for Rugeley's Mills at exactly the same hour as Gates began his march toward Camden—10:00 P.M. Early on the morning of

August 16, 1780, the advance guard of British Legion cavalry contacted a patrol of the American forces, exchanging a few wild shots with them and preventing the two armies from literally stumbling into one another in the dark.

When Cornwallis was informed that his enemy was at hand, he was pleased. He wanted no part of a night encounter but was satisfied with his position; swamps on either side of his main body protected it from enveloping movements. His Lordship called a halt and deployed his forces on both sides of the road, extending them in a long skirmish line to the edge of each swamp. Then he waited.

For Horatio Gates, an illusion was shattered. He had expected to sweep overpoweringly into Camden, routing Rawdon and his relatively few troops in short order. Now it was another situation entirely. The latest intelligence put the British force at 3000 men under the respected and feared Cornwallis, with the pathologically feared Tarleton thrown in for good measure. Gates might have retreated had not his subordinates, perhaps convinced that the troops simply could not move, urged him to stand and fight.

It was muggy and hazy as the sun rose. The British found their American enemy similarly strung out on both sides of the Camden Road. There were vital differences, however, which Cornwallis and Tarleton quickly noted. In the center of the American line and to the immediate left were the Virginia and North Carolina militias under Edward Stevens and Richard Caswell. Directly opposite, Cornwallis had posted his most seasoned regulars under Lieutenant-Colonel James Webster.

On the American right, Gates had placed his own best troops, the Continentals, under DeKalb. They faced some of Cornwallis' less esteemed forces, including the Loyalist militia under the command of Lord Rawdon. Thus each commander had, again coincidentally, arrayed strength against weakness, and it quickly shaped up as a battle to be won by the side that refrained from being overrun.

Had there been a premium on audacity, the Americans might have carried the day, for orders came down from Gates to Stevens: let the Virginia militia attack Cornwallis' seasoned veterans. Spurred on by Stevens, the Virginians advanced with bayonets ready, but when they got within 50 paces, the sight of the oncoming British professionals reduced them to panic and, as was so often the case, they made straight for the gum swamp to the rear.

On the British left, Rawdon's less experienced troops set

forth a withering fire which soon left the battlefield in acrid, clinging smoke. On the right, Webster wisely refused to chase the Virginians, and instead hit the exposed flank of the North Carolinians and quickly routed them.

That left DeKalb and the Continentals to face the full fury of Webster's men, bearing down on their left. DeKalb had twice repulsed Rawdon's charges but now the scales were weighted against him. Still, the issue remained in doubt until Cornwallis himself rode serenely among the Irish Volunteers, lauding and rallying them to the fight.

The Marylanders, from the reserve position, now struggled forward to help DeKalb, but it was too late. With the full power of the British, including Tarleton's dragoons, unleashed against his shattered forces, DeKalb might well have surrendered, but this was not his nature. Others around him fled but the brave Baron, almost alone, fought on. When his horse was slain, he continued to wield his sword. Stabbed from all sides, he finally went down, his body torn three times by musket balls. Some of his men trailed off into the swamps, but most of them died at Camden.

Mortally wounded, DeKalb lay on the battlefield too weak to be moved, and it was there that Cornwallis reined up to pay his respects, saying: "I am sorry, sir, to see you, not sorry that you are vanquished, but sorry to see you so badly wounded."

DeKalb must have been too weak to reply: he died three days later. His remains lie today in a Camden churchyard and there are no quotation marks around the word Baron on his monument. The field on which he died is remote and neglected, but Baron DeKalb, who proved his nobility of spirit there in 1780, lives on in the hearts of Camden's citizens.

Gates himself seems to have fled farther and faster than any of his men, putting nearly 200 miles between himself and the fighting before he stopped. Of this Nathanael Greene was to remark: "His retreat was equal to that of Xenophon but only a little more rapid." Rapid, too, was the demise of Gates's military stature. Camden was too much for George Washington and the Continental Congress to swallow, but Gates wasn't. Greene was soon to come south and take over Gates's command.

For Charles Cornwallis, Camden was a victory beyond expectation. The Earl's army had killed about 900 of the enemy and taken 1000 prisoners. They had taken all the American artillery and most of the baggage, wagons and military stores. Gates had fled in disgrace and the only American army in the Southern Colonies had been shattered.

As if that wasn't enough, Cornwallis detached Tarleton and the dragoons to pursue Sumter. On August 18, the hard-riding cavalry caught the Americans unaware at Fishing Creek and, as Tarleton described it, "totally destroyed or dispersed his detachment," killing 150 on the spot and taking 300 prisoners.

When news of the victories reached London, Cornwallis and Tarleton were the heroes of the hour. British arms had carried the day from Charleston to Camden. The provinces were quiet, the Patriot spirit quelled, the Americans routed. Surely, now the end was in sight. Surely, now British soldiers could soon return to their homeland.

Nadir

THE PATRIOT CAUSE AFTER THE BATTLE OF CAMDEN WAS DESPERATE. Gates's army was scattered and Americans of all persuasions were either bitter, disheartened or neutral. Food and forage were scarce, uniforms tattered or discarded. No home was safe from raids. Patriots slew Loyalists; Loyalists retaliated and called their vengeance a mark of "patriotism" in itself. Defection and treachery were accepted ways of life. Personal interests and personal loyalties underwent continuing, often agonizing, reassessment. Through it all on both sides ran the pervasive fear of sudden, ugly death at the hands of a supposedly friendly neighbor or from a marauding stranger, in uniform or out. If the whole dreadful charade had a name, it was survival.

Curiously, to those fighting for freedom the very word "rebel" was anathema. The most dedicated Patriots gloried in their rebellion but took offense at being labeled "rebels." They disowned "English" as their language and were likely to compliment a Frenchman with a good command of English for speaking "American" so well. In all, 1780 was an unsettling time for labels and values.

When battle action dwindled, as it did after Camden, the Revolution seemed to many to be a war of never-ending petty violence. Transportation was uncertain, and news of the sporadic and often isolated fighting traveled slowly. At Hillsborough, North Carolina, 200 miles from the scene of his disastrous defeat, Horatio Gates waited for stragglers to rejoin him. They came slowly, tattered and beaten in body and spirit. Under no circumstances could the several hundred Americans at Hillsborough be described as an army; an army no longer existed that summer. Thus for critical months the outcome of the war in the South, if not the entire nation, lay in the hearts and hands of the fabled Southern guerrillas, Francis Marion, Henry Lee,

Thomas Sumter and Andrew Pickens. These men, with their small groups of die-hard Patriots, lived in the swamps, sniped at the Redcoats, attacked baggage trains and harrassed patrols. They had grown up in a back-country society where political organization had been casual. Most were descendants of German, Scotch or Irish settlers, to whom such machinery as courts and legislative proceedings meant little. They had not been raised on London tradition and did not now aspire to be a part of it. By and large, they were not tea drinkers. It is remarkable that from this society men emerged to fight fanatically for such abstractions as the right of men to be taxed only by their elected representatives.

Preeminent among the Patriot guerrillas was Francis Marion, a mature and seasoned veteran of 48 by the time Camden fell. He had been fighting since 1775, having gone to war as a captain in South Carolina's first mustered regiment. Rising to the rank of colonel and the command of his own partisan regiment, the "Swamp Fox," as he was known to friend and foe, was a fearsome figure to the British. At times he commanded hundreds of men, including former black slaves as well as white Patriots. At other times his forces dwindled to only a few dozen. Marion deeply resented any efforts made by landowners to reclaim slaves from his partisans, and was often quoted as refusing to "suffer blacks to be removed from my brigade."

The evidence is meagre but it seems likely that Marion, who had little time for morning reports and the formalities of the military, thought even less of the South Carolina legislature's edict against slaves bearing arms. Many slaves went off to war with their **Southern** masters to serve as batmen, spies and men of all work. Throughout the war in the South, blacks built bridges, carried ammunition and endured equal hardships in the field with the white troops. In the partisan forces of Francis Marion, the color of a man's skin would never disqualify him in a fire fight. That he could shoot straight was all that counted. The legislature was not out in the swamps fighting the war.

Marion was a small, wiry man, hardy and even-tempered. He inspired an almost fanatical loyalty in his troops. When **South Carolina** made him a brigadier, it surprised no one that he decided to continue in command of his partisans. Loyalty in Francis Marion flowed downward as well as up. He was described as handsome, daring and brave, but at the same time cautious and always willing to retire when the odds dictated it. This was a quality which Generals Washington and Greene demanded in their subordinate commanders; with Marion it was a way of life.

He spoke seldom because his actions spoke for him. He did not drink. He was a strict disciplinarian and a great tactician; a man who struck the enemy as a lightning bolt, and as quickly disappeared. Unlike Tarleton, he was not known for inhumane acts to unarmed men, although his raiding tactics often put unarmed men at his mercy.

On August 20, Marion and 16 of his phantom horsemen fell upon a party of British and Tory troops escorting more than 150 American prisoners back to Charleston from Camden. Marion's men thundered in at daybreak making as much noise as possible, thereby suggesting that they were out in great strength. The British forces, caught by surprise, threw down their arms. The Americans could have wiped out the enemy, but Marion insisted that all be taken prisoner even though they outnumbered his attacking force. The American prisoners were freed and many made their way painfully back to Gates at Hillsborough. Ultimately, Marion exchanged his British prisoners for Americans of similar number and rank. Raids of this type, carried out with split-second timing and great verve, established Marion in the judgment of history as the greatest partisan leader in the Revolution.

Henry Lee, not often included among the Southern partisans because he commanded regular forces and fought extensively in the North, is recognized here because of his daring cavalry attacks which at times resembled the actions of Marion, Pickens and Sumter. He was a pugnacious and arrogant young man about Tarleton's age, and was sometimes given to rash statements and judgments. He was not offended by his nickname of "Light Horse Harry." On the contrary, he reveled in it and its implied image of hell-bent-for-leather daring. It was Light Horse Harry who won a daring victory over the British on August 19, 1779, at Paulus Hook (now part of Jersey City, New Jersey). In effect, this action ended the active military engagements of Washington's and Clinton's forces that year, and set the stage for the British drive south late in 1779.

Like so many of the "victories" in the Revolution, Paulus Hook had scant significance beyond the bag of prisoners and the always sought-after heartening of the troops. But at the time, with the country desperate to cheer for something, a cheer went up for Lee. The Congress voted him its thanks—and a gold medal. Now Lee's name was mentioned in the same breath with Anthony Wayne's. "Light Horse Harry" and "Mad Anthony" became household phrases, counter-curses to such fearsome words as "Bloody Tarleton." It goes without saying that Lee took south a military reputation that did not want for luster.

Thomas Sumter was in his 47th year when Lord Cornwallis began his drive to subjugate the South. He had been fighting for six years and had risen to the rank of brigadier in command of a special corps of irregulars. He was a man of large and rugged frame, imperious by nature and, like Lee, a daredevil who stood ready to risk much with audacious action. He, too, commanded troops ferociously loyal to him and his way of doing things. His discipline was casual and he relied on leading by example, eschewing whatever passed at the time for by-the-book regulations. Sumter's unwillingness to subject himself to another officer's command was a quality which he passed along to his troops. More than most, Sumter's outfit was a "special force." They did it their way—or not at all.

Sumter was considered to be less compassionate than Marion in the treatment of prisoners. Of him it is written: "...He was apt to make considerable allowances for a state of war....He did not occupy his mind with a critical examination of the equity of his measures, but indiscriminately pressed forward to his end—the destruction of the enemy and the liberation of his country." Henry Lee, in his memoirs, compared Sumter to "Ajax, relying more upon the fierceness of his courage than upon the results of unrelaxing vigilance and nicely adjusted combination."

At the very time of Gates's defeat at Camden, Sumter was having a small moment of glory. In command of a mixed force of 700 of his own partisans, plus Continentals and militia, Sumter made a whooping raid on a British wagon train on the Wateree, capturing 150 of the enemy along with 40 fully provisioned wagons.

Lack of the "unrelaxing vigilance" noted by Lee quickly undid Sumter's daring victory, however. At noon on the 18th of August, camped at Fishing Creek with their arms stacked, Sumter's forces were surprised by Tarleton's dragoons. Some of the Americans were sun bathing, some sleeping, some swimming in the creek. Tarleton fell upon them without mercy. His 160 dragoons killed 150 Americans, captured more than 300 and released all of the British and Loyalist prisoners. Had Sumter taken the trouble to post adequate security, he might well have defeated Tarleton, since he had a numerical edge of about four to one. As it was, the "Gamecock," as Sumter was known, barely made good his own escape and arrived in Charlotte two days later without his hat.

Andrew Pickens, like Marion and Sumter, entered the war as

a captain and advanced steadily to become a brigadier general
of militia in 1781 at age 43. He was humorless and taciturn,
deeply religious and an elder in the Presbyterian Church. He
had a long, craggy face, was lean of build and slow to anger.
The possessor of unusual strength and a rugged constitution, he
was said to have been able to go long hours without rest or
food. He lacked the flamboyance and the education of Lee, was
less dashing than Sumter, and not as well known as Marion. But
he had the reputation of being a good man to have around when
the going got rough. He, too, inspired great confidence in his
men and was particularly good at recruiting militia. Under the
loosely written Articles of Confederation, nobody could be
"drafted" and enlistments were often for brief periods, sometimes no more than three months. In practice, just about anybody could quit anytime he wanted, and a good many did.
When Camden flushed the summer soldiers, men like Andrew
Pickens kept resistance alive with their appeals to Southern
Patriots to join up and give it "one lick more."

Even the hardiest of the Patriots despaired at times, however.
Before the year was out, Henry Lee confided to Anthony Wayne
in a letter from his camp on the Pee Dee River: "The troops
are destitute of every article of clothing. Their only covering is
an old shirt and trousers. The whole are without shoes, nor can
any sort of manufacturing be established in this country, therefore our hides are useless to us. Our two regiments of horse are
reduced to half a regiment and illy supplied with accoutre-
ments. Our provisions are from hand to mouth. The present
camp affords good support of every kind; but when we are
forced from this, Heaven only knows how we are to employ our
teeth."

During the summer of 1780, an uneasy calm settled over the
Southern theatre of war. Major General Marquis de Chastellux
was to report his dismay at the business-as-usual atmosphere in
these words:

"The indolence and dissipation of the middling and lower classes
of white inhabitants are such as to give pain to every reflecting
mind....These landowners cleared only so much ground as their
slaves could effectively cultivate, yet would sell no parcel because
they hoped to acquire more slaves after the 'War for Independence.'

"Horse racing, cock-fighting and boxing matches are standing
amusements for which they neglect all business, and in the latter of
which they conduct themselves with a barbarity of their savage
neighbors.

"Free for all fighting, unless specially precluded, was the order of the day, which operations, when the first onset with fists is over, consists in fastening on the nose or ears of their adversaries with their teeth, seizing him by the genitals and dexterously scooping out an eye...

"The rage for dress among the women in America, in the very height of the miseries of war, was beyond all bounds; nor was it confined to the great towns. It prevailed equally on the seacoasts and in the woods and solitudes of the vast extent of the country, from Florida to New Hampshire...

"Mighty little, mighty few, mighty weak...are (expressions) much used."

Widely heard in the first days of autumn was the prediction that the Patriots could not last out the winter, that Britain's Southern strategy had at last begun to pay off and that Cornwallis was prepared to offer acceptable peace terms. To all these rumors, Patriot guerrillas, shivering in the swamps and back-country hideouts, turned deaf ears. It was a time of hanging on, of hoping for a miracle.

King's Mountain

A S THE SUMMER OF 1780 WORE ON CORNWALLIS, DESPITE THE BRITISH victories at Charleston and Camden, found himself facing a dilemma. He was not able to recruit the hordes of Loyalists the Crown had so confidently expected to join him in South Carolina. Soldiering in the South in the dead of summer, as future generations of Americans were to learn, is no fun and it was no different in Cornwallis' campaign. When Cornwallis sent out patrols, foragers or recruiting parties, there was always the fear that the hated partisans would fall upon them, inflict casualties and fade away. Illness, particularly fevers, dogged the ranks. Supply became a problem. Wherever he turned, he could see the result of attrition on his army. While Cornwallis pleaded for pacification, the American guerrillas stoked the fires of rebellion.

His Lordship retained the hope, however, that all might still be well. After all, there was no real army opposing him. Many rebels from the shattered army of Gates had taken on the protective coloration of neutrality. Some pledged allegiance to the King, some stole off to fight another day, while others never took up arms again. In this period of eerie tranquility, the British may have believed that, apart from the guerrillas, there was a new submissiveness in the South.

There remained, however, one curiously intact stronghold which had not been impressed by Cornwallis' victories. This was the region including northwestern South Carolina, western North Carolina and a segment of what today is eastern Tennessee. There in the Appalachian Mountains resided the tough, independent frontier people, mainly of Scotch-Irish descent. To them, the war against Britain had been dwarfed by the more immediate problem of protecting their homes and families from the Indians. From time to time, the "over-the-mountain" men fought skirmishes with the Loyalists, but to many the Revolution was a remote cause.

Cornwallis, worried about this indeterminate force of potentially hostile manpower on his flank, directed Major Patrick Ferguson to cross into North Carolina, snuff out Patriot opposition and recruit as many Loyalists as he could. The problem of the mountain men was still very much on Cornwallis' mind as he marched toward Charlotte in late September, but His Lordship was diverted there by the disquieting performance of one of his subordinate cavalrymen, Major George Hanger.

In Charleston, Hanger had caught Tarleton's eye. They shared similar interests and tastes and together had pursued the young ladies of the area with, if one can rely on their own accountings, no small degree of success. Hanger had already been passed over for promotion in the British army and was lately separated from His Majesty's forces. Fluent in German, Hanger came to America with a commission purchased in the German Jagers and the reputation of having deflowered British womanhood at indiscriminate levels.

Of his early life, Hanger confessed:

"I had a most decided preference for female society and passed as much time in the company of women as I have ever done since. A carpenter's wife was the first object of my early affections; nor can I express the nature of my obligations to her. Frequently have I risked breaking my neck in getting over the roof of my boarding house at night, to pass a few hours with some favorite grisette of Windsor. During the latter part of my time at Eton, to perfect my education, I became attached to, and was very much enamoured of, the daughter of a vendor of cabbages."

This was a style that appealed to Tarleton, of whom Horace Walpole reportedly said: "He has butchered more men and lain with more women than anybody else in the Army." Tarleton's old schoolmate, playwright Richard Brinsley Sheridan, came to Banastre's defense: "Lain with! What a weak expression! He should have said ravished. Rapes are the relaxations of murderers!"

In any case, with Tarleton abed with fever, Hanger was ordered to cautiously reconnoiter the approaches to Charlotte. The impetuous Hanger, trying to upstage Tarleton, instead led his cavalry on a charge into town, leaving the infantry to walk unsupported behind him. Colonel William Davie, a brave and resourceful officer, defended the city with a little band of 150 men and made Hanger and the British pay a high price for this bit of stupidity. Had not Cornwallis angrily come forward, taking over this rudimentary operation himself, far worse damage might have been done. As it was, the British suffered needless casualties, Hanger was wounded and Cornwallis left with no fit cavalry commander. Some authorities have argued that in all the Southern Campaign, he never did have one.

Once ensconced in Charlotte, Cornwallis again turned his attention to Ferguson. The Scot had been named by Clinton to take command of all Loyalist militia after the fall of Charleston and by now he led a force of well over 1000 men. At 36, he was ambitious, talented and impulsive. These qualities might have proved winning attributes in another man but in Ferguson they were subverted by fierce resentment of what he regarded as unfair treatment of him by the British army hierarchy. A case can be made for Ferguson's point of view. He was 10 years older than Tarleton and Rawdon and vastly more experienced, yet the latter two were more esteemed by Cornwallis and were given greater responsibilities.

In knowledge of weapons and tactics, perhaps not even Cornwallis excelled Ferguson. He had already invented a rifle which was superior to any Britain was to turn out in the eighteenth century, only to have the government inexplicably refuse to mass-produce it. Born of Scottish parents, he learned to ride and shoot at an early age, and at 14 he joined the Royal North British Dragoons with a cornetcy purchased by his father.

Ferguson was six years younger than Cornwallis but, like him, had fought in the Seven Years' War. He came to America a captain and quickly earned for himself a reputation for being both brilliant and erratic. Legend has it that in 1777 at Brandywine a senior American officer rode slowly past Ferguson's outpost at dusk, presenting an easy target for one of the British army's finest marksmen. Ferguson let him pass, refusing to shoot the officer in the back. The officer, according to some of Ferguson's colleagues, was George Washington.

The relationship between Cornwallis and Ferguson was correct but cool. Ferguson's enthusiasm for and confidence in the Loyalist militia was not shared by his chief. Nor did Cornwallis think Ferguson to be particularly suited emotionally to command. Cornwallis also sensed in Ferguson a certain impatience, a desire to plunge ahead rather than move cautiously.

Ferguson's impatience was understandable. His rapid-fire rifle had been rejected for no good reason. He had received but a single promotion in four years. Now he regarded his post as head of all Loyalist militia as a kind of independent command and he was anxious to cut loose and make his name. Cornwallis of all people should have understood and sympathized with this desire; it was curiously similar to his own feelings after years of playing a secondary role to Clinton and Howe. But Cornwallis appeared neither to like nor trust Ferguson—one more example of the Earl's inability to get along with his commanders above or below him. This particular example was to contribute to a debacle of major proportions.

As Ferguson and his Loyalists moved into North Carolina to recruit more troops, reports reached him of violence done by over-the-mountain Patriots to Loyalist and British forces. Following earlier examples of Cornwallis and Rawdon, Ferguson decided to send the mountain men a measured threat. He paroled a prisoner, one Samuel Phillips, and dispatched him to Colonel Isaac Shelby, commander of Patriot militia in Sullivan County, North Carolina. Ferguson warned Shelby and the mountaineers that "he would march his army over the mountains, hang their leaders and lay their country waste with fire and sword, if they did not desist from their opposition to the British arms."

Suiting action to word, Ferguson pursued a Patriot raiding party to the very slopes of the Blue Ridge Mountains before returning to his base at Gilbert Town on September 23. The mountain men were on notice.

Back in the headwater country of the Watauga, Holston and Nolichucky rivers, Ferguson's threats quickly began to rankle. Why wait, the mountaineers asked, until the Loyalists come after us? Instead, why not go after them? In the eye-for-an-eye code of the hills, this made abundant sense. Not unlike the Indians around them, the mountain men raised their own war cry and called for the assembling of volunteers at Sycamore Shoals, near the present-day site of Elizabethton, Tennessee.

On September 25, about 1000 men came together, intent on catching and finishing off Ferguson and his Loyalists. It was a motley crew. Many wore buckskin, breeches and gaiters of home-dyed cloth, wide-brimmed hats and long hair tied at the back in queues. Each had a knapsack, blanket and long rifle. Some were on foot, others on horseback. Sycamore Shoals had the air of a revival meeting picnic about it. Many of the men had brought their wives and children to see them off on this dangerous mission to the other side of the mountains. On the eve of their departure, the Reverend Samuel Doak, a pioneer Scotch-Irish clergyman, addressed the mountaineers. In ringing rhetoric, he likened their mission to the Biblical rise of Gideon's people against the Midianites and predicted, as in Gideon's cause, total victory. "The sword of the Lord," thundered the Reverend Mr. Doak, "and of Gideon!" It became the battle cry for this quickly formed, rough-hewn little army.

On September 26, the mountain men began a five-day march which was to carry them to Quaker Meadows on the Catawba. A few days later, they would join with South Carolina Patriots at Cowpens, South Carolina, now the staging area for the battle to be fought at King's Mountain and later a famous battlefield in itself.

The early stages of the march were the hardest because the mountaineers followed obscure Indian trails over rugged terrain. But each group was fiercely loyal to its own leader, and the leaders themselves were men of iron.

There were men such as Joseph McDowell, a well-born Virginian who had forsaken the easy life for the wilds of the Piedmont; Benjamin Cleveland, another Virginian who had moved west and acquired an exalted reputation as an Indian fighter; and James Williams, a long-time Tory-hater who was a delegate to the provincial legislature of South Carolina. Others included William Chronicle, a veteran of the 1780 skirmishes and a resident of the south fork of the Catawba; Joseph Winston, a leather-tough frontiersman who had been fighting Indians since he was 17; and Edward Lacey who ran away from his Pennsylvania home at 13 to fight with Braddock in the Indian campaigns.

Isaac Shelby, another leader, looked fat but he was agile, and no man to threaten, as Ferguson would shortly learn. In addition, Shelby would become the first governor of Kentucky just as his colleague, John Sevier, would become Tennessee's first governor. Finally there was William Campbell, a large-framed man, six feet, six inches tall, who had raised one of the first Patriot militia companies in Virginia and whose wife was a sister of Patrick Henry. In solemn council, the mountain men chose Campbell as their commander-in-chief, but it was clearly understood that when the fight began, each of the clan leaders would play a distinctly personal role.

Patrick Ferguson had reasonably good intelligence on the movements of the mountain men. As early as September 27 he marched south, sensing danger and being reluctant to fight until he had more precise information on the numerical strength of his enemy. Ferguson at this stage was not so sure that the men trailing him were the "backwater plunderers" he once called them. Hoping to confuse his pursuers, he made a feint toward the British and Loyalist stronghold at Ninety-Six, so-called because it was 96 miles from the nearest settlement at Fort George. On October 2, he crossed the Little Broad River and sent word to Cornwallis that if he were not greatly outnumbered he would stand and fight. With what trepidation Cornwallis must have received that message. If the Loyalists under Ferguson couldn't whip backwoods militia, it would be a fateful day for Britain and the whole philosophy of getting the Americans to do the fighting.

On October 6, Ferguson wrote that he had taken his position on King's Mountain, "a post where I do not think I can be forced by a stronger enemy than that against us." Supremely confident to the point of foolhardiness and lusting for recognition, Ferguson made the decision to fight without consulting Cornwallis, who was only 35 miles away in Charlotte. Inexplicably, Cornwallis did nothing to reinforce Ferguson. Instead he sent messages urging Ferguson not to fight but to join him in Charlotte.

As soon as the mountain men learned that Ferguson had gone into a defensive position, they moved forward to close with him. King's Mountain Ridge, where the battle took place, extends some 600 yards in a northeasterly direction and is a small segment of the 16-mile-long King's Mountain Range. The summit of the ridge, stony and exposed, stood about 60 feet above the countryside surrounding it and varied in width from 60 to 120 feet. The trees thinned out near the crest.

Ferguson no doubt felt he held commanding ground with his 1104 men. Many had been with Ferguson since the fall of Charleston; they respected him personally and had confidence in his military expertise. The mountain men, however, saw it another way. From concealed positions behind trees and brush of the valley, the sharpshooters had a clear view of Ferguson's men at the crest.

When scouts came back with this description of the enemy's position, the mountaineers called a halt about a mile from the ridge. Horses were hitched and final instructions were given the men. Each detachment was to form in two-column lines and proceed quietly on foot to given positions at the base of the ridge, in effect encircling Ferguson and the Loyalists. On the right flank were posted detachments under Major Winston, Colonel Sevier and Major McDowell—with Winston's forces making up the point. In the center were columns commanded by Colonels Campbell and Shelby. Heading the column on the left were

Major Chronicle and his men, followed by Colonels Cleveland and Williams. As the march began, Major Winston was detached with a small group of men to make a big right-hook movement, closing off Ferguson's most logical line of retreat. From the outset, the over-the-mountain men were thinking of doing to the Loyalists what Ferguson had threatened to do to them: wiping them out.

The attackers moved with professional skill to their pre-assigned positions. Seeking cover as they advanced through the wooded ravines, the Patriots surrounded their quarry. Campbell and McDowell passed through the gap at the southwest of the ridge, taking positions on the southeastern and eastern slopes. Sevier's men formed along the western slope and Shelby took his position to the northwest. At the same time, other Patriot detachments formed at the bottom of the ravine which led around the northern and northeastern base of the ridge.

Patrick Ferguson's command post was near the northeastern section of the ridge but he had a picket line all along the crest. By midafternoon on October 7, as the Patriots below locked him in, Ferguson must have felt some nagging doubts about his position. When the pickets commenced firing, he did nothing to deter them.

It remained for Campbell and Shelby to open the battle proper. Exhorting their men up the hill with Indian-like war whoops, these Patriots fired their flintlock pieces and charged. Here Ferguson and his defenders enjoyed a clear advantage: they had bayonets; the mountain men didn't. At close quarters, there was nothing for the Patriots to do but give ground, running back down the hill. It was to be a contest between the dead-eye mountain marksmen picking off the visible enemy, and Ferguson's well-trained Loyalists who had learned their relish of cold steel from him.

Retreating back down the mountain, the Patriots rallied at the foot, reformed, fired and charged up the hill again. Attacks and counterattacks raged all around Ferguson. It was as if a dozen battles were taking place all at once and the casualties were heavy on both sides.

It soon dawned on the defenders that something desperate was happening to their position. It was shrinking. Each charge by the mountain men in effect drove the Loyalists together on the crest, into an ever diminishing pocket. The defenders seldom saw the enemy until they charged into view near the tree line and fired. The Loyalists then counterattacked with bayonets and the Patriots fled for the thickets to reload.

A 16-year-old boy with one attacking party told why the Loyalists were ineffective: "Their great elevation above us had proved their ruin; they overshot us altogether, scarce touching a man except those on horseback." When those few Patriots on horses saw what was happening, they quite logically dismounted and took cover.

Ferguson's bayonets took a heavy toll, but each countercharge and subsequent retreat by the Loyalists exposed them further to the deadly marksmanship of the mountaineers who picked them off in droves. In less than an hour, some of the defenders began to run out of ammunition and to give way, but there was no place to go. As a result, the pocket on the crest kept shrinking, and the shrinkage provided better and more concentrated targets for the Patriots.

Out of ammunition, beaten and dazed, the Loyalists were ready to surrender. But not Ferguson. This warrior's reputation and career were at stake. In a desperate effort to break out of the trap he had entered so freely and shouting, "Huzza, brave boys, the day is our own," Patrick Ferguson, on horseback and followed by a handful of Loyalists, charged directly down the southeastern slope hacking at any and all who stood in his way. Patriot eyes and Patriot guns were on him. In a veritable hail of fire, Ferguson fell. It is recorded that "seven rifle balls had passed through his body, both his arms were broken and his hat and clothing were literally shot to pieces."

The day was indeed Ferguson's own; his last. His body lies today a short way down that southeastern slope at King's Mountain, his grave marked by a simple stone, a cairn, and an inscription attesting to the noble qualities of Major Patrick Ferguson—a Scot who died a long way from home.

After Ferguson fell, Captain Abraham DePeyster surrendered to save the surviving Loyalists from the slaughter. Many of them would have been better off dead.

The victory of the mountaineers was complete and crushing. Many authorities consider the rout of the Loyalists at King's Mountain to be the real turning point of the Revolution. Never again would the British be able to make a large-scale recruiting drive in the South. Part of the reason for the inhibited recruiting was the vengeance taken on the Loyalists by the over-the-mountain men.

Cries of "Tarleton's Quarter" echoed over the battlefield after the Loyalists surrendered and many were shot after the order was given to cease fire. The dead lay in heaps on all sides. With no place to go and no place to hide, the defenders of

King's Mountain stood like "a herd of deer in a corral" and were slaughtered.

In a way, they were the lucky ones. The wounded were carted to a glen a few miles from the battlefield, dumped on the ground and left to die without food, blankets or competent attendants. Nearly every defender was either killed, wounded or captured while the Patriots, virtually untrained in formal warfare, suffered the comparably miniscule loss of 28 dead and 62 wounded.

There were to be further trials for the Loyalist prisoners. On October 8, they were herded toward Gilbert Town in a two-day forced march without food or water. The mountaineers constantly threatened to kill their prisoners in event of Loyalist or British attack. On the third day, the mountain men divided up their prisoners' baggage. By October 13, the grisly column had reached Bickerstaff's Plantation in the vicinity of Rutherfordton, North Carolina.

The victors were clearly intent on avenging atrocities against their own forces by commiting a few of their own. A drumhead court sat in judgment on the cowed and starving prisoners and selected nine men for execution. On the night of October 14, the nine were hanged from a giant oak by the eerie light of torches before a captive audience of their horrified comrades.

On the next day, the prisoners were kicked awake before dawn and forced to march without food for 30 miles over a quagmire road. When a Loyalist fell, he was either trod upon or slain. It was a minor miracle that several hundred prisoners were tough enough to survive Patriot brutality and reach Bethabara near Salem on October 24. Along the way at least a hundred managed to escape. Eventually, many other Loyalists escaped as their captors lost interest and went back to their mountains. As winter neared, only about 125 Loyalist prisoners remained and these were marched off to confinement at Hillsborough.

Although Nathanael Greene was to express his deep disappointment at the melting away of Loyalist prisoners, it may have served the Patriot cause to have those unfortunate and brutalized men return to their homes. It is hard to imagine that any Loyalist participant in the Battle of King's Mountain could muster sentiment toward the British or the Patriots beyond a devout wish for a plague on both their houses. In the eyes of their own countrymen, the Loyalists were traitors and villains; in the eyes of Lord Cornwallis, they were dastardly and pusillanimous. Truely, these were now men without a country, men who had fought bravely for what they believed to be right. Theirs was the damnation which afflicts the losers.

At Charlotte Cornwallis received sporadic word of the King's Mountain fighting. What had been a rout became a holocaust in the retelling. Ferguson was dead; his army had ceased to exist. These were the chilling facts, and there were more. Every effort to raise militia to fight for Britain had failed. Marion was running wild, burning houses and bringing violence to areas heretofore considered secure and pacified. Even Ninety-Six, the British bastion, feared trouble. From Camden came word that the garrison was short of flour. Worse, the news from King's Mountain had broken the morale of the Loyalists, who whispered among themselves that one could expect no help from the British when the going got tough.

In Charlotte, the presence of Cornwallis and his veteran troops had done nothing to encourage enlistment. Former Loyalists backed away from the British and became neutralists, or joined the Patriots. The regulars and provincials in Cornwallis' crack units came down with fevers and the garrison lacked medical facilities to cope. The Earl himself was stricken. The situation was not hopeless, the British reasoned, only because their enemy faced many of the same problems as well as some special ones of its own.

Cowpens—Prelude

WHAT I HAVE BEEN DREADING HAS COME TO PASS."
Those were the words of Nathanael Greene to his
wife when, on October 14, 1780, George Washington asked the
Rhode Islander to take command of all American troops in the
South. It had been a long, hard war for Greene and now the pros-
pect of taking over the job Gates had bungled and nobody else
wanted was a bleak one. But there was no way to say no to
Washington.

The more Greene studied his problems, the more impossible
they appeared. Cornwallis was getting reinforcements at a time
when he already enjoyed numerical superiority over the Americans. With Baron von Steuben, his inspector general, Greene
went to Philadelphia and conferred with the Congress, quartermaster agents and department heads. There were all kinds of
supply problems because the Patriots were short on uniforms,
weapons, blankets and shoes. Greene pleaded eloquently for
support, arguing that if the Carolinas could not be saved, Virginia was doomed, too. Enroute to Charlotte, which Cornwallis
had evacuated after King's Mountain in favor of Winnsboro to
shorten his line of communications with Rawdon, Greene made
additional stops in Maryland and Virginia to seek aid for the
tattered Southern forces. That Greene was nowhere impressed
with his reception was reflected when he wrote: "They all promised fair but I fear will do little; ability is wanting with some,
and inclination with others."

On December 3, Greene formally took command of the
Southern Department from Gates—and in such a way as to put
the elder man at ease. First, Greene quashed a congressional
effort to hold a board of inquiry into Gates's conduct at the Battle of Camden. Brusquely, Greene dismissed this bit of mid-war
vengeance, arguing that vital witnesses were either in captivity
or too busy to testify. Next, Greene wrote an intimate, friendly

letter to Francis Marion. The Rhode Islander had never fought with the Swamp Fox but he had done his homework on Marion and knew him to be an indefatigable leader and a vital cog in the South at a time when Greene needed to devote every moment to reorganizing the American will to resist. Marion with his slashing raids would become invaluable to Greene as the prime source of intelligence on enemy strength; Greene told Marion he was depending on him for that function.

On reaching Charlotte, Greene spent some time with Daniel Morgan who had been "ordered" back into combat by the Congress in June. The Congress, however, refused at first to promote Morgan to general so Morgan declined to obey the order.

After the Camden debacle, Morgan had a change of heart and hastened to Hillsborough, where he joined Gates in late September. On October 2, the Old Wagoner took command of a newly formed corps of light infantry and on the 13th Congress belatedly promoted him to brigadier general.

If there was any feeling on Greene's part that he was dealing with a man of lesser intellectual stature, he never revealed it. On the contrary, Greene's orders to Morgan showed a disarming deference, and Greene himself was later to copy Morgan's unorthodox tactics. He looked upon Morgan as a man who might do something constructive with the militia. A back-room brawler and frontiersman, Greene reasoned, might be just the man to mix the militia with the Continentals and make them work and fight together.

Greene had less than 2000 men fit for duty. Cornwallis had perhaps twice as many active troops and more on the way. Throwing aside the book, Greene decided to split his forces and thus pose threats to the British in several directions. His orders to Morgan read:

"Sir: You are appointed to the command of a corps of light infantry, a detachment of militia and Lt. Colonel William Washington's regiment of light dragoons. With these troops you will proceed to the west side of the Catawba River, where you will be joined by a body of volunteer militia under the command of Brigadier General Davidson of that state, lately under the command of Brigadier General Sumter.

"This force and such others as may join you from Georgia you will employ against the enemy...either offensively or defensively as your own prudence and discretion may direct, acting with caution and avoiding surprises by every possible precaution. For the present I give you the entire command in that quarter, and do hereby require all officers and soldiers engaged in the American cause to be subject to your orders and command. The object of this detachment is to give protection to that part of the country and spirit up the people...."

Spiriting up the troops and those loyal to the Patriot cause was a good trick in that bleak December. Torrential rains were falling and all rivers were swollen, many out of their banks. But just before Christmas the weather cleared and Greene's strategy jelled. Morgan was to take off with about 600 men, ferry across the Catawba and keep moving, directed solely by his "prudence and discretion." Greene, with less than 1400 troops, would push north to Cheraw Hill.

For the two American commanders and their weakened, underclad and often homesick men, the approaching Yule season could only be melancholy. The December rains had reduced the trails to quagmires and rendered travel of any kind extremely difficult. Morgan's old ailments assailed him again and it is copiously recorded that every stride of his horse sent rheumatic pains through his lean, leathery body. Still, on Christmas Day, Morgan's raiders bedded down on the Pacolet River in the northwestern part of South Carolina. The Old Wagoner had brought his men about 60 miles in four days. That was scarcely a record but, as Morgan himself explained it, there had been "deep swamps and very steep hills which rendered our march very unpleasant."

Most sources agree that the movements of Greene and Morgan thoroughly befuddled Cornwallis. Possessing about a two-to-one superiority in manpower and a considerable edge in combat experience, Cornwallis found it difficult to understand what his enemy was trying to do. Their divided forces that Christmas were some 140 miles apart, Morgan on the Pacolet and Greene in north-central South Carolina. Cornwallis was in between at Winnsboro—and transfixed.

Had Cornwallis but known, keeping him on the horns of a dilemma was precisely the effect Greene hoped to achieve. The division of Greene's army posed threats toward Ninety-Six, which the British vowed to hold at all costs, and toward Camden. Greene obviously hoped that these potential dangers would confuse Cornwallis and keep him pinned at Winnsboro, uncertain of which way to jump.

For a while at least, it worked. Cornwallis was reluctant to engage either Greene or Morgan until Tarleton was in fighting condition. Since early December, Tarleton and his dragoons had rested near the Broad River at Woodward's Lowland Plantation. The rains, which had so hampered the movements of the Americans, had not been friendly to the British either. Tarleton's raids had been curtailed and he himself recovered slowly from a persistent fever. By Christmas, however, Tarleton was chafing for action, and for a promotion which he felt to be long overdue. After all, he had chased, fought and defeated the wretched Americans all the way from Goose Creek to the Pacolet. Now if he could close with and destroy Morgan, Tarleton's fame, burgeoning in Britain, would know no bounds.

Morgan, too, was restive; a lesser man might have been nervous. His intelligence reports on Tarleton's movements were spotty, and Tarleton, who could cover prodigious distances with his dragoons and take an encampment by surprise, was the commander Morgan feared most. The Old Wagoner was under no illusion about his military position. He knew he could count on his Maryland and Delaware Continentals and some of his experienced riflemen. In all, they numbered about 520 men. He also respected Colonel William Washington and the approximately 80 light dragoons he commanded. But Tarleton, Morgan knew, had a larger force, more cavalry and very likely some field pieces which could deal wholesale destruction if brought into sudden play from a point of vantage.

As it developed, Morgan was soon too busy to indulge his fears. Two days after pitching the Pacolet camp, one of Morgan's spies rode in to report that a contingent of Georgia Loyalists, 250 strong, was shooting up Patriot patrols and civilians of Patriot persuasion to the south. Morgan conferred with William Washington, then sent the cavalry and about 200 mounted militia on a Tarleton-like raid.

Most of the militia were from the Carolinas; they rode off with great determination, fired up by Morgan to avenge the rapes of their womenfolk and the violence done their unarmed collaborators. After a hard, 40-mile ride, Washington's force burst upon the Loyalists at Hammond's Store, not far from Ninety-Six. In one of the fiercest small engagements of the Southern Campaign, 150 Loyalists were slain and another 40 captured. The rest of the Tories fled in confusion while Washington sped back to the Pacolet without losing a man.

This trial by fire for the raw militia went a long way toward raising Patriot morale but Morgan was well aware that such an event could not long escape the attention of Cornwallis and Tarleton. Fearing a sudden reprisal, Morgan remained convinced that he still lacked the strength to confront either man.

and he wrote to Greene: "Were we to advance and be constrained to retreat, the consequence would be very disagreeable." He added: "Could a diversion be made in my favor by the main army, I should wish to march into Georgia....Packsaddles ought to be provided, let our movements be what they may...It is incompatible with the nature of light troops to be encumbered with baggage."

Clearly, Morgan wished to avoid any major engagement until he could muster a force at least as large as Tarleton's. Nor could he be certain that Tarleton, persuasive in his dealings with Cornwallis, might not be massively reinforced at any time. Above all, Morgan's overriding fear was that he might be caught between Tarleton's mounted dragoons and Cornwallis' main force. In such a situation, the Americans would be outnumbered at least four to one, and heavily outgunned.

Further complicating life for Morgan and Greene was the chilling news that Britain's General Alexander Leslie had arrived in Charleston with a Redcoat force estimated at 2000. The scales had tipped dramatically in favor of Britain but Greene refused to panic. Instead he argued patiently with Morgan against a retreat into Georgia. In Greene's view, it was better to utilize Morgan as a knight ready for a surprise thrust, leaving Cornwallis to wonder what he should do.

At last Cornwallis did something. If Greene could divide an inferior force into two contingents, His Lordship, with reinforcements from Leslie in immediate prospect, could go the Americans one better. Orders went out from Cornwallis to divide Britain's forces into three contingents. He himself retained command of the main body and decided to march toward Morgan. A second group was detached to reinforce Camden. Tarleton, also reinforced and maneuvering in the vicinity of Ninety-Six, got this exhortation from his chief in early January: "If Morgan is still...anywhere within your reach, I should wish you to push him to the utmost...No time is to be lost...."

It was the sort of message Tarleton liked to hear. Jubilantly, he replied: "I must either destroy Morgan's corps or push it before me over Broad River towards King's Mountain."

Cornwallis, from a secure position at Winnsboro on the other side of the swollen Broad, responded that Tarleton had "perfectly" understood the situation—and so it appeared. But then the rains set in again, slowing considerably the communication between camps. Before long, neither side had up-to-date knowledge of the whereabouts of friend or foe, a situation which was to influence profoundly the outcome of the impending battle.

On January 4, 1781, from his camp on the Pacolet, Morgan wrote Greene:

"My situation is far from being agreeable to my wishes or expectations. Forage and provisions are not to be had. Here we cannot subsist, so that we have but one alternative, either to retreat or move into Georgia. A retreat will be attended with the most fatal consequences. The spirit which now begins to pervade the people, and call them into the field will be destroyed. The militia who have already joined will desert us, and it is not improbable but that a regard for their own safety will induce them to join the enemy."

Before Morgan's somber appraisal reached Greene, Cornwallis prepared to march, and his message to Tarleton, dated January 6, said: "I shall march Monday for Bullock Creek. Leslie will march on Tuesday by the River Road for the same place." The record shows that Cornwallis and Leslie moved their troops very slowly. Both were encumbered with artillery, ammunition, baggage and stores, the continuing heavy rainfall slowed their advance and the pace itself was leisurely.

Meanwhile, Greene still haggled with his rheumatic and unhappy subordinate, Daniel Morgan. "It is my wish that you should hold your ground if possible," Greene wrote, and then he observed laconically: "Colonel Tarleton is said to be on his way to pay you a visit. I doubt not but he will have a decent reception and a proper dismission." Greene seemed to grasp that Cornwallis was in no position to help Tarleton for a few days and he also apparently liked the idea of letting "that boy," as some detractors called Tarleton, try to take the measure of the battlewise Old Wagoner.

Out of touch with Cornwallis, Tarleton bulled ahead, intent on closing with Morgan. This time, the Green Dragoon was convinced, the Americans could not escape him. Unmindful of Morgan's experience and reputation, Tarleton chased after him with three possible courses of action in mind: catch and fight Morgan before the latter could reach Broad River; chase him to the Broad and cut him up in front of that raging torrent; or drive him over the river into the guns of His Lordship. There was only one flaw in the third of Tarleton's alternatives: Lord Cornwallis wasn't there.

On January 9, Tarleton pitched camp at Duggins and waited for the rain to stop and the Enoree River to fall. There he received the news from his scouts that Morgan held the ground at Grindal Shoals, only 12 miles away. Unflustered and unhurried, Cornwallis continued his march along the north side of the Broad, spending the night of the 14th—appropriately enough—on the Tardy River. In the six-day march from Winnsboro, Cornwallis had covered only 30 miles.

Incredibly, Morgan himself wrote as late as January 15 from Thicketty Creek that he had no intention of fighting. He knew Tarleton was a mere day's march behind him—yet wrote to Greene: "The enemy's great superiority in numbers, and our own distance from the main army will enable Lord Cornwallis to detach so superior a force against me as to render it essential to our safety to avoid action."

On January 16, Cornwallis stepped up his advance and covered the 10 miles to reach Turkey Creek, but he was still 25 miles from Cowpens. In his final note prior to the battle—which Tarleton was to receive about a week later—His Lordship stated that he had been out of touch with Tarleton for five days. Glumly, Cornwallis expressed the conviction that Morgan had escaped them again.

Had Cornwallis but known, the Old Wagoner was even more discouraged with his lot. Tarleton was at his heels and ahead lay the Broad River with its difficult fording problems. If there was one thing Morgan wished to avoid, it was getting caught with his back to that turbulent water while Tarleton's cavalry went to work on his troops. In one of the most abject messages he ever wrote, Morgan asked Greene to recall him and his detachment. Before the message could be sent, the situation changed for the worse. One of Morgan's mounted patrols galloped in with word that Tarleton was a mere six miles away with 1200 men, many of them British regulars.

Backed into a corner, out of touch with Greene and reluctant to cross the Broad where he feared Cornwallis awaited him, Morgan quickly changed his mind: he would fight. There was another compelling reason for making a stand at Cowpens. For several days, Morgan's scouts had ranged the countryside, desperately trying to round up as many able-bodied men with firearms as they could find. In all the vastness of western South Carolina, one place stood out as a recognizable point of reference. Cowpens had been the American staging area for the Battle of King's Mountain. Every man for miles around could find Cowpens and Morgan had reason to hope that many would find it before he had to fight Tarleton.

The battleground was known as Hannah's Cowpens from the name of the man who for years had grazed his cattle there. It was a rolling, gentle slope of waving grass dotted with scrub pine, oak and chestnut trees. From the tree line at the foot of the hill, the area in which Tarleton's forces could be expected to emerge, the ground sloped upward gradually for about 1000 yards.

Rigid in his saddle, tight-lipped and uncomplaining of his aches and pains, Morgan broke the news to his officers: the retreat had ended. One can believe the Old Wagoner truly said: "On this ground I will defeat the British or lay my bones."

Numb with surprise, his officers followed Morgan as they reconnoitered the battlefield on the evening of January 16, 1781. The route the attacking British forces would have to take was uphill for about 400 yards. Then it leveled off slightly before rising again for another 600 yards. At the very top was a grassy knoll, behind which the ground sloped downward toward the Broad River. Behind the knoll, troops could stand without being seen by the attackers. A man on horseback standing in his stirrups could view the approaches all the way down to the tree line 1000 yards below. It was in this hilltop declivity that Morgan placed his command post.

What dismayed Morgan's officers at the decision to fight on such terrain was the apparent ease with which Tarleton's vaunted cavalry could ride in among the scattered trees to hack up the infantry. The flanking terrain, too, was open and exposed with no obvious natural obstacles to deter an attempted envelopment. Morgan, perhaps, took a more perceptive look at this situation than did his subordinates. The creek heads to his right and left, some 2000 feet apart, were swollen and deep. These would prevent any flanking movement from gaining a broad field of envelopment. There was another factor. Morgan was fairly certain that Tarleton would come straight at him up the hill, intent on wiping out the Americans with a frontal assault.

That evening, Morgan's fellow officers reportedly urged him to reconsider his decision to fight there. Some wanted to push on to the Broad, try to get across and worry about Cornwallis later. Morgan remained adamant and immediately spelled out to the officers his battle plan. Then, as he reported later in a personal letter, he went into the woods alone and in the lowering twilight ascended a tree and "poured out my soul in prayer for protection."

Throughout the rest of the night, he lost no opportunity to be the swashbuckling, confident, devil-may-care leader, instilling in his troops his own confidence and pledging over and over that come morning the Old Wagoner would "crack his whip" over "Ban." It is significant that Morgan never referred to "that boy" by name. To Morgan, Tarleton was "Ben" or "Ban" or "Benny."

Morgan and the whole encampment got a tremendous lift when Andrew Pickens thundered in on horseback, greeted his comrades and reported that he had 150 (some say only 70) of his best men in the vicinity and ready to join the fight. One can imagine what this must have meant to Morgan on the eve of the battle; Pickens was a man who had earned his credentials the hard way. Morgan also noted that far into the night other reinforcements trickled in steadily, singly and in groups of three or four and he did some quick calculating. He had been prepared to face Tarleton outmanned perhaps by something like three to two. Now Pickens and his men and those who had been told to assemble at Cowpens were beginning to redress the balance. Tarleton might be in for a surprise.

In all the accounts of the battle, much is made of Morgan's tireless efforts to bolster the courage of his men. It is widely reported that, as he moved from one campfire to another, he stripped to the waist to show his horribly scarred back—a reminder of the 499 lashes the Old Wagoner took for rudeness to a British officer during his days with Braddock. A lesser man might have died from such punishment. Morgan joked about it, saying that the sentence had been 500 lashes but that the drummer had missed a beat and thus King George owed him one more lash.

Throughout the Revolution, and indeed, through all the history of American warfare, one cardinal principle has been sacred to the military: the American soldier is at his best when thoroughly briefed and totally conversant with what the overall objective is and what he is supposed to do. It is doubtful if any American troops ever went into a fight with a better knowledge of the battle plan than did Morgan's men at Cowpens. In addition, Morgan joked, cajoled, back-slapped and bantered as he went tirelessly among the campfires. He was fond of saying: "The Old Wagoner will crack his whip over Ben in the morning as sure as he lives. Just hold up your heads, boys. Three fires, three cheers and a charge, and you are free. And then, when you return to your homes, how the old folks will bless you, and the girls kiss you, for your gallant conduct."

A young volunteer in Colonel William Washington's cavalry attested to Morgan's performance in his memoirs: "We were very anxious for battle and many a hearty curse had been vented against General Morgan during that day's march (January 16) for retreating, as we thought, to avoid a battle. Night came upon us, yet much remained to be done....It was upon this occasion that I was more perfectly convinced of General Morgan's qualifications to command militia than I had ever before been. He went among the volunteers, helped them fix their swords, joked with them about their sweethearts, told them to keep in good spirits and the day would be ours. And long after I laid down, he was going among the soldiers encouraging them...I don't believe he slept a wink that night."

Morgan was indeed busy. He ordered the militia to make sure a sufficient supply of ammunition was on hand. He arranged to have the baggage sent well to the rear and he pushed out scouts and patrols to keep watchful eyes on the approaching British. This was the first time Morgan commanded troops in battle as a general officer and he was leaving nothing to chance.

Banny, too, was busy. He ordered his buglers to sound off at 2:00 A.M. and his travel-worn troops grumblingly prepared to make their nightmare march through the dark swamps and thickets. In a short time, Tarleton's men were on the move in the dank, dripping morning. Scouts were sent forward and to the flanks to provide security against surprise. In advance, Tarleton placed three companies of light infantry; then came the Legion Infantry followed by the 7th Royal Fusiliers Regiment. Next came the "grasshoppers"—two three-pound artillery pieces—perhaps the most traveled and traded guns in the Revolution. Behind the artillery came the 71st Highlanders, followed by Tarleton's cavalry and the mounted infantry. It was an impressive force stumbling along in the dark, eager to overhaul and destroy Morgan. The odds on bringing that off, Banastre Tarleton believed, were in his favor. Not since King's Mountain had such a large engagement with the enemy loomed.

This time, though, there was an important difference. At King's Mountain, Tories from the Carolinas had been overwhelmed by over-the-mountain militia. This day, the 17th of January, 1781, the British troops were in large part His Majesty's regulars. Morgan, on the other hand, had a mixed assortment. In veterans, Tarleton enjoyed something like a three to one edge.

Because of the darkness, the British force moved slowly. Nonetheless, it reached Thicketty Creek (recorded on British maps as Thickelle Creek) before dawn. Tarleton paused. It was time to sniff out the enemy. Intelligence reports indicated Morgan was nearby so a party of cavalry was ordered out and it soon made contact with one of Morgan's probing patrols.

It was still dark when Morgan's patrol broke and ran with its news: Tarleton was on the march with his entire force, infantry, artillery, dragoons—and he was less than five miles away. "Boys, get up," bawled Morgan from his command post. "Banny is coming!"

The Americans had prudently cooked their breakfasts the night before and now Morgan told everyone to eat hearty. The last of the baggage wagons rumbled to the rear among the trees and the mounted militia tethered their horses behind the knoll. As Tarleton's first mounted patrols reached the tree line, they could scarcely believe their eyes. In the faint streaks of early dawn they could make out Morgan's skirmish line on the forward slope of the hill!

A detachment raced back to Tarleton with the news. The Americans were out in force in exposed positions on an open hill, free of swamps and trees with their flanks unprotected. Tarleton was incredulous. Could this be the way the great General Morgan chose to receive him? Incredulity changed to jubilation as Tarleton himself reached the tree line. It was shortly before 7:00 A.M. and the first rays of a pale sun were breaking through to the east. In front of him, some 400 yards distant, were the Carolina and Georgia militia—sitting ducks for a cavalry strike. To Tarleton, this couldn't have been better if he had arranged it himself and it confirmed the message he had sent Cornwallis a couple of days earlier: "At last," he had written, "Morgan is within our grasp." Tarleton determined to make the most of it. With the three-pounders, with superior cavalry, and with his very considerable forces, Tarleton reasoned, he would gain the victory alone—and should he not have quite the capacity to bring it off by himself, there was Lord Cornwallis on the Broad to come to the rescue.

On the part of Lieutenant-Colonel Banastre Tarleton, these were miscalculations of staggering proportion.

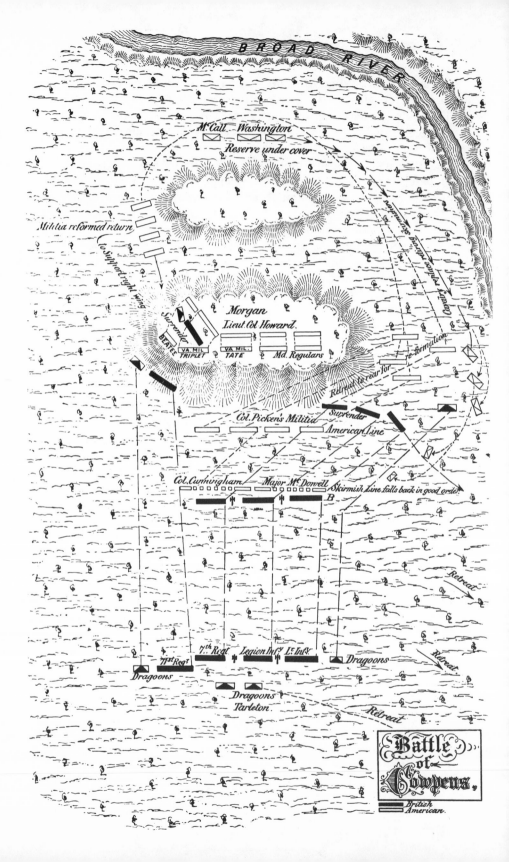

Battle of Cowpens.

Cowpens—The Battle

THE AMERICAN MILITIA, PRONE ON THE FORWARD SLOPE OF THE HILL, blew on their hands to warm them as they waited for the British attack. They were the pawns in Daniel Morgan's game plan. Hold your fire, the Old Wagoner had told them, until the British come out of the trees and get within easy range.

As they waited in the dark, the militia could hear sounds of the approaching enemy, a shouted order, a curse, the neigh of a horse. How far away? Half a mile? Less? All along the thin line of irregulars there were whispered exchanges. Banny was coming; he'd be on them soon, just as sure as the morning sun. All eyes were fixed on the openings in the tree line and an eerie silence descended on the battlefield.

Daniel Morgan had deployed his men to the right and left of the Old Mill Gap Road. At the top of the hill the general, with his 450 seasoned Maryland and Delaware Continentals, looked down to the tree line. The Continentals were commanded by Colonel John Eager Howard, a man in whom Morgan had profound trust. This line would hold at all costs; anything else was unthinkable. Augmenting the Continentals and manning their flanks were some handpicked militia from Virginia and Georgia.

Down the hill, some 150 yards away, Pickens was in command of about 300 North and South Carolina militia. Morgan counted on Pickens to get the most from these men, many of whom were expert marksmen. They were spread thinly across the field in the knee-high grass, behind bushes, trees and rocks —waiting. In front of them, taking advantage of similar concealment were about 150 Georgia and North Carolina militia under the command of Majors John Cunningham and Charles McDowell.

Behind everything, including his own command post, Morgan prepared a little surprise for the British. Here were posted

Colonel William Washington and his 80-man cavalry force, augmented this day by 45 Georgia infantrymen, who had volunteered to fight on horseback, commanded by Lieutenant James McCall. Tarleton had counted on having a vastly superior cavalry. Now Morgan was shaving the odds by putting foot soldiers on horseback.

The Old Wagoner's battle plan, laboriously and intricately explained to every man the night before, was deceptively simple. The skirmishers out front in the waving grass were to await the first onslaught, take two shots, then retire in good order through Colonel Pickens' line. This line was to hold its fire until the attackers neared, take two shots and withdraw laterally to their left, circling behind the Continentals to take new positions on the American right flank. From there, the militia was to support the Continentals with flanking fire. Thus, the less experienced troops, after firing briefly, were to be pulled out of the action, leaving the all-in fighting to the Continentals.

Morgan made some basic assumptions in his deployment which might have weighed more heavily on a lesser commander. First, he was dead certain that Tarleton would come straight at him. Second, he counted on his greenest troops in the very front to pick off some of the British, slow their advance and move in good order through Pickens' line. Third, and most important, Morgan relied on Pickens to move more than 400 men all the way around the field of battle, keeping control enroute and forming up again on the opposite flank. This was perhaps the trickiest element of the plan. Once these troops headed for the rear, Morgan knew the temptation would be great to keep right on hightailing it for the Broad River.

All was in readiness shortly after 6:00 A.M. but the field was too quiet to suit Morgan so he bawled an obvious question at the top of his teamster's voice: "Are you ready to fight?" The reply, in roaring unison: "Yes!" The Old Wagoner was reassured. He had done all he could; his human chess pieces were on the board.

Banny arrived with the sun. Some of the dragoons, their brass helmets gleaming, cantered out of the trees to survey the field. Then Tarleton himself rode into the clearing and a long line of Redcoats commenced to form up behind him. Ban liked what he saw and with typical verve he hastily ordered the deployment of his forces. The 7th Regiment took the left. The kilted Highlanders and about 200 of the cavalry were designated as reserve. Some 50 dragoons were sent to each flank and the "grasshoppers" were positioned in the center, slightly to the left. The remaining British were strung out in a long skirmish line, and with a wave of his sword Tarleton indicated he was ready. The British troops gave off with a mighty, challenging roar.

Morgan wanted to be sure no one was intimidated and from the top of the hill, at the top of his lungs, he howled: "They give us the British halloo, boys, give them the Indian halloo, by God!" When the voices of some 1000 Patriots responded in the blood-curdling yips and yells of the true native Americans, it may have given His Majesty's forces pause, but it did not deter Tarleton who decided to see how quickly he could dislodge the first skirmishers. Impetuously, he ordered 50 mounted Legionnaires to charge the prone Americans. Sabres flashed in the thin light of dawn. Hoofbeats drummed as the horsemen charged up the slope. Then the long rifles spoke. The British could see nothing but puffs of smoke rising from the grass, but saddles were emptied and horses fell. Others reared and turned. Fifteen cavalrymen were already down and the others raced back to the tree line. The militia had done the job and Tarleton was on notice: this was to be no Fishing Creek.

But then Tarleton saw the dim figures in the grass arise and walk toward the rear. Perhaps, he must have reasoned, they had had enough after all. Well, he would make certain that they kept moving by ordering the artillery to fire at point-blank range. A few militiamen fell but the line moved in good order through Colonel Pickens' positions.

To Tarleton it looked as if a retreat had begun. British drums rolled, the fifes shrilled and the entire British line moved forward on the run. When it got within 150 yards of the reinforced second line of Americans, Andrew Pickens gave the order to fire. It was a brisk exchange but more Redcoats than Americans dropped and, according to plan, Pickens led his men in a crab-like withdrawal to the side and rear, firing as they cleared out. Now Tarleton was certain that, despite his considerable number of casualties, British pluck was carrying the day and, sensing a kill, he ordered 50 dragoons into the fray. As they charged toward Colonel Howard's main line, they overran the last of the Pickens contingent which was making its lateral movement around the American left flank. There was an understandable panic which hastened this withdrawal and Tarleton became further convinced that victory was within his grasp.

It is generally established that some of the militia ran fast enough to get all the way back to the tethered horses. These men, despite all threats and blandishments, rode off to live and fight another day. That they constituted a small segment of Morgan's forces was due in large part to the bravery and resourcefulness of Morgan and some of his officers. One of these, Lieutenant Joseph Hughes, was a large man of great strength and fleetness of foot. In the words of one historian: "With his drawn sword he would outrun his men and passing them, face about and command them to stand, striking right and left to enforce obedience to order; often repeating with a loud voice: 'You damned cowards, halt and fight! If you don't stop and fight you'll all be killed!'"

From the top of the hill, Morgan saw the British dragoons making for Howard's main line. Morgan wanted no part of that, having just seen some of his militia turn tail. Without hesitation, he waved Washington and his cavalry into the fight. The 50 dragoons were quickly driven off but the main British line, still running, roared a fresh challenge as it neared the Continentals.

Each of Howard's men had a knee to the ground to steady his aim and as the enemy came into range the Continentals unleashed deadly fire. Many "epaulette men"—a term Morgan used in singling out British officers for his snipers—went down, and for the next half hour the two lines traded round for round on the smoke-shrouded slope. By all accountings it was one of the fiercest fire fights of the Revolution and it was climaxed when the lines came together and went at each other with bayonets and hand-to-hand.

Tarleton, dismayed at this unexpected resistance, called up his Highlanders who immediately gave the British the necessary strength to dislodge Howard. Concern for his threatened right flank prompted Howard, as he later explained, to alter his position. "I attempted to change the front...In doing this, some confusion ensued," he said. That was understating the case considerably. Most accounts of the battle credit Howard with trying to get one company to face to the right and ward off the onrushing Highlanders. Instead, in the "confusion," these Continentals turned to the rear and marched away. The rest of the Continentals interpreted the withdrawal of the flank company as a signal for a general retreat and also moved to the rear. The following stilted conversation is widely reported to have taken place:

Morgan: "Are you beaten?"

Howard: "Do men who march like that look as though they were beaten?"

Morgan: "Right. I'll choose you a second position. When you reach it, face about and fire."

It is difficult to credit this exchange when it is simultaneously argued that Howard could not clearly convey his orders to the flank company. This Highlander charge, no doubt, put great pressure on the Continentals who were already tangling hand-to-hand with the British. It is no wonder that Howard could not convince men under frontal assault that, for the larger good, they should turn away from cold steel to repel some other fellows rolling up their flank. No matter how nor why, the Continentals fell back, knowing that several hundred militia were just over the crest of the hill ready to pour flanking fire on their pursuers.

As the Americans withdrew, Tarleton must have been certain he had won. So were his troops. They had marched all night through the swamps, attacked on empty stomachs, run nearly 1000 yards uphill and routed three lines of Americans. Now, still running, the British screamed out their blood lust.

Behind the knoll Daniel Morgan wheedled, cajoled and browbeat his militiamen to form for another fire or two. Washington, who in routing the dragoons was now in the British rear, is said to have cried: "They're coming on like a mob. Give them one fire and I'll charge them."

Morgan screamed orders to the Continentals to face about and fire. They did. And from the American right the militia raked the British with flanking fire, shooting from the hip. The attack suddenly stalled and once again, as at King's Mountain, the British had no place to go, not even to the rear, for Washington's cavalry was upon them howling promises of "Tarleton's quarter!"

While Pickens kept the militia firing, Washington was slashing and hacking at any Redcoat that moved and the reformed Continentals poured shot after shot at the center. Above the furor rose the voice of John Eager Howard: "Give them the bayonet!" The British, overwhelmed, threw down their arms, and now the much maligned American militia charged into the fray also roaring threats of "Tarleton's quarter." It is quite remarkable that the American officers were able to restrain most of these vengeance-bent troops.

The battle had gone against him so suddenly that Tarleton could scarcely realize all was lost. His cavalry reserves were a bit more perceptive because they absolutely refused to be committed. In his later accounts of the battle, Tarleton claimed his troops panicked and declined to launch the attack he ordered.

In any case, as the Legion Infantry and light infantry dropped their arms and scurried down the hill, Washington's cavalry quickly rode in among them and took them prisoner. Slaughter was averted when Morgan, Howard, Pickens and the other officers ordered their men to spare the British.

What was left of the action centered around a grim, fighting withdrawal by the Highlanders. They might have made it had not Howard's Continentals been freed by the surrender of most of the British infantry. When the Continentals turned in strength on the Highlanders, promising them quarter, they surrendered too.

Colonel Washington, flushed with victory over Tarleton, was anxious to close with and cut down the "Green Dragoon." So diligently did he pursue Tarleton that he outrode most of his cavalry and suddenly found himself upon Tarleton who, with two of his own officers, wheeled to fight. As Washington slashed at one of Tarleton's companions he broke his sword, whereupon that Englishman prepared to strike the American colonel a mortal blow. Another Patriot, joining Washington, saved him by shooting the British officer in the shoulder. This American has been variously identified as "a lad named Collins," "a waiter," "a servant," "a bugler," and "a boy of 14." There may be other versions. In any case, the arrival of more of Washington's men caused Tarleton and his friends to cut and run. A parting shot from Tarleton missed Washington but struck his horse, thus giving the colonel two close calls within a matter of seconds.

It was a complete victory for Morgan. In laconic style, he reported the body count to Greene: Americans dead, 12; wounded 61. British dead, 110, including one major, 13 captains, 14 lieutenants and nine ensigns; wounded, 200; prisoners, 830. Tarleton had lost nine-tenths of his attacking force, about a fourth of Britain's troops in the South.

As Colonel Washington mounted a new horse and took off with some of his men in a futile pursuit of Tarleton, the Americans tidied up the field. They had captured 60 black slaves who had served as batmen and bearers for the British. They also took ample British stores, the "grasshoppers," assorted weapons, ammunition, and the enemy's colors, fifes, drums and music.

Tarleton, after giving Washington the slip, returned to his baggage train and found it being looted by a group of Loyalists. The dragoons, who had found no stomach for a fight with Washington, Morgan and Howard, efficiently hacked up their fair-weather friends and drove them off. It is interesting to note that Tarleton, in his account of this action, prudently refrained from identifying the looters, thus contriving to leave the impression that they had been Patriots.

Daniel Morgan did not tarry to celebrate his victory. No time was to be lost. The hated Banny was banished, but Cornwallis might be waiting in the wings. The Old Wagoner quickly reformed his able-bodied men and moved out before noon. Later in the day they crossed the Broad River and with infinite relief learned that Cornwallis and his army were nowhere in the immediate vicinity.

At Cowpens Andrew Pickens, the silent hero who had first blunted the British attack, remained with the wounded and made them as comfortable as he could in tents, attended by surgeons. The next day he caught up with Morgan across the Broad.

A kind of unbelieving euphoria swept the Colonies after Morgan's victory. Greene himself, filled with awe, wrote: "After this, nothing is impossible." George Washington was jubilant. He shared Greene's view, regarding Cowpens as a vital victory. Cornwallis, crushed, felt his chances for continuing a successful campaign had been grievously damaged. He wrote in a letter to Lord Francis Rawdon (reproduced on page 138):

Buffalo Creek Jan: 21st 1781

My Dearest Lord

    The late affair has almost broke my heart.
Morgan is at Gilbertown, I shall march tomorrow with
1200 Infantry & the Cavalry to attack or follow him
to the banks of Catawba. Gen. Howard remains at
Cherokee Ford with all Baggage knapsacks
included, ready to meet us at Ramsoures.
I was never more surrounded with difficulty & distress,
but practice in the school of adversity has strengthend
me....

Your truly affectionate friend

Cornwallis

The Cowpens action ranks among the most important of the entire war for three significant reasons. First, it was a clear-cut victory for Patriot arms over British regulars and, apart from King's Mountain, the only American victory in the entire Southern Campaign. Second, the defeat was such a jolt to Cornwallis that, vengeance-bent, he departed from his grand strategy, made a futile chase after Greene and further weakened his increasingly isolated army. British rage and frustration were best put to words by Britain's able Brigadier General Charles O'Hara:

"...Without baggage, necessaries, or provisions of any sort for officer or soldier, in the most barren inhospitable, unhealthy part of North America, opposed to the most savage, inveterate, perfidious, cruel enemy, with zeal and with bayonets only, it was resolved to follow Greene's army to the end of the world."

Finally, the political climate in the Southern Colonies warmed to the Patriot cause after Cowpens, bringing with it a trickle of volunteers. At the same time, the British encountered fresh difficulties in mustering Loyalists. It was an old story for all old soldiers: everybody wanted to be with the winner.

Historians have taken the position that had Britain not lost so many good troops at Cowpens, Cornwallis might have won handily two months later at Guilford Courthouse. If so, then Cowpens deservedly ranks as the turning point in the campaign because the Guilford standoff left Cornwallis' forces so badly mauled that they turned toward Virginia—and Yorktown.

General Morgan's own reaction to Cowpens was modest. "Our success," he wrote to Greene, "must be attributed, under God, to the justice of our cause and the bravery of our troops. My wishes could induce me to mention the name of every private centinel in the corps. In justice to the brave and good conduct of the officers, I have taken the liberty to enclose you a list of their names, from a conviction that you will be pleased to introduce such characters to the world."

Greene was equally generous in his report to Washington: "The event is glorious....The brilliancy and success with which it was fought does the highest honor to the American arms and adds splendor to the character of the general and officers."

Congress agreed. It praised Morgan for a "complete and important victory" and it awarded him a gold medal. The Old Wagoner did not receive the medal for a decade but it was a large gesture. Congress also presented William Washington and John Eager Howard with silver medals and swords. Pickens, geographically a little farther away from Congress, got only a sword. In all, it was heady stuff for the Patriots—too heady to last.

Guilford Courthouse

BROODING AND BITTER (BUT NOT TOO DISTRACTED TO THINK OF SALVAG -ing his military reputation), Banastre Tarleton fired off a letter to Earl Cornwallis soliciting his approbation for the conduct of the Cowpens battle or his leave to retire "till inquiry could be instituted."

Whatever he thought, Cornwallis' reply to Tarleton was generous. He wrote: "You have forfeited no part of my esteem as an officer by the unfortunate event of the action of the 17th: The means you used to bring the enemy to action were able and masterly and must ever do you honour. Your disposition was unexceptionable; the total misbehaviour of your troops could alone have deprived you of the glory which was so justly your due."

How Tarleton must have treasured and guarded that letter! It was, he may well have imagined, his safe-conduct pass through the burgeoning fury of Britain's army hierarchy. As it developed, the letter was not enough to get Tarleton off the hook. He was to answer for his role at Cowpens for years to come.

However, as January of 1781 was expiring, there were more immediate problems. In Cornwallis' view, Greene and Morgan had to be caught and punished. King's Mountain had been bad enough but Cowpens was worse because it had involved a defeat for British regulars led by the heretofor invincible Tarleton. Cornwallis, intent on rectifying that grievous aberration as quickly as he could, set off in pursuit of his adversaries. Before long, he was chasing only Greene, for Morgan was destined to quit the fray.

In early February, Greene and Morgan moved slowly north in wretched sleet and rain. At Abbot's Creek the main body paused while Greene pushed out patrols to gather intelligence

101

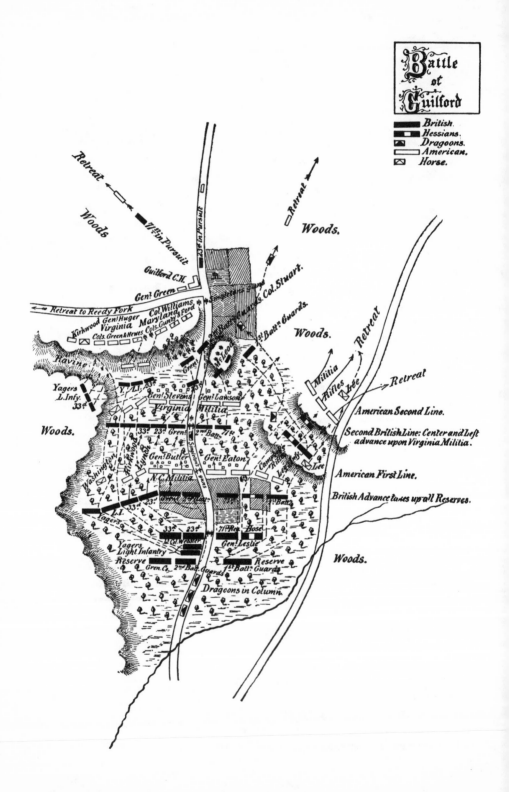

on Cornwallis and Tarleton. Then Greene turned eastward—and the sleet turned to snow. Greene's plan was to keep moving, draw Cornwallis away from his supplies, avoid a fight, keep the army together and stay alive. Along the way he would look for a battlefield which might yield advantage to his rabble in arms.

Not all of Greene's men had shoes. Those lucky enough to be shod soon found their footwear coming apart in the mud, slush and swamps. The condition of these freezing Americans, "with only one blanket to four men, their shoes worn out and their bleeding feet tracking the ground," was reminiscent of the darkest days at Valley Forge.

The spirit of the Old Wagoner was near the breaking point. It must have been a blow to his pride to admit to the hard-pressed and suffering troops that he could no longer ride a horse. That is what he did, however, and he availed himself of a carriage to precede Greene to Guilford. There he busied himself procuring food and forage, but when Greene arrived Morgan candidly stated that his endurance was at an end. Even then, Morgan's wry sense of humor survived. He told his commander: "I am much indisposed with pain and to add to my discomfort am violently attacked with the piles, so that I can scarcely sit upon my horse. This is the first time that I ever experienced this disorder and from the idea I had of it, sincerely prayed that I might never know what it was."

Greene tried to wave off Morgan's problems in the hope that the Old Wagoner could pull himself together. He even prevailed upon young Henry Lee to talk Morgan into staying. Then Greene offered Morgan the command of a new special force made up of Washington's cavalry, Howard's Continentals and Lee's Legion. Most of the men in the former two units had been with Morgan at Cowpens but neither their adulation nor the blandishments of Greene and Lee could dissuade Morgan. Reluctantly, then, on February 10, 1781, Greene issued this terse order from Guilford Courthouse: "General Morgan of the Virginia Line has leave of absence until he recovers his health as to be able to take the field again."

In his lonely trek to Virginia, Morgan's mind was back in the lines with Greene. Several times the Old Wagoner became so weak he could not continue his journey. At one stopping point he wrote his commander:

"I have been doctoring these several days, thinking to be able to take the field again. But I find I get worse. My pains are now accompanied by a fever every day. I expect Lord Cornwallis will push you until you are obliged to fight him, on which much will depend. You have, from what I see, a great number of militia. If they fight, you will beat Cornwallis; if not, he will beat you, and perhaps cut your regulars to pieces, which will be losing all our hopes. I am informed that among the militia will be found a number of old soldiers. I think it would be advisable to select them from among the militia and put them in the ranks with the regulars, select the riflemen also, and fight them on the flanks, under enterprising officers who are acquainted with that kind of fighting; and put the militia in the center, with some picked troops in their rear, with orders to shoot down the first man that runs. If anything will succeed, a disposition of this kind will. I hope you will not look on this as dictating, but it is my opinion on a matter I am much concerned in."

For the next several weeks, while Greene waited for reinforcements from Virginia, his bedraggled troops led the equally bedraggled forces of Lord Cornwallis on a wild goose chase, never permitting the British to close with them. Here the game favored the Americans. They knew the terrain and, more important, they knew the swollen rivers. They built boats and hid them in swamps and creekheads. When the British got close, the Americans made for their makeshift rafts, forded a raging torrent and thumbed their noses at their pursuers. As Brigadier General Charles O'Hara, one of Cornwallis' officers, describe it: "The two armies were never above twenty miles asunder, they constantly avoiding a general action and we as industriously seeking it. These operations obliged the two armys to make numberless moves which it is impossible to detail."

During this period of inconclusive maneuver, Greene detached Light Horse Harry Lee to harass British outposts and discourage Loyalists from joining Cornwallis. Lee had a singular success on the Haw River where a bizarre feat of daring (the British called it treachery) wrote finis to overt aid to the Crown throughout the area.

A Loyalist doctor, Colonel John Pyle, had painstakingly raised a force of some 300 Loyalists and was enroute, Lee heard, to join Cornwallis. Somewhere along the line, the Loyalist force was to be met by none other than Tarleton's Legion and grandly escorted to Cornwallis' command post.

For Henry Lee, the situation seemed intriguing. He was Tarleton's age and had Tarleton's style and rank. But he had a better education, equal daring and a burning desire to establish himself as the superior military leader of the two.

When Pyle's Loyalists were approached by green-jacketed horsemen led by an intense young man whose long hair was tied in the back Tarleton-style, they quite naturally thought the escort party was at hand. It was a disastrous misconception. As Lee's marauders went to work on the horrified enemy with sabres, the conviction that a terrible mistake was being made swept the Loyalists. Tarleton, they reasoned, simply did not recognize them. But loud huzzahs for good King George brought only death to those who so marked themselves. A Tory sergeant, deceived to the end, said: "Bless your soul, Mr. Tarleton, you have this day killed a parcel of as good subjects as ever His Majesty had."

"You damned rascal," snorted Light Horse Harry. "If you call me Tarleton again I will take off your head....I am Lee of the American Legion." The next day, Lee's men reported 93 Loyalists dead.

In all of his maneuvering, Nathanael Greene never strayed very far from Guilford Courthouse. He had long ago picked it as the spot for a showdown with the British and now he felt that time was drawing near. Despite the ill condition of his troops, he considerably outnumbered the British, who were suffering too. When reinforcements reached Greene on March 13 and 14, he quietly moved his entire army to Guilford Courthouse and took up defensive positions.

Cornwallis received word of Greene's deployment on the 14th and early the next day marched from his camp on Deep River. Cornwallis had bobbed and feinted with Greene five years earlier in New England and now had done the same for nearly two months since the fight at Cowpens. It was time the lines were drawn.

Greene took Morgan's letter and the Cowpens battle plan to heart. He formed three lines about 400 yards apart, facing west. The first two lines extended north and south and crossed the New Garden Road. The third line, north of the road, followed along the crest of a low hill. Heavily wooded terrain would inhibit the effectiveness of Tarleton's cavalry, and British artillery would not be able to get a clear field of fire against this deployment. The flanks of the first line were exposed but Greene didn't worry about this because the battle plan, as at Cowpens, called for an orderly retreat by these troops after the first shots were exchanged. Greene expected the heavy woods on both sides to canalize the British attack and, like Morgan, he kept his Continentals well back to bear the brunt of the advance long after the battle had begun.

In the first line, Greene put his North Carolina militia. On the left were Harry Lee's Legion and Colonel William Campbell's riflemen, the latter of whom had made their mark against the Loyalists at King's Mountain. On the right, he put Colonel William Washington's cavalry, some Delaware Continentals and Colonel Charles Lynch's riflemen.

In the second line were the Virginia militia, relatively inexperienced but spoiling to make up for the failure of their fellow Virginians at Camden. Behind them were the men of Brigadier General Edward Stevens to insure against any wholesale withdrawal.

The third line was made up of Greene's four Continental regiments. The First Marylanders were a seasoned unit. The Second Marylanders and the two regiments of Virginians had been reorganized and muscled up with replacements, but the officers were proven veterans and there were some old soldiers in among the rookies. In all, Greene had some 4400 men on the field of which perhaps 1500 were regulars. Other estimates of his strength, especially those of British orientation, ran higher.

Arrayed against the Americans was a much smaller British force, perhaps 2000 in all, but most of them were veterans of long years of fighting in America and on the continent. The Guards were represented by two battalions, a Grenadier unit and a light infantry company. There were two regiments of foot, the 23rd and 33rd, the former of which was the justly famous Welch Fusiliers. There were the 71st Highlanders, the Hessian Regiment of Bose, some Hessian riflemen, Tarleton's Legion cavalry and some elements of Royal Artillery.

Before the battle began, there was an inconclusive skirmish about three miles west of Guilford in which Lee's cavalry engaged Tarleton's. Each of these flamboyant commanders claimed victory, but it was costly to Tarleton whose right hand was shattered by a rifle ball. To his credit, Tarleton never left the field: he continued to direct his segment of the attack, personally defenseless, his right arm in a sling.

Gingerly, as befits a commander advancing against an enemy of indeterminate strength on strange terrain, Cornwallis moved forward. His troops, the Highlanders, the regiment of Bose, and the 23rd and 33rd Regiments were spread out in a single line. In support were the First and Second Battalions of Guards and the Grenadiers of the Guards. Other units were held in reserve.

The general thrust of the British attack was east toward the brow of the hill. Firing erupted from both flanks where Greene had posted his most seasoned troops. As a result, the British threw in their support elements early. General Leslie on the right committed the First Battalion of the Guards to oppose the American left and thereby extended his own line. On the British left, Lieutenant-Colonel James Webster, one of Cornwallis' ablest officers, pulled his whole line leftward to make way for the Second Battalion and Grenadiers of the Guards.

Staying on top of the action, Cornwallis brought up the light infantry and the Hessian riflemen to protect the extreme left. He surveyed the next development with wonder. On each flank the British were taking—and dealing out—heavy casualties. In the middle they were advancing almost without any deterrance. Then the American left under Lee and Campbell commenced to give way, pursued by the Regiment of Bose and the First Guards. The Americans fought a determined withdrawal, however, and in effect this became a small, separate battle which was not broken off until the parent engagement ended.

On the American right confusion existed. These troops apparently fell back to become an extension of the right flank of the second line, then withdrew with that line to the flank of the third. But meanwhile, Cornwallis was intent on exploiting the breakthrough in the middle, which saw his men proceed east along the road and through the woods until they met the American second line. There the Virginians stood fast, inflicting heavy casualties on the British. Under relentless pressure from Cornwallis' veterans, however, the Virginians finally gave way in an orderly withdrawal.

At the third American line, the British hit the backbone of the Southern Continental army—some 1500 strong. Here ensued the hardest fighting of the entire engagement. Heavy woods and deep gullies served to slow the British advance. Also, the stout resistance of the Marylanders and a cavalry charge by the intrepid William Washington at one juncture threatened to drive the British from the field. When the Marylanders advanced on the British, bayonets at the ready, Cornwallis knew the issue hung in the balance. Remorselessly, he broke up this hand-to-hand conflict with point-blank use of his artillery. The Americans gave way and, miraculously, the British suffered minimum casualties. Tarleton galloped off to retrieve the Hessians and the First Guards from their private battle and Greene could see that Cornwallis was about to throw everything at his regulars.

Some historians have faulted Greene for leaving the field at this juncture. The truth of the matter is that he had no Daniel

Morgan on the ground to round up the militia and secure from them some much-needed flanking support. On the other hand, Greene knew that a general retirement from the battle with his best troops still intact would leave him in a position to renew the fighting at some future date on his own terms. He had dealt the British a blow while suffering relatively few casualties himself. Why not leave the field to the British? Of what value was it? Thus, Nathanael Greene left Cornwallis his "victory."

Greene explained his actions in a later report: "The enemy having broken the Second Maryland Regiment and got into the rear of the Virginia Brigade, and appearing to be gaining our right would have encircled the whole of the Continental troops, General Greene thought it most advisable to order a retreat."

Among the American heroes of Guilford Courthouse was one Peter Francisco, who rode with William Washington. This mysterious giant of a man, six feet, eight inches tall, carried a five-foot sword given him by George Washington himself. Little is known of this furious man's origins. A Virginia foundling, he became a blacksmith and was said to be the strongest man in the colony. At Guilford Courthouse he reportedly slew 11 men with his great sword. At one point, a British guardsman is said to have pinned Francisco's leg to his horse with the thrust of a bayonet. Calmly, the giant helped the guardsman withdraw his cold steel, but then the Britisher made the fatal mistake of turning his back on Francisco. The Virginian neatly "cleft the poor fellow's head down to his shoulders."

After the Americans fled the field, it was a melancholy night for Cornwallis. In his lonely vigil at Guilford Courthouse, he was forced to listen to the screams of his wounded and dying men. In all, the British suffered about 600 casualties, the Americans only half that many. In the chessboard concept of war, Cornwallis had won. He had faced long odds in coming to battle at all, being outnumbered and not informed of the terrain. At every critical juncture he had made cool decisions and when the battle looked darkest he had persevered and carried the day. None of this mattered back in London, however, where Charles James Fox drily commented: "Another such victory would ruin the British Army."

March to Virginia

I F NATHANAEL GREENE LACKED THE FINESSE—OR THE LUCK—TO COME OFF with brilliant victories, it must at least be conceded that his perseverance and ability to hold his army together were qualities which largely contributed to Britain's undoing in the South.

Guilford Courthouse also forced Cornwallis to come to an immediate decision. With his weakened forces, he had several possible courses of action: he could stay in the area, rest and refurbish his battered forces and seek another showdown with Nathanael Greene; he could withdraw to a defensive position in Wilmington; he could strike back into South Carolina and join Lord Rawdon at Camden; or he could abandon the Carolinas for Virginia. That he took the Virginia route suggests he was confident Britain's strong outposts in South Carolina would keep Greene occupied. Besides, Cornwallis seemed to have convinced himself that if only Virginia could be subdued, resistance to the British would disappear. After all, they held Charleston, Camden and a half-dozen other strong points in the Carolinas. Again Cornwallis was beguiled by the prospect of a single, smashing victory which would put an end to the war: this was the phantom dream which Cornwallis pursued with the fanatic dedication of a Ponce de Leon seeking the fountain of youth. He needed help from Clinton now before he could come to grips with a large American force in the field.

Greene, on the other hand, could never be quite sure that Cornwallis would not return to attack him. For the moment the Americans could pause and rest, certain that the British were as spent as they and certain also that only Rawdon in far-off Camden had the manpower to engage them. As the militia which had fled at Guilford straggled back, Greene determined to turn his attention to South Carolina. He sensed even then that Cornwallis would have his hands full in Virginia and that if the Patriots could harass the British in South Carolina and prevent their sending sizable reinforcements to Virginia, the war might be brought to a swift and happy conclusion.

To mask his plans Greene sent two detachments after Cornwallis, who had marched toward Wilmington. These were to give the impression that Greene had begun a full-scale chase with his entire army, which in actuality had struck south toward the interior posts held by the British. When Cornwallis learned of this trickery, he fired off a letter to Clinton explaining that he was powerless to help Rawdon, by then some 150 miles away. To retrace his steps through that hostile terrain, fording all those dreadful rivers, would mean exposure to another blow from Greene's will-o-the-wisp army.

General Clinton, ever pleased to note Cornwallis' shortcomings, complained in reply that he would have preferred Cornwallis to stick with Greene. But Sir Henry did not order the Earl to go back to South Carolina, which suggests he meant only to imply that the damage was already done.

Critics of Greene have said that by turning his attention to South Carolina he was avoiding a more important clash with Cornwallis. The reasoning there seems specious. Greene was cautious, perhaps overly so at times, but he would fight when he viewed the conditions as favorable to his cause. His maneuvers in the next weeks were to keep some 7000 British troops tied down at a time when they were desperately needed in Virginia.

On April 7, Cornwallis reached the Wilmington area with his ragged and exhausted army. The march had been slow from Guilford. There were about 400 sick and wounded in the ranks and enroute the brave Colonel Webster and four other officers had died. The whole of Cornwallis' army was now without shoes.

While the troops rested and scrounged items of clothing and equipment, Cornwallis planned his next move. It is doubtful if he ever surprised an American commander more completely (with the possible exception of Horatio Gates at Camden) than he did his own commander, Sir Henry Clinton, when he made that move two weeks later into Virginia. Evidence is lacking, but the march from Wilmington must have been undertaken by Cornwallis with something between a sneaking and a certain conviction that Clinton opposed it.

In a letter to General William Phillips, whose troops were in the vicinity of Portsmouth, Virginia, Cornwallis pointed out that the Carolinas could not be held unless Virginia were subjugated. To Clinton, the Earl said much the same: "North Carolina is of all the provinces the most difficult to attack unless material assistance could be got from the inhabitants, the contrary of which I have sufficiently experienced." On May 13, before Clinton had had time to reply, Cornwallis crossed the Roanoke with Tarleton raiding and foraging in front of him. When the Earl's forces made the juncture with those of Phillips at Petersburg, bad news awaited them: Phillips had died five days earlier of fever. The new commander was Benedict Arnold, for whom Cornwallis, with his avowed dedication to personal loyalty, could hardly have had great regard.

Nonetheless, Cornwallis found himself once again commanding a rather sizable field army. Arnold had 2000 men and orders to fortify a naval base and put pressure on the provinces, thus taking some of the heat off Cornwallis in South Carolina. But here was Cornwallis at Arnold's side. Arnold earlier had joined Phillips, who himself had commanded some 2500 men. Now more reinforcements were arriving up the James River. Cornwallis now had about 7500 men under his command, but, and this was galling, he was dismayed to find himself once more inhibited by the clammy, defensive hand of Sir Henry Clinton.

Cornwallis still wanted to find the enemy and give him a proper thrashing, and now he had enough men to try it. Instead, he was forced to contend with the armchair strategy of his superior: fortifying naval stations and making little raids in the provinces. Sir Henry rather favored the naval station at Portsmouth, but Arnold opposed this and said so before returning to New York. Without Clinton's approval, however, Cornwallis was stuck with the orders given Phillips, at least until Clinton could modify them. In the meantime, the Earl kept busy with harrassing raids on Lafayette's patrols.

It was, on the whole, an unproductive exercise. Lafayette had learned a lot from Greene and Washington about retreating, and he kept his small army—one third the size of the forces under Cornwallis—on the move and out of British clutches. In June, General Anthony Wayne arrived with some veteran troops, making Lafayette's army more formidable. In July, after a period of inconclusive feints and thrusts on both sides, Lafayette was joined by a living legend, a gaunt and hollow-eyed General Daniel Morgan, determined to fight once again.

The great-hearted Lafayette received Morgan and the men who followed him back to the war with rejoicing. On the spot, Morgan was given command of the light troops and cavalry. It is one of the small ironies of history that, shortly after Morgan returned to the field, Lord Cornwallis dispatched a special force to probe Lafayette's lines. In command of that force was Banastre Tarleton.

The action was never joined. Either a sixth sense on Tarleton's part or a few well-placed rounds from some strangely familiar long rifles put him on notice that this might not be a good day to fight. The Green Dragoon returned to the main body and Cornwallis without fighting.

Lafayette, watching Morgan's troops flush the British, was full of admiration. He wrote George Washington: "The riflemen ran the whole day in front of my horse without eating or resting."

Morgan, who understandably wanted to serve under Washington and be in the line at the finish, was denied both ambitions. Soon the old ailments returned and he was forced to retire once more. This time he wrote Washington personally, saying that the great disappointment of his military career was in never having served directly under his commander-in-chief.

Washington was clearly pleased and touched. He wrote the Old Wagoner: "I most sincerely lament your present situation, and esteem it a peculiar loss to the United States that you are, at this time, unable to render your services in the field."

Washington learned in June that Cornwallis was in Virginia, but shortly thereafter he got another bit of intelligence that caused him considerable elation. The French Count Francois de Grasse, now in the West Indies, would bring his fleet north to the Chesapeake as soon as he could outmaneuver and outrun the British fleet. To the American commander, this instantly suggested an exciting possibility. If he and the French commander, Jean Baptiste Rochambeau, could sneak around Clinton and join Lafayette, and if De Grasse could seal the British off from the sea, Cornwallis could be starved and hammered to death.

Cornwallis, meanwhile, was having his troubles with Clinton. Sir Henry was urging him to take a strong defensive position, either at Williamsburg or Yorktown, then detach six infantry regiments, including Rangers, cavalry and every other ablebodied man he could spare, and send them to New York! Cornwallis must have seethed inwardly—but he moved promptly to comply with Sir Henry's orders.

On July 6, at Green Spring Farm, Cornwallis scored one of his most satisfying small-scale victories of the war. By ruse, he convinced Mad Anthony Wayne that a small detachment of British guarded the baggage of the main army northwest of James-town. In truth, Cornwallis had quietly deployed a large part of his army to commanding ground, reachable only by a narrow causeway. If Wayne could be induced through faulty intelli-gence to cross the causeway, Cornwallis could envelop Wayne's flanks and cut up the attackers as they retreated through the bog. For once, everything went according to plan. Wayne's forces advanced into the trap, Cornwallis sprang it and Wayne, ever audacious, decided his only hope was to attack on line with bayonets and perhaps make Cornwallis think reserves were coming up to help. Wayne's ploy failed and many of his panic-stricken men made good their retreat only because of the merciful descent of darkness. Cornwallis took about 75 casual-ties; Wayne roughly twice that figure.

Cornwallis' elation was soon dimmed by the arrival of a let-ter from Sir Henry which suggested to the Earl that his commander in New York had taken leave of his senses. Clinton prattled about plans for an attack on Philadelphia: he wanted Cornwallis to march into Pennsylvania. He also had a grandiose plan to trap the French squadron in Rhode Island. And he wanted still more of Cornwallis' troops detached.

As July dragged on, Cornwallis sent various units destined for embarkation to New York to General Leslie at Portsmouth. The Earl left himself only 10 boats for the use of his own infan-try and cavalry. And dutifully he dispatched Tarleton on the raids Clinton favored, destroying or capturing enemy stores.

Before the troops sailed, however, Clinton blandly counter-manded his own orders. Now it was top priority for Cornwallis to hold Old Point Comfort which secured Hampton Road. In addition, Clinton both gave back and took away again the troops which had almost been enroute to him. The Earl, Clinton wrote, could keep all the troops he needed. But after Cornwallis had decided what was needed and made Old Point Comfort secure, all troops surplus to those needs should be sent to New York. That Cornwallis retained his sanity at this juncture seems quite remarkable. He had never even intimated that holding a defensive post such as Sir Henry proposed required an entire army. He had, however, time and again expressed the convic-tion that the war could be won only by coming to grips with a large force of Americans and destroying them. Now Sir Henry was putting words in the Earl's mouth, arguing that Cornwallis had pleaded to keep his forces intact in order to comply with Clinton's wishes to protect ships of the line.

While Cornwallis looked for a position to fortify in conformity with Clinton's wishes, he was harrassed with letters from Sir Henry urging haste and castigating Cornwallis for leaving the Carolinas in the first place. In spite of the petty needling, Cornwallis went about the business of seeking the required strong point—a port which would accommodate deep-water vessels and a position which could be defended effectively. Cornwallis' reluctant choice: a Virginia village named Yorktown.

"We Get Beat …. And Fight Again"

As Cornwallis' men progressed toward Virginia, Greene moved with all deliberate speed for Camden. News of Greene's march into South Carolina swept the back country like wildfire and spurred Sumter, Marion and Lee to new peaks of activity. Lee and Marion found each other and together embarked on a siege of Fort Watson, which stood 30 feet high on an Indian mound on the Santee River at Wright's Bluff. Surrounded by three rows of abatis, the fort was held by a mixed force of 100 regulars and Loyalists. The attacking force cut off the garrison's water supply, but the defenders immediately dug a well inside. Then, for five days, the raiders built a 40-foot tower from logs. On the night of April 22, sweating Patriots pulled the tower into position and in the morning the defenders found themselves looking up into the barrels of Patriot rifles. There was no place to hide and Fort Watson ran up the white flag.

Meanwhile Greene, 30 miles away at Hobkirk's Hill, was deploying his forces in such a way as to invite an attack from Rawdon in Camden. On the morning of April 25—the same day Cornwallis marched his rested army toward Virginia—Rawdon made for Hobkirk's Hill and a showdown with Greene.

Lieutenant-Colonel Francis Rawdon at 26 was a rather fearsome figure. He was a gangling, glowering man who had spent much of the war in holding operations. This day he was spoiling for a fight, eager to whip Greene who had become an international figure after his standoff with Cornwallis at Guilford.

Greene had deployed his men on Hobkirk's Hill with the Virginia Continentals under General Isaac Huger on the right. To the left were the Marylanders; behind them the North Carolina militia. On the extreme left were posted Colonel Washington and his dragoons, who at once circled behind Rawdon to prevent his escape back to Camden.

As soon as Greene saw Rawdon coming straight at him, he

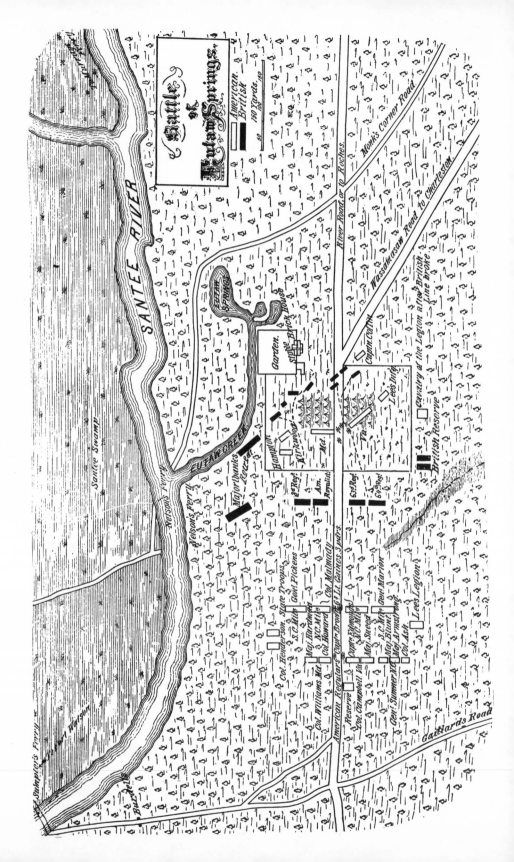

ordered his six-pounders to pour grapeshot into the advancing column. Rawdon's troops dropped like flies in the withering fire, whereupon Greene ordered Colonels John Gunby and Benjamin Ford, commanding on the left, to launch a bayonet attack. Colonels Richard Campbell and Samuel Hawes moved forward to hit Rawdon's forces on the flank and Greene had reason to believe that at last he had a chance for the type of clear-cut victory which had always eluded him. But Rawdon was wily and tenacious: he extended his lines and fought back. Then, unaccountably, Greene's fabled Marylanders gave way and the British came on with renewed verve. Compounding Greene's problems, Colonel Washington's encircling movement had been too wide and, unlike at Cowpens, he was far in the rear of the British when he was most needed to apply critical pressures.

Once again, Greene had fought a bloody, inconclusive battle, causing the enemy some 250 casualties and taking about the same himself, but leaving the field to the British. Clinton and Cornwallis hailed Hobkirk's Hill as a great victory over Greene; in truth it was just another standoff, the type from which the Americans always seemed to recover more quickly than did the British. To Chevalier de la Luzerne, the French minister to the United States, Greene wrote: "We fight, get beat, rise and fight again." It remains a fair appraisal of how Greene retreated to victory.

As Greene's raiders—Marion, Sumter, Pickens and Lee—rode to one success after another in the small engagements which characterized the fighting at this period, the British began to realize that Greene's presence now totally jeopardized their hold on South Carolina. By mid-May, Greene and his raiders had taken 800 prisoners and mounted threats to both Ninety-Six and Augusta.

Greene sent Lee to aid Pickens in besieging the strong points around Augusta and himself led his main body toward Ninety-Six. This fortified town was surrounded by a stockade fence, a ditch and an abatis. The jail, a small fort in itself, overlooked the stream which gave Ninety-Six its fresh water. Across the stream stood two blockhouses, both heavily armed and defended.

The fighting which took place at Ninety-Six followed the Nathanael Greene pattern: bloody and inconclusive. Defenders of the fort crept out at night and attacked Greene's detail which was attempting to dig a parallel siege trench just 200 feet from the stockade. American casualties were heavy; the British lost but one man. Preparations for the siege continued at a more prudent distance. By June 11, Greene got word that Rawdon, heavily reinforced, was on the way to relieve Ninety-Six. On the 14th, Sumter and Washington attacked Rawdon, trying to slow him down, but were driven off with heavy casualties.

With Rawdon almost upon him, Greene made one more effort to reduce Ninety-Six. In a savage, half-hour battle Greene lost 150 men, and by failing to commit reserves at a critical moment, lost the siege as well. Greene wrote that he had to "lament that such brave men fell in a unsuccessful attempt."

Cautiously, Greene made his way with the main body toward the High Hills of the Santee for a much-needed respite from war, heat, mosquitoes, hunger and thirst, leaving his tireless and faithful guerrillas to harass the low country. Colonel Peter Horry, a little-publicized but highly competent officer who served the South Carolina state cavalry, led slashing forays to the very outskirts of Charleston.

Despite setbacks, Greene had all of South Carolina in turmoil. Cornwallis was already in Virginia and moving inexorably toward his final disaster. In South Carolina, the British were confined largely to Charleston, except for Rawdon's army which could never quite pin Greene down where it wanted him. With a kind of sixth sense, Greene knew he could help George Washington most effectively by staying in South Carolina, out of harm's—and Rawdon's—way. It was a strategy that Greene stuck with until a singular opportunity for a showdown presented itself.

At the outset of the last half of 1781, Nathanael Greene devoted much of his time in the High Hills of the Santee to the emerging problems of restoring Patriot rule in South Carolina. The High Hills were ideal for this brief interlude. The weather was less hot and the defensive position was strong in the event of an unexpected British attack. At the same time, Greene was close enough to the enemy to pose a constant threat—and close enough to his guerrillas to have good and continuing intelligence on the British.

All around him Whigs and Tories continued to murder one another and Greene was vexed at his inability to reduce the hatred and fear which imbued the countryside. He called in and conferred with officials of Georgia and South Carolina, pleading with them to organize new governments and promise amnesty to any who had not borne arms. The war wasn't over, Greene reasoned, but it was long past time to start binding up the wounds. He called on his guerrilla leaders to exert sweet reason. In effect, Greene said, be Robin Hoods; take only from the well-to-do and help the destitute, and by all means give receipts for what you take.

From Virginia came reports that buoyed up the little army on the Santee. The Compte de Rochambeau and the Marquis de Lafayette were maneuvering into positions against Cornwallis. This suggested that Greene could perhaps discount the persistent stories of an impending return of Cornwallis to South Carolina. Still, that was the thing that Greene most feared. He was determined to guard against another juncture between Cornwallis and Rawdon. To deny them a united front, he would even face another of the battles he seemed always destined to lose.

Greene himself had become quite acclimatized to his role as the running general. In a letter to Henry Knox he confided: "There are few generals that has run oftener or more lustily than I have done, but I have taken care not to run too far, and commonly have run as fast forward as backward, to convince our enemy that we were like a crab, that could run either way."

On August 13, Greene received intelligence from Light Horse Harry Lee that tended to move him forward. The British, Lee said, were tuckered out from the heat and therefore the time was propitious for attack. To incite the fight he was always looking for, Lee sent another message to Greene on the 17th: he expected Cornwallis to strike back toward Charleston. That settled the matter. Without delay, Greene moved toward Camden and a showdown with Colonel Alexander Stewart, who commanded some 2300 British troops then maneuvering in the area and who was expecting reinforcements from Charleston.

In the fierce heat of that South Carolina summer, Greene marched by night. At Stoutemire's Plantation on September 5, he urged Marion to join him. Rations were short but the time for a fight was at hand. In easy stages, Greene moved his main body, about 2400 strong, to a position several miles from Eutaw Springs and about seven miles from the enemy.

Early on the morning of September 8, Greene moved quietly toward his foe. The British, unaware of the approaching army, had an unarmed forage detail in the line of advance. Not even last minute intelligence reports convinced the British that Greene was on their heels. When Stewart finally sent Major John Coffin out to reconnoitre with 200 horsemen, the British made a whooping charge on what he regarded as a party of mounted American militia. It was a bad judgment on Coffin's part; he was attacking Light Horse Harry Lee.

Supported by heavy fire from the infantry, Lee ordered a bayonet charge by the Legion while his dragoons thundered off to
envelop Coffin. In disordered flight, many of the British threw
down their weapons. Including the unarmed detail digging
potatoes, Lee took more than 200 prisoners, and in holiday
spirit Greene's army trudged toward the fateful clash at Eutaw
Springs.

When the Americans first met resistance from a British skirmish line near Eutaw Springs, Greene deployed his men and
took personal command. He saw from his position in the center
with the militia that Stewart had drawn up his forces in an un-
broken line, with his left anchored to Eutaw Creek and his re-
formed cavalry under Coffin on the right. In the center were
contingents of New York and New Jersey Loyalists.

Lee and his men, supported by infantry under Colonel John
Henderson, formed the American left. Marion, Pickens and the
Marquis de Malmady fanned out with the militia across the cen-
ter and to the right.

Stewart clearly planned a bayonet charge, confident that the
American militia would break and run as it had on some occasions in the past. This time, however, he faced seasoned militia
as ably led as it had been at Cowpens. To the surprise of the British, the militia held and returned their fire in calm order. As
the cannons shook the ground with terrible blasts, Greene
moved the North Carolina Continentals up to reinforce the center. They also acquitted themselves nobly. It was not until Colonel Henderson suffered a severe wound that the American left
began to buckle. Greene was having no part of that. This was
his chance to break the back of the British war effort in the
South. To seize that chance, he ordered his entire second line—
the Continentals from Delaware, Maryland and Virginia—to
move through the wavering militia and mount a bayonet
charge. With a mighty, challenging roar, the Patriot veterans
swept forward, and at the same time the hard-riding Lee cut
and slashed at the British right. In exultation, Greene surveyed
what he took to be a rout. All along the line the enemy was on
the run.

Then occurred one of the unforseen developments which
dogged the battles run by Nathanael Greene. The Virginians
paused in line to get off a few rounds at the retreating British.
Lee was appalled, as well he might be, for his flanking attack
left him directly in the line of the Virginians' fire. Thundering
up on horseback, he demanded an explanation from Lieutenant-Colonel Richard Campbell. He never got it for the next in-

stant Campbell took a bullet in the chest which was to prove fatal. In those brief moments, the American pressure on the British flank was relaxed, and before his horrified eyes Greene saw the British defenses harden.

Two pockets of British resistance emerged; one was in dense undergrowth where the men fired from concealment, another in some sturdy buildings bordering the creek. To make matters worse, many of the Patriots, unaware of the renewed resistance and seeing only that the camp had been vacated, set to work on an abundant supply of rum and soon were in no condition to continue the fight. Seeing this, Coffin settled his score by leading a cavalry charge on the tippling Americans. In a confusing fight with many casualties on both sides, Greene's big victory was snatched from him again. The four-hour fight ended with the Americans in full retreat. It was a ghastly march, impeded by scores of wounded on litters. Many of the imbibers had neglected to refill their canteens with water. The entire army, which had suffered about 25 per cent casualties, reached the comparative safety of Burdell's Plantation in a state of shock and exhaustion.

But as Greene looked back on it, he decided things had not turned out too badly. He could scarcely afford the 500-or-so casualties his army took—but no more could the British endure theirs, which were considerably higher. No British force had pressed forward to finish Greene off, and that alone suggested that the enemy had been mangled too. In the months and years ahead—for Greene and his army were to fight on long after Cornwallis gave up the ghost at Yorktown—Nathanael Greene was the man for the job. He could be beaten. Almost everyone, in fact, beat him at one time or another. But he could not be exterminated. He was there, a presence, Godlike—remorseless and implaccable to the end.

Indeed, for the British, Greene was the wraith who haunted and perverted their dreams of victory. The field and the day belonged to Britain but the future belonged to Greene.

Siege of Yorktown.

American.
French.
British.

YORK RIVER.

Guadaloupe
Charon
Sunken Vessels taken by Americans.
Vessels taken by French.

Rangers by Reg'
Gloucester

F. Fusileers
Simcos

Reg' of Touraine
Reg' of Agenois
Royal Valenois

Town British occupied by French

Second Parallel

F

A

A

Moors House
First Parallel

Soisonois
Deux Ponts
Bourbon

Place of Surrender.

Baron Viominil

French Artillery

L! Infantry
Virginia Militia
Gov! Nelson
American Hospital

MARYLAND
VIRGINIA
Lafayette
Baron Steuben
NEW YORK

Adj! Gen!
Guards
Rochambeau

Qr. Master Gen!
Rhode Island
New Jersey
Sappers and Miners
Gen! Clinton

Road to Hampton.

Washington

□ Artificers
□ Laboratory
□ Magazine

Yorktown

I N THE EARLY SUMMER OF 1781 ANY MAN WHO MIGHT HAVE HAD THE temerity to predict that General George Washington in New York and Earl Cornwallis in the far-away South would shortly clash in Virginia, and that the battle would all but end the Revolution, would have been immediately confined as a lunatic.

That was before several things fell into place all at once for Washington, who was long overdue for a little luck. The early intelligence on De Grasse's move toward the Chesapeake was confirmed. Washington assessed his situation in the North and found it to be somewhere between desperate and hopeless. In his own words:

"Instead of having magazines filled with provisions, we have a scanty pittance scattered here and there in the different states. Instead of having our arsenals well supplied with military stores, they are poorly provided, and the workmen all leaving them. . . . Instead of having a regular system of transportation upon credit, or funds in the quartermaster's hands to defray the contingent expense of it, we have neither the one nor the other; and all that business, or a great part of it, being done by military impress, we are daily and hourly oppressing the people—souring their tempers and alienating their affection. Instead of having regiments completed to the new establishment, scarce any state in the Union has, at this hour, an eighth part of its quota in the field, and little prospect, that I can see, of ever getting more than half. In a word, instead of everything in readiness to take the field, we have nothing: and instead of having the prospect of a glorious offensive campaign before us, we have a bewildered and gloomy defensive one, unless we should receive a powerful aid of ships, land troops, and money from our generous allies; and these at present are too contingent to build upon."

That Washington, less than two months after this abject

assessment, could put in motion his plan to throttle Cornwallis is a testimonial to his rebounding courage. In July Rochambeau, who had been active in the initial planning, joined Washington on the Hudson. Every care was taken to deceive Clinton. Under no circumstances, Washington and Rochambeau agreed, must Sir Henry gain the first inkling of the plan to drive south.

In all, Washington had about 12,000 men at his disposal, including some 8000 French army and Patriot units designated for the Southern trek. The other 4000 under Major General William Heath were to be left behind to guard West Point and to deter Clinton should he make a move.

On August 19, a few days after Washington received word that De Grasse was committed to full sail to the Chesapeake with a substantial fleet and more than 3000 troops, the stealthy withdrawal began. Washington's men melted away using back country roads and regrouped at Princeton, New Jersey.

Clinton was not the only person confused by these movements. Washington's secretary, Jonathan Trumbull, wrote: "By these maneuvers and the correspondent march of the troops, our own army no less than the enemy are completely deceived. No movement perhaps was ever attended with more conjectures, or such as were more curious than this....Not one, I believe, penetrated the real design."

After the juncture at Princeton, the march continued to Trenton where Washington was shocked to find that there were not enough ships available to transport the troops south. After a hasty consultation with the field commanders, the decision was made. If the ships had not come for the men, the men would march to the ships. The army continued on foot to the head of the Chesapeake, marching through Philadelphia, Chester, Pennsylvania, and Wilmington, Delaware. The battered Patriots and their French allies were given heroic welcomes all along the route and at Chester, Washington got the best news of all: the Comte de Grasse, with 28 ships of the line, was in position off Virginia, and 3200 fighting men had debarked and were at Jamestown, ready to join Lafayette. Sir Henry Clinton, to the attacking force's relief if not its surprise, had yet to move.

Jubilantly Washington, Rochambeau and the Chevalier de Chastellux left the movement south by ship to subordinate commanders and proceeded overland to Mount Vernon. It was the first time Washington had seen his home in six years. On September 14, the commanders arrived in Williamsburg and it was announced that Washington was taking command of the rapidly burgeoning and combined Franco-American forces.

Comte François de Grasse, an uncommonly good sailor, was also a good politician and a sound bargainer. He had, in a later century's parlance, an eye for the main chance. He had reached the French West Indies in April, after a 38-day Atlantic crossing from Brest. There had been a brush with the British fleet under Rear Admiral Sir Samuel Hood who, along with his superior in the American theatre, Sir George Rodney, showed little stomach for a major naval engagement with the French. That fitted in nicely with De Grasse's plans in any case. He moved on to Santo Domingo and completed negotiations for additional ground troops with the new commander there, M. de Lillancourt.

From the West Indies garrison De Grasse took detachments from the Gatinois, Agenois and Touraine regiments, along with some artillery pieces, dragoons, siege and field ordnance. De Grasse agreed that the troops would be returned to the Indies by October 15. He also made arrangements for additional financial aid for Washington's destitute forces.

As he approached the Virginia capes on August 30, De Grasse encountered the British frigate *Guadaloupe* and the corvette *Loyalist*. He made quick work of these lookout ships, boarding the corvette and bottling up the frigate in the York River. The next day, De Grasse sailed into Chesapeake Bay for anchorage, and individual ships were designated to block the mouths of the York and James rivers. French ground forces disembarked and under the command of the Marquis Saint-Simon, proceeded along the James River to join Lafayette's command.

De Grasse, aware that he had enjoyed a lucky passage from the Indies, wanted to get the fighting over as quickly as possible before the British came after him in force. He urged Lafayette, reinforced by Saint-Simon, to attack but Lafayette, who had been dodging Cornwallis for many months, decided to wait for Washington and Rochambeau. As Lafayette put it: "Having so sure a game to play, it would be madness, by the risk of attack, to give any thing to chance." Cornwallis, Lafayette already sensed, was a fish in a barrel.

De Grasse was less sure. He and his ships of the line, confined as they were in the Chesapeake, might look like ships in a bottle to the British. Where was the British navy, anyway? De Grasse had no way of knowing that a bit of luck had entered into the game there, too. In July, Rear Admiral Thomas Graves, commanding British navy units in New York, had gotten word that a big convoy of goods and supplies for the Patriots had sailed from Europe and that it was vital that it be intercepted.

This caused Graves to put to sea with a sizable fleet, confident that if the French struck north from the West Indies, Rodney and Hood would take care of them.

In truth, Rodney and Hood tried. Rodney was ill and had turned over his command to Hood, urging him to intercept De Grasse and have it out with the Frenchman. By a quirk of fate, Hood had sailed into the Chesapeake ahead of De Grasse and finding no enemy there had gone on to New York. Nobody, consequently, took care of De Grasse—an error fatal to the fortunes of Lord Cornwallis.

The noose tightening around Cornwallis' forces was, if not of British make, at least bartered to the executioners by the Crown's military leadership.

First, Sir Henry dawdled in New York for precious weeks long after it was apparent to everyone, including British intelligence, that Washington and Rochambeau were moving against Cornwallis.

Second, Admiral Graves, back from his unsuccessful attempt to find the phantom convoy, waited until August 31 to sail for the Chesapeake to challenge De Grasse. When he arrived off the capes on the morning of September 5, he divided his fleet into three sections. Graves directed the battle from his flagship *London*, which mounted 98 guns. The other two sections were led by Rear Admiral Samuel Hood and Rear Admiral Francis Samuel Drake.

De Grasse knew full well that the outcome of this battle would determine the fate of the British forces in Yorktown and he was determined to drive the enemy off. At noon, when the tide was right, De Grasse moved out into the Atlantic to intercept his foe. He commanded from the bridge of his flagship the *Ville de Paris*. His subordinate commanders were Le Sieur de Bougainville, De Latouche-Treville and Le Sieur de Monteil.

Superiority in both ships and guns lay with the French that afternoon. De Grasse took 24 ships of the line carrying some 1700 guns and 19,000 sailors into action. Against this force the British mustered 19 ships with 1400 guns and some 13,000 seamen. Here again, the initiative lay with the French. De Grasse attempted to maneuver in such a way that the entire British fleet would become engaged, but evasive tactics by Graves avoided such a clash. In the end, only 15 French ships got into the fighting. At five o'clock, with the winds varying, De Grasse made a determined run at the *London*, and with guns blazing caused Graves to break off the action. The battle lasted more than two hours and Graves took advantage of the wind to sail out of contact at sunset. The British later reported that De Grasse's guns had worked over their flagship so thoroughly that Graves had been obliged to change all its masts.

Britain lost 90 killed and 246 wounded in this action, which came to be known as the Battle of the Virginia Capes. French casualties totaled about 200, but several British ships were heavily damaged and one, the *Terrible*, had to be scuttled.

The fleets stayed in visual contact the next day but Graves decided he had taken too much damage to renew the action. De Grasse, too, had reservations about getting too far away from Yorktown where his principal function was to keep the British bottled in. There followed several days of inconclusive maneuverings in heavy winds which made it difficult for De Grasse to come to grips with the British, who in any case were reluctant to resume the fighting. On September 10, Count Paul François de Barras, commanding a squadron of ships which had sailed down from Newport to reinforce De Grasse, arrived off the capes. Graves, now badly outnumbered, knew he had lost. On September 14, he turned tail and headed back for New York.

Cornwallis, aware that forces were closing in on him, might have done something to help himself by attacking Lafayette but he, too, waited—beguiled by promises of action from Sir Henry—until Washington and Rochambeau and the troops from the West Indies were on the ground. By then it was too late. It is a prime irony of the war that Cornwallis, Britain's ablest and most aggressive field commander, spent the last months of his luckless campaign burrowing, molelike, to resist the siege of Yorktown.

By mid-September, Cornwallis received word that Graves had deserted him, that Lafayette was receiving reinforcements and that Washington and Rochambeau were marching against him—and not far off. The Earl sent Tarleton with a nine-man patrol to gather intelligence on the size of the enemy forces. Banastre returned to camp with a realistic estimate of Lafayette's strength and urged Lord Cornwallis to press an immediate attack. It was typical that Cornwallis may have allowed his reservations about Banny to cause him to discard the idea. In retrospect, it appears to have been Cornwallis' last chance to break out of the coffin which American daring and British dallying had fashioned for him. In fairness to Cornwallis, he gave the idea consideration. There were two possibilities: he could take the road to Williamsburg, advancing several thousand troops at night and hope to surprise Lafayette before he could go to work on them with his artillery; or he could ferry troops up the York River to a position above and behind Williamsburg hoping for the same element of surprise. The British also considered executing these movements simultaneously, hitting Lafayette from both front and rear.

Just as Cornwallis was settling for the first plan, he received a message from Clinton that caused him to postpone the attack. Help was on the way, Sir Henry said, in the form of Admiral Digby who could be expected off the coast "any day." Also, Sir Henry confided, he was detaching 4000 men to come to relieve Cornwallis. It was already quite late, but the letter caused Cornwallis to hesitate—and in effect sealed his doom. When Washington and Rochambeau arrived in force on September 26, Cornwallis must have known that without reinforcements the game was over. He had let slip his only chance of breaking out of the siege lines, and now he pressed ahead with the digging to defend what quickly would become an untenable position.

There were outer and inner lines of fortification running in arcs around Yorktown from east to west. The outer line was the easier to defend. It was a good half mile in front of the inner line and was flanked by ravines, marshes and creeks. It also offered good fields of fire against the four roads which approached the defenses from the outside. Cornwallis augmented these natural defenses by building small fortifications on his left flank near the head of Wormsley Creek. On his right, he was stronger. The Fusiliers' redoubt commanded the main road to Williamsburg and could be supported by any ships brave enough to stand motionless in the York River.

Between the outer fortifications and the city, Cornwallis built 10 strong points to cover the conceivable routes of enemy advance. Redoubts 9 and 10 protected Cornwallis' left flank. The Earl also stripped guns from the navy and in all had some 65 guns in the 14 batteries along his formidable earthworks on which British troops and Negro slaves had toiled night and day for many weeks.

Even Cornwallis must have realized that he had not enough of anything to face the forces ganging up on him. With little more than 5000 troops to confront an enemy who now had three times that many, Cornwallis could not even effectively man the defensive positions he had devised. But the Earl, good soldier that he was, was determined to do the best he could in a bad situation. He placed his headquarters in a large house on commanding ground in the southeastern section of Yorktown, well behind Redoubts 9 and 10. These were critical points in

Cornwallis' defensive plan. If they held, he could concentrate on whatever enemy came down the Williamsburg Road. If they fell, the attackers would quickly threaten his rear.

Despite the odds against him, Cornwallis was reluctant to sit still and let the enemy come at him. The British still toiling at the earthworks were under sporadic sniper fire, so Cornwallis sent Tarleton out to harass those militiamen. The result was negligible. Meanwhile, the work continued. Fields of fire were cleared and the earthworks and trenches beefed up with logs. Then on September 28 came the fateful word. The enemy was moving forward in force.

The French came down the main road from Williamsburg to Yorktown and fanned out to form a front on both sides of that road. The Americans broke off to the right so that the attackers had a semicircular front, sealing Cornwallis off from relief—were there any—by land. The sea, with De Grasse's formidable fleet unchallenged, offered no escape to the British.

Quietly Cornwallis watched these maneuvers, hardly knowing what to do. If he defended his outer perimeter with determination, he would suffer heavy casualties and have less strength to hold Yorktown. If he abandoned those positions, he would find himself fighting on a diminishing front ill-suited to defensive action.

Once again, Sir Henry Clinton played a role in Cornwallis' planning. Another message from him promised that 5000 men would sail on October 5 to relieve Cornwallis. The Earl calculated the odds. It was September 29. As he saw it, the better part of valor would be to abandon the outer defenses, concentrate on holding the town, and endure the siege and its attendant artillery barrage until Clinton's reinforcements arrived. On September 30, General Washington observed that the British had pulled in their lines. He immediately occupied the vacated defensive positions and the preliminary skirmishing began.

Tarleton sent a raiding party out to take some prisoners: they captured a few. Saint-Simon's light infantry closed with some of Cornwallis' pickets and drove them in. Then Washington set about digging trenches inside the British defensive positions while Cornwallis harassed them with his artillery. The Patriots digging the trenches kept one eye on the vicinity of Cornwallis' guns. Each tell-tale flash from a British muzzle sent the workers diving into their unfinished ditches. It was slow going.

Soon, the British saw, this steady cannonading was depleting their ammunition supply and not causing many casualties. The tire was reduced. The Americans continued to dig parallel lines which brought them closer and closer to the British strong points.

On October 2, Cornwallis sent Tarleton to Gloucester where it was hoped he might raid and forage in front of the British defensive positions. This proved impracticable because Washington had already reinforced General George Weedon and his 1500 Americans there with troops led by the Marquis Claude Gabriel de Choisy. In one brush with the French, Tarleton lost a horse and was nearly captured, narrowly making good his escape when he was rescued by several of his men. Characteristically, Tarleton wrote he had been denied victory because of an inept performance by his troops.

Up to now, the bombardment had all been outward bound from Yorktown. Washington was about to redress the balance. He brought up his own siege guns, emplaced them and, on October 6, commenced some cannonading of his own. The siege was on.

Washington concentrated his parallels on Cornwallis' left flank where Redoubts 9 and 10 seemed to pose the strongest resistance. From the first parallel trench, which covered about 2000 yards of the front, the Patriots dug ancillary trenches toward the fortifications. Then, in the classic pattern, the attackers branched out to dig a second parallel, this one closer to the defenses of the British where cannon could be emplaced to deliver point-blank fire.

One thing disturbed Washington. He knew he would have to eliminate Redoubts 9 and 10, perhaps by frontal assault. Once they fell, he could pour fire on the defenders almost at will. On October 9, the first parallel was complete and Washington began his bombardment in earnest. Yorktown soon became a shambles, the orderly life in neat tents was disrupted and the defenders were forced to seek any kind of cover they could find. Casualties mounted; the screams of the wounded and dying could be heard in the siege lines. The firing was so intense that many on both sides were deafened.

The next day British Major Charles Cochrane slipped through the French sea blockade in a small boat and delivered a message from Sir Henry Clinton. In placating terms, Sir Henry expressed his concern for Cornwallis' position, but regretfully announced he had postponed his departure with a relief force until October 12 or so; he was not quite sure. Cornwallis' hopes were dashed. He and his men had endured a dreadful bombardment sustained only by the hope that Sir Henry had departed New York on the 5th, as earlier promised. Now if the armchair general were coming at all it would be days, maybe weeks, before he arrived.

The French and Americans stepped up their fire. On the 11th, the French brought two more batteries with six 24-pounders into play and that night the Americans began digging the second parallel.

What Cornwallis saw on the morning of the 12th must have convinced him that the drama was drawing to a climax. The Americans, who had a strong, native facility for digging, had all but completed the second parallel—and it extended menacingly toward the key Redoubts.

The American barrage continued unabated while the British, low on ammunition, could make· only token responses as gun after gun in the Yorktown defensive line was silenced. Redoubts 9 and 10 bore the brunt of the concentrated fire and, on the night of October 14, Washington decided to storm them.

Cornwallis had fortified the Redoubts as best he could. Sharp stakes protruding from the earthworks would have to be surmounted. A hodge-podge of fallen trees and sharpened branches also faced the attackers. Defending Redoubt 9 were about 120 Hessians and British commanded by Lieutenant-Colonel Henry Johnson. Some 50 men under Major James Campbell held Redoubt 10.

Lafayette was chosen by George Washington to command 400 American light infantry in the attack on Redoubt 10. The gallant Frenchman, not unmindful of the honor, turned over to Lieutenant-Colonel Alexander Hamilton the role of field leader of the storming party. Washington turned to Rochambeau for the assault on Redoubt 9. Rochambeau delegated this distinction to Major General the Baron Charles-Joseph-Hyacinthe du Haux Viomenil, who in turn entrusted it to Lieutenant-Colonel the Comte Guillaume de Deux-Ponts. To prevent the defenders from escaping, Colonel Laurens took a sizable party to the rear. The Redoubts were encircled.

The brave Colonel Hamilton led his silent storming party to a quick and easy victory at Redoubt 10. The British, hearing the Americans approaching, rushed to the parapet edge to throw down explosives, but Hamilton and his men clambered up the sides and engaged the British in a bayonet fight in the dark. It is no reflection on Major Campbell that he saw the hopelessness of his situation and surrendered. Redoubt 9 saw brisker fighting with the British pouring heavy fire on the French forces, but here again the British gave up when they saw how badly they were outnumbered. The attacks on the Redoubts were the only major hand-to-hand actions of the siege and were vital to the subsequent victory of the combined French and American forces.

In his last message to Clinton before the surrender, Cornwallis pluckily advised his commander-in-chief that the position of the British at Yorktown was not worth the effort to relieve it. Still, the Earl refused to give up. On the morning of the 16th, he sent Lieutenant-Colonel Robert Abercrombie with some 300 men out of the British lines in a desperate gamble to spike some of the siege guns. The raiders knocked out seven cannon before French Grenadiers under the command of Comte Louis-Marie de Noailles drove them off, killing eight and taking a dozen prisoners.

Within hours, however, the guns were back in operation and the fearful pounding of Yorktown resumed. Now all hope was gone. There was to be clearly no relief from the dallying Sir Henry. Casualties mounted. There was no place to protect the sick and the wounded. Cornwallis, a fighter to the end, made what for him was a logical decision. He would attack.

That evening, Cornwallis sent orders to Tarleton to prepare for an attack on Choisy in the morning. The Earl would ferry as much of his army as he could across the river to augment this audacious maneuver. Tarleton sent every boat he could muster back to Yorktown for this purpose. The first wave crossed over and reached Gloucester before midnight. Then fate struck Cornwallis a damaging blow. A storm came up, scattering the boats which carried the second wave of troops. Several precious hours were lost and by then it was too late. Cornwallis, part of his diminished force in Gloucester, part in Yorktown and part scattered in the river, was at the end of his resources. Grimly he ordered all to return to Yorktown where, on the morning of the 17th, the bombardment reached a new peak.

Shortly after 10:00 A.M., Cornwallis did the only thing left for him to do: he proposed a surrender. An emissary with a white handkerchief courageously walked out into view of the American lines and was escorted to Washington with this note from the embattled Earl:

Sir;
    I propose a cessation of hostilities for twenty-four hours, and that two officers may be appointed by each side, to meet at Mr. Moore's house, to settle terms for the surrender of the posts of York and Gloucester.

All along the siege lines the guns fell quiet. George Washington, on the threshhold of the victory so long denied him, was prepared to be lenient—but not sentimental. He replied to Cornwallis that he would grant the British general two hours in which to draft his terms.

In the eerie silence Cornwallis prepared his proposals and at 4:30 P.M. they were in Washington's hands. The American commander found them at least partially satisfactory and responded that the British could count on the same consideration for their surrendering army as had been granted the Americans at Charleston. With what irony Cornwallis must have read that portion of Washington's response! At Charleston, Cornwallis had been denied even the role of minor leadership he sought. At Yorktown, he was to bear the full humiliation for capitulation alone.

Both sides, in any case, agreed that differences of opinion were to be negotiated at a meeting of commissioners at the home of Augustine Moore in the rear of the first siege line, as Cornwallis had proposed. The British were represented by Lieutenant-Colonel Thomas Dundas and Major Alexander Ross. Washington nominated Colonel Laurens for the American side and, in consultation with Rochambeau and Lafayette, the Viscomte de Noailles for the French.

On October 18, the commissioners met and in a lengthy, tedious session drafted the Articles of Capitulation. Washington reviewed them on the 19th. He balked at one stipulation made by Cornwallis. Washington flatly refused to grant immunity from punishment to Loyalists serving in the British forces at the time of surrender. That, Washington declared, was a matter entirely in the jurisdiction of the United States of America.

Washington had the surrender document transcribed and sent over to Cornwallis with the stipulation that he sign by 11:00 A.M. The Earl put his signature to the paper at the appointed time, as did Captain Thomas Symonds on behalf of Britain's naval units in the York.

With a kind of psychological flourish, Washington and Rochambeau went to the battered Redoubt 10 to sign. Acting on behalf of Admiral de Grasse and the French fleet, the Comte de Barras then put his signature to the document.

Under the articles troops, seamen and marines from the British side were surrendered as prisoners of war. Officers were allowed to keep their sidearms, private papers and property. The soldiers were to be sent to prison camps in Virginia, Maryland and Pennsylvania. Washington was particularly generous with Cornwallis once the articles were signed. The Earl and some of his ranking officers were placed on parole with the widest freedoms. The sloop *Bonetta* was made available to Cornwallis to carry dispatches to Sir Henry Clinton, after which it was to be surrendered to American authorities.

There was to be no shilly-shallying with the surrender. At noon on October 19, with the ink scarcely dry on the Articles of Capitulation, allied forces made ready to receive the arms of their beaten foes. In order to prepare even one rank of suitably attired troops, the Americans had to cannibalize uniforms. The French, according to most records, managed to field some exceedingly well-dressed troops.

Promptly at 2:00 P.M., in the vicinity of what is today a national cemetery, the British army marched somberly out of Yorktown along the York-Hampton Road to the measured tread of an old British marching song: "The World Turned Upside Down." At the head of the column was not Earl Cornwallis who had led these troops all the way from Charleston. The Earl sent word that he was indisposed and confined to his quarters and, instead, sent Brigadier General O'Hara to act in his behalf.

O'Hara was an emotional man. One can imagine he had no more relish for turning over his sword to a conqueror than had Lord Cornwallis, but he bravely sought out Rochambeau. There ensued a bit of military protocol which must have been galling to O'Hara. The French leaders, in deference to their commander-in-chief, referred O'Hara to Washington. O'Hara very likely had thought it presumptious to approach Washington—after all, O'Hara was only filling in for Cornwallis—but on French advice, he now went to the commander-in-chief. Washington, in turn, referred O'Hara to General Lincoln, his second in command and the man who had surrendered Charleston to Clinton. Now everything was tidy and O'Hara offered his sword to Lincoln as a token of defeat and surrender. Lincoln, who had been through something like this before, returned O'Hara's sword.

Following this, the British army marched down Surrender Road between columns of American and French troops to Surrender Field. A British soldier wrote of this procession in his diary: "We came directly onto a level field or large meadow where we marched, one regiment after another, stacked muskets and lay down all our arms."

On this very day, Sir Henry Clinton set sail from New York to "relieve" Cornwallis. Five days later the armada arrived off the Virginia capes. Sir Henry stayed long enough to ascertain that Cornwallis had surrendered, then scuttled back to New York.

Washington's report of total victory reached Congress on October 24 and it set off celebrations throughout the land. Lafayette wrote America's allies in France: "The play is over; the fifth act has come to an end." King Louis XVI ordered "illuminations" to celebrate this great victory of French arms. And in England there was a sigh of relief that the long conflict had ended. Britain, said the man in the street, should not have been in this war in the first place.

It had been six years from Lexington to Yorktown. At last, America was to gain her independence—but not immediately. Not until November 30, 1782, did commissioners from Britain and America sign the articles of provisional peace. And it was September 3, 1783, before the Treaty of Paris was ratified. Still, Yorktown marked both an end and a beginning.

III
AFTERMATH

Buffalo Creek Jan: 21st 1781

My Dearest Lord

    The late affair has almost broke my heart. Morgan is at Gilbertown, I shall march tomorrow with 1200 Infantry & the Cavalry to attack or follow him to the banks of Catawba. Gen: Howard remains at Cherokee Ford with all Baggage Knapsacks included, ready to meet us at Ramsoures. I was never more surrounded with difficulty & distress, but practice in the school of adversity has ~~taught~~ strengthened me. Write to me, & to Howard, & communicate with 96. England is with Howard.

I would have the Cape Fear business go on — Communicate this to Balfour

        Your truly affec:ate Friend

R:t Hon:ble Lord Rawdon &c &c &c   Cornwallis

The letter from Cornwallis to Lord Rawdon following the Battle of Cowpens. (Courtesy of the Public Record Office, London.)

Cornwallis

C HARLES CORNWALLIS RETURNED TO LONDON SOMETHING SHORT OF the conquering hero, but by and large he was received as a capable officer who had done his best in a war which probably should not have been fought in the first place. Of the principal protagonists of the American Revolution, none was to match the dazzling career of Cornwallis in the last decades of the eighteenth century.

As early as May of 1782, while Cornwallis was technically still a prisoner of war on "parole," there was talk in London that he would go to India as Britain's governor-general and commander-in-chief. The military and civil services of India were in a deplorable state and Cornwallis, who had emerged from the Revolution with the reputation of a sound administrator, was regarded by the King and his counselors as the man for the job. At last Cornwallis accepted the post on February 23, 1786, "with grief of heart." Thus, the man who surrendered at Yorktown moved on to greater glory with the same reluctance which always seemed to mark his advancement to new levels.

Cornwallis had his work cut out for him in India. He quickly perceived that the civil service was corrupt because civil servants could not live on the pittances they received as salaries, and he noted many problems of lax discipline and disorganization in Britain's military forces. At once Cornwallis began a series of reforms. He called for more regular troops from Britain to supplement and replace the officers and soldiers of the East India Company. He raised the pay of the Indian civil servants so that they were not obliged to steal to survive. For more than three years he devoted himself tirelessly to the mass of problems of colonial administration, winning respect both in India and at home for his efforts.

Through it all, a wistful loneliness for Britain and his only son, Lord Brome, then a boy at school, is much in evidence. The

Earl's letters to his son also reflect fatherly fears and deep compassion. Cornwallis wrote on September 17, 1786: "You must write to me by every opportunity and longer letters than I write you; for I have a great deal more business every day than you have on a whole school day, and I never get a holiday. I have rode once upon an elephant, but it is so like going in a cart, that you would not think it very agreeable."

In Cornwallis there was also a humility and self-denigrating quality which was revealed in another letter to Lord Brome just after Christmas the same year:

> "You will have heard that soon after I left England I was elected a knight of the Garter, and very likely laughed at me for wishing to wear a blue riband over my fat belly....But I can assure you upon my honour that I neither asked for it nor wished for it. The reasonable object of ambition to a man is to have his name transmitted to posterity for eminent services rendered to his country and to mankind. Nobody asks or cares whether Hampden, Marlborough, Pelham or Wolfe were knights of the Garter. Of all things at present I am most anxious to hear about you. The packet that was coming to us overland, and that left England in July, was cut off by the wild Arabs between Aleppo and Bussora...."

Cornwallis was to have no time to luxuriate in the success of his reforms of the civil and military functions. When the Rajah of Travancore, an ally of Britain, was attacked in force by the Tippoo Sultan in 1790, Cornwallis at first left the field command to Britain's senior officers in Madras but, when the campaign bogged down, he went there himself before Christmas and took charge. The campaign of 1791 was typical Cornwallis: methodical, calculated and by and large successful. The Earl knew that he would have to take Seringapatam—the Tippoo stronghold—but first he would have to reduce the bastions in between. In March, British forces under Cornwallis stormed and took the pettah and the citadel of Bangalore. In May, Cornwallis reached Arikera—within 10 miles of Seringapatam. But it was too late in the season to undertake such a long siege. He destroyed his heavy baggage and fell back to Bangalore, where he devoted himself to planning a big campaign the following year.

Here again, Cornwallis displayed his talents as a politician. He made alliances with both the Nizam and the Mahrattas, thus isolating Tippoo from potential help. The campaign of 1792 brought Cornwallis the big victory he had always been denied in the American Colonies. Forts long considered impregnable fell to British forces courageously led by Cornwallis. When he left Severndroog on January 25 with his own army reinforced by troops from Mahrattas and Nizam, there was little doubt that Cornwallis would crush Tippoo. In about 10 days, they arrived before Seringapatam and on February 6 a major assault was launched against the whole line of forts to the north of the Kaveri River.

A few days later Cornwallis was joined by General Robert Abercromby and his men who had come up from the west coast, and the siege of Seringapatam began. Britain's heavy artillery quickly frightened the defenders and, on February 10, Tippoo surrendered two of his sons as hostages to indicate his firm intent to negotiate a surrender. After the treaty of peace was signed, Cornwallis went back to Calcutta and there occupied himself with completing the reforms he had begun. In England, the Earl's entire conduct of Indian affairs was highly approved, and on August 15, 1792, he was created Marquis Cornwallis in recognition of his services to the Crown.

There was to be more glory for Cornwallis in the field. In 1798 when the Irish rebellion posed a threat to peace, it was Cornwallis who took charge as viceroy and commander-in-chief. The old American hand and the old Indian hand was by then widely accepted as his country's ablest trouble shooter on any front. In humility, Cornwallis took this sticky job, won the key skirmishes, tracked down the rebels and pacified the country. In victory he was compassionate, following one simple rule; punish the ringleaders and spare their dupes.

Nor did Cornwallis find peace in retirement. Trouble was brewing again in India and the Crown turned to Cornwallis, once more asking him to take up the dual role of governor-general and commander-in-chief. At 66, Cornwallis regarded the proposal with faint enthusiasm but the sense of loyalty and duty which had beset him all his life forbade him to refuse. He left England in March, 1805.

The Marquis found India much changed when he landed at Calcutta on July 29. As always, Cornwallis had a specific course of action in mind. This time it was to mediate among the warring factions and, as he expressed it upon arrival: "to put an end to this most unprofitable and ruinous warfare."

At once, he set out by ship up the Ganges to open negotiations with Indian leaders but was overtaken by an illness whose symptoms were described as a failure of "powers of mind" followed by a lapse into unconsciousness. He was put ashore at Ghazipore, but his strength never returned and he died there on October 5, 1805.

Cornwallis does not want for monuments to his memory. A mausoleum, erected over his remains at Ghazipore, has ever since been attended by the Indian government. Statues of the mausoleum, erected over his remains at Ghazipore, has ever since been attended by the Indian government. Statues of the Marquis stand in St. Paul's Cathedral in London as well as in Madras and Bombay. His niche in history was firmly carved— and widely accepted, even in his own lifetime.

Sir Henry Clinton, by comparison, went into near total eclipse after the Revolution. He never held another army command. Well-born and moderately well off, he lived out his days unexceptionally and was devoted to his children, five of whom were by his wife who had died in childbirth and several more illegitimate ones born of later romances.

Clearing his reputation for being "the commander who lost the war" became an obsession with Sir Henry but, as in the war itself, this was to be an uphill, losing proposition. He complained in 1789: "I have been disgraced for trying to save what others have been rewarded for losing." This clearly was an allusion to the rewards and laurels bestowed on Cornwallis, Howe and even Tarleton. Toward the end, Sir Henry became almost a caricature of the long-winded, boring old soldier avoided by friends and acquaintances who long since had been content to let memories of the debilitating war recede.

In 1794, Sir Henry was named Governor of Gibraltar, a sinecure post which he was never to take up. He died in England just before Christmas, 1795, of what has been described as an abscess of the knee. He provided as well as he could for all in his family, whether they legally bore the name of Clinton or not.

Greene

For Nathanael Greene, still controlling the High Hills of the Santee, the news of Cornwallis' surrender at Yorktown was nostalgically welcome. Greene's men had suffered an epidemic of dysentery and fever that October, and the camp was short of every type of supply, including quinine and alcohol, trusted remedies for most of what ailed them.

After Yorktown, everything changed for the better. Reinforcements and fresh supplies came in from North Carolina. Fevers vanished. Cornwallis was beaten, his whole army in captivity. Greene's army, the unconquerable ragamuffins of the Patriot cause, staged an unforgettable celebration. Parade lines were formed, chins up, eyes prideful. There were extra rations for the men, and the ladies of the neighboring plantations, many of them long separated from their warrior husbands, entertained Greene's officers in their homes. Many lasting friendships were forged.

But the war was not over for Nathanael Greene: not everybody trusted the British to stay beaten. Greene who never won —but never lost—was given the taxing job of holding his army together against the possibility of a renewed British effort to subjugate the states and make them colonies again. That he succeeded, that he kept an army in the field for many months after Yorktown, was a tribute to his leadership and the esteem in which his men held him. It was no doubt galling for Greene to play his cat-and-mouse game with the British in the Carolinas when the war for all practical purposes had ended at Yorktown, but there was one great compensation: Kitty would soon come south to join him.

What was left of the war in the Carolinas soon became a kind of standoff with neither side anxious to commence a major action, and Greene, with Kitty at his side, was able to turn at least part of his attention to making the transition to civilian life.

In these endeavors, as in war, Greene's problems all but over-whelmed him. He was beset by debts, harassed by charges of misusing army funds and had but little time for his beloved Kitty. Indeed, the man who gave so much of his life to the nation's fight for independence had precious little time left for himself.

Both South Carolina and Georgia—in appreciation of the Yankee general who had lived and fought with them—offered Greene sizable plantations. One of the first New England fami-lies to settle in the South after the Revolution, he and Kitty moved into Mulberry Grove Plantation near Savannah. Despite this largesse, Greene did not distinguish himself as a business-man or a planter, and was never able to establish himself on a sound financial footing. Although he later acquired vast timber rights in Georgia, Greene could not muster a sufficient labor force to exploit those resourses; to the end Nathanael Greene, outspoken foe of slavery and a man of stubborn principles, refused to use slave labor.

On June 12, 1786, Nathanael and Kitty Greene journeyed to Savannah where Greene met with friends to seek aid in the settlement of one of his pressing debts. Coming home the next day he complained of a headache which got steadily worse. At Mulberry Grove he went directly to bed, but the pain persisted and the following day his forehead appeared to be swollen. A doctor was summoned, drew some blood and predicted that Greene would soon commence to rally.

It was not to be. Greene fell into a stuporous sleep. By the night of June 18, it was clear to Kitty and a few close friends at his bedside that the general who couldn't be beaten was at last in a losing fight. He died about 6:00 A.M. on June 19, 1786, in his 45th year.

The South never forgot the man who helped deliver it from the hands of the British. In 1820, the citizens of Savannah, by private donation, built a monument to their adopted son. Under it lie the remains of the one-time Rhode Island Quaker, the young man with the limp who vaulted from private to general and who, in the judgment of history, contributed perhaps as much as any single person in the last, fateful Southern Cam-paign to the establishment of the United States of America.

Tarleton

AFTER THE BRITISH TROOPS STACKED THEIR ARMS AND MARCHED AWAY to prison camps, Yorktown became a center of protocol in which bruised egos were salved at command level. Both Washington and Rochambeau entertained their distinguished enemies at elegant camp dinners, but it is intriguing to note that this camaraderie was never freely extended to Lieutenant-Colonel Banastre Tarleton. Nobody, it seems, invited "Bloody" Tarleton to dine—nor would anyone join him at table.

Whatever his shortcomings, Tarleton was never wanting in audacity. Collaring the Marquis de Lafayette, Tarleton inquired if the neglect of his person were accidental. The Marquis, ever the gentleman and with no stomach for a contretemps, passed the buck to John Laurens, the distinguished and able young South Carolinian.

Laurens was Tarleton's age, a brave officer, better educated and at least as articulate. He had been thwarted in his efforts to raise a fighting force of blacks for the Patriot side, but this day he was more than a match for Tarleton. When confronted by the Green Dragoon, who brusquely repeated his question, Laurens replied: "No, Colonel Tarleton, no accident at all; intentional, I can assure you and meant as a reproof for certain cruelties practiced by the troops under your command in the campaigns in the Carolinas."

Bristling, Tarleton replied: "What, Sir, and is it for severities inseparable from war which you are pleased to term cruelties, that I am to be disgraced before junior officers? Is it, Sir, for a faithful discharge of my duty to my King and my country that I am thus humiliated in the eyes of three armies?"

"Pardon me," interrupted Colonel Laurens. "There are modes, Sir, of discharging a soldier's duty, and where mercy has a share in the mode, it renders the duty more acceptable to both friends and foes."

Laurens made a lasting point. The "mode" of discharging a soldier's duty is always best remembered by those who have experienced it on their own skins. The French, by contrast, had no searing memories of Waxhaws and Fishing Creek, of burning homes and unarmed men struck down, of unheeded cries for quarter. Tarleton dined with the French. Still, the antagonism toward Cornwallis' cavalry commander simmered on. Shortly after the surrender, Tarleton told his French captors that he had reason to think he might be murdered by Southern Patriots in reprisal for some of his raids. Confirmation that these were not idle fears came after the French, humoring Tarleton, moved him to new quarters. On the following day it was found that "the bed upon which he was to have slept had been stabbed in several places."

Back in London, Banastre Tarleton soon returned to his old ways and old haunts, chasing the girls and gambling at the Cocoa Tree. The dashing colonel became a landmark figure in the capital, clad in his green jacket, tightly fitted trousers, black boots and tall helmet with black feathers. It wasn't long before Ban embarked on a tempestuous affair with Mary Robinson, a leading figure of the London stage, and sat for a portrait by Sir Joshua Reynolds.

It was not long either before Tarleton became the center of a raging controversy which was to titillate London for years. Britain had accepted the loss of the American Colonies fairly philosophically, but there was still much rancor in military breasts which surfaced in the form of letters to the newspapers. Tarleton, more than most, was the subject of these letters as the participants in the campaign of 1780-81 felt constrained to launder their war records in the public prints.

An anonymous letter addressed to Tarleton appeared in the *London Morning Chronicle* on August 9, 1782. It accused him of winning battles only against those "whom you luckily attacked when cooking their dinner" and it also charged him with slaughtering unarmed men. Further, it laid at Tarleton's door full responsibility for the defeat at Cowpens because "you got yourself and the party completely ambuscaded, completely surrounded, upon all sides by Mr. Morgan's riflemen." The letter concluded: "Thus fell, at one blow, all the Provincial Legion, with about three hundred veterans!"

The writer very likely was Lieutenant Roderick MacKenzie, a junior officer on the British side at Cowpens who, unfortunately for Tarleton, recovered from the wounds he suffered there. In the years ahead, he was to badger Tarleton, chapter and verse, with his conduct of the battle. In any case, this letter was the opening salvo of a grim barrage which extended to Cornwallis and Sir Henry Clinton, both of whom reacted sharply to the allegations that they were responsible for the disaster.

The nimble Sir Henry rushed quickly into print with his side of the story, a windy alibi entitled *Narrative of Lieutenant General Sir Henry Clinton, K.B., relative to his command of King's Troops in North America: Particularly to that which respects the unfortunate Issue of the Campaigns of 1781.*

The particularization in Sir Henry's accounting kept popping up in the newspapers. He himself took the lofty view, stated and restated, that "none of the misfortunes of the very unfortunate campaign of 1781 can, with the smallest degree of justice, be imputed to me." It was an astonishing position for the commander-in-chief of the King's troops and it pointed directly to his subordinates, Cornwallis and Tarleton, as the ones to whom the "misfortunes" could be "imputed." After all, the "unfortunate campaign of 1781" began at Cowpens in January and ended at Yorktown in October. Tarleton's reputation and Cornwallis' heart had been broken at the former; both had capitulated to Washington at the latter.

Cornwallis, still on "parole," fired off his rebuttal: "I acted under positive orders," he wrote. But he admitted that "Cowpens was the turning point of the campaign," and then he denied responsibility for it. In hindsight, it appears that Cornwallis' position was more defensible than Sir Henry's but the net result was devastating for Banny. The lieutenant-generals had spoken and now the young lieutenant-colonel was out at the end of a long, slender limb. "The unfortunate day at the Cowpens" became a household phrase that summer and implied that the pride of the Cocoa Tree, Banastre Tarleton, had somehow managed to lose the war all by himself!

Banny wasn't taking any of it. He defended himself against Clinton, Cornwallis and MacKenzie with the greatest vigor, and that defense culminated in the publication of his book *A History of the Campaigns of 1780-81 in the Southern Provinces of North America* which appeared in 1787. Naturally, a lengthy section offers Tarleton's view of the critical Cowpens battle. It would appear to show that at best even ranking warriors bring only a worm's eye view to their eyewitness accountings. At worst, the view seems highly parochial. In Tarleton's words:

"Lieutenant-colonel Tarleton...thought it incumbent on him to lay before His Lordship by letter the probable accounts of Morgan's forces and designs; the necessity of waiting for the baggage of the light troops...and the plan of operation which struck him as equally necessary and advantageous for the King's service. He represented the course to be taken, which fortunately corresponded with the scheme of the campaign: He mentioned the mode of proceeding to be employed against General Morgan: He proposed the same time, for the army and the light troops to commence their march: He explained the point to be attained by the main body: And he declared that it should be his endeavour to push the enemy into that quarter....

"At three o'clock in the morning of the 17th, the pickets being called in, the British troops, under the command of Lieutenant-colonel Tarleton, were directed to follow the route the Americans had taken the preceding evening, and the baggage and waggons were ordered to remain upon their ground till daybreak, under the protection of a detachment from each corps."

In great detail Tarleton then described the disposition of his forces, the terrain and his impression of the force awaiting him. He continued:

"The (American) militia, after a short contest, were dislodged and the British approached the continentals. The fire on both sides was well supported and produced much slaughter: The cavalry on the right were directed to charge the enemy's left: They executed the order with great gallantry, but were drove off by the fire of the reserve, and by a charge of Colonel Washington's cavalry....Upon the advance of the 71st, all the infantry again moved on: the continentals and the backwoodsmen gave ground: the British rushed forwards: An order was dispatched to the cavalry to charge: An unexpected fire at this instant from the Americans, who came about as they were retreating, stopped the British and threw them into confusion. Exertions to make them advance were useless....An unaccountable panic extended itself along the whole line....The cavalry did not comply with the order (to advance)....All attempts to restore order, recollection or courage proved fruitless....Another party of the Americans, who had seized upon the baggage of the British troops on the road from the late encampment were dispersed....

"On the route, Tarleton heard with infinite grief and astonishment, that the main army had not advanced beyond Turkey creek, he therefore directed his course to the south east, in order to reach Hamilton's ford, near the mouth of Bullock creek, whence he might communicate with Earl Cornwallis.

"The number of the killed and wounded, in the action at the Cowpens, amounted to near three hundred on both sides, officers and men inclusive: This loss was almost equally shared; but the Americans took two pieces of cannon, the colours of the 7th Regiment, and near 400 prisoners...."

Tarleton's body count stood in wild variation with the facts. So did his effort to saddle Cornwallis with responsibility for the failure of the British attack, and no one sounded off in refutation more loudly than Lieutenant MacKenzie. If one takes exception to the premise that Lieutenant MacKenzie loathed his commanding officer, it is entirely feasible to substitute any other verb which means roughly the same thing. MacKenzie's letters ultimately were gathered together and printed in book form under the title *Strictures on Lieutenant-colonel Tarleton's History of the Campaigns of 1780 and 1781 in the Southern Provinces of North America.* The following excerpts from MacKenzie's book deal with Tarleton's version of Cowpens:

"I now proceed to examine the account which our author has given to the world of his defeat at Cowpens, but previous to this investigation it will be necessary to inquire, what degree of credit is due to his description of the advance to the field of battle. The traits of self-importance which it contains are too apparent to escape the notice of any reader; in his relation of circumstances antecedent to this disaster, he says...that in a letter to Earl Cornwallis, 'He *represented* the course to be taken, which fortunately corresponded with the scheme of the campaign: he *mentioned* the mode of proceeding to be employed against General Morgan: he *proposed* the same time, for the army and light troops to commence their march: he *explained* the point to be attained by the main body: and he *declared,* that it should be his endeavour to push the enemy into that quarter.' How rapid was the advance of this gentleman to the summit of military knowledge!"

In a lengthy, truculent passage, MacKenzie next pointed out that Tarleton knew on January 14 that Cornwallis was at Bull Run, 45 miles from the rendezvous point. Further, Cornwallis had to contend with difficult creeks and rivers and could not move rapidly because of the "incumbrance of a train of artillery, military stores, baggage and all the other necessary appointments" of the main body. In short, according to the MacKenzie version, Tarleton was imprudent to assume that Cornwallis was in the vicinity on the 17th.

Then MacKenzie ticked off Tarleton's "errors:"

"The first error in judgement to be imputed to Lieutenant-colonel Tarleton is the not halting his troops before he engaged the enemy....The British infantry, fatigued with rapid marches, day and night for some time past, might have had rest and refreshment... The artillery all this time might have been playing on the enemy's front, or either flank, without risque of insult....The second error was the un-officer-like impetuosity of directing the line to advance before it was properly formed and before the reserve had taken its ground....The third error in this ruinous business was the omission of giving discretional powers...to (subordinate officers) to advance the reserve....The next and most destructive, for I will not pretend to follow him through all his errors, was in not bringing up a column of cavalry and completing the rout, which, by his own acknowledgments had commenced through the whole American infantry....

"I have now done with the action at Cowpens, and on this occasion confess that I am not without my feelings as an individual for so wanton an attack on characters and entire corps, whose conduct had been, till then, unsullied. There is not an officer who survived that disastrous day who is not far beyond the reach of slander and detraction; and with respect to the dead, I leave to Lieutenant-colonel Tarleton all the satisfaction which he can enjoy, from reflecting that he led a number of brave men to destruction, and then used every effort in his power to damn their fame with posterity."

As the years passed, so did the rancor over who lost the war, and Banastre Tarleton, riding out the storm, went on to an illustrious career of his own. But to the American South he would always be "Bloody." Some regarded him as the arch villain of the Revolution, a "butcher," a "reckless bully" and a "harsh, brutal, vain man."

To the ladies of two continents, however, Ban was something else—handsome in a sharp-featured way, gracious, even gallant. Unfortunately for Banastre Tarleton, very few ladies wrote histories of the miserable, dirty war which crested in the Carolinas and ended in Virginia.

Eventually, after keeping London's gossip writers busy for years, Tarleton was to marry, prosper and sit in Parliament. There he was best known as the spokesman of the Liverpool shipping magnates who busily carried black African slaves to the New World. It is perhaps the crowning irony of this violent man's life that he was to take his leave of it on January 16, 1833—on the eve of the 52nd anniversary of "the unfortunate day at the Cowpens." He was in his 80th year.

Morgan

IN WINCHESTER, VIRGINIA, DANIEL MORGAN KNEW IN HIS ACHING BONES that the end of the war was near. He found it galling to be on the sidelines rather than with General Washington as the climax approached, but he consoled himself and did what he could to help out. Several times, in 1781, he had refurbished some of Lafayette's troops, getting them uniforms and supplies and seeing that their horses were properly shod. Since there was no money, Morgan personally guaranteed the local tradesmen that they would eventually be paid. Morgan's word was quite enough. When news reached Virginia that De Grasse controlled the sea approaches to Yorktown, nobody crowed louder than Morgan. It was an event, he noted, to make "a good man's soul feel happy." And he added his own prognosis: "I am in hopes that we have that old fox, Cornwallis, pretty safe." The events of October quickly confirmed his judgment.

When the American units of the allied armies began their return march to the Hudson towards the end of the month, one of the most immediate problems was finding winter quarters for British prisoners of war. Once again the army turned to Morgan as the senior resident military man in the Winchester area, and Morgan was active in securing shelter for the prisoners. The French, always cognizant of life's more agreeable aspects and how best to enjoy them, stayed on the peninsula, wintering in Yorktown, Williamsburg and Hampton, before departing for Rhode Island. De Grasse sailed off for the West Indies, arriving only a little behind his original schedule. Cornwallis and Tarleton set sail for New York. At Yorktown then, except for the hordes of friendly Frenchmen, everything gradually settled back into what the natives undoubtedly spoke of as "business as usual."

At Winchester, Daniel Morgan fretted in his idleness, but it wasn't long before he commenced to prosper. He had large

151

land holdings and he steadily acquired more. His military reputation as architect of the only American victory over British regulars in the Southern Campaign was vast, and it was only human if the rough-hewn general traded on it a bit. With the passing of time, Morgan gloried in the retelling of the Cowpens events and, in his recall, the American forces seemed to contract while Tarleton's expanded. In truth, Morgan probably never knew how many men he had in the fight, given the piecemeal reinforcement of his little band on January 16 and 17, 1781. Years later, Morgan seemed satisfied to say he had around 800 men while Tarleton fielded about 1200. If this was an exaggeration, it still was nearer the truth than Tarleton ever got. He put Morgan's force at about 1500 and suggested that the dead and wounded on each side were about equal.

In his advancing years, Morgan became fond of denigrating the role of his militia at Cowpens. It was a trait which did not endear him to his Southern neighbors in the Carolinas. After all, the militiamen from the Carolinas and Georgia who took exposed positions on an open slope were directly under Tarleton's guns and in the path of his cavalry. They held their ground, turned back the first tentative cavalry charge, fired their two rounds and retired in order to the right flank—all on command—from whence they delivered the volley which finally routed the British.

Yet Morgan was to say: "I would not have had a swamp in view of my militia on any consideration; they would have made for it and nothing could have detained them. As to covering my wings, I knew my adversary and was perfectly sure I should have nothing but downright fighting. As to retreat, it was the very thing I wished to cut off all hope of....When men are forced to fight, they will sell themselves dearly."

One man who particularly wanted to meet Morgan was the Marquis de Chastellux, who wrote of Cowpens: "This event, the most extraordinary of the whole war, has always excited my curiosity." When the Marquis arranged an interview with the Old Wagoner, shortly after his retirement, the two discovered they had a rather high mutual regard. The Marquis described Morgan as "a man of about 50, tall and of a very martial appearance."

Morgan apparently found De Chastellux a good listener. The Marquis was to write that Morgan "admitted very candidly that the retrograde movement he had made (at Cowpens) was not premeditated. His troops were intimidated when the English, with more confidence than order, advanced to the attack: observing them keeping their ranks, he suffered them to retreat a hundred paces and then commanded them to halt and face the enemy, as if the retrograde movement had been really preconcerted."

The Marquis, in this little-noted reminiscence, wrote that Morgan's account of the maneuver might "teach philosophers and critics to suspect those who have written history...all the copious and elegant historians who delight in multiplying and varying the description of battles, or what is yet more reprehensible...borrow from historians the events and strategems of war...."

In any case, premeditated or extemporaneous, Morgan's success at Cowpens kept him in the public eye for years and when Americans on the frontier resisted paying duties on whiskey—foreign and domestic—President Washington turned to his old friend for help.

Morgan shared Washington's determination that the fledgling nation should have a strong central government. He took to the field with troops once again in 1794 to put down the rebellion, and it was largely through his personal authority and stature that the leaders of the rebellion surrendered. Morgan insisted that they be allowed to return to their homes without prejudice.

The rapid movement of Morgan into Pennsylvania to put down the rebellion was lauded by Henry Lee, then the Governor of Virginia: "When...the inhabitants of Pennsylvania menaced by force of arms to prostrate the majesty of the laws, and consequently reduced President Washington to the mortifying necessity of arresting their folly and wickedness by the bayonet, Morgan was summoned...."

The Old Wagoner promised Washington he would march against the rebels with a hastily mustered army "to show them our determination to bring them to order and to support the laws."

Washington responded warmly: "Although I regret the occasion that has called you into the field, I rejoice to hear you are there...."

The rebellion collapsed before any major action could be joined and Morgan himself played a personal role in preventing a tavernkeeper from selling booze to the troops at exorbitant prices. As Morgan was to explain it: "When I told him his fault, he began to treat me with indignity, and I broke his mouth, which closed the business." At 58, Morgan could still lash out with either hand.

When he was 60, Daniel Morgan stood for the Fifth Congress and won a seat. There is little to show that he distinguished himself in any way during that session but he is remembered for coming down four-square on one position when he wrote a friend: "The Democrats is a parsell of egg-sucking dogs!"

Morgan died of his assorted infirmities on July 6, 1802, surrounded by his family and old soldiers from his beloved Virginia units of Revolution days. Even in death, however, this fighting man was to find no peace. Buried at Winchester in the Shenandoah Valley, the Old Wagoner's very bones became an issue. First, the handsome slab which commemorated his resting place was chipped away by souvenir hunters. Then, in 1865, a rumor circulated that Union troops planned to dig up Morgan's remains and take them back to Pennsylvania. The South was having no part of such villainy. Late one night, six prominent Winchester citizens dug up Morgan, placed the remains in a new casket and reinterred him at his present place of rest in the Mount Hebron Cemetery in Winchester.

The general became a strictly Southern issue in 1951 when the villagers of Cowpens, South Carolina, sought to have his bones moved to the site of his greatest victory, but Winchester stood firm: Daniel Morgan had chosen Virginia; Virginia would not suffer his removal.

At Spartanburg, South Carolina, in the main square not far from the battlefield, there is an imposing monument to the Old Wagoner. Made of granite, 21 feet high, it is topped with a stern bronze statue of Morgan. In 1959, sentiment was voiced in Spartanburg to move the statue and the monument to facilitate the flow of traffic. The automobile and the twentieth century lost that decision to the Daughters of the American Revolution, who rallied on Morgan's flanks and told the world where the traffic could go. Today, the cars drive slowly around the Old Wagoner—just as men walked cautiously around him in life.

INDEX

REAWAKENED

ALSO BY COLLEEN HOUCK

Recreated

The Tiger's Curse series

COLLEEN HOUCK

REAWAKENED

EMBER

Text copyright © 2015 by Colleen Houck
Cover art copyright © 2015 by Chris Saunders

randomhouseteens.com

Educators and librarians, for a variety of teaching tools, visit us at RHTeachersLibrarians.com

The Library of Congress has cataloged the hardcover edition of this work as follows:
Houck, Colleen.
Reawakened / Colleen Houck. — First edition.
pages cm
Summary: "A visit to an Egyptian exhibit brings teen Lilliana Young face to face with a recently awakened mummy-turned-handsome-sun-god as she gets caught up in an adventure with more twists and turns than the Nile itself"— Provided by publisher.
ISBN 978-0-385-37656-3 (hc) — ISBN 978-0-385-37657-0 (glb) — ISBN 978-0-385-37658-7 (ebook)
1. Amon (Egyptian deity)—Juvenile fiction. [1. Amon (Egyptian deity)—Fiction. 2. Gods, Egyptian—Fiction. 3. Adventure and adventurers—Fiction. 4. Supernatural—Fiction. 5. Egypt—Fiction.] I. Title.
PZ7.H81143Re 2015
[Fic]—dc23
2014023498

ISBN 978-0-385-37659-4 (trade paperback)

Printed in the United States of America
10 9 8 7 6 5 4 3 2 1
First Ember Edition 2016

For my dad, Bill, who left us all too soon

THE WINE OF LOVE

An Ancient Egyptian Love Poem

Oh! when my lady comes,

And I with love behold her,

I take her into my beating heart

And in my arms enfold her;

My heart is filled with joy divine

For I am hers and she is mine.

Oh! when her soft embraces

Do give my love completeness,

The perfumes of Arabia

Anoint me with their sweetness;

And when her lips are pressed to mine

I am made drunk and need not wine.

PART ONE

In the great city of Itjtawy, the air was thick and heavy, reflecting the mood of the men in the temple, especially the countenance of the king and the terrible burden he carried in his heart. As King Heru stood behind a pillar and looked upon the gathered people, he wondered if the answer his advisers and priests had given was their salvation or instead, their utter destruction.

Even should the offering prove successful, the people would surely suffer a terrible loss, and for him, personally, there was no way to recover from it.

Despite the simmering heat of the day, he shivered in the temple's shadow, surely a bad omen. Uneasily, he ran a hand over his smoothly shaven head and let the curtain fall. To quiet his nerves, he began to pace the temple's smooth, polished dais and ponder his choices.

King Heru knew that even should he defy the proposed demands, he needed to do something drastic to appease the fearsome god Seth. If only there was a way out, he thought. Putting the proposal to the people was something no king had ever done before.

A king held his position precisely because it was his right, his duty, to see to the needs of his people, and a king who could not make a wise decision, however difficult, was ripe for deposing. Heru knew that by allowing the people to decide, he proved himself to be a weakling, a coward, and yet there was no other outlet he could see that would allow him to live with the consequences.

Twenty years before King Heru's time, all the people of Egypt were suffering. Years of terrible drought further complicated by devastating sandstorms and plague had almost destroyed civilization. Marauders and old enemies took advantage of Egypt's weakness. Several of the oldest settlements had been wiped out completely.

In a desperate act, King Heru invited the surviving leaders of the major cities to come to his home. King Khalfani of Asyut and King Nassor of Waset agreed to a one-week summit, and the three of them, along with their most powerful priests, disappeared behind closed doors.

The results of that meeting had been a decision that tipped the balance in the pantheon of the gods. Each city worshipped a different god—the residents of Asyut, which played host to the most famous magicians, were devoted to Anubis; those of Waset, known for weaving and shipbuilding, to Khonsu; and King Heru's people, skilled in pottery and stone cutting, worshipped Amun-Ra and his son, Horus. The kings had been convinced by their priests that their patron gods had abandoned them and that they should come together as one to make offerings to appease a new god, namely, the dark god, Seth, in order to secure the safety and well-being of the people.

And so they did. That year the rains came in abundance. The Nile overflowed its banks, creating fertile lands for planting. Livestock flourished, tripling in number. Women gave birth the following year to more healthy babies than had ever been recorded. Even more astonishing was when the queens of each city, who had been the most outspoken against the deity change, were appeased when discovering that they, too, had conceived.

As the three queens each gave their husbands a healthy son, they acknowledged their blessings, especially the wife of Heru, who had never had a child and was well past her bearing years. Though in their hearts, the new mothers still paid homage to the gods of old, they agreed that from that time forward they would never speak ill of the dark one. The people rejoiced.

The people prospered.

The three kings wept with gratitude.

In an age of peace and harmony, the sons of each queen were raised as brothers in the hope that they would someday unite all of Egypt under one ruler. The worship of Seth became commonplace, and the old temples were essentially abandoned.

The sons considered each king a father and each queen a mother. Their kings loved them. Their people loved them. They were the hope of the future, and nothing could keep the three of them apart.

Now, even now, on the darkest day of their fathers' lives, the three young men stood together, waiting for the kings to make a surprise announcement.

In a moment, the three kings would ask the unthinkable. A favor that no king, no father, should ask of his son. It made King Heru's blood run cold and left him with vivid nightmarish dreams of his heart being found unworthy when weighed against the feather of truth in the final judgment. The three kings stepped into the glaring sunlight that reflected off the white stone of the temple. King Heru stood in the center while the other two men took their place at his side. King Heru was not only the tallest of the three but also the most skilled speaker. Raising his hands, he began, "My people, and visiting citizens from our dearly loved cities upriver, as you know, we, your kings, have been in conference with our priests to determine why the river, which has lapped our shores so gently for the last twenty years, does not flourish as it should in this most important season. Our chief priest, Runihura, has said that the god Seth, the one we have worshipped wholeheartedly these past years, demands a new sacrifice."

King Heru's own son took a step forward. "We will sacrifice whatever you think is necessary, Father," he said.

The king held up his hand to quiet his son and gave him a sad smile before turning back to the crowd. "The thing that Seth asks this year as a sacrifice is not a prized bull, bushels of grain, fine fabrics, or even the best of our fruits." Heru paused as he waited for the people to quiet. "No, Runihura has said that Seth has given us much, and for the things we have received we must return that which is most precious.

"The god Seth demands that three young men of royal blood be sacrificed to him and that they serve him indefinitely in the afterlife." Heru sighed heavily. "If this does not happen, he vows to rain destruction upon all of Egypt."

House of Muses

"Fifteen fifty," the driver demanded in a heavy accent.

"Do you take credit?" I responded politely.

"No. No cards. Machine's broken."

Giving a slight smile to the heavily browed eyes staring at me in the rearview mirror, I pulled out my wallet. As many times as I'd ridden in a New York City cab, I'd never gotten used to the attitude of the taxi drivers; it irked me every time. Still, it was either that or our family's personal driver, who would shadow me around, reporting every move I made to my parents. All things considered, I much preferred independence.

I handed the driver a twenty and opened the door. Almost instantly, he sped off, leaving me struggling to maintain my footing while coughing in the cloud of gray exhaust he left behind.

"Jerk," I mumbled as I smoothed my cropped trousers and then bent down to adjust a strap on my Italian leather sandals.

"Do you need help, miss?" asked a young man nearby.

Standing up, I gave him the once-over. His department store jeans, I ♥ NEW YORK tee, and scruffy boy-next-door appearance instantly told me he wasn't from the city. No self-respecting New Yorker, at least none

I knew, would be caught dead in an NYC tee. He wasn't bad-looking, but when I considered his likely determinate stay in the city coupled with the fact that he would obviously not be parental approved, I surmised that any further dialogue would be a waste of time. Not my type.

I hadn't figured out exactly what my type was yet, but I figured I'd know it when I saw it.

"No thanks." I smiled. "I'm good."

With a no-nonsense stride, I headed toward the steps of the Metropolitan Museum of Art. The girls at my school would think I was an idiot for passing up a cute boy/potential boyfriend—or at the very least, a fun distraction.

It was easier not to make any promises I didn't plan on keeping, especially with a boy who hadn't met any of my requirements for the perfect guy. The list wasn't complete yet, but I'd been adding to it for as long as I'd been old enough to be interested in boys. Above all else, I was careful and thoughtful about my choices.

Even though I was very picky, wore only designer clothes, and had a monthly allowance bigger than what most people my age earned in a year, I was by no means a snob. My parents had certain expectations of me, and the money was used as a means to fulfill them. I was always taught that the image one portrays, though certainly not one hundred percent accurate, was an indicator of the type of person you were. Despite my efforts to find evidence that this wasn't always the case, among the people I went to school and hung out with, it often was.

My father, a successful international finance lawyer, always said, "Bankers trust the suit first and the man second," his version of "Dress for success." He and my mother, who spent most of her waking hours in her skyscraper office at one of the largest media companies in the city, dictating orders to her personal assistant, had drilled into me that image was everything.

Mostly, I was left on my own as long as I did what they expected, which included attending various functions, portraying myself as a doting daughter, and getting straight As at my all-girls private school. And, of course, not dating the wrong type of boy, which I accomplished by not dating at all. In turn, I was given a generous allowance and the freedom to explore New York. A freedom I cherished, especially today, the first day of spring break.

The Met was one of my favorite hideouts. Not only did my parents approve of the institution—a definite plus—but it was a great place to people-watch. I wasn't sure what I wanted to do in the future, but this was the week I had to figure it out. I'd already been accepted to a number of parent-approved universities. Mother and Father—they hated being called Mom and Dad—wanted me to major in something that would make them proud, like medicine, business, or politics, but none of those really interested me.

What I really enjoyed was studying people. People of the past, like the ones I read about at the Met, or even just the people walking around in New York City. In fact, I kept a little book full of notes on the most interesting people I saw.

How I would turn this admittedly strange hobby into a career, I had no idea. My parents would never approve of my becoming a counselor, mostly because they believed a person should be able to take charge of their own mental health by merely willing themselves to overcome any obstacle they might face. Consorting with those they considered beneath their station wasn't something they encouraged, and yet becoming a counselor was the one career path that made the most sense to me.

Any time I thought about the future, my parents came to mind. What they had planned was a constant drumming on my consciousness, and if I entertained the idea of deviating from their plans even an iota, I was filled with guilt, which effectively choked the life out of any little seeds of rebellion.

One of those seeds was where I applied to college. Technically, it wasn't a mutiny, since they knew about it. I was allowed to apply to places that interested me as long as I sent in the paperwork to the ones my parents approved of as well. Of course they'd been thrilled when I was accepted to them all, but there was no doubt that they were pushing me in a certain direction.

Now spring break of my senior year was finally here, a time most teens loved, and I was dreading it. If only everything didn't have to be decided right now. Mother and Father had given me until the end of the week to choose my college and my major. Starting college as undecided was not an option.

Stopping at the counter, I flashed my lifetime membership card and swiftly walked through the roped entrance.

"Hello, Miss Young," said the old guard with a smile. "Here all day?"

I shook my head. "Half day, Bernie. Meeting the girls for lunch."

"Should I be watching for them?" he asked.

"No. I'll be alone today."

"Very good," he said, securing the rope behind me and returning to help with the line of tourists. There were definitely some perks to having parents who donated annually to the Met. And since I was an only child, I was lucky enough to receive the full "benefit" of their monetary donations, wisdom, and experience. They were loving, too, if love looks like a stiff upper lip of pride and approval. But I was often lonely, and at times felt trapped.

Whenever I started to feel like I needed a real mom type to bake cookies with, I asked to visit my paternal grandmother, who lived on a small farm in Iowa, a woman my parents checked in on exactly once every two months. They visited her annually, though they stayed in a nearby city hotel and worked from their room while I stayed on the farm with her overnight.

Speaking of grandmas, a very interesting-looking older woman was seated on a bench ahead of me and staring at one of my favorite pictures, *She Never Told Her Love,* by Henry Peach Robinson. The photograph was controversial. Critics said it was indecent and indelicate for a photographer to capture a dying woman in print, but I found the photo dramatically romantic. It was said that the photographer was trying to illustrate a scene from Shakespeare's *Twelfth Night*. I knew the quote on the picture's description by heart.

SHE NEVER TOLD HER LOVE,
BUT LET CONCEALMENT,
LIKE A WORM I' THE BUD,
FEED ON HER DAMASK CHEEK.
TWELFTH NIGHT, 2.4.110–12

Consumption. That was supposedly what the woman in the photograph was dying of. I reasoned it was appropriate. Dying of a broken heart must feel like a type of consumption. I imagined it to be a squeezing pain that wrapped itself around a person like a boa constrictor, tightening more and more, crushing the body until there was nothing left but a dry husk.

As fascinated as I was by the photo, I was even more fascinated by the woman who sat staring at it. Her cheeks sagged, as did her heavy body. Strands of limp gray hair hung from a messy bun. She clutched a worn cane, which meant it was well used, and she wore a floral-patterned, butterfly-collared dress (circa 1970). Her feet were planted shoulder width apart in thick-soled Velcro-closed sneakers. The woman was leaning forward, resting her hands on the edge of the cane, her chin propped on her hands as she studied the picture.

For the better part of an hour, I sat at a distance, watching her and sketching her silhouette in my notebook. At one point, a tear ran down her face and she finally moved, digging into a giant crocheted bag for a tissue. What caused her tears? I wondered. Did she have a long-lost love of her own? Someone she had never shared her feelings with? The possibilities and questions swirled in my head as I adjusted my backpack and headed down the hall, shoes clicking on the marble floor. Noticing a familiar guard, I stopped.

"Hi, Tony."

"And how are you today, Miss Young?"

"I'm well. Hey, listen. I need to do some serious work. Is there a less-trafficked place around here that I can go to before I meet my friends for lunch? The people are too distracting."

"Hmm." Tony rubbed his chin and I heard the bristly sandpaper sound that meant he hadn't shaved that morning.

"The Egyptian wing is roped off," he said. "They're adding some new pieces. But they shouldn't be in there today. The boss lady is at a conference, and nothing in this museum moves without her."

"Do you think I could go in there and sit? I promise not to touch anything. I just need a quiet spot."

After a brief frown of consideration, his brows drew apart and he smiled. "All right. Just make sure you're careful. Stay out of view of the tourists, or they might get the idea to follow you in."

"Thanks, Tony."

"You're welcome. Come back and see me again when you get a chance."

"Will do," I said, and headed toward the special-exhibitions exit, then turned back, "Hey, Tony, there's an old woman over by the photography exhibit. Can you check on her in a little while? She's been there a long time."

"I will, Miss Lilliana."

"Bye."

I sped past the wall of photographs and headed downstairs to the main floor. The Medieval Art and the Hall of Cloisters, full of tapestries, statues, carvings, swords, crosses, and jewels, led to the museum store and then, finally, to the Egyptian wing.

When no one was looking, I slipped under the fabric rope. Despite the air-conditioning, the dust from thousands of years ago had a sharp enough tang to be noticeable. Perhaps the recent remodeling of the exhibit had released centuries of dust into the air, giving the effect of old things being stirred to life.

The overhead lights were off, but sun came through the large windows and lit up displays as I continued. Tens of thousands of artifacts were housed in a couple dozen rooms, each room focusing on one era. I felt adrift in a black ocean of history, surrounded by little glass boxes that offered fading glimpses of time gone by.

Displays of cosmetics boxes, canopic jars, statues of gods and goddesses, funerary papyrus, and carved blocks from actual temples, all gleaming with hidden stories of their own, captured my attention. It was as if the artifacts were simply waiting for someone to come along and blow the sandstone grit of time from their surfaces.

A sparkling bird caught my attention. I'd never seen it before and wondered if it was part of the new display or just on rotation. The rendering, a beautifully made golden falcon that represented the Egyptian god Horus, was called *Horus the Gold*.

After finding a cozy corner lit well enough for me to see, I sat with my back against the wall, turning to a blank sheet in my notebook to list all possible majors and major/minor combinations in groupings my parents would approve of. I was matching up my top three choices with their universities when I heard a scrape.

Wondering if a tourist had followed me in, I listened carefully for a few minutes. Nothing. This wing of the museum was as silent as a tomb. Smirking at my own stupid cliché, I went back to my notes and examined a glossy college brochure.

Before I made it through the first page, there was a thumping sound, followed by the same scraping noise. Though I considered myself a rational person, not easily frightened, a chill ran from my scalp down the length of my spine, as if icy fingers were caressing my vertebrae.

I set down my pencil and notebook carefully, trying to not make any sounds of my own, and listened with increasing alarm to the scrapes, scuffs, and distinctly nonhuman groans coming from the other side of the wall. Someone or something was definitely there. Calling forth my sensible mind to dispel my fear, I considered that perhaps the sounds were being made by an animal.

An eerie moan made my hands tremble, and the sight of my shaking fingers steeled me. I was being silly.

"Hello?" I ventured quietly. "Is someone there?"

I stood and took a few steps forward. The sounds abruptly ceased and my heart stilled. Was someone hiding? A museum employee would have answered me.

Sucking in a shaky breath, I rounded the corner only to come face to face with a wall of plastic. *This must be the section they're working on,* I thought. It was too dark to make out any shapes inside the room, so I stood there for a full minute gathering my courage.

I ran my fingers along the thick plastic lining until I found an opening, gasping when I saw a figure staring back at me, not inches from where I stood. But the frightened girl clutching the plastic drape was just me: her slightly wavy, product-enhanced, long brown hair, pale skin, and white designer blouse now marked with dust. Yep, me. The tile beneath the large artifact read ANCIENT COPPER MIRROR. I shook my head as I tried to make out what else was in the room.

The polished floor was protected by a heavy drop cloth, which was covered with sawdust, and several boards, cut in various shapes, lay haphazardly on the floor. I used one to prop open the plastic curtain, taking advantage of whatever meager light I could get, and moved deeper into the room.

Dark shapes and statues filled makeshift shelves, with stacked crates blocking every path. Now that I knew this shipment was so recent, I rationalized that what I'd heard was most likely a rat or a mouse making its home in one of the boxes. That would explain the silence since I'd come in.

I saw nothing that looked out of place in a museum. A box of tools here, a circular saw there. Opened crates filled with Egyptian treasures resting on the straw. True to my word, I didn't touch any of the pieces, and moved through the space carefully and quietly until a golden light behind some boxes caught my eye. I let out a small gasp as I came upon an enormous sarcophagus.

The lid, resting at an angle on the lower half of the coffin, was breathtaking. As I focused on all the little details—the handsome carved face, with polished green stones for eyes, the crook and flail he held crossways on his chest, the precious gold details that meant he was likely someone of importance—my fingers itched for my pencil and notebook.

Right away I noticed the patterns of three—three birds, three gods, three sets of wings, three bands on the arms. I wondered what they signified and began coming up with possible scenarios as I continued exploring. The packing slip on the coffin-sized crate nearby read:

UNKNOWN MUMMY
DISCOVERED 1989
VALLEY OF THE KINGS
EGYPT

Despite my fascination with the upcoming exhibit, I didn't notice anything out of the ordinary. No rat tails or droppings that I could see. No squeaking mouse hiding in a corner. No grave robbers or cursed mummies. Not even any museum employees.

As I turned to leave, I looked down and suddenly realized two things: first, the straw-filled sarcophagus didn't contain a mummy, and second, there was a set of footprints other than my own in the sawdust, ones made by two bare feet, and they led *away* from the coffin.

An intense curiosity took hold of me, and ignoring strong reservations, I followed the footprints. They led me on a path between boxes and crates until I met a dead end. No climactic movie music was triggered. No rancid scents of decay or death assaulted my nose. No creepy monster leered at me from the darkness.

Recognizing I'd let my imagination get the best of me, I began making my way back toward the plastic curtain. I was passing the copper mirror when a hand shot out of the darkness and locked on my arm. My choked scream echoed, the shriek bouncing off relics. The golden gods and stony statues kept their icy eyes forward, remaining as still and dead as everything around them.

Stranger in a Strange Land

The hand, which was extremely warm and not covered in ancient mummy wrappings, let go the instant I screamed. I dashed through the plastic curtain and around the wall to grab the can of pepper spray I kept in my bag. I stood there, can aimed, finger on the trigger, as the bare feet that were poking out beneath the curtain retreated into the darkness.

The sound of rummaging soon became obvious as the mysterious person began cracking open boxes. Something, most likely a box, crashed to the floor, and a metallic ringing indicated that a precious object of some kind had also been heedlessly dropped.

"I'm warning you. I'm armed," I threatened.

Whoever was in there paused and said a few words I didn't understand before they went back to whatever it was they were doing.

"What was that? What did you say?" I asked. When they didn't respond, I tried another tack. *"Qui êtes-vous? ¿Quién es usted?"* The only response was a grunt of frustration and the unmistakable sound of a crate being tossed aside.

"Look, I don't know who you are or what you're doing in this exhibit," I said, switching back to English while I knelt and threw my papers into my bag, "but you really shouldn't be in there."

Hoisting my bag over my shoulder without taking the time to zip it, I kept my eyes trained on the sheets of plastic ahead while inching toward the entrance. I hid behind the displays until I reached the main walkway, still holding up the pepper spray in case the stranger jumped out at me. When the plastic sheet came into view, I scanned the area for a sinister shape, but nothing emerged from the closed-off section.

Was the person hiding? Was I being stalked? "Please come out and explain yourself," I called bravely. Keeping my back to the wall, I waited for an answer.

What I should have done was leave and report what was happening to the security guards, but as I stood there, curiosity overwhelmed me and I couldn't. If the person had wanted to attack me, they already had had ample opportunity.

Perhaps he or she was lost. What if it was a transient who had wandered into the exhibit and was trying to catch a nap? Maybe it was an employee. Maybe they were hurt. I lowered my aching arm and slowly walked back toward the plastic curtain.

"Hello? Do you need help?" I ventured. I didn't sound as confident as I had hoped.

I heard a sigh as someone came toward me. Even though I was no longer pointing the can of pepper spray, I was still clutching it, nervously running my forefinger in little circles over the trigger.

"Who are you?" I asked again quietly, more to express the thought out loud than because I expected an answer.

A hand grasped the curtain, pushing it aside as the object of both my fear and curiosity stepped through, mumbling an assortment of words that sounded very much like expletives in another language. Stopping just outside the curtain, he—it was most definitely a he—let the plastic fall and faced me with an irritated expression.

Though we were in the darkest part of the exhibit, I could clearly make out the pleated white skirt that ended just at his knees and the wide expanse of a tanned and very bare chest. His bare feet were covered with sawdust. He seemed young, maybe just a few years older than me, yet his head was bald.

Crossing muscular arms over his wide chest, he boldly looked me up and down and I got the feeling that he found me both surprising and disappointing. "Stay back," I said, raising the can of pepper spray and feeling like an idiot for getting into this situation. He just raised an eyebrow and smirked, seeming to taunt me.

Jabbing a finger toward me, he uttered something that sounded like a command.

"I'm sorry. I don't understand you," I answered.

Noticeably frustrated, he repeated himself, more slowly this time, as if he were talking to an imbecile.

I answered back just as slowly, first gesturing to myself, "I," then shaking my head, "don't understand," and finally pointing at him, "you."

Crying out in exasperation, he threw his hands into the air and kept them there. At that exact moment, the overhead lights came on. A little squeak escaped my mouth as I got my first real glimpse of the guy I'd assumed had been living with the relics. He was definitely *not* a transient.

Who are *you?* I wondered as I studied the person, who was not a man and yet not a teen. He seemed . . . timeless. Hooded hazel eyes, at that moment more green than brown, beneath a strong brow pinned me with a gaze that was both intelligent and almost predatory. I felt like a mouse looking up at a swooping falcon, knowing death loomed but utterly unable to look away from the beauty of it.

His physical splendor was undeniable: brooding eyes, miles of muscles beneath smooth, golden skin, and full lips that would send any girl swooning. But there was something deeper behind the beauty, something very different about him that made my fingers itch for a pencil and paper. I wasn't sure I could even capture the indescribable thing I felt when I looked at him, but I really wanted to try. As easy as I found it to put people in categories based on the things I noticed about them—

their clothes, the way they moved, the people they were with, or their patterns of communication—I thought that for him I just might have to come up with a new system. He didn't belong in any particular group. He was unique.

I blinked and realized he was smirking again. Even if the rest of him was a mystery, I could identify the expression. I'd met dozens of boys with expressions like that. International or not, they were all the same. They thought their wealth and good looks made them powerful. This guy was practically dripping with power. *Definitely not my type.*

"So what are you supposed to be?" I lashed out, heat stinging my cheeks in response to his arrogance. "Are you some international model taking photos down here and now can't find your pants?" I scoffed, indicating his costume or lack thereof. "Well, believe me," I said, using my best condescending voice and punctuating each word with a dramatic gesture for emphasis, "nobody would look twice at you, so just . . . move along."

Sighing, Model-boy mumbled a few words as he swirled his fingers in the air. Suddenly, there was a funny taste in my mouth, a kind of fizzing, like an effervescent candy had just dissolved on my tongue. The sensation quickly disappeared and I was trying to figure out what he was doing when he said a word I finally understood.

"Identify."

"Identify?" I repeated dumbly. "Are you asking my name?"

He nodded once.

Shifting my weight, I answered tersely, "Lilliana Young. What's yours?"

"Good. Come along, Young Lily, I have need of your assistance," he said, forming his lips around the words like they left a bad taste in his mouth, and effectively ignoring my question.

Presuming I'd follow, he turned and plunged back through the plastic curtain. After a brief hesitation, my insatiable nosiness got the better of me, and unable to come up with another good option, I threw aside the curtain and followed. Light filled every corner of the once-dark room, and I found Model-boy sifting through items in a crate, tossing the discarded ones aside like rubbish.

"What exactly are you doing? Why are you dressed like that? And how can you suddenly speak English?"

"Too many questions, Young Lily. Please pick one."

He lifted a heavy jar from the box. Closing his eyes, he spoke softly, melodically, in another language. After a moment, he shook his head, put the item back, and selected another.

"What are you doing?" I asked as he repeated the chant.

"I am seeking my jars of death."

"Jars of death?" I paused. "Do you mean canopic jars? And what do you mean, 'my'?"

"No more questions, Young Lily."

"So," I mumbled, stalling as I tried to figure out what exactly was going on, "you're looking for canopic jars, aka death jars. I read about those recently in *National Geographic*. They're the kind used for mummies. The ones their organs are kept in."

"Yes."

"Are you stealing them?"

He moved to another crate. "I cannot steal that which belongs to me."

I crouched and peered into the guy's face. I was pretty good at reading people, so I usually knew when someone was lying. This guy wasn't. Which meant he either actually believed he had some claim on these Egyptian relics or he was crazy. I was inclined to go with crazy.

"Look," I said quietly. "These items belong to the museum. You're not supposed to be touching them. You can't just come into a museum and take whatever you like."

"Museum?"

"Yes, museum. As in, collection house of antiquities, displayer of old documents and art of great value."

Pulling the top off yet another crate, he squatted to examine the contents. "Ah," he said. "A House of Muses."

"A what?"

He ignored me and, after a brief perusal of the box's contents, rose with a grunt of frustration. "They are not here."

"The death jars?" I asked.

"Yes. These are replicas. They do not hold my life force."

"Life force, right." *Definitely crazy.*

Mumbling a few excuses, I stood and began my retreat, but he followed me.

"Without my life force, I am merely a walking shadow on borrowed time," he stated gravely.

His eyes locked with mine in a disturbingly determined way as I backed away nervously. "I need sustenance, Young Lily," he said while advancing.

"Sustenance, okay." *Please don't let hot foreign-model guy turn into Hannibal Lecter.* "Well, there are a lot of places where you can get something to eat. May I recommend the Roof Garden Café on the fifth floor?" I backed around a stack of crates as I gave him directions, but he pressed forward.

"Do not run away, Young Lily."

"Run?" I tittered anxiously. "I'm not running. But speaking of running, if the Roof Garden is too far, there's always the American Wing Café. It's right next to this Egyptian exhibit. You can't miss it. Well, I've got a meeting to get to. I've really got to go."

"You do not understand. Without my jars I must share your life force."

"Share my . . . Well, see, that's the thing, I'm using mine just now, thank you. Really wish I could help you, I do," I said, realizing he'd backed me up against a wall of crates. When my backside hit the barrier, he smiled. Without a second thought, I blasted him in the face with the pepper spray. Howling, he doubled over. At the same time a wind began to swirl around him, lifting little pieces of dust and construction material into the air.

Panicked, I spun and ran toward the curtain. But before I reached it, the lights went out and I banged my knee against the golden sarcophagus. Stumbling to catch my balance, I heard him coming toward me. "Come back, Young Lily," he groaned. "I need you."

Oh, I don't think so. There was no time for my eyes to adjust. Gripping my bag with one hand, I felt along the coffin until I'd skirted the massive object, and then hurried out as fast as I could. He followed me, emerging from the curtain just a few seconds after I did.

My open bag was bouncing, and pens and pencils scattered all over the floor. When my notebook fell out, I had to stop for it despite the danger. I chanced a look back.

Crazy model-boy was standing there, arms raised in the air, eyes closed. He was chanting like before, his voice echoing through the exhibit as I dashed toward the exit. A mysterious wind lifted my hair, blowing it around my face and blinding me as I ran. His words pierced my consciousness, like hieroglyphs being chiseled into stone. He chanted:

Protect me, God of the Morning Sun.
Rebuff those who work evil.
Turn aside this calamity.
With the power of my mouth,
The power in my heart,
I utter a spell.
As our forms are bound this day,
So are our lives.
Tirelessly, she will serve me
Whilst I serve Egypt.
As I wander this land,
Make light my feathers,
Make swift my wings,
Make steady my heart.

I take her strength of body,
And, in doing so,
Pledge to reward the gift given
Where I am unknown, she will attend.
Where I am alone, she will be.
Where I am weak, she will sustain,
Even unto death,
That the darkness might be locked away
And all things remain in the light of the everlasting sun.
My heart is firm.
My soul is triumphant.
My service is eternal.

I'd reached the exhibit doors, but the moment he finished, I was blasted backward onto the tile floor.

I had no idea what was happening. All I felt was pain. My heart beat erratically, and my stomach quivered with nausea when my lungs couldn't take in air.

Did he shoot me? As I tried to fill my lungs, I felt around on my back. There was no blood. No bullet hole. Carefully, I stood up. I needed to get out. Now.

Reaching the side exit, I checked my watch. Eleven-thirty-five, just a few minutes late for my date. If I missed out on the pretty much mandatory lunch, I'd never hear the end of it from my dad. He wanted me to make friends with the daughters of some very important people he wanted to "work with," meaning rub elbows with, in the future.

Darting through the foot traffic, I entered one of my favorite restaurants and was ushered to a table next to the large bay windows that looked out over the street. Sinking into the chair, I blew out a breath as three pairs of critical eyes stared me down. My classmates. Their perfectly plumped glossy lips made little O shapes as they set down their menus to study me.

"What happened to you?" Redhead asked.

"You look like something the cat dragged in," said Blonde.

"Dragged in, scratched, coughed up in a hairball, and tinkled on, maybe," added Blonder.

The girls laughed. "No, even better," Blonde said. "You look like a windblown tourist left too long on an open-top bus. Aw . . . did you lose your map?" she added in a syrupy-sweet voice.

I smiled my best nice-to-see-you-but-I-really-want-to-kill-you smile at my three "friends," but they were nowhere near finished.

"I mean, seriously, who did your hair this morning? Albert Einstein?"

"Yeah, and your clothes." Blonder twitched her nose. "I've seen fewer wrinkles on a shar-pei."

Redhead leaned over and picked at my shirt. "Is that sawdust?"

Grimacing, I replied, "Yes."

"I knew it!" Blonde gasped facetiously. "Lilliana is having a secret affair with a rodeo clown." All three girls burst out laughing.

"Well, that explains the hair," said Redhead.

"Okay, back off. I've had a rough morning, all right?" Picking up the menu, I tried to covertly smooth my hair and brush some of the sawdust from my clothes. "I was involved in a hit-and-run at the museum," I mumbled from behind the menu.

"You mean outside the museum?" Redhead asked with a hint of actual concern.

My lips twitched sheepishly. "No, I mean inside the museum."

Blonder gasped for real this time and then lowered her voice. "Were you . . . mugged?"

In an instant, all three girls became very serious at the mention of the deep-seated fear they shared, which was to be the victim of a purse snatching. The belief that everyone else in the world had designs on their money and, for most of them, their person, was almost a required understanding at my elite private school.

"You poor thing," Blonde clucked as Redhead rubbed my back for a minute, then quickly dusted off her fingers on her napkin. "You just relax. We'll take care of you."

While Blonde was going on about the merits of a new designer she loved, I stared absentmindedly out the window. Immediately, I felt something. My gut twisted, muscles spasming as my breath quickened for no apparent reason. Then, at the edge of the window, a man came into view. A man who was stopping traffic. A bald man wearing a white pleated skirt and no shoes.

Though New Yorkers are used to just about anything, the man caused a stir. The crowd parted for him as he tilted his head skyward, spinning in a circle to look at the surrounding buildings as if he'd never seen one before. When he stepped into traffic I stood up involuntarily.

Then a cab hit him.

"Cassie, Christy, Courtney, I'm sorry, but I've got to go."

Picking up my bag in a panic, I ran out of the restaurant and into the street. A strange compulsion drew me toward this person who both fascinated and terrified me, and I wasn't sure I wanted to find him still among the living.

Heart of a Sphinx

I pushed forward with alarming urgency, shoving people out of the way, even knocking a kid over to get to the man. *What is wrong with me?* It was like someone had taken over my body and I was just along for the ride.

When I finally wrenched my way to the man's side, what I saw made me forget all about our first encounter. The impact from the taxi had sent him rolling into oncoming traffic, and he'd been struck at least twice. Blood dripped from his mouth and from a large gash on his head. Road rash ran down his side, and his feet were covered with cuts.

One of his hands was crushed, his very nice abdomen was already bruising, and his right shoulder was ripped up. Onlookers couldn't seem to figure out what to do except take photographs with their phones.

"Back off!" I screamed uncharacteristically at the crowd. I started edging away a bit when some of them began turning their cameras on me. To be fair, they probably didn't know what to make of the man. Heck, I didn't know what to make of him myself. He was alert, which surprised me, considering the state of his body.

From the moment he saw me, his eyes, more amber now than green, never left my face. He was afraid, confused, and in pain. I could feel the emotions coming off him in waves, and the empathy it stirred within me was tangible. It licked my skin with a panicked heat. I felt as if my own body had just gone through the same painful experience. I had to help him.

Though severely injured, he tried to sit up as I approached. "I've found you, Young Lily," he said, the words seeming to carry more weight, more meaning than just the obvious. He looked like an ancient warrior dying on a concrete battlefield.

Kneeling beside him, I touched the smooth skin of his arm lightly and, despite my uncertainty, said gently, "You sure did. And look what you've done to yourself."

The fact that he was hurt, perhaps even dying, coupled with my strange new insight into his feelings made whatever remaining fearful thoughts I had about him dissipate, like little bubbles popping into watery nothingness in the bright sunshine.

He was still crazy, no question about that, but now I believed he was more a pitiable type of insane than an I'm-going-to-kill-you-slowly type. The dark menace and exaggerated sinister qualities I'd branded him with earlier seemed silly to me now. He looked so harmless lying in the street.

Moaning, he shifted and then hissed in pain. I guessed that his leg or maybe even his hip might be fractured. Pulling out my phone, I had just begun dialing 911, when he lifted his non-crushed hand. "Help me," he pleaded.

I pointed to the phone. "That's what I'm doing."

"No." He shook his head, closing his eyes as he gritted his teeth. After panting for a few seconds, he focused on me again. I stared into his eyes and felt inexplicably mesmerized. The noise of New York City washed away. The world ceased to exist except for the two of us, me and him. And for a moment I imagined sinking into the deep pools of his eyes and being lost forever. *Oh, boy, what have I gotten myself into?*

"Help me," he repeated. His words snapped me out of the strange, dreamlike trance and the city's sounds assaulted my ears once again. Automatically, I dropped my phone on the pavement, barely noticing the cover popping off, and reached for his hand.

A burning jolt seared through my fingers and into my veins, the pain bringing tears to my eyes, and I wondered if this was what electrocution felt like. I cried out between chattering teeth as a strange scent, like scorched perfume or incense, assaulted my nose. Just as quickly as it had come, the agony began to diminish, turning into a warm, tingling sensation that lifted my hair at its roots and caused wispy tendrils to float with a static charge. There seemed to be an invisible barrier between us and the crowd. Though they snapped pictures, no one approached.

My muscles trembled from aftershock. I felt wrung out, like I'd been shoved into a dryer and tumbled around until I emerged in a fried, wrinkled heap. Someone squeezed my hand.

My eyes flew open, and suddenly remembering where I was, I yanked my hand from the man's grip. "What *was* that?" I demanded. The euphoria of being a Good Samaritan had abruptly faded, replaced by shock at what had just occurred between us.

"What did you do?" I half questioned, half accused. I felt as if I had been violated, but I couldn't really figure out why, and the uncertainty brought fresh tears to my eyes.

He studied me for a moment, and I got the distinct impression that he regretted what he'd done. Not deigning to give me an answer, he sighed, wiping the blood off his lip, and carefully stood up, testing each leg as if unsure it would hold him. The people around us gasped in amazement, snapping dozens more pictures of this miracle man.

That he was healed enough to walk was not nearly as surprising as how he handled the crowd. He was model-tall, and since I was still kneeling, I had to crane my neck to see him. The sun was right over his head, which, from my perspective, gave him a halo effect so bright I could barely look at him.

Seeming to enjoy the attention he'd brought to himself, he nodded to the people, smiling as he turned in a slow circle to look at all of them.

When he was satisfied, he stuck out his hand imperiously. "Come, Young Lily," he said in a rich voice. "There is much to do."

I was about to tell him where he could go stick his arrogant attitude along with his sexy accent, when he gave me the piercing gaze again. My vision blurred as everything around me took on a dreamlike quality, the urge to fight leaving me just as quickly as it had come. Feeling very unlike myself, I gathered up my phone like I didn't have a care in the world, shoved it into my bag, and allowed him to help me up.

Standing so abruptly made me woozy, and he put his hand on my back to steady me. I was uncomfortable with his forwardness and attempted to stagger away from him to wrestle my own way through the crowd, but he wouldn't have it. "You will stay by my side, Young Lily."

He took my hand and placed it on his arm, as if he were escorting me to a ball, before moving forward. The people parted like the Red Sea, and he strode through the crowd as boldly and as regally as a prophet. In the now filthy and torn pleated kilt-thing he very much looked the part.

As we walked, I tried to focus. I knew there was something very fishy going on and that my behavior was out of character, but I couldn't seem to break away from the guy or the haze that I was swimming in. Still, I vowed that, miraculous recovery or not, he would have to think twice if he presumed I was going to morph into a faithful follower, despite my actions to the contrary.

When we reached the sidewalk, we passed my openmouthed trio of classmates, their noses pressed up against the restaurant's glass wall.

"I am sorry to involve you in this, Young Lily, but it is necessary," he said, after we were a few blocks from the incident.

"What exactly am I involved in?" I hissed, still uncomfortable around him and itchy to escape yet compelled to stay by his side.

He covered my hand with his now-healed one and sighed. "There is too much to explain, and this is not the right place."

"Then what place would suit you in giving me an explanation?"

He pursed his lips and scanned our surroundings, taking in the skyscrapers with an amazed expression. "I do not know," he said, shaking his head.

"What kind of an answer is that? And how did you heal? What did you do back there?"

With a grunt of frustration, he pulled me into the shadow of a building with enough roughness that I fell against him. My heart beat in a prickly half-fearful, half-excited way that was very unusual for me. My free hand was splayed over his chest and my skin tingled where it touched his. My body seemed to leach warmth from his. The guy was hot. Literally. Perhaps he was feverish.

The fact that I was now feeling feverish too irritated me. I didn't go for dangerous guys, especially bald guys wearing skirts who I couldn't figure out. He was different from any guy I had ever met.

As he squeezed my shoulders to help me regain my footing, he murmured, "You ask too many questions, Lily. Your thoughts are too busy. It is an extra distraction for me in a world already full of chaos." He patted my shoulder gently. "Try to put your mind at ease. I mean you no harm."

"That's probably what all alien abductors say," I muttered, wondering why my tightly controlled sarcastic thoughts were suddenly escaping my lips.

"I must rest for a few moments," he explained matter-of-factly, and then easily let me go when I squirmed in his grip. He slid away a few inches so his body was fully enveloped in the hot sunshine and then leaned back and closed his eyes, trusting that I wouldn't leave. I smiled, tightening my grip on my bag and preparing to run, only to find that I couldn't lift my feet. *What is going on?* I thought. I needed to calm down. When I finally stopped thinking about leaving, I could take a step.

For several minutes, I tested my ability to move. I could walk in circles, sit on a nearby bench, walk over to a garbage can, but if I took too many steps away from him, my body seized up. It was like there was an invisible chain keeping me tethered to him. *Something is seriously wrong with me!*

I tried to flag down someone to explain that I was sort of a prisoner, but the words kept coming out wrong. Instead of pleading for help, I'd ask to borrow a pen. When I tried to report the man to a passing cop, I said, "Nice day, isn't it, Officer?"

I needed to get away from him. *No. That's wrong. Why would I want to leave him?* My mind seemed to be playing tricks on me. Eventually, I accepted the fact that I had to stay with him for the time being. When I did, I felt like I could breathe more easily and my thoughts became more focused. Sitting on the wooden bench, I studied him and waited, struggling to understand what kind of hold he had over me.

If I were like the other girls at my school, I would have been in tears, but instead, my mind filled with questions. This was how I dealt with stressful situations. I calmly thought things through until I found a solution.

How does a guy who has just been in a serious accident heal so quickly from his injuries? Who is he? What is this strange power he uses to manipulate me? What does he want from me? I rubbed my shoulder. I needed some pain reliever. The headache of all headaches was coming on; I could feel it inching up the back of my neck. *And why do I feel like I've been run over by a freight train? I don't even know this guy's name.*

After several minutes of watching him recline against the wall, I grew restless. Pulling out my notebook and pen, I turned to a fresh sheet of paper and then paused, not knowing where to start. He either didn't mind or didn't notice me studying him, so I took my time perusing his face.

He was handsome, but his good looks seemed . . . otherworldly. Even when a passing cloud shrouded him in shadow, his body appeared to glow. Not like a neon sign or anything like that; it wasn't noticeable unless you were really paying attention, but there was a faint shimmer to him, as if he were in a constant spotlight.

I lifted my head to start drawing his picture, only to find him watching me with cool green eyes.

"It is time to go, Lily," he announced.

"Go where?" I asked.

Squaring his impressive shoulders, he straightened to his full height and looked at the surrounding buildings. He studied both sides of the street as if assessing our options. "I do not know. I have never seen monuments of this size before." Cocking his head, he queried, "What is the distance to Thebes?"

"Thebes?" I snickered softly. "Uh, let's just say it's a little farther than I would want to walk in these shoes." I clapped both hands over my mouth, utterly shocked that I'd said exactly what I'd been thinking. Snarky, acerbic comments were definitely not mother-approved, and I'd worked hard over the years to develop the habit of waiting an extra moment before responding.

I'd long ago learned that my natural response to most situations was humor in one form or another, and there was no place in my parents' circles for a quick-witted daughter.

Oblivious to my thoughts, he glanced down at my shoes, frowning. "Very well. We shall find another means of transportation."

Leaving the wall, he approached me with catlike grace, hand stretched out. I jerked my head away and he appeared hurt by my action.

"Remain still," he said softly, stroking my cheek lightly. His fingertips felt like they were filled with liquid sunshine, and at his touch, heat seemed to seep into my cheekbones. I got the distinct impression he was assessing my body, and not in a boy-checking-out-girl way.

"You are weakened," he said finally. "The accident has diminished our strength. We both need sustenance."

"There's that word again."

Cocking his head, he asked, "Is there a different word you would prefer?"

"No, it's fine, as long as I'm not the one on your menu," I quipped uncertainly.

"I do not consume human flesh. Is this practice common in your city?"

"Uh, no."

He looked relieved. "That is good. I would rather starve on my sojourn."

"Well, at least I can cross 'cannibal' off the list. I was worried you were going to slice me up into little pieces and pull out your sauté pan." His brows lowered in concentration and then lifted as his mouth curved up into a genuine smile. His expression was so bright and full of delight that I found myself wanting to bask in the display. It was as if he'd been covered by storm clouds, but in that brief moment the sun peeked through, warming me in a way that made me want to see him smile all over again.

I'd been very wrong in my initial assessment of him. He wasn't a cover model, a lunatic, an axe murderer, or any of the other labels I'd tried to make fit. The power that settled on his shoulders didn't come from money or good looks, though it was obvious he had at least one of those. No, this guy's confidence wasn't based on a superiority complex. It wasn't superficial.

"Perhaps later," he said with a twitch of his lips. "Tell me, what harvests are gathered in this iron city? I do not see farms, but I smell food everywhere."

Harvests?

Taking hold of my hands and pulling me up from the bench, he asked, "Will you help me find it, Lily?"

I got the sense he was asking for much more than directions to the nearest fast-food joint, and was suddenly sure of a few things. First, he was way out of his element, literally a stranger in a strange land. Second, although he was definitely comfortable in his own skin, he was experiencing moments of confusion and doubt, which made him unsure of himself and hesitant, and he chafed at those feelings. Third, he really seemed to need me. That above all else rang loud and clear.

Maybe the solution was simple. Perhaps if I just bought him a burger and pointed him in whatever direction he needed to go, this pseudo-hypnosis thing would end, we could amicably part ways, and I could head home and try to make sense of all this. I hypothesized that perhaps some unknown force had brought the two of us together, and my role as this guy's guardian angel would soon be over. If that wasn't the case, I had no idea what was going on.

I often found that the most obvious solution was the right one. He wanted to eat, so I'd feed him and then take it from there.

"Well"—I scanned the street for a place to eat—"in New York City they have a little bit of everything."

"This city is called New York?"

"Yes," I said slowly, watching his expression. If he was playing at not knowing where he was, he was an exemplary actor.

"Excellent," he said. "Take me, then, to a little bit of everything."

I gave his skirt a pointed look. "Um, I think the only place you would fit the dress code for would be a hot dog stand."

Wrinkling his nose, he exclaimed, "You eat . . . dogs? That is almost as bad as people!"

"No!" I snickered. "Boy, you *are* from out of town. Hot dogs are made from pork or beef."

"Ah, I understand. Then I would like a hot . . . dog."

"You got it, Ali Baba."

"Why do you call me this?"

"I have to call you something. You still haven't told me your name."

I spotted a food cart across the street and indicated for him to follow me to the crosswalk. He tagged along placidly, and while we waited to cross, he said, "Amon. My name is Amon."

"Right. Amon." He didn't pronounce it like *Ammon*. His version was a much more swoon-inducing "Ah-*moan*," providing, of course, that one would swoon over a guy who was obviously not all there. "Well, it's nice to meet you, Amon from Thebes."

"I am not from Thebes."

"No?"

"I was born in Itjtawy in the time of the Dark One's reign."

"Right. And Itjtawy is in what country, exactly?"

"You would likely know my land as Egypt."

Really, why did the good-looking, interesting guys always have to end up being MIA upstairs? His body had reached cruising altitude, but the pilot had obviously called in sick. "So should I call you Pharaoh Amon or King Amon?" I teased, playing along.

"I was to be a king, but the time of the pharaohs was after my own."

"Uh-huh." This was getting easier. I finally felt like I was getting back in control. "Well, that's okay. You shouldn't feel bad. Titles don't make the man. Am I right?"

Amon folded his arms across his chest and regarded me. "You are laughing at me."

"Never. I wouldn't mock an almost-king-slash-non-pharaoh."

His expression was doubtful and a little more shrewd than I felt comfortable with, but he let it go, watching the action on the street instead. He seemed fascinated by the traffic—the honking, noisy, fist-waving, tire-screeching action. It was almost like he'd never seen a car before. Which was impossible. There were maybe—*maybe*—only a handful of people in the entire world who didn't know what a car was.

When the light changed, Amon waited for the traffic to come to a stop. He didn't move until I took his hand.

"Come on!" I entreated. "The light will change soon and the drivers don't really care if you're still in the way."

After I mentioned the possibility of another accident, he rushed forward, gripping my hand and tugging me along as he weaved quickly among the other pedestrians to get safely to the other side. "I do not trust those golden chariots," he declared, while giving the taxis the evil eye.

"Yeah, well, travel by golden chariot is pretty much essential in Manhattan."

"I thought you said we were in the city of New York," he said as I guided him to the hot dog cart.

"We are. Manhattan is the name of the island."

"Island?" he mumbled. "We are indeed far from Thebes."

"Yes, we are," I said in an exaggerated voice as if I were talking to a child. Gently, I patted his arm as if he were an invalid. "So let's get you a hot dog, put my phone back together, and call social services to come pick you up." I hadn't decided on a course of action until that moment, but it felt like the right one. I was suddenly exhausted. This guy was in need of more help than I could give him, and I wanted to remedy the situation as soon as possible.

"Why is there a service to lift people? I can walk. Ah . . . you mean a litter. Yes, that is appropriate."

"Indeed it is." I smiled at him, utterly confused by our conversation.

"Whaddya want?" the hot dog vendor barked after giving Amon the once-over.

"Two dogs with the works and a soda," I replied.

Amon, if that was his real name, stood right behind me as if guarding my back from the people passing. He watched with curiosity as the vendor got my order together. When the vendor was finished I handed Amon the food before fishing out a ten-dollar bill from my wallet. After stuffing the change into the guy's tip jar, I walked Amon to an empty bench and put my bag between us as he began fiddling with the hot dog wrapper.

Amon took a bite and seemed to like what he tasted, but when I unscrewed the top of the soda bottle things really got interesting. He chugged a mouthful of soda and a second later he was choking on CO_2, soda spraying everywhere as his eyes watered.

I grabbed some napkins from the vendor and began cleaning the soda from Amon's chest and arms.

He was looking at me with a half-frustrated, half-amused expression. "I can take care of it, Young Lily."

Cupping my hand, he wriggled the wad of napkins from between my fingers while I blushed violently and apologized. "Sorry, I didn't mean to do that."

He took both the sticky soda and my fumbling words in stride. Still, I forced myself to look away as he finished cleaning up because I was enjoying the process just a little too much. Being physically attracted to Mr. Almost-King/Non-Pharaoh just wasn't acceptable, and I refused to allow even a glimmer of interest to take root.

When he was done cleaning his chest, Amon thrust the soda bottle into my hands. "This drink is vile. Is there no juice of the grape, or perhaps water?"

"Hold on." I left and returned a moment later with some bottled water. "Here. Now, why don't you tell me how you came to be in New York and yet have never heard of the place?" Instead of answering me, he drained his beverage.

Raising the empty bottle, he exclaimed, "This water is more delicious than the soft kisses from the daubed lips of a dozen nubile maidens."

Suddenly, I couldn't remember what I'd just asked him. Seeing that my only response was to stare at him like I'd forgotten how to think, which, incidentally, wasn't too far from the truth, he waved a hand to get my attention. "May I have more, Lily? My throat is as dry as a sandstorm in the desert."

What a coincidence. My throat had suddenly gone dry, too. "Uh . . . sure."

Leaving my bag on the bench beside him, I pulled out some cash and headed back to the vendor. When I turned around, my hands full of bottles, I saw a man in a hoodie grab my backpack and begin to run. *Seriously? Is this the day I'm having? Surely I'm being punked!*

"Hey!" I shouted, and immediately dropped the bottles, two of which split, spraying their contents on my legs. Without a second thought, I ran after the thief.

"Stop him!" I called out, and was pleased to see several pedestrians make an effort to slow the thief down. Before I reached him, the man abruptly halted in his tracks, as if he had no control over his body. He turned around to face me as a voice behind me said, "You will return her belongings."

I grunted, "Not now, Amon. I can handle this." To the thief, I proclaimed, "Give it back and I won't call the cops."

The thief nodded, his eyes glazed over, and passed me my bag. Afterward, he started as if jerking awake and lunged through the crowd, desperate to get away. Glancing briefly at Amon, I shook my head in disbelief and unzipped my bag to check its contents.

Once again a crowd had gathered around us, and Amon played to the masses. Some people even cheered, and Amon raised his hands, seeming to enjoy the praise.

Everything accounted for, I angrily zipped my bag closed and swung it over my shoulder. "Unbelievable," I muttered to myself. "I mean, really. Un-freaking-believable! Craziest day *ever!*"

I spun around, very much needing to get away from everyone. Amon quickly caught up. "Where are we going, Young Lily?"

"I don't know where you're going, but I'm going home."

"To *your* home?"

"Yes."

He matched my stride easily even though I was practically running by now. At the corner, I raised my hand to hail a cab and one immediately pulled over.

As I yanked open the door, Amon said warily, "I do not trust the golden chariots."

I sighed and turned back around. "Look, the best thing for you to do is to head back to the museum. It's a straight shot down, six blocks or so. Ask for Tony. He's a friend of mine. Tell him you're trying to get to Thebes and they'll help you out. He can get you another hot dog and put it on my tab."

"I do not understand, Young Lily. You wish for me to leave you?"

"Yes. I need to go home, take a bath, and sleep for a long time."

"Then I will go with you."

"No, you—"

"Hey, you coming or not?" the impatient driver asked.

"Hold your chariot!" I shouted back, adding bellowing at cabbies to my new repertoire.

The driver shut up and satisfied himself after that with giving me annoyed looks.

At Amon's expectant expression, I lost it. There was already enough pressure on me without adding this guy to the mix. It was time to get off the insane train. Last stop. Everybody off.

Rubbing my temples, I explained, "I'm really sorry, but I just can't do this, whatever *this* is, anymore. My head hurts. I was almost robbed. I had to eat lunch with the Three Weird Sisters. I channeled so much static electricity that my mouth tastes like the outside of a burned marshmallow. And to top it all off, I've been escorting the Captain of Crazytown around New York. Do you see why I need to go home?"

Amon brushed a fingertip against my cheek, like he had earlier, and, with a very subdued demeanor, he nodded. "Yes. I understand. You must rest tonight."

"Will you be okay?"

"I will not come to any harm, Lily."

"Good." The weight of responsibility for him was like a heavy blanket that suddenly slipped from my shoulders. Still, I bit my lip and called out as he turned away, "Wait!"

Riffling through my wallet, I pulled out several twenties and pressed them into his hand. "If you get hungry or thirsty, give the hot dog man one of these."

"*Hakenew,*" he said as he tightened his fist, crushing all the bills in the middle. At my look of confusion, he clarified, "My thanks."

"Ah. Well, goodbye. And, good luck."

"May luck be with you as well," he replied.

Climbing into the cab, I shut the door, telling the driver to head to Central Park. As he waited for the traffic to clear so he could pull out, Amon gripped the frame where the window was rolled down and leaned closer to talk to me.

"Young Lily?" he asked.

"Yes?"

He gave me one of his special sunlit smiles. "You have the heart of a sphinx."

I was about to ask him what that meant, when the driver pulled away. Amon stared after me as the distance between us increased, and despite the certainty of my decision to leave him there, I remained uncomfortably twisted in my seat, watching until he was swallowed up in the jumble of people moving like ants through the dark jungle of Manhattan.

4

The Ties That Bind

As the driver turned the corner, bringing Central Park back into view, I asked him to drop me off at the Hotel Helios, my home. When I was young we'd lived in the suburbs and my parents would take the train into Manhattan every day. But as soon as my mother got her big promotion and my father scored a huge moneymaking deal, they traded in our upscale, more-rooms-than-we-knew-what-to-do-with suburban home for an even more upscale, snooty penthouse that was easily ten times the price and had even more rooms that we never used.

There were definite perks to living in Manhattan, and even more perks to living in a hotel—like maid service, room service at all hours, doormen, valets, access to the hotel pool, the steam room, and the gym. Still, it was hard for me to think of this residence as a home.

The streets of New York were constantly filled with noise. A drilling, jackhammering, honking, police-whistling, bus-squeaking, and exhaust-hissing cacophony that never faded. Then there was also the fact that "homes" in NYC came with apartment numbers and shared walls with various eateries, or, in my case, floor levels and room service. And then add to that, that my parents preferred to keep our residence looking magazine perfect, stiff, and unlived in. I didn't crave a place where the grass was greener—heck, I just wanted grass, period. It was no wonder I felt a bit disenchanted.

To me, a home was a quiet place with a yard, a fence, and a dog. And not one of those sissy dogs that ride in purses, either. A real home needed a real dog, like maybe a German shepherd or a Doberman—a big dog that would slobber all over its owner, dig up the yard, and wait patiently by the window to welcome its master home.

Now, my grandmother's farm was the perfect place for a dog. I had fond memories of chasing her various pets through fields of tall grass, wet noses being pushed into my hands, the smell of sun and wind and wood and fur as I kissed the tops of their heads and played with their ears. She'd had several dogs over the years, but her last dog, Bilbo, had recently died of old age and she didn't have the heart to replace him yet.

As soon as the driver pulled up, Herb, the hotel doorman, made his way over and opened my door.

"Did you have a nice day, Miss Young?" he asked politely.

I allowed him to help me out. "Herb, it was one of the worst days of my entire existence. You wouldn't even believe me if I told you," I said as I squeezed his hand.

Chuckling, Herb walked me to the hotel's golden doors. "I'd believe anything you told me. You aren't one of those dramatic young women always vying for attention."

I laughed. "Well, drama can sneak up on you, Herb. I have officially received more attention today than I'd ever want. The result is a killer migraine and a hankering for chocolate. Have a nice evening."

"You too, Miss Young. I hope you feel better." He gave me a puzzled look before opening the door.

"Me too," I replied over my shoulder as I entered the hotel. *When did the lights get to be so bright?* I squinted to minimize the stabbing pain behind my eyeballs as I made my way through the lobby toward the private elevators, where Stan stood guard and let me up to floor fifty-two.

There was nothing modest about the place where I lived. My parents owned the entire floor and had spared no expense in decorating it with highly fashionable pieces—rugs selected by famed interior decorators, art that was carefully chosen not only to complement the rooms but also to show potential clients, tastefully, just how much money we had, and a big-enough-to-get-lost-in refrigerator disguised to look like an expensive cabinet—items that were as cold and impersonal as the rooms themselves. My bedroom being the only exception. That was the only place I felt comfortable enough to kick my shoes off and drop my keys on the table.

One of the only purchases my parents had made that I actually liked was a Chihuly chandelier, which hung in the dining room. It felt chaotic somehow, which was a very unique feeling in my otherwise straitlaced life. The softly lit golden balls, drawn curlicue ribbons, and twirled shells had a wild kind of beauty that beckoned me to stretch beyond myself, to use the heat of experience to shape the grains of sand in the emotional desert that was my life into something as rich and precious as the Chihuly's spun glass.

As I entered the kitchen, I called out, "Marcella, are you here?" The only sound I heard in reply was the fading echo of my voice in this empty tomb of a home. Selecting a perfectly chilled diet ginger ale from the fridge, I headed to my room, my sanctuary in what I liked to call "the ice palace." When I entered, I let my bag fall heavily to the floor and leaned over to undo the buckles on my sandals.

I loved my room. I'd decorated it in cream, ivory, and the palest shades of pink. The bed and nightstand were a tawny gold and carved in a style reminiscent of Victorian England. The posts at each corner of the bed curved in beautiful arches, with sheer curtains hanging from them in soft folds.

One side of the room was floor-to-ceiling windows, which led out to my own private veranda with a magnificent view of Central Park. The opposite wall was offset with geometric shapes: frosted glass squares and rectangles in various sizes that were lit from behind with muted pink lights.

Catching a glimpse of myself in the huge gilt mirror convinced me that a bath was absolutely necessary before I climbed into bed. I padded across the room, my feet sinking into the thick carpet. I staggered toward the bathroom, massaging the back of my neck along the way.

My shoulders were stiff and sore, especially the left one. The throbbing in my head was getting worse, and to top it all off, my skin felt slightly swollen and itchy. I ran my tongue over my lips and tasted a coppery tang, as if my lips had been bleeding. *Maybe I'm allergic to something,* I thought. *Probably all that ancient dust in the museum.*

I popped four ibuprofen, then stared at my reflection and got an up-close view of just how haggard I looked from every possible angle.

"How about that? The Twisted Sisters were right. I do look like something the cat coughed up."

Praying that the ibuprofen would work its magic quickly, I sank into the luxurious tub and commenced scrubbing. The hot, bubbly water made me realize just how tired I was. With my head cushioned by a thick towel, I fell asleep. It didn't seem like I'd been out for very long when my eyes suddenly snapped open.

The windows were frosted for privacy, so light could come in and heat would be deflected but no one could see inside. The spa-style shower, closed off with a wall of etched glass, functioned in a similar way, letting in light but allowing only an opaque view of the person bathing.

I hadn't bothered to turn on the lights because I wanted to enjoy the warmth from the setting sun, a rare treat in a town full of skyscrapers. That was one of the biggest perks about living in a skyscraper near Central Park. The dimming light must have been playing tricks on my eyes, though, because, for a moment, it seemed as if someone was there, moving in the shadows.

After staring fixedly at the spot for a solid minute, I decided it must have been the clouds that caused the shifting shades; either that or the long shadows of the buildings across the park. I settled my head back against the towel. "Paranoid much?" I mumbled.

I tried to relax and enjoy, but the perfectly warm water chilled me. Darkness seemed to leach the sunlight from the room, and I suddenly felt as if I were entombed in a large sarcophagus instead of reclining in a spacious tub. A strong scent of incense mixed with the sharpness of coppery blood. I heard the faint sound of someone sobbing and then a scream. Gasping, I sat straight up, causing water to slosh in violent waves that spilled over the rim and onto the marble platform.

With a burst of energy, I scrambled out of the tub and stood staring at it in horror. Trembling, water pooling at my feet, I pushed my dripping hair out of my eyes, and tried to calm my breathing and slow my heart rate. *What is wrong with me?* I'd never heard of migraines causing hallucinations, but I supposed it could happen. An even more logical explanation would be that I'd nodded off and had a bad dream.

Maybe I have low blood sugar. I'd had only tea before heading off to the museum. *That must be it. Low blood sugar,* I rationalized, chalking the experience up to delusions due to hunger, but even after pushing the crazy things that had happened that day to the back of my mind, I couldn't deny that something very strange was going on.

Unplugging the drain and deciding to let our housemaid, Marcella, clean up—something very abnormal for me, and something I knew she would devise a secret punishment for later—I wrapped a thick towel around my hair, slid on my plush robe, and headed to my room, taking a seat at my desk.

The first thing I did was extricate the giant mishmash of papers that I'd stuffed into my bag when I made my hasty retreat from the museum. After sorting and stacking them into neat little piles and placing them on the corner of my desk for easy access, I felt much better. There was something about those piles, along with lists that had heavy black checkmarks and calendars with full days crossed off, that gave me a sense of control and, even more, a sense of achievement.

Perhaps I was more my parents' daughter than I liked to believe. The organized me, the meticulous me, the good little soldier, fit perfectly into their lifestyle, and I seemed to find comfort of sorts in the routine. Though in my heart I longed for some chaos and adventure, the truth was that I very much depended on order to function.

Opening my notebook, I found the page where I'd begun the sketch of Amon. I tried to tackle drawing his face but kept erasing his features, frustrated that I couldn't get them right.

Why I was so picky about Amon, I didn't know. Eventually, I gave up and just drew the outline of his head.

I heard the ding of the elevator, followed by the staccato clicking of high-heeled shoes indicating that my mother was home. I'd been focused on Amon's sketch far longer than I thought. My mother ducked her head into my room, and the flowery fragrance she always wore tickled my nose.

"Mother," I said, not lifting my head from my sketch.

She entered my room and put a hand on my robe-clad shoulder. "How was your day? Herb said it was a rough one."

I shrugged in response and tried to remind myself that Herb was just looking out for me, while Mother picked up a college brochure, homing in on the one she found least desirable. I could almost hear the frown in her words as she perused the paper. "I see you've been giving some thought to your choices."

"Yes. I haven't decided on anything yet, though."

Squeezing my shoulder in a way I found more controlling than comforting, she said, "I'm sure you'll select the right option." She undid the clasp on her necklace and began taking off her bracelets as she queried, "How did your meeting about the senior class project go?"

"It ended abruptly."

"So I heard."

Twisting in my chair to look at her, I asked, "Who called?"

"Cassie's mom. Cassie was worried about you. She said you left the meeting to help some boy in the street?"

To the layperson, my mother probably sounded genuinely concerned, but I felt the bitter sting of her disapproval and immediately attempted to placate her. "It wasn't as dramatic as she made it sound."

"Oh?" was the only response. A single syllable that conveyed a myriad of meanings carefully dropped into the conversation. It was an old television producer's trick used to make guests uncomfortable enough to fill the silence, and potentially hang themselves in the effort. Though I was aware of my mother's interview technique, I rose to the bait.

"She's right that there was a boy in the street, but what she didn't say was that there had been an accident. He was badly hurt."

"And you were attempting to help," she said with a raised eyebrow, more an accusation than a question.

"I didn't feel there was a choice," I remarked, giving a direct, if not fully truthful, answer.

"Weren't there any police around? Didn't someone call an ambulance?"

"I don't know. He was gone before any authorities arrived."

"I thought he was badly hurt."

"He was. But . . . he stumbled away." My voice drifted off lamely.

Her keen eyes spotted my notebook and she pulled it closer, trailing her finger down the page. "Is this your mystery boy?"

I nodded while laying my arm over the notes about him at the bottom, hoping it would be interpreted as a casual, nonconcealing gesture.

"Hmm. Perhaps I should place a few calls, try to track him down so he can get some medical help."

She was heading into the realm of making Amon her business, and I couldn't allow it. It wasn't that she would do something to hurt him, but my mother had very strong feelings about people needing to be shuffled into what she considered their proper place.

In her care Amon would likely end up in an institution. I wasn't sure he didn't belong in one, but the idea of him being put away felt very wrong. Needing to throw her off the trail by agreeing, I swallowed thickly and squeaked, "I'm sure he could use it."

I experienced a brief moment of panic as she hesitated over my sketchbook. If she decided to confiscate it, I didn't know what I'd do. Instead, she closed it and pushed it to the corner of my desk.

"You know how tolerant I am of your little hobbies," she began. "I just hope that you weren't rushing into a dangerous situation for the sake of documenting someone . . . new?" Her sentence was part command, part warning, and part query. Smiling back, I just shook my head, as if the notion were entirely unwarranted.

After a painful moment of my mother's scrutiny, during which I was sure she could somehow read my mind and discover each and every little secret thought, she dropped the subject and gave me her social-media smile. A small part of me was panicked that she would search for footage of the incident with Amon.

As long as I didn't jostle the frame too much, I could safely cross between the world my parents lived in and the world I'd fashioned for myself. The incident with Amon was the most dangerous, and admittedly exciting, thing that had ever happened to me, and as much as I wanted him to find his home, and he could probably do so with their help, I also wanted to keep the events of the day all to myself.

"Well, we have a little humanitarian in the family, then, don't we?"

Quickly, I turned my grimace into a small smile and hoped my mother didn't notice the difference.

"Just be sure to reschedule your meeting," she continued. "You know how important it is to your father."

"Yes. I know. I'll give the Weird Sis . . . the girls a call tonight."

Her eyes narrowed shrewdly. She caught my sarcastic slip but magnanimously chose to ignore it. "That's my girl." She smiled, patting my cheek as if I were a prize pony, before turning and disappearing for the evening.

Letting out a deep sigh of relief that the interrogation was over, I stood and groaned, massaging my lower back. I felt like an old lady. Even worse, like an old lady who had been run over by a car. Little prickles of pain erupted all over my back, sending goose bumps of aches up and down my body, which made me feel like a porcupine being kicked around by a tiger—bristly, dizzy, and slightly gnawed-on.

Deciding to skip dinner and retire early so as to stave off whatever bug had invaded my system, I climbed into my four-poster bed and settled in, hoping for a long, rejuvenating sleep. Instead, I dreamed of strange things. Large, colorful beetles crawled up my arms and kept coming no matter how many times I brushed them off. I sank into a murky river full of snapping crocodiles. And then, when I thought I could stand the nightmares no more, I was wrenched into a dark place where an unseen evil tried to pry away something that was precious and perfect.

I woke abruptly at dawn as air shifted over the bed, and I sensed movement by the French doors. The sheer curtains billowed in the breeze, and I could hear the comforting sounds of beeping trucks many stories below. *I must've opened the door to the terrace last night,* I thought.

Rubbing my arms, I stepped into a pair of soft slippers and padded toward the door. Dew coated the wrought-iron patio furniture. Stepping onto the veranda, I caught the scent of the planted flowers in their hanging boxes and inhaled deeply as I looked out over the park.

I rubbed the head of the large stone falcon that the hotel had placed there long before we moved in. I believed, though I'd never admit it, that the gesture brought me luck. There was one bird guarding each side of the hotel—north, south, east, and west. My personal falcon seemed to be watching over Central Park, protecting it like a gargoyle, and sometimes I liked to imagine that he was watching over me, too.

Pink rays of sun hit my skin, and though my body still ached and my head throbbed painfully, I swore that just standing in the sun siphoned off some of the pain. I heard the flutter of wings behind me and would have immediately shooed away the pigeons if standing in the sun hadn't felt so perfect.

Gripping the balustrade, I closed my eyes, basking in the feeling and momentarily forgetting my surroundings until I heard an all-too-familiar voice. "The sun makes us feel strong, Young Lily. As I am bound to it, you are bound to me."

A Feast in the New Kingdom

Whirling around, I whispered in an incredulous voice, "Amon? What are you doing up here? Wait. No. More important, how did you get up here?" I kept my voice low as I glanced nervously at the open door to my room. It was unlikely my parents or Marcella would be checking on me so early, but then again, they enjoyed changing up the routine every once in a while to keep me off guard.

"I need you, Lily," he said simply.

"What you really need is to go home," I replied. "Look, why don't I just call the police and see if they can locate someone who knows you?" I turned toward the veranda door.

"No." His quiet command stopped me, and I felt a familiar warm glow filter through my mind, just like when I hadn't been able to leave him in the street. When I made the mental decision not to call the police, I regained control of my limbs.

My eyes lifted to his questioningly and I felt his emotions rise within me. "You don't have a home anymore, do you?"

"My home has long since turned to dust."

Tilting my head, I asked, "Are you controlling me with hypnosis?"

"What does that mean?"

"You know, like taking over my mind, making me your Renfield?"

He concentrated on my eyes and then raised his eyebrows as if he'd discovered the answer to a question. "Ah, I understand," he said. Pacing behind the couch, he clasped his hands behind his back. "The answer I would give you is, not exactly. It is not my intention to make you a slave to my will, Young Lily."

The dawn light spilled over Amon's body, giving his skin a warm glow. Though it was definitely strange and all kinds of wrong to find him not only in the building I lived in but also on the same floor *and* just outside my room, I was surprised that I felt happy to see him, crazy stalker or not.

If I'd been logical, I would have been figuring out a way to alert the police or, at the very least, building security, but my desire to do so was weak, and I couldn't bring myself to feel anything but relief. Amon, too, seemed reassured upon seeing me unharmed.

Of course, I also had to acknowledge that his answer to my Renfield question was "not exactly," which meant that I *was* somehow bound to him like Renfield had been to Dracula. It was entirely possible that he was placing these placating thoughts in my head. Did I really trust him, or was he just coercing me to feel that way? At the same time, if I couldn't rely on my own emotional response, what *could* I trust?

I took a few steps forward and then stopped, my mind at war with my feelings. Sunshine pooled around Amon, and I swore I could almost see the heat radiating from his body. The cold that had seeped into me since my bath hadn't gone away, despite the thick down comforter I'd buried myself under when I went to bed, but Amon looked all kinds of warm—like a hot summer day at the beach mixed with sun-kissed tropical breezes all wrapped up in a heated blanket.

He appeared to sense my thoughts and smiled, his teeth dazzling and bright against his golden skin as he stretched out a hand. For a moment, I wondered if that warmth of his would encompass me, too, if I held on to him. But I immediately gritted my teeth, determined not to allow him to manipulate me, and stood my ground.

Folding my arms across my chest, I suppressed a shiver and hissed, "Answer my question. How did you get up here?"

Amon lowered his hand and frowned. "The man who guards the golden box showed me how to find you."

"Stan?" I shook my head. "No. That's not possible."

He gave me a long look and sighed. "Many more things are possible than you can imagine, Lily."

Apparently. And now common sense told me I needed to get away. I backed up a few steps and sidled a little closer to the open glass door. "What do you want from me, anyway? Why are you following me?"

"We are . . . connected, Lily."

"Connected," I repeated flatly.

"Yes. I have done a spell that has tied my *ka* to yours."

"Your ka? What the heck is that?"

"Ka is like . . ." He slapped his palm against his head and walked away, his white skirt swishing around his muscular thighs.

With his back turned to me, I got a good view of his broad shoulders and his strong arms, which were only slightly less distracting than his wide chest and very nice abs. I shook my head to clear it. Was he really the most attractive guy I'd ever seen, or was he just manipulating me into *believing* that he was?

He spun around quickly and though he didn't seem to notice my gaze redirecting from his body to his face, my cheeks burned. This time I didn't get the sense that he was aware that he found him attractive. I frowned as I acknowledged that those feelings had come from my own head and not his.

"It's like a life force," he continued. "My life force is tied to yours."

"I still don't understand. Are you trying to say we're soul mates?"

"Mates?" This time color stained *his* cheeks. "No. We are not coupled in that way."

I couldn't help it. I snickered. Biting my lip, I wondered if I should be glad or insulted that he didn't like me like that.

Amon suddenly seemed nervous and dropped his eyes. "Your"—he gestured to my midsection—"inner workings, your viscera—the stomach, lungs, liver, intestines, even your heart—are linked to mine. This connection has caused you pain. I am sorry for this, but I was desperate. You see, I cannot survive long in this world without my jars of death, and since—"

I held up my hand. "Wait. A. Minute," I said, punctuating each word. "Are you saying that you're borrowing my 'inner workings' because you couldn't find your canopic jars?"

"Yes."

"And you're serious?"

"Yes."

There wasn't even a hint on his face to say he was anything but sincere. *All right.* I decided to go along with the craziness for just a moment and try to figure out what exactly was getting lost in translation. At least I was now getting *some* answers.

"So you're saying that I've been feeling sick because of this spell you cast."

"Your thoughts are correct."

"And so . . . you're what, exactly? An organ vampire?" A mind-melding vampire was something I understood if not believed in.

"I do not understand 'vampire.'"

"You know. A bloodsucker. A garlic hater. Turns into a bat. A sparkly demon that avoids sunlight. That sort of thing."

"I do not avoid sunlight; the sun strengthens me. And I do not drink blood."

"Uh-huh. So that makes you a . . ." I did the mom trick and waited for him to fill in the blank, but he just stood there looking at me.

"Okay," I said, embracing my inner sarcasm. "Then choose the answer that best applies to you. 'I am (a) crazy, (b) a tanning-slash-workout junkie, (c) an ax murderer looking for a place to put his organs, or (d) a figment of Lily's very inventive imagination.'"

He frowned. "I am lucid of mind, Lily. I do not understand 'tan-ning,' and the only lives I have ever taken were those of evil men."

I was about to ask a question about the killing of evil men when Amon strode boldly toward me. Again, I found I couldn't move, though his increasing proximity was setting off alarms in my brain. He gently pressed his palm to my cheek and gazed at me with eyes greener than the grass in Ireland.

Instantly, I became aware of his unique scent—liquid amber with a kiss of cashmere and a hint of myrrh warmed in the sun. I liked it. A lot. I didn't want to. My cheek burned where his palm rested, and I found I couldn't turn away from him.

With the utmost earnestness, he asked, "Does my touch prove to you that I am a real man and not someone found only in your dreams?"

My throat had suddenly gone dry. I made an effort to swallow and reply, but instead I focused on his full lips and merely nodded, especially when I realized that I didn't really know how to answer his question.

His hand slipped down my face to cup my chin, and he studied my expression for a moment before saying, "You do not need to fear me, Lily. You are hurting because of my actions. Please let me help."

After he said that, I was able to focus once again on the throbbing at the base of my neck, the ache in my limbs, and the nauseating quiver in my stomach. I nodded, confused but trusting at that moment, despite the other half of my mind protesting to the contrary.

Amon took a step closer, miles of bare chest mere inches from me, and even without coming into full-body contact, I felt prickles of warmth sink into my frame like I'd been shot with little solar arrows.

Closing his eyes, Amon placed his hands on my neck and cupped it gently. The thought briefly occurred to me that I might soon be stran-gled, but he held me as carefully as a butterfly. He began murmuring and his hands burned in a VapoRub kind of way. My skin tingled as heat ran through my body, shutting off the pain and leaving a blessed numb-ness in its wake.

When Amon lifted his head and staggered back a few steps, I could see the cost of whatever it was he had done. His golden skin now had a gray, pasty tinge and his bright eyes looked tired, more brown than green.

Sinking on to the nearest piece of patio furniture, Amon buried his face in his hands, his chest rising and falling quickly, his breathing as shallow as if he had just run a race.

"What did you do?" I asked, trying to make sense of what had happened.

"I gave back some of the energy I stole. Unfortunately, it is only a temporary reprieve, Young Lily."

"Temporary?"

"Yes. The pain will return, but I will share the burden of it for as long as I am able. You must believe that it was never my desire for you to share my fate."

"Look, I'm not really following you, fate-wise. I'm just going to assume that you did some kind of hypnotherapy on me, and it worked. So thank you. I feel much better."

After a brief moment of hesitation, I sank onto the cushion next to him. His emotions tasted bitter. Assuming he was telling the truth and we were connected, then what I was feeling now could, in theory, be coming from him. Pain. Weakness. And something else . . . something beneath the surface. It finally came to me: loneliness. As quickly as I made sense of it, the emotion was smothered.

"Do not delve too deeply, Young Lily." Amon leaned his head back against the cushion and added softly, "You may not like what you find."

He closed his eyes, long lashes casting shadows across his cheekbones. Tentatively, I pressed the back of my hand against his forehead. His skin, which had been full of heat a mere moment before, had turned as cold as ice. "You're freezing," I declared.

I rushed into my room and scooped up my down comforter, stopping to close and lock my bedroom door just in case a parental figure decided to check on me, and headed back to the veranda. After tucking the comforter around Amon, I asked, "Were you serious when you said the sun makes you stronger?"

"Yes, Lily," he whispered.

"All right, then. Let's get you back into the sun." I didn't understand what was happening between us, but his weakness had created an even stronger tangible pull. It was gentle but persistent. It came at me in little waves, slowly sapping my strength.

"Your thoughts are correct," Amon said as I shuffled him to a bench bathed in sunlight. "But I will attempt to use as little of your energy as possible."

"Can you read my thoughts?"

"I understand you in the way you understand me," he explained cryptically. After he was settled, he mumbled, "Thank you, Lily."

The sun really did revive him. The difference was noticeable and undeniable. His draw on me lessened until I could barely feel it. After a few moments of observing him, I said, "Okay, here's what I'm thinking. You probably have a condition. Like one of those rare sun allergies, except you're the opposite. You've got a problem with shade." But if that was really the case, then how had Amon given his strange sun condition to me? "Amon? You mentioned sharing my energy."

"Yes. That is right," he replied.

"So yesterday when you were injured, you borrowed my energy to heal yourself. Is that correct?"

"Partly. You are my tie to this world. Like an anchor on a boat. I can draw all my power only when I am fully formed. Until I am in my proper frame, I must remain linked to you."

This was getting weirder by the second. "Okay, let me see if I understand. Your body works like a solar panel, with the sun functioning as your own personal miracle cure, you're in desperate need of an organ transplant, and for the time being you need me to be your Energizer Bunny."

I didn't realize I'd been gesturing until Amon took my hands in his.

"Lily, your words are confusing to me. Though I do get power from the sun, it is not enough to do the things I must do in the time allotted. Without the jars that hold the remainder of my essence, I will soon die."

"You're dying?"

He nodded. "It is not the right time. I need to remain in this world until I have accomplished my purpose."

Oh.

My half-realized attempts at minimalizing his symptoms vanished, tamped down by the seriousness of his condition. Common sense and practical Lilliana took over. I squeezed his hand. "Of course you do. You are far too young to die."

Everything suddenly fit into place. He was still lost, but now I knew that he was also terminally ill.

The organ business was likely because he was in organ failure, and he must have been put on heavy medication, which made him a little loopy.

Testing alternative healing methods would explain his obsession with healing and energy transfer. Someone probably hadn't kept an eye on him, and he had wandered off wearing nothing but a white sheet, which had likely come from his hospital bed. That also explained the bare feet and the hair loss for a guy so young. I wondered if he had gone to the museum as a dying wish.

"Lily?"

His simple utterance of my name made the spinning wheels in my mind come to a complete stop. "Yes, Amon?" I replied softly, with an apologetic sort of smile.

"I sense your thoughts. Though it is true that my body is weakened, there is no sickness in my mind. I do not have much time in your world, and the ceremony must be completed while I have strength. If I can raise my brothers, they will help me finish what I must do, but to do that I need your help finding them."

"You want me to help you find your brothers?"

"Yes."

Relief flooded through me. "Of course. I'll do whatever I can. Were they at the museum with you?"

He shook his head. "They are lost like me."

So he wanted to reconnect with his brothers. Well, if he needed help with his bucket list, then that was something I could do. Leaving him in the sun, I headed back into my room and returned with a pad of paper and my trusty mechanical pencil.

"Okay, let's start with names."

He nodded. "One is named Asten."

I penciled in *Asten.*

"He is the son of Khalfani."

"Right. Last name Khalfani."

"No. His father's name is Khalfani."

"Okay, good. That's very good, Amon." I smiled brightly. "What's his last name?" I asked slowly.

Amon's eyes narrowed, but he answered my question. "He is known only as Asten, but sometimes he is also called the Celestial Magician or the Cosmic Dreamer."

"Um . . . okay." I jotted down *possible magician/check Vegas,* and then asked about his other brother.

"He is named Ahmose, and he was once the prince of Waset."

"Waset. Is that a country?"

"It was once a great city."

"I see. Go on," I said as I wrote *possible politician.*

"He is the Great Healer, and the Master of both Beast and Storm."

"Gotcha." I adjusted my notes. Crossing off *possible politician,* I wrote *veterinarian or perhaps weatherman.*

"When was the last time you saw either of them?"

"It's been a millennium."

"Uh-huh." For a moment the only noise was the scratching of my pencil.

Closing my book with a pop, I said, "I think I have a good place to start." I put my hand on Amon's bare shoulder and squeezed gently. "I promise I'll do my best to find your brothers and get you where you need to be."

"Thank you, Young Lily."

"You're welcome. Now, how about some sustenance?" Pausing briefly, I added, "Can you eat solid food?" *I should never have fed a cancer patient a hot dog. What was I thinking?*

"Do you have a hot dog?" he asked, as if reading my mind.

"Hot dogs aren't very nutritious, and it's unlikely there'd be any here, but I'll order something for you. Something soft that will be easy on the stomach."

"My teeth are sound. I do not require mush. My arrival is often celebrated with feasting and song, but you can sing for me at another time. I confess that at the moment I am hungrier than an outcast jackal and would not put off a feast for any entertainment, no matter how riveting."

"Right. I'll hold off on the riveting singing. A feast, though, I can arrange. You just stay right here in the sun until I get back."

He nodded, the fatigue on his face obvious.

Carefully closing the sliding door behind me and drawing the curtains, I grabbed my robe and headed toward the kitchen, stopping to check my reflection in the mirror. My dark hair hung down my back in thick, messy waves. The blue eyes looking back at me were bright, and my cheeks sun-kissed.

I was definitely not looking like the poised, elegant, controlled girl I usually was. I appeared excited, wild, and a little frenzied. Making a deliberate effort to calm myself and smooth my hair, I proceeded slowly to the kitchen. It was empty. My parents must have left early. Then it hit me that it was Marcella's day off, too. Perfect.

I called room service and placed my order, then headed back to the veranda.

"Have you soaked up enough sun?" I asked.

"I have taken in all I can for the moment."

"Great. Let's get you inside, then."

He followed me into my room and watched with interest as I hastily grabbed a lacy black bra from the back of a chair and tossed it and my comforter in a wrinkled heap on the bed.

"So, your breakfast is coming, but that will take a half hour or so. I'm going to raid my father's closet for some clothes for you. In the meantime, do you want to take a shower?"

"A shower?"

"Unless you prefer a bath?"

"Ah. Yes, I would enjoy a good scrubbing."

"Great. So I'll get the clothes, and the bathroom is just through there."

Amon gave me a quizzical look before heading into the bathroom. I left him to his own devices while I scrounged up something for him to wear.

My parents' bedroom and bathroom were even bigger than mine, and their closet was ginormous. I knew that Father had some old T-shirts and jeans in drawers in the back. I dug up a pair of sneakers, socks, a workout tee, sweatpants, and a lightweight jacket, and was headed back into my parents' room when the thought occurred to me that Amon might need underwear.

Going through my father's underwear drawer was not something I ever thought I'd have to do, but I was even more out of sorts when I considered which pair would best fit Amon. Finally, I settled on some generic boxers and headed to my bathroom.

When I returned, it sounded like Niagara Falls was thundering over a cliff in my room. All the fixtures were streaming water at full force. Amon stood by the sink staring at his reflection with fascination.

"This bathroom"—he tested out the word—"is unique."

I turned off the water in the sink. "I suppose it is. Here are your clothes. Did you decide on a bath or a shower?"

"Which is the shower?" he asked.

When I pointed to the spa-style shower, which was currently pounding water from every one of its multiple body sprays and jets,

Amon glanced in that direction but turned to the tub instead, reaching for his man skirt. He began playing with a tie on one side.

I held up my hands, spinning around, and involuntarily squeaked when I could still see him in the mirror attempting to disrobe. Quickly shutting my eyes, I said, "Whoa, there. Could you at least wait until I leave?"

"Why would you leave?"

"Um . . . a little thing called modesty?"

"Mod . . . esty?"

"Yeah. You know. Not showing what the Egyptian gods gave you. That sort of thing."

"I do not understand. Then who will wash me?"

A burst of laughter came out before I could stifle it. "Uh, yourself?" With eyes still shut, I felt my way over to the sink and then from there to the door. "Amon, I realize you probably had nurses in the hospital giving you sponge baths and all, but I am just not prepared to take that step with you. Okay?"

I heard the unmistakable sound of clothing hitting the floor and then the swoosh of water as he sank into the tub. "Very well, Lily. You may keep your mod . . . esty."

"Thanks." I backed far enough away so that the only thing I would be able to see was his head and then opened my eyes.

"Here." I tossed him a washcloth and a bar of soap. "If you want the jets on, push that button on the side. Over on the left, by your hand."

The look of amazement on his face when the jets came on was priceless.

"Towels are on the heated rack on the left side of the tub. Food will be here in twenty minutes." I shut the door behind me and then added, shouting, "And make sure you come out dressed!"

I quickly straightened up my room, and not long after the phone rang, indicating that the food was ready. I met the server by the elevator, signed the form, and took the cart from him. "I'll call when you can come pick it up, okay?"

"Very good, miss."

Wheeling the cart into the kitchen, I set two places and got out milk, a variety of juice bottles, and two mugs for the hot chocolate I'd ordered. After setting the platters of food on the table, I shouted, "Amon! Breakfast is here! Are you dressed?"

I jumped when I heard his voice right behind me. "I am having a problem."

"You scared me." I turned around and found him holding the shoes in one hand and his sweatpants up around his waist with the other. "Are they that loose?" I asked.

To prove it, he let go and the pants slid dangerously low on his hips. There were no white boxers in sight. "Um . . . Amon? Where are the rest of the clothes I gave you?"

"This is the one I chose. It covers the most."

"Ah, I see. Then you made a good choice, but I meant for you to wear all of the clothes."

"All of them?" His eyes roved over my body, still clad in pajamas. "But you do not wear that many."

"No, not when I'm sleeping, but when I dress for the day I will wear clothes like the ones I gave you."

"Very well. May I eat first, Lily?"

"Sure. Have a seat."

While he sat down I uncovered the dishes. Fragrant steam rose as I removed each domed lid. "There. Now you eat while I go get dressed. I'll bring back your other clothes, too, okay?"

Amon stared at the food with wide eyes, and he could only nod in response.

As I turned to leave, I smiled. My parents would raise their eyebrows when they saw how much food I had ordered for just one meal, but it was worth it to see the look on Amon's face. He'd requested a feast, and a feast I gave him. One worthy of anyone's bucket list.

He was now surrounded by eggs done eight different ways, hash browns and skillet potatoes, country ham, apple sausage, maple bacon, biscuits slathered with honey and melted butter, caramel-apple-topped pancakes with whipped cream, crème brûlée French toast, malted Belgian waffles, a fruit platter, and a basket full of croissants, Danishes, and streusel-topped blueberry muffins. If he couldn't find something he liked among those dishes, then he was past helping.

I dressed in what I called designer casual and smiled as I assessed myself in the mirror. Though my eyes were still bright, I looked much more like the poised, calm, and in-control version of myself. Heading back to the kitchen, I dumped Amon's clothes on the chair next to him. I put my hands on my hips and laughed as I took in the scene before me. "Which one did you like best?"

"All of it," Amon mumbled with his mouth full. "Here, Lily. Sit." He pulled out a chair and took my arm, tugging until I sat down. "Eat."

I scooped some fruit onto my plate and nibbled on it while he filled his plate again. Halfway done, he paused and looked at me. "Why are you not eating?"

"Too many carbs."

"What is a carb?"

"Uh, too fattening."

"You are not fat." Amon looked me up and down in a way that made me feel slightly uncomfortable. "You are too thin. Eat."

He picked up a serving spoon and began filling my plate until the plate could hold no more.

"Okay!" I threw up my hands. "That's enough."

Grunting, he turned back to his food, but kept a vigilant eye on me and pointed to my plate every time I set my fork down.

When he poked my arm for the third time, I said, "I can't eat any more. Usually I just have tea for breakfast."

"Tea is not food."

"It's all I need."

"No. A woman needs more than tea," Amon stated, looking into my eyes. I suddenly felt very exposed, as if we were talking about much more than just breakfast. I got the distinct impression that he was studying me from the inside out and could see all my insecurities. Hunger and sustenance seemed to take on a different meaning in that moment.

"Yes, I suppose she does," I answered, turning my eyes away.

Finally finishing his food, he pushed back from the table and declared he was ready to begin the search for his brothers. He struggled with the T-shirt, so I helped him twist it around. As I did, my hands brushed against his rather nice chest. I blushed and turned to pick up the jacket. After I thrust it into his arms, I noticed that the sweatpants were once again threatening to slide off his hips.

I cleared my throat. He'd been examining the jacket's hood with a curious expression but looked up. "It's, um, your pants. There's a string, see? At the waistband? Just pull it tight and tie it."

Casting aside the jacket, Amon found the drawstring and pulled it on one side, then the other. I left him to finish dressing and returned to my room to grab my bag and fill it with all the things we might need.

I put in my laptop, my cell and charger, my notebook, and my wallet. Then I returned to the kitchen and added some bottled water. Amon tossed in a few apples and oranges and I threw in a bag of crackers. After looping the strap across my body, I knelt at his feet, helping him tie his sneakers, and thought about where we should go.

Logically, the first step would be to take him to the hospital nearest the museum and see if anyone recognized him, but I bit my lip as I considered that he might not get a chance to find his brothers if we did. Odds were they'd lock him up after this escape. Taking him back just seemed wrong.

"Are you ready, Young Lily?"

Amon offered his hand to help me stand. "Thanks. Yes, I'm ready if you are."

"Very well."

He kept hold of my hand and closed the distance between us. Wrapping his arm around my waist, he said, "Hold on to me very tightly."

"Amon . . . what are you—" My question turned into a scream as wind swept around our bodies, gritty sand stinging my skin like thousands of needles. I watched in horror as my body unraveled, piece by piece, to join the tumult, and my cry was cut off because I no longer had a throat, let alone a voice.

Panicked, I reached out to grab on to something and became aware of another presence nearby. Amon responded to my fear. He soothed me, holding me together, though I knew it wasn't his arms that I felt. The storm swirled around us as we descended into a place that grew darker with each passing second.

Then I drowned in the quicksand.

Unwrapping the Truth

Light penetrated the darkness, and where I once felt nothing, I could now sense the pressure of Amon's arm around me, his hand clutching mine. The swirling sand became sluggish and started sticking together, and in the process, the grains re-formed my arms, legs, and torso. Risking the possibility that I might be horrified at the sight of my own flesh, I opened my eyes and was greatly relieved to find my skin still attached to my body. Not only were there no gaping wounds or scratches, but my skin gleamed with health. I realized then that the sand blast must have exfoliated my entire body, a thought that left me feeling slightly queasy.

We were standing in a park—Central Park, in fact—on a path I'd walked several times over the years. There was no one around to see us materialize and I wasn't sure if that was good or bad, but one thing was for sure: Amon was definitely not the person I had believed him to be.

In the distance I could make out Hotel Helios. Amon's chest heaved against my hand, which was splayed across it, his head angled toward the sun, his eyes still closed.

"Amon?"

He opened his eyes and looked down at me and then at our surroundings with an expression of confusion that quickly turned into something else.

"*Mehsehhah ef yibehu hawb!*" he shouted, and threw up his hands in a gesture of intense frustration. He slowly turned in a circle, mumbling to himself in another language. When he recognized the hotel, a few more words that sounded suspiciously like expletives escaped from his lips.

Emotion was building up inside me that I couldn't restrain. My very structured life was spinning out of control.

I was smart. I was cultured and tactful. I got along easily with adults. I was the epitome of cool, calm, and collected. And I was always, *always* in control. I was Lilliana Jailene Young, and I was in danger of losing my wits over a boy—a crazy, fascinating, inexplicable, impossible-to-understand boy.

Amon eventually circled back to me and said, "My powers are weakened and my brothers are too distant. We are going to need help."

"Help?" I spat, and then shouted incredulously, "Help? Really? You think? Because personally I'm feeling a little bit beyond help!" I had never shouted at the top of my lungs before in my life. Since meeting Amon, shouting seemed to be becoming a new habit of mine, but the upside was that yelling at Amon actually felt good.

Amon zeroed in on me like *I* was the mental patient. "Young Lily, calm yourself."

"I don't think so!" I shouted.

"Lily, we need to—"

"We need to nothing! I don't know who you are or what kind of crazy drugs you've been feeding me, but you're done. We're done. Do you get it? I am *finished* helping you."

Turning toward home, I stalked away, an action that felt immensely satisfying. Each step, every small unit of distance I put between us, helped me gather myself and get back to feeling normal. I shifted my bag so it wouldn't bounce so much and hoped Amon wasn't following me.

The few passersby who came into view gave me a wide berth as I stomped along, mumbling about lost, dying, homeless boys who were far too attractive for their own good. I couldn't describe what had just happened without using *Star Trek* references.

I'd tried to rationalize everything that had happened, placing each strange event into a neat little box, but this, whatever it was that Amon had just done, had set off a bomb in my tidy mental office. This one wasn't going to fit. In fact, it was way, way outside the box. The best thing was to get some distance and then try to figure out what was going on with me, because clearly I wasn't right in the head. I wondered if Amon would come after me. If he did, I'd simply scream. There were usually people all over the park and someone was bound to hear me.

"Lily!"

Speak of the sun devil. Amon *was* coming after me.

"Young Lily, come to me now!" he called out as if I were a disobedient puppy.

"Leave me alone or I'll scream!" I yelled back, picking up the pace to a half-jog, half–power walk.

I could hear him following me, and I took in a breath to shriek for help, when, with an imperious voice, he cried out, "Lily, you will stop!"

My legs froze with a jolt so sudden that my bag flopped around to my front and pulled me off balance. I fell in a heap on the grass, unsure what had just happened. In the few seconds it took for me to gather the items that had fallen out of my bag, Amon was upon me and offered a hand. When I stubbornly refused, he used his controlling voice again. "*Lily,* take my hand."

This time I made a concerted effort to refuse his command and was rewarded with pain—stabbing, knife-twisting-in-my-gut pain. It made me gasp, and I absolutely knew Amon had caused it somehow. It actually hurt to disobey him. When my determination weakened and the pain overwhelmed me, I whimpered and gave in. My traitorous hand shot into his and he pulled me up. *Resentment* was an insufficient word to describe what I felt toward him at that moment.

"You *will* sit down and talk with me," he ordered.

Gritting my teeth, I took a defiant step away and staggered, hunched over in wrenching agony. The rage I felt grew with each passing second. My whole body shook with it, and in that moment there was not a person or a thing on earth that I hated more than him. I was seething, and I'd never felt that way about anyone before. Not in my entire life.

"Let me go!" I hissed as he guided me to a nearby bench.

"No. You will not run away and you will not scream."

Angry tears filled my eyes, and I let them run silently down my face, desperate not to give him the satisfaction of seeing the effect his actions had on me and yet unable to do anything to prevent it. "What are you going to do to me? Is this a kidnapping? An assault?"

He looked at my face then and noticed the tears. Tentatively, he wiped one from my cheek with his thumb, his expression full of regret. "Sit," he said, but then changed the tone of his voice. "Please."

Amon took the bag from my shoulder and set it on the bench next to me, then paced in front of me for a few moments. "I am sorry to use my power to control your actions. I know how deeply you abhor it, but—"

"You don't know anything about me," I spat.

He sighed. "I know more about you with each passing minute, Young Lily. Even without our connection I can see how you despise the idea of submitting your will to another, but you must understand, I cannot let you leave. You do not need to fear me. I have no desire to hurt you."

"I don't understand what you're doing to control me, but I will fight you. In fact, I . . . I will hate you for this forever." I'd never actually said those words to anyone before and I wasn't really sure I could follow through with the threat. I'd never had cause to feel hate.

Sure, there were people I didn't like, but I just categorized them in little boxes labeled Needy, or Low Self-Esteem, or Bully. It never affected me emotionally. I was always able to distance myself and keep my emotions in check, but with Amon it was different. The idea that the boy I took under my wing would manipulate me hurt more than I thought possible.

Amon's look became stony. "Hate me, then. Struggle. Rail against me. Rebel at every turn, but it will do you no good. You will cause yourself only more pain. I told you, Lily, you are bound to me and you will remain by my side for as long as I wish it."

The indignation and rage I felt melted into something else. My body shook and I felt like a dog that had been kicked by its master. "That's a fine thing to do when all I've done is help you," I said.

He shrugged as if he didn't care how I felt, but I could see that he did, and that confused me even more.

"It is necessary," he finally acknowledged.

"But why? Why can't I leave? What do you want from me?" I sniffled loudly and, with a groan of vexation, rummaged through my bag until I found a pack of tissues.

"I told you. I need to find my brothers."

"You must be heartless to take advantage of the kindness of a stranger like this." Teardrops clung to my lashes, making Amon blurry. Why was I crying? I never cried. Crying was ugly. It was a sign of ingratitude. My emotions were too close to the surface. Attempting to tamp them down, I blew my nose and wiped my eyes. "Do you even have cancer?"

Amon knelt in front of me, taking a new tissue to dab at my sticky cheeks, and sighed. "I have found over the centuries that my heart is of very little use to me."

He trailed the tip of his finger over the curve of my cheek and warmth began to seep into my skin. For a brief moment, I allowed myself to enjoy his gentle touch, but then I froze, and realized he had, too.

His hand dropped to his side and I sensed that he was as surprised by his gesture as I had been. He was trouble. He was my enemy. *Wasn't he?* One thing was certain, though: he made me . . . feel. And I wasn't comfortable with that.

Amon was charming enough on his own, but I sensed there was more than just me being physically attracted to him. I'd never been affected by a boy like this before, and the sensation was disturbing. Not in a creepy, horror-show kind of way, but the kind of disturbing that left me feeling unanchored. He had uprooted me from a very comfortable life and was holding my fragile frame in the palm of his hand.

Still, as I studied his handsome face, I recognized that part of me, a part that I didn't want to claim or acknowledge, longed for the warmth his touch brought. That even if I was uncomfortable with the emotions he evoked, I'd never felt more alive. More like a real girl and less like the porcelain doll my parents had molded me into.

Amon seemed to have the ability to both cause confusion and chase it away. Being with him was exhilarating and frightening, and at the same time that it gave me a sense of power, it left me utterly weak. Overall, I felt unhinged and jittery, with a side dish of guilt."I don't like this power you have over me," I said quietly. "It makes me feel not quite like myself. Like I have no control over my body."

"I am sorry for this. Again, I do not wish to exercise this power, but I cannot continue on my path without you. I need you. You have no idea how desperately." He took my hands, rubbing his thumbs over my knuckles. "Lily, please know that I do not wish to make you sad or cause you harm. Can you at least believe that?" he asked.

For a long moment I looked into his hazel eyes. Amon was a lot of things, and there were many parts of him I didn't understand at all, but I somehow knew he wasn't a liar. I could sense it. "Yes," I answered grudgingly. "I believe you."

"Good." Amon nodded. "Now, what is cancer?"

"It's a disease of the cells. How do you not know this?"

He sighed. "You have so many questions."

I closed my mouth and sat back, turning my head and shrugging.

"Why do you do this?" Amon asked.

"Do what?"

"Retreat inside yourself?"

"I don't understand what you mean."

He studied my face and said finally, "I did not mean to insult you.

Your questions are welcome. Perhaps I can answer yours and ask for some answers in return?"

Hesitantly, I nodded.

"First, there are many things I do not understand about your world, but I do know that my body is not diseased."

I started laughing and soon began to cry, hiccupping between sobs. I had thoroughly lost it. Uncontrollable giddiness overwhelmed me; I felt like I hadn't slept in a week. When I grabbed a second and then a third tissue, he said, "Lily, take my hand."

Eyeing his open palm suspiciously, I sniffled loudly.

"Please, Lily. I can offer you peace."

Sensing that it wasn't a command this time and realizing that it didn't hurt to disobey, I let his hand envelop mine.

"Draw upon my energy," he said. "Try to find balance."

I took a deep breath in an attempt to center myself and felt something shift between the two of us. It was as if the tugging sensation was reversed and warm sunlight trickled slowly into me. It calmed and relaxed me in such a way that my confusion and anger became less important. I still remembered that I was mad, but it seemed distant, buried, like I had to reach deep within myself and work to pull it to the surface.

"Who *are* you?" I whispered. His lashes fluttered and green eyes rimmed with golden brown opened and looked straight into my soul. "The way you look at me . . . It's like you . . . you know me," I said.

"Yes."

"I mean . . . I mean all of me."

"Not . . . everything."

"But you can read me . . . somehow."

Amon nodded. "This is our connection, Lily."

"You are not what I think you are, are you?"

"I am more. And perhaps less."

I sighed. This was downright confusing. "All right. Then why don't we start over and try this the old-fashioned way." I stuck out my hand

and he took it. "My name is Lilliana and yours is Amon. So, Amon, where are you from?"

Amon gave me a quizzical look and then nodded. "I am from Egypt."

"You were born there?"

"Yes. Many years ago."

"How did you get here?"

Amon sat at my feet in the grass. "I am unsure, exactly. But my sarcophagus was in the House of Muses, so I would suppose that I was brought here. For what purpose, though, I do not know."

"Your sarcophagus?"

"Yes."

"I don't understand. Do you own the sarcophagus? Are you a curator of some kind? Where does your power come from?"

Amon laughed. "I will do my best to answer your questions in the hope that by doing so you will begin to trust me." He held up his hands and then ticked off his answers on his fingers. "I do not understand 'curator.' My power is a gift from the sun god Amun-Ra and his son Horus. And that sarcophagus is one of many I have slept in over the centuries."

I stared slack-jawed at him for several seconds and then murmured, not quite believing I was saying the words, "Are you trying to tell me that you're a . . . a mummy?"

"A mummy." His lips formed the word as if tasting it. Slowly, he answered, "Each millennium, when I pass through your world, my body is encased in the wrappings of Anubis. Is this what you mean?"

I sat back against the bench, hard. "Mummification means a dead body gets wrapped from head to toe and is placed in a sarcophagus that usually gets hidden in a pyramid or a temple," I explained.

"Then yes. I am a mummy."

When I was able to speak, I remarked, "You don't look dead."

"I am not dead," he declared, then added, "at the moment."

I suddenly remembered entering the Egyptian exhibit and finding the sarcophagus empty. "Do you swear you are telling the truth?"

"I swear on the heart of my beloved mother as to the veracity of my words."

When Amon had asked me before if I believed him, I'd told him truthfully that I did. There was absolutely nothing insincere about him. I could tell that he believed what he was saying, but that didn't mean that what he was saying was one hundred percent true.

To find out, I channeled the hard-nosed police interviewers I'd seen on television. Leaning forward and narrowing my eyes, I began peppering Amon with questions. "What were your parents' names?"

"King Heru and Queen Omorose."

"What was your favorite childhood toy?"

"A wooden carving of a horse."

"What is your favorite food?"

"Honey and dates from my country and the sweet round discs filled with fruit from yours."

"Uh-huh." So he liked Danishes. "Favorite music?"

"The sistrum, the harp, and the lute."

"If you're an Egyptian mummy, where are your wrappings?"

"My body does not need the wrappings now. I have risen, as I do once every one thousand years."

Blinking after absorbing that statement, I continued. "But I didn't see any strewn about the exhibit. What happened to them?"

"When it is time for me to rise, I waken and use my power to disintegrate the wrappings. Otherwise it would be difficult for me to move about."

I grunted. "Right. I guess that would be difficult," I mumbled. Cocking my head, I continued. "How is it that you understand English?"

"A spell." When I just blinked, he explained, "I did not understand your language at first. Do you remember when you gestured to me in the House of Muses?"

I nodded.

"I invoked a spell from the Book of the Dead to be able to communicate my thoughts to you. This is how we understand one another."

"Then you can understand anyone, from any country?"

"If I need to, yes."

"Why did you choose me?"

He didn't answer for a few seconds but looked at me. Then he plucked a blade of grass and twirled it between his fingers. "You were there," he answered simply.

Sitting back on the bench, I folded my hands in my lap and studied his face. With each answer he gave, my incredulity grew. It wasn't possible. "Can you show me something?" I gestured with one hand. "You know . . . something magical?"

"Transporting you to the park and controlling your actions is not proof enough of my power?"

"Well, I've been operating under the assumption that you were hypnotizing me somehow, so I need to see something else to be convinced."

"What would convince you?"

"Oh, I don't know. The ten plagues of Egypt, raising an undead army, resurrecting your long-lost love, something like that."

Amon frowned. "Why would I do any of those things?"

Shrugging, I answered, "That's what mummies do in the movies."

"What is a movie?"

"It's like a play. A drama."

"I see. I do not wish to bring a plague to your city. To raise an army of the undead, I would need to channel a great deal of power, which I do not have at this time, and I have never found a woman to love."

"Really? So there's no mummy girlfriend out there?"

He cocked his head. "My brothers await me, but there is no one else. No other friends that are females."

"Hmm. Interesting." I mentally shelved that piece of information. "Okay, so then do something else, something different."

After a moment of thought, he said, "I need to conserve my power, so I will do something small."

"Okay."

Shifting forward, I watched Amon with hawk eyes as he raised his hands and cupped them together. Nothing was happening. He closed his eyes in concentration and then slowly pulled his hands apart. Light filled the space between them and I felt the sting of little particles brushing against my face as tiny grains of sand flew toward his fingers.

I watched in fascination as the sand swirled and the outline of a sphinx began to take form. A jogger crested the hill and I jumped off the bench, catching Amon's hands in mine. The light disappeared and the sand fell around us in a gritty shower.

"I believe you," I whispered. I suddenly became very aware of how close our faces were, the attraction between us tangible and warm. My breath caught and I blushed as my gaze drifted from his eyes to his lips. He didn't back away or move at all, but I felt a shift, as if the air between us had suddenly become very warm.

Any slight movement and we could be kissing. With a twinge of alarm, I realized that I wanted to experience his lips pressed against mine, and I wondered if it was something I truly desired for myself or if he was making me want it.

I couldn't understand how I could go from absolute hatred—well, as close as I got to it, anyway—to trusting a guy who was an ancient mummy, complete with powers, to wanting to make out with said ancient mummy in just a matter of minutes. Boy, I was . . . Out. Of. My. Mind.

Backing away a few inches, I felt a breeze cool my stinging cheeks.

Clearing my throat, I squeezed his hands and said, "Amon, whatever powers you have, you can't show them to anyone but me and your brothers. Promise me."

"Why do you ask this?" he queried softly, lightly stroking my fingers with his thumbs. The movement sent warm pulses shooting through my veins and tickled my nerve endings in a very good way. Nervously, I withdrew my hands and shifted a bit farther away. Amon didn't seem disappointed by my actions, just curious.

I looked around and waited until the jogger disappeared into the trees before saying, "It's just dangerous, okay? Like when you healed yourself and then stood in front of the crowd letting people see your power. You need to be more careful. Try to blend in. Otherwise, people will see you as crazy, like I did, or assume you're on drugs and lock you up. There are people who would try to hurt you, or at the very least cart you off to Area 51." At his look of confusion, I said, "I'll explain Area 51 later. I still have a billion questions to ask, but I believe you are who you say you are, as impossible as it seems."

Amon nodded. "Good."

"Now tell me why you need me to go with you."

"As I said, without your inner workings supplying me with strength, I will die before my purpose is accomplished."

"And what is your purpose?"

"To waken my brothers and complete the ceremony to align the sun, the moon, and the stars so that the Dark One, Seth, the god of chaos, may be kept at bay for another thousand years."

"Uh-huh. Hold that thought." I grabbed my notebook from my bag and began scribbling. "One thousand years . . . sun . . . moon . . . stars . . . and Dark One. Hmm, you're going to have to tell me more about that guy Seth later. So are your brothers mummies, too?"

"Yes."

"You do realize we are very far away from Thebes, right?"

"How far away exactly?"

"Let me check." I pulled out my smartphone and thumbed through several pages. "Egypt is like . . . over five thousand, six hundred miles away," I announced.

"What is a mile?" he asked as he stared with interest at my phone.

"Oh, boy. What units of measurement did you use in Egypt?" Amon captured my hand and my pulse jumped. "What are you doing?" I asked nervously.

Amon smiled. "Showing you our units of measurement." He traced the lines on my palm and then ran the pad of his finger down my pinky. "This is called *djeba*, or the width of a finger. The next is *shesep*, the width of your palm. *Meh niswt* is a royal cubit, which is seven palms." Amon placed his palm next to mine and demonstrated the widths stacked on top of each other.

Flushing, I punched the numbers on my phone. "So, it says here that one mile is three thousand five hundred and twenty cubits. That means that to get to Thebes it would be roughly . . . nineteen million, seven hundred twelve thousand cubits."

He gasped. "That's almost a thousand *iteru*!"

"Yes, and that's not crossing land, either. It's over an ocean. Have you ever seen the ocean?"

He nodded. "I have seen the great seas that are fed by the Nile."

"Believe it or not, Amon, that great sea is actually small when you compare it with others."

Amon looked away and said quietly, "I have not had much opportunity to explore the world."

A melancholy expression stole over his face, and I found myself missing his warm smile. "Amon?" I touched his hand and scooted closer so he could see my phone. "Look." I showed him a picture of Earth. "We are on this continent called North America. Egypt"—I used my fingers to turn the globe and then zoom in on Africa—"is way over here on the African continent. So you can see you are a long way from Kansas, Dorothy."

"What is this box of magic?"

"Uh, it's called a phone. It has apps that work kind of like a computer."

"I do not understand."

"I can seek answers to questions with it."

"It is like an oracle?"

"I suppose in a way."

"How did you acquire this gift of the gods? Did you defeat a monster in battle?"

"Not exactly. Pretty much everyone has one."

"May I look?" I handed him my phone and he scrolled his finger across the world map, watching in fascination as the perspective changed. "We are truly on the other side of the world?" he asked.

"That's right. And don't forget, we are assuming that your brothers are still *in* Egypt. Actually, they could be anywhere—China, France, the U.K.—Egyptian exhibits are very popular."

Amon ran his hand over his bald head as he said thoughtfully, "This is why my power could not take us to them." His eyes met mine. "I cannot use my power to cross over great waters. The desert sand becomes too heavy when it meets the water. It would sink us into the bottomless ocean."

I swallowed. "Well, technically the ocean isn't bottomless, but I get the picture."

Playing with the phone, he began pressing various buttons and exploring different apps. I was shocked at how quickly he was picking up modern technology.

"There are too many oceans, you are right," he declared. "But if we could get to Egypt, I could ask Anubis for aid."

"Can't you ask him for aid from here?"

"No. The ritual to call upon him must be performed in a certain place."

"Right." The idea that this perplexing, fascinating man from another time was leaving was a relief, but at the same time, I'd be very sorry to see him go. How often does a girl get to go out with an Egyptian prince?

Amon was looking at me expectantly. Biting my lip, I suddenly realized what he wanted. *The date isn't over yet.* "Um . . . look, Amon, I'm not packed for an extended vacation, and I can't just go gallivanting across the globe. My parents wouldn't approve, and I have school next week. Spring break is over on Monday, you know.

"Why don't you just hypnotize some guy at the airport who is going to Egypt and you can borrow his 'inner workings' until you get there. Then, presto changeo, you sandblast your way to your brothers, raise them from the dead, finish your ceremony, and dust your hands of it all, so to speak."

"What is an airport?" he asked.

"An airport is a place that has lots of white chariots that can fly in the sky, even over great waters."

Amon rose immediately. "Yes. We will take a flying chariot to Egypt."

"Whoa, wait a minute," I cautioned as he pulled me to my feet. "What happened to connecting with some other person who's already going?"

He lifted my bag and secured the strap across his chest before taking both my hands in his. "I can connect to only one person, Lily." I'm sure he saw the alarm on my face, because he quickly added, "Do not worry. Once the ceremony is complete, our need to be connected will be gone and you may return home to your family and your school. At that time I will have my full power and I will be able to manipulate time and send you back to your home so that you will arrive just a moment after we left. No one will miss you. Your family will never even know you were gone."

As he started pulling me along the path, I grew more anxious. "But what if your special location to do the Anubis ritual thing isn't there anymore? I mean, there's been a lot of archaeological digging in the last one thousand years, you know. Uh, that means they've been excavating tombs," I added in case he misunderstood. "The whole thing is a long shot." I tried to wriggle my hand out of his grip and continued, "I mean, the remains of your brothers could be anywhere. And speaking of that, why do *you* have to raise them? Why can't they raise themselves, like you do? And another thing—"

"Lily." Amon stopped and turned, placing his hands on my shoulders. Warmth seeped directly into my bones, my muscles relaxing so completely that every question I had melted away. I wondered if he was doing that on purpose again, or if it was just a natural part of being around him. "I promise you that I will answer all of your questions," he said. "But I must complete the ceremony before the full moon has risen directly above the ancient temples of Giza. Those monuments still stand, do they not?"

"You mean the pyramids? Yes, but—"

"Then we need to get there as soon as possible."

"But with the full-moon restriction that gives us only a month at best."

"I fear our time is much more limited," Amon said after glancing briefly at the sky. "By my calculations we have approximately one week." He took hold of my hand again and guided me expertly out of the park.

The honking of horns grew louder and we were soon surrounded by people. If I was going to escape it would have to be now. The thing was, I wasn't sure I wanted to. Yes, my emotions were erratic. Yes, Amon was using me like an energy bar. Yes, he was an Egyptian mummy come to life. But I couldn't deny that I'd never felt more . . . alive in all of my seventeen years than I had in the past twenty-four hours.

Amon stopped in front of the horse- drawn carriages, smiled widely, and raised his eyebrows.

"Sorry, Spartacus, they only travel around inside the park," I explained.

He sighed. "It is probably for the best anyway. Those horses look fat and lazy. It is likely they do not have the stamina for the speed I wish."

"Hey!" an eavesdropping coachman protested. Ignoring the carriage driver, Amon spotted a cab and stepped boldly in front of it, holding his hands up in a commanding gesture, despite the fact that the off-duty light was on. "Stop, golden chariot!" he shouted.

Amon headed around to the driver's side and spoke with him for a moment, ignoring the honking and rude gestures coming from the other drivers. Then he indicated I should come forward.

The driver shot out of the taxi and opened the door for me. "Please make yourself comfortable, miss. I'll have you two to the airport in record time." Amon handed my bag to the driver.

I hesitated by the open door. Lifting my eyes, I found Amon holding out his hand as he watched me and I wondered if he was using his power to read my mind.

"Will you come with me, Lily?"

Not *"You will come,"* or *"Come with me,"* but *"Will you come?"*

Amon was giving me a choice. Which I wasn't sure was exactly the case, but it was a nice gesture. This was the moment. I had, if not all the facts, enough details to make an informed decision. Amon still had the power to control me and he was desperate enough to force me to do his bidding, but at the same time, he was offering me a precious taste of free agency.

I knew I was a coward—a privileged, self-deluded, spineless coward who preferred sitting in her pretty little mansion, in her prim little room, placating her preppy fake friends, and all the while fooling herself into believing that she was as free-spirited as the people she drew in her notebook.

But, I wasn't. And right now, looking into Amon's eyes, I was panicked. Not only because what he was asking me to do was way, *way* beyond my comfort zone, but also because I was deathly frightened that this adventure might be my one and only opportunity to break out. To choose something different. To *be* someone different. It was all too easy to picture my life five years in the future.

A gritty determination filled me. I wasn't sure if it was Amon's influence or if a switch in my mind had finally been flipped, but suddenly I *wanted* to go. I wanted to jump off a cliff. Leap from a plane. Grab the opportunity, as crazy as it was, to do and see things nobody else could.

Though my hand shook, I slid it into Amon's and said, "Let's go." Taking a deep breath, I released all my reservations, feeling a sense of pride that I'd had the courage to say yes. Now I just had to get into the cab before my second thoughts became overwhelming.

Gifting me with a sunshine smile, Amon pulled me close and whispered in my ear, "You are braver than you think. Truly, you do have the heart of a sphinx."

"What does that mean, exactly?" I asked as I climbed into the cab and scooted over to make room for Amon.

"In my country a sphinx is often depicted as a man, but the Greeks believed the sphinx to be female: half lioness, half human. I appreciate their version more. You see, a lioness is brave and smart. She is a huntress who provides food for her cubs. Each animal she hunts has the potential to end her life, but she still hunts just the same, for there are others who rely on her. To have the heart of a sphinx is to have the heart of a lioness. But the sphinx is also a protector, a defender. As she raises her great wings, she creates a powerful wind that wards off evil."

"So are there real sphinxes? I mean, if Anubis is real and mummies are real, then it's a possibility, right?"

Amon finally turned to me and rubbed his jaw. "I have never seen one, but there is a legend told among warriors that a woman brave of heart who proves herself in battle will be embraced by the spirit of the sphinx."

"Right. All things considered, I'm not sure that's something I'd want to aspire to. Battling isn't really on my list of things to do, and I'm also not too fond of the idea of having a tail."

Amon glanced at my body with interest as if considering the possibility.

"What?" I sputtered as my face turned red.

"Nothing," he answered, unable to hide his grin.

I sank my elbow into his side and said, "Quit it. And while I'm thinking of it, stop reading my mind, too."

"Believe it or not, I try to avoid it, but sometimes your feelings are so overwhelming, even I, with all my powers, do not have the ability to defend myself from the onslaught."

I peered at the driver, wondering what he thought of this conversation, but he didn't seem to be paying much attention. In fact, his expression was almost . . . giddy.

Quietly, I asked Amon, "What did you do to him?"

"Are you controlling him?"

"I am manipulating his vision," Amon said as he leaned closer.

"What do you mean?"

"What he sees are the two most important people he will ever drive."

When we arrived at JFK, I pulled out my credit card to pay, but the driver was insulted that I'd even suggest such a thing. He even dusted off my backpack and offered to carry it in for me. When we were finally able to break away from him, he shook hands with Amon, offered him a business card, said he was a big fan, and added that if Amon was ever in New York again to please not hesitate to call upon him for any reason.

As he drove away, I couldn't help but laugh. "Who did he think you were?"

"I am not sure of the name, but the image of a young male singer with lots of hair came to my mind."

The idea that a NYC taxi driver's dream client was a member of a boy band kept me smiling all the way into the airport terminal.

Flying Chariots

We entered the airport without any trouble, and Amon watched the other travelers with an expression of deep fascination. How different and strange we must have seemed to him, what with our gleaming windows, spacious, airy buildings of chrome and metal, and everyone bustling from place to place with their wheeled luggage.

"Now, you have to be careful about what you do in here. You have a knack for drawing too much attention to yourself. Try to blend in. There are cameras everywhere." At his confused look, I explained, "A camera takes pictures. You know, like the carvings on the walls of temples and pyramids? They're like that, only much, much more accurate. See?"

I took a picture of myself with my phone and showed it to him. With fascination, he traced the image with his finger.

Turning my phone around, I clicked a picture of Amon, but the screen was blurred. "Hold on. Let me try again."

I shut off the flash and touched the button again and again, but each shot was the same. In the spot where Amon should be, there was a burst of light.

"Your technology cannot carve my image. It is likely because I am a walking shadow."

Staring at the bright blur on my phone, I mumbled, "More like a walking supernova."

Amon continued to study the other travelers and then asked suddenly, "How do you see me, Young Lily?"

"I don't know. I mean, I have no way to classify you. Are you an Egyptian god? A mummy? Are you human? A ghost? Immortal obviously, but really there's just no frame of reference."

"No. I mean to ask you, what is wrong with my appearance?"

"Um . . . nothing, really." *At least, no girl I know would have a problem.*

Amon frowned. "Do you know if this . . . airport has a room for baths?"

"You want to take a bath right now?" I asked, confused.

"*No.*"

And then it hit me. "Oh, a *rest*room. Sure."

"I do not wish to rest, either."

"No, I know. That's just what it's called—a bathroom, a restroom, or a men's room." I looked around and spied one not too far away. "Do you see where that man is going? That's the restroom for men."

"Will you wait for me here?"

"Yes."

As I watched him walk away, an idea popped into my head. On a whim, I headed over to a cart that sold earbuds. I knew Amon would find them very interesting and was buying him a pair when I felt a tug in my gut.

Signing the receipt quickly, I gave in to the pull and was drawn back in the general direction of where we'd been sitting. The chairs were now occupied by other travelers, and Amon was nowhere to be seen. Turning in a circle, I tucked my hair behind my ears and looked for him.

The tugging sensation was gone. I assumed it had been generated by Amon, so its abrupt absence worried me.

A familiar voice called my name quietly and I spun around. "Amon? What . . . what have you done?" He'd changed out of my father's baggy workout clothes, and as I glanced around I realized how he'd gotten a different outfit. Three young men stumbled from the bathroom wear-

ing articles of clothing that had once been my father's. Each had a confused look on his face and one of them plucked at the old T-shirt as he
walked away.

The fact that Amon had switched clothes with them was the least
startling part of his transformation. The young man with the devastat-
ingly gorgeous smile had somehow added hair to his head. "Is that a wig?"
Reaching up, I tugged on the hair and found it solidly stuck to his head.

"It is my own hair. Is the style correct?"

If I thought Amon was handsome before, he was handsome to the
nth degree now. His hair was dark brown, short in the back and on the
sides, and a little longer on top. It was thick, layered, voluminous, and a
little messy. The sort of hair a girl could bury her fingers in as she kissed
him. *Stop it, Lily!*

"It's . . . not bad," I finally said. "How did you do it?"

"I just accelerated the natural growth."

"I thought you were bald because you couldn't grow hair."

"No. Egyptian princes shave their heads."

"I see. So . . . why did you change clothes and grow your hair?"

Amon shrugged. "It has not escaped my attention that I do not look
like other men my age. It will be easier for me to move about if I'm less . . .
noticeable. There is not much I can do to alter my behavior except to follow your example, but I can attempt to at least look like I am from your
world. I have not seen any men my age with shaven heads."

"Right, but—"

"Do I look better?"

"You look great," I said, and he did. He now wore a pair of dark,
straight-leg jeans, a fitted blue blazer, a white henley shirt, and gray
Converse sneakers.

"I have a new belt, too. See?"

He lifted his shirt to show me, but I was too distracted by the tight
muscles of his abdomen to notice the belt. "That's . . . that's nice," I murmured, and turned away to hide the red warming my cheeks.

Dropping his shirt, he asked, "Does it not meet your expectations?"

I waved a hand. "Believe me . . . you are above and *beyond* my expectations." I cleared my throat uncomfortably, realizing what I'd just said. He didn't seem to notice anything abnormal. "Well. Now that you are attired comfortably, shall we figure out which plane will take us to Egypt?"

Leaving behind a trail of dreamy-eyed airline employees entranced by Amon's power, his *GQ* looks, or a combination of the two, and, clutching two tickets to Cairo that we had neither paid for nor showed passports to attain, we made our way through the airport. It wasn't long before I noticed the effect Amon had, not just on employees but on almost every person of the female gender he met.

Amon had an aura of power, and, at least to me, he radiated all things warm and sunny. I suspected this was either a natural part of him or a reflection of the gifts of the sun god. We were all like sunflowers turning our heads toward a very handsome sun. The idea irritated me and I realized it was because I selfishly wanted to keep all of Amon's warmth for myself.

Once we were on board, the flight attendants began showering us with a little too much attention. Amon basked in it.

The first hour passed and the flight attendants had become a constant annoyance. By the time the fourth attendant came by just to check on Amon a second time, I was fed up and interrupted her before she said anything. "We're fine, thanks." I hissed at Amon, "I liked you better bald."

Amon thought my reaction was hilarious. In response, I grabbed the pillow off his armrest and jammed it behind my head, folding my arms across my chest and closing my eyes so I didn't have to watch the never-ending parade of Amon devotees.

Still chuckling, Amon grabbed the blanket given to him by one of the attendants—whose perfume he'd declared rivaled an Egyptian queen's—tucked it around me, and leaned over to whisper, "A desert lily need not turn jealous eyes toward the common violet."

I didn't respond and was soon lulled to sleep by the drone of the engines.

Sight for Sore Eyes

The clattering of silverware and the soft murmur of voices woke me. Opening my eyes, I saw a large man across the aisle digging into his dinner and was jolted back to reality. Bringing my palms to my eyes, I rubbed and wondered if I had just dreamed these past two days.

"Excuse me," the flight attendant said as she practically shoved her ample bosom in my face so she could have better access to my traveling companion. Obviously, it wasn't a dream. I was alert enough to hear Amon exclaim over the dinner she was going to be bringing him. Rolling my eyes, I tapped her on the shoulder.

"I'd like to use the restroom, please."

"Oh, of course."

Once in there, I locked the door and wet a towel to press against my cheeks. I didn't look like myself. My normally confident, shoulders-back stance and healthy frame looked hunched and sickly. There was a definite gray tinge to my skin, made worse by a sheen of sweat. My chestnut-brown hair hung in limp, fettucine-like strands, the shine long gone. My carefully applied makeup was smeared, and the circles under my eyes looked like wrung-out tea bags.

Taking out the small makeup case I'd fortunately brought with me, I fixed my face the best I could and pulled my hair up into a loose ponytail. *What have you gotten yourself into?* I allowed myself a brief moment of hysteria for agreeing to go to—I could barely even think it—*Egypt*, with a who-knows-how-many-thousands-of-years-old mummy prince who was too hot to handle in more ways than one.

When I had repeated the mantra "It is what it is" to myself a dozen times, I was ready to return to my seat.

I found a middle-aged woman sitting next to Amon, asking him all kinds of questions about his homeland. When he saw me, he said to her kindly, "My Lily has returned and it is time for us to dine. Perhaps we can speak of Egypt some more at a later time."

"Oh, yes, I'd like that," the woman said, grinning from ear to ear before she returned to her row.

Scowling, I dropped back into my seat and tucked my makeup bag on the floor under me. Amon leaned over to buckle my seat belt. "You must wear this at all times until the captain says it is safe to walk about the cabin."

I pushed his hands away. "Yeah, I got it. And I'm not *your* Lily, by the way."

Cheerfully ignoring my comment, he asked, "Do you know how to lower your table?"

"Yes. I was *born* in this century."

He seemed both fascinated and a bit confused by my sarcasm. I wasn't sure why I suddenly felt so prickly. Once again, my emotions were running amok. When my table was arranged, the flight attendant brought our meals. I saw the special smile she gave to Amon and I narrowed my eyes, and then froze, realizing why I'd been so irritable. I was feeling . . . possessive of Amon. After I cleared my throat loudly, the flight attendant set down the trays with heavy clunks and asked Amon if he needed anything else. When he said he would let her know, she left us alone. Not one, not two, but three dinners sat before each of us. "What is this?" I sputtered.

"A feast. Or at least, the best that Gloria could provide under the circumstances."

Apparently he'd ordered the vegetarian lasagna, the chicken dinner, a chef's salad, and a fruit and cheese platter for each of us.

"She said she will bring our desserts later," Amon said as he picked up a bunch of grapes and started pulling them off, one by one, with his teeth.

I shook my head. My dark mood lifted at seeing him eat grapes like an ancient god, which I suppose he was, and my lips curved into a smile despite my attempt to remain irked. "Like this," I whispered, and picked off a few grapes from the bunch and then placed them in my mouth. Amon lowered the bunch and watched me, focusing his attention on my lips. I'd just begun to feel awkward, embarrassed, and a little warm, when he pointed to the lasagna.

He copied my every move, from using the knife and fork, to opening the little packages of salt and pepper, to using the napkin, to drizzling the dressing over the salad. He soon noticed that I'd placed my napkin over my tray and was immediately concerned.

Brushing his fingers across my cheek, his Egyptian-god version of a diagnostic tool, he asked, "Are you ill?"

"No. Just a little tired," I answered as he studied me with his hazel eyes.

"Then why haven't you finished eating?"

I shrugged. "I don't usually eat this much. I told you before, remember?"

"I remember."

Amon turned back to his food but soon pushed the remainder of his meal away as well. When I asked him why, he answered, "Feasting is not meant to be done alone. It is a time for celebration, renewal. If you will not indulge with me, then I will also abstain."

"What exactly are you celebrating?"

"Life," he said simply.

"I don't understand."

The attendant took away our unfinished meals and refilled our drinks. After trying every noncarbonated beverage available, Amon declared orange juice to be his drink of choice, which made sense for a sun god. He watched my drink warily as I sipped from my recently refilled diet ginger ale. I repeated, "Why are you celebrating life?"

"When I . . . wake, I find I have a great hunger for life. During the weeks before the ceremony, I feast. I dance. I surround myself"—as he continued, he touched his fingertips to a loose lock of my hair and trailed his fingers down the length of it until the wisps fell against my cheek— "with beauty. I relish every moment of being alive. Then I have something to reflect upon, to warm me during the long years of darkness."

"Where do you go after the ceremony?"

His expression changed from peaceful to grim, and he turned away as he replied, "I do not wish to speak of it."

"All right." It was so strange to look at Amon and not see the warmth I'd come to know so well. "Well, how about a movie?"

"What is that again?"

"Would you like to see the modern interpretation of mummies?"

"Yes."

We stayed awake late into the night watching film after film, pausing only for restroom breaks. I started with old school: Boris Karloff's *The Mummy*. Amon's only response when it was over was "Another." I found myself watching his expressions more than the movies as we saw the 1999 version of *The Mummy* and the 2001 sequel, *The Mummy Returns*.

Amon frowned at scenes that were supposed to be humorous and scoffed openly at others. He fixated on costumes and backgrounds and once whispered, "I do not know this place."

I tried to explain how the scenes were often false, created by artists who work on the computer, but he shushed me and kept watching. I nodded off during the third film and woke up near the end. "Did you like it?" I asked.

Not answering my question, he began asking his own. "Why do your people view Egypt in this way? I am made out to be a monster when my role is to save mankind from darkness. I am not evil, Lily."

I took his hand and said, "I know that."

"This is why you were frightened of me in the House of Muses? You thought I would consume your flesh and split your spirit self from your physical body, or cause a plague to rain down upon you?"

"Not . . . exactly. But I was afraid, yes."

Amon sat back in his seat and mumbled, "The ancients were not fearful of our rising. They anticipated our awakening. Garlands were draped round our necks. We were treated as gods, princes. They offered us their love and devotion. Now we are shunned, feared, made into creatures of death and stench.

"We are at best forgotten, at worst vindictive demons. We are unknown. Unworthy. Unloved. Perhaps we are meant to waste away to nothing, to truly become the relics we are, and give ourselves over to dust and decay."

The emotions Amon was feeling—despair, loneliness—came at me in waves and I couldn't help but respond.

"Amon." I cupped his hand in mine and said quietly, "I know you haven't risen in ideal circumstances, and you're right that your . . . kind hasn't been thought of by the masses as heroes, but that doesn't diminish what you are, who you are, or what your purpose might be. Even though the people you've met don't know you, they sense something special and they gravitate toward you. Look at these flight attendants! They might not recognize you as a prince, but they still fall all over themselves worshipping you. It's like they can't resist. Your warmth draws them to you."

My words made an impact. I sensed it in him as he considered what I said. Little by little, his dark thoughts dissipated, and it wasn't long before he gifted me with a chagrined smile.

"Lily, are you perhaps a goddess residing in a modern form? You have the wisdom of one."

I scoffed, "I'm no goddess, believe me. I'm just a good observer of people."

"You observe, but you do not interact?"

"As a rule, no. I try not to interfere or get involved with other people's lives."

"Why not?"

"I suppose it would ruin the mystery."

"For me there is nothing of the mysterious. When I focus on a person I can perceive their thoughts."

"So you can read everyone's mind, not just mine?" I asked.

"I have been gifted with the Eye of Horus."

"Who exactly is Horus, and what does his eye have to do with anything?" I asked, glancing around nervously and lowering my voice.

"Do not worry, Lily. Most of the people around us are asleep, and if I wish it, they cannot hear us. I can . . . disrupt their hearing."

"Like with your photo?"

"Yes. It is the same. They will know we are talking, but they will not understand us." He concentrated for a moment and then said, "It is done."

The dark plane coupled with the fact that no one could hear us made me feel like I was trapped in an intimate little bubble with Amon, and I found I liked the feeling. "Okay, so tell me about Horus."

Amon's smile flashed in the dark. "Are you not tired, Lily?"

"Exhausted, but I really want to hear this."

"Very well." Amon paused for a moment, and then began. "Horus is the son of Amun-Ra. He was called the Golden Sun; whereas his father was the Risen Sun, Horus was the light that broke forth over the hills at the beginning of a new day, filling the world from one end to another."

"The horizon," I murmured. "He's the horizon."

Amon tilted his head, considering my words. "Yes. I believe that is an accurate definition."

"Tell me more," I said, and got out my notebook to draw, turning on the little overhead light so I could see. "Can you describe him?"

"In carvings, he is often represented with the head of a falcon, but as your . . . movies have shown, this concept is misunderstood. He does not have an actual falcon head, just as Anubis does not have a dog's head. These animals are their companions."

Amon peered at my sketch and continued. "The gods and goddesses were often depicted with the heads of their token animals so they could be discerned from one another and from other important leaders."

"That makes sense. What color is Horus's hair?"

"I have not seen Horus personally."

"Oh. Well, just tell me what you know about him and his eyes or whatever," I said, pencil poised to take notes.

"Horus is the son of Isis and Osiris—"

"Hold up. I thought he was the son of Amun-Ra."

"He is."

"How can he be the son of both?"

"I will explain. Perhaps it is better to start with Osiris. He married his sister, Isis."

"His sister?"

"Yes."

"Is incest common among the Egyptian gods?"

"It is, and also later, among the pharaohs."

"Yuck, but okay . . . go on."

"Osiris was a good and wise ruler of Egypt, and when it was time for him to take a wife, he found no woman he loved more than his sister, Isis. The goddess Isis was as soft and as lovely as a moonbeam, and she had a gift for magic unlike any other. Their union was happy and was celebrated by all except one—their erstwhile brother Seth."

"Wait. Isn't he the bad guy? The Dark One, or whoever, that you have to overcome?"

"He is the very same."

"Interesting." I started making a new list as Amon went on.

"The dark god Seth did not always have a heart so black, but he was jealous of his brother Osiris. Seth wanted to rule, but even more, he wanted Isis. Seth was bewitched by her beauty, and though he took many different women to be his wife, he did not think any of them as desirable as the one he couldn't have. The need to possess his sister consumed him. In anger he turned away from all that was good and allowed the seeds of corruption, bitterness, and lust to fester in his heart.

"Isis told her husband that Seth's advances had become more and more intolerable and that their brother had finally gone too far—he actually attempted to lay his hands upon her. Fortunately she was able to use her magic to deflect his unwanted attention. Osiris questioned Seth, but the ruler's brother had become a smooth liar. He accused Isis of misunderstanding his intentions and assured Osiris that he was happily married to not only one wife but several. He asked, 'What need have I to take my brother's wife as well?'"

"Devious," I murmured as I made a note.

"Osiris, a good-natured man, believed the best of everyone, including his brother, and he soothed his wife, telling her she must have misunderstood. But Isis was clever. She guessed that Seth was up to something, and soon she was proved right."

"What did Seth do?" I asked, fascinated by the story.

"He ordered a beautiful wooden chest made. It was exquisitely crafted, overlaid with pure gold, and built to the exact dimensions of Osiris."

"A chest for a body? Like a coffin?" I waved my hand. "I mean, a sarcophagus?"

"Exactly. Seth threw a great feast in honor of Osiris and then offered this beautiful chest to whoever could fit in it. Several people tried, probably thinking of winning all that gold, but there was no one who fit exactly."

"No one except his brother."

"Correct. Soon everyone had tried to fit into the chest, but no one had yet won the item. Seth taunted his brother, saying that perhaps it was only 'fit for a king,' and invited Osiris to try his luck. Isis begged her husband not to attempt it, for she sensed a deception, but Osiris saw no harm in it and was delighted that his brother would bring him such a prize.

"Osiris climbed into the box, and immediately Seth and his servants sealed the lid with molten lead. As the men carried the box containing Osiris out of the palace, Seth cornered Isis. He had an amulet that protected him from her magic, and he was determined to take possession not only of the throne but of his sister as well. The only thing Isis could do was to use the power of the moon to escape. She leapt upon a moon-beam and vanished.

"Later, she discovered that the chest had been thrown into the Nile. By the time she was able to raise the box, it had been broken into by crocodiles and her husband's body had been torn to pieces."

"That's horrible!"

"Yes."

"I don't understand. If Osiris was dead, how was Horus born? Was he a child when it happened?"

"Ah, well, you see, Isis was a very determined woman. She did not accept the demise of her husband. She called upon all the power at her disposal and was able to gather the pieces of his body, slaying many crocodiles in the undertaking."

I wrinkled my nose. "Ew. For what purpose?"

"Resurrection." At my raised eyebrow, Amon shifted toward me and explained, "After all the pieces were gathered, Isis summoned Anubis and told him she needed his help to get her husband back."

"Did it work?"

"After a fashion. Anubis carefully wrapped the pieces together, plac-ing foot to leg and leg to torso until he formed the shape of a man. If a leg or an arm was too mangled, or if a finger or a toe was missing, Isis filled the body in with the limbs of the crocodiles she'd cut her hus-band's remains from.

"With Isis chanting spells the entire time, Anubis embalmed the remains of Osiris and was able to unite the five components of her hus-band. He had re-formed the body, had loaned his own *ba*—his power—connected the *shuwt*—the shadow—and called the ka to return, naming the bound form with its *ren,* or name: Osiris.

"Together Anubis and Isis generated a powerful wind that swirled around the form, raising it into the air. The figure moved and was brought gently down to stand upon its feet. Osiris was Egypt's very first mummy. Weeping, Isis removed the wrappings from her husband and found him once again whole and perfect except for his skin, which had become as green as a crocodile's. She rejoiced, but Anubis sadly informed her that the magic that brought her husband back to life came with a price.

"Anubis explained that Osiris must be forever bound to the afterlife. Isis and Osiris were allowed to remain together one night, and then he had to depart from her side and take his place with Anubis. There he watches over the scales of judgment and commands the Land of the Dead."

"So during that one night she got pregnant?"

"Correct. Seth, thwarted in the pursuit of his sister, took possession of the throne. He was confident that there was no one to rival him since Osiris had never fathered an heir."

"But then Horus was born."

Amon nodded. "Horus was the delight of his mother, and he inherited a portion of her power. His mother channeled the moon in her magic, and Horus was granted a great gift from the moon. He was born with filmy eyes that could see in the darkness. It was said that his eyes could create light. Horus could see great distances and he could discern the tiniest detail. Prey could not hide from him and he could find the truth amidst lies.

"Isis nurtured her son and his gifts. He was raised in secret, and his mother took on a new identity to prevent Seth from finding them. When Horus was of age, Isis took her son and approached Amun-Ra himself, asking for his help in returning her son to his rightful place as a ruler. Amun-Ra was disinclined to help. Horus had no experience and Seth had become very powerful.

"Frustrated, Isis turned to magic. She called an asp from the desert and hand-fed him a rat that she had poisoned with magic. The vermin did not kill the snake, but the poison made the asp's venom powerful enough to harm a god, even one as potent as Amun-Ra.

"Knowing where the god liked to walk every evening, Isis placed the snake in his path. He ignored it as he did most creatures since he could not be harmed, and when the snake bit, he chuckled and continued on his walk.

"At sundown, Amun-Ra rode the ceremonial barque through the underworld, and just as he emerged to begin a new day, he collapsed, a victim of Isis's poison. Runners were sent out to find a cure, and Isis quickly made her way to Amun-Ra's side. She whispered in his ear that if he told her his true name, she would give him the antidote. Desperate, he agreed."

"What was his true name and why did she want it?" I asked.

"I do not know. As part of their arrangement Isis was never allowed to reveal it. Isis healed Amun-Ra and then used his true name to force him to help her son. When you know the true name of a being, be they god, human, or animal, you gain power over them."

"But I have only one name."

"That is because you have not yet discovered your true name."

"I'm not sure I have one."

"Every living thing does. Your true name represents your ideal self. The person you are at the center. The name that is engraved upon your heart."

"Do you have a true name?"

"I do."

"And it isn't Amon?"

He shook his head. "I was given the name Amon when I was called to my purpose."

"Then why wouldn't Amon be your true name?"

Amon took my hand and pressed my palm against his chest. "In my heart, I know it is not."

With his hand wrapped around mine, I could feel the familiar warmth from his fingers, but I could also feel a more intense heat coming from his chest.

I moved my hand away, though he seemed reluctant to let go of it. Clearing my throat, I picked up my notebook and skimmed through my scribblings. "The eye power you were talking about seems different from what you do."

"It is both the same and different. Shall I continue the story?"

Nodding, I nibbled on the pencil eraser and crossed my legs, shifting the notebook to my lap.

"Isis invoked the true name of Amun-Ra in a spell that would release him only when three demands were met. Her first request was to instate Horus to his father's position. Second, she asked to accompany Amun-Ra on his nightly journey to the underworld as often as she wished so that she might visit Osiris."

"And third?"

"She asked for something no other had ever dared. Isis told Amun-Ra that she wanted her son not only to be the rightful heir of Osiris but also to be named the heir of Amun-Ra himself."

"That's how he became the son of Amun-Ra?"

"Yes. Amun-Ra had to grant the three wishes of Isis, and, as a result, adopted Horus as his own son."

"I'll bet Seth didn't like that."

"Not at all. Seth immediately challenged Horus and they began a series of tiresome battles."

"Didn't Amun-Ra try to stop it?"

"No. He thought battling Seth would be a good opportunity for Horus to prove that he was worthy of the great god's attention. Three tests were arranged—a test of strength, a test of skill, and a test of power. To show strength, they fought for three months as hippopotamuses, but they were evenly matched. Next, they were both to build ships of stone and race them down the Nile, but Horus cheated and painted a wooden ship to look like stone. While Seth's boat sank, Horus won the race, but his trick was discovered and once again there was no winner.

"Finally, a hunt was organized. Whichever man could find Nebu, the golden stallion that roamed the desert, tame him, and bring him to Amun-Ra would be declared the winner.

"Seth had heard the rumor that Horus had very powerful eyes and he worried that Horus would likely be the first to find Nebu, so in an act of desperation, he stole upon Horus while he slept and ripped his eyes from their sockets. He hurled the orbs across the dunes and left a blind Horus to die while he went in search of the famous horse.

"Without his eyes, Horus was stripped of immortality. For months, he wandered the desert alone but for a falcon he befriended. The bird brought him meat, which he ate raw, and it became his faithful companion. Horus realized that his ambition and power had made him arrogant. Every day he turned his face to the desert sun and promised his new father, Amun-Ra, that he would change his ways and become the kind of leader the people needed.

"Weeks passed and Amun-Ra decided that Horus had been punished enough. Disguised as an old woman, he approached Horus and cried out for help. Horus sent his falcon to find the woman and followed the call of the bird until he came upon her. He offered what assistance he could and, to his surprise, the woman changed form. Feeling the warmth of the sun god, Horus knelt at Amun-Ra's feet and begged for forgiveness. He asked not to be instated but to be taken to his mother so he could be comforted by her love before he died. Amun-Ra took pity on Horus and exclaimed that not only would he see his mother with his own eyes, but his power would be restored as well.

"This time one eye, his left eye, retained the power of the moon, but in his right eye, Amun-Ra bestowed the power of the sun and made Horus his heir in truth. The Wadjet, or Eye of Horus, can be seen in art and carvings all over Egypt. It is said that an amulet made with the Eye of Horus can ward off evil, shielding its bearer from harm. The symbol is a sign of the protection of the god Amun-Ra and is a reminder that when we are stripped of all we hold dear, we can finally see the truth."

"So, in a way, you are under the protection of Amun-Ra and you can see the truth when you look at people?" I asked.

"There are other powers associated with it as well. I can draw energy from the sun, see in the darkness, and seek out things that are hidden."

"Is that how you found me in New York?"

"Yes, that and my connection to you. I probably could have found you without our connection, but it would have taken a long time. Your city is the largest I have ever laid eyes upon."

I grunted. "It's one of the biggest in the world, but I think there are a few in China that are bigger."

"It is hard to conceive of."

"It's hard for a lot of people, even for many who have been born in this time. So did Seth ever find the golden horse?"

"He did, but he could not capture it. After Amun-Ra healed Horus, he banished Seth, who was enveloped by a desert storm, never to appear again until my own time. Nebu the golden stallion became a legend. Many men died seeking him in the desert. Amun-Ra's challenge has never fulfilled, and there were many who thought they could become the heir of the sun god if they captured and tamed the famous horse."

"Will you tell me about that, too?"

"Perhaps later, Young Lily."

"I didn't know sun gods needed rest."

Amon closed his eyes and murmured, "Your questions have finally tired me."

"Well, you are *very* old," I teased.

Opening his eyes to slits, Amon turned his head toward me. "Not old enough that I cannot rein in lovely tormenters who bedevil me with questions and delight in afflicting me with all manner of inducements."

I was going to ask him what he meant by inducements, but then he sighed and nestled his head against my shoulder. My nose was pressed into his hair. It was as soft as a newborn's and I couldn't help but inhale the scent of him—warm amber and myrrh. Adjusting himself by shifting even closer, he covered both of us with a blanket and quickly fell asleep.

My body was lulled by the contact as little pulses of warmth sank into my skin. Questions still swirled in my mind, but I turned off the light and let the darkness of the plane envelop me. I tried to quiet my thoughts, but instead I imagined what it must have felt like to wander the desert, blinded. A falcon cried and I jerked awake just as the captain announced our descent into Cairo.

Walk Like an Egyptian

With his sunshine smile, Amon bade each crew member best wishes before disembarking. By the time he was finished, he was confident enough to not only find his way around the airport, which would have been challenging even for me, but to gain us access to a VIP lounge where we could refresh ourselves.

After I'd rinsed out my mouth, brushed my hair, and washed my face, I met Amon in the waiting area, where he handed me a bottle of water. I was exhausted, and not just because I hadn't slept very long. It was something deeper, and I sensed that my connection to Amon was a primary cause. Amon noticed my exhaustion, too.

"You are weary, Young Lily."

Sipping my water, I nodded.

"Come," he said, leading me to some very comfortable-looking chairs next to large windows. I sat in one while he stood directly in front of me. The sunlight helped a bit, but my eyes still felt swollen and, despite my having downed my water, my mouth felt gritty and dry.

Amon pressed his fingers against my cheek and his eyes remained closed for several moments. "Well, doctor? What's the diagnosis? Am I going to live?" I asked, half joking and half fearing his answer.

Frowning, Amon picked up my hand and squeezed it lightly. "You need to rest," he announced.

"I already knew that."

Though concern was written all over his face, he tried to hide it. "Then let us be on our way," he said gently.

Amon helped me stand and then wrapped his arms around me. Immediately, I panicked. "Whoa, there! Wait a just a minute, Mister *I Dream of Jeannie*. Why don't you save the sand travel for when we really need it?"

Pausing, Amon took stock of our surroundings. "Perhaps you are right. Let us find a golden chariot."

Tagging along behind him, I said, "They might not be golden in Egypt, you know."

"Ah, yes. Cairo is likely much more advanced than your city of Manhattan. We will find some fast horses."

"Um, you might want to prepare yourself for a little culture shock," I cautioned as we headed toward the doors. "I don't think you'll find Egypt like it was a thousand years ago."

"They are still my people. I am sure the city will be much like I remember."

"Okay, don't say I didn't warn you."

Amon's face darkened when we stepped out into the bright sunshine. The city stretched before us, and it was undeniably not what Amon had been hoping for. He glared at me when I quipped, "See? Not even a camel."

Approaching an airport security guard, Amon adjusted my bag on his shoulder and began speaking with the guy. When he returned, I saw the guard on his walkie-talkie. "What's up?" I asked.

"He will arrange a VIP chariot for us." Pointing to one of the small black-and-white taxis that sped by, Amon added, "I will not bend my body to fit into a chariot so small. My sarcophagus was more spacious."

I laughed, shifting closer to him so a large group of people could pass us, and Amon wrapped his hands protectively around my shoulders. There were many tourist groups from several different cultures and countries. Amon cocked his head and listened as they passed. "There are so many languages," he said finally.

"Egypt is a pretty popular tourist destination."

"What does this mean, 'tourist destination'?"

"Well, many visitors come to Egypt to see the pyramids or other relics of the past."

"What kinds of relics?" The car arrived, and the driver rushed out to take the bag from Amon.

"Artifacts like pottery, art, jewelry, old writings on papyrus, mummies, that sort of thing."

Amon had my door halfway open but halted. "They visit Egypt to view the dead? See the bodies of those who have left this life?"

Suddenly, I became aware of how disrespectful that seemed. "Um, yes. Though I think some of the more fragile mummies are kept locked away from the public. I suppose you could think of it as the people of this time paying their respects to the kings and pharaohs of old. No one is allowed to touch them, and they're usually preserved under glass."

Amon didn't say anything for a moment, and I could tell he was rolling the idea around in his head.

When we were settled in the car, Amon said to the driver, "We are VIP travelers seeking respite from our journey. We require refreshment, new clothing, and supplies."

The driver raised his eyebrows at Amon, chanced a look at me, and asked in English, "Where do you like to go?"

"Take us to a nice hotel."

"Cheap nice, or pay-the-money nice?"

Amon leaned forward. "The fee is immaterial."

"Pay-a-lot-of-money nice," I clarified.

"Very good."

The driver sped off, taking what I suspected was the long route, but I didn't complain. It was nice to watch Amon as he took in the changes to the city.

"How far are the pyramids of Giza?" I asked the driver.

"Not far. Maybe thirty-five, forty kilometers. You want to go today?"

"No. Today, we rest."

"Very good."

"The weather is cooler than I expected. Is this normal?"

"April is spring in Cairo," the driver explained. "Very nice."

I played with my phone and discovered that the pyramids were about twenty miles from the airport. Converting to cubits, I whispered, "Sixty-seven thousand five hundred cubits."

Amon just grunted in response, totally transfixed by the scenes outside the window. Modern Cairo was a bustling city. Like New York, it had a mix of both old and new buildings, except that *old* had an entirely different meaning in Egypt.

We passed mosques and bazaars, cemeteries and museums, luxury towers and apartment buildings, and theaters and shops, but unlike New York, Cairo had an ancient feel, and it wasn't hard to imagine that if the people slowed down enough, the desert dust that constantly lapped at the edges of the city would rise up like a hungry wild beast and consume civilization, dragging it back into the sand and burying it so completely that Cairo would quickly be lost, like the cities of old.

The driver finally pulled up in front of a large hotel with a beautiful circular pool and fountain. Palm trees lined the drive, and two large columns, carved to look like ancient obelisks, stretched to the sky on either side of the pool.

We got out, and as Amon spun in a slow circle, I fumbled for my credit card. Amon then turned his attention back to us. Fixing his gaze on the driver, he murmured a few words, and without further comment, the man turned his head, put the car in gear, and drove off. *I wonder how long we're going to be able to keep doing this.*

The hotel was opulent, and other than the decor, I could have easily mistaken it for an upscale building in Manhattan. The lobby boasted a five-star restaurant, and the outer sections were lined with expensive shops selling women's clothing, designer handbags and luggage, and souvenirs; a bar; and an after-hours lounge. There was even a perfumery.

Amon hypnotized the guy at the front desk, and we were soon swept with our meager belongings up to the top floor. They gave Amon keys to the minibar and to a VIP lounge where we could dine in private if we wished. After teaching him how to order from the room service menu, I disappeared into the shower.

Donning a robe and thinking I'd head to bed wearing it instead of my rumpled clothes, I ducked my head into the next room to find Amon surrounded by dishes of food. He sat in the sunshine coming in from the window, not eating. Our view was incredible. Far below was the beautiful Nile, sunlight twinkling across its surface. Though his hair and skin were gleaming, I'd never seen him so melancholy.

"I see you've ordered a feast. Aren't you hungry?" I asked.

"I have no passion for food."

"That's very unlike you."

"Yes. Do you see, Lily?" Amon pointed to the Nile. "I have ridden on this very river countless times and yet I do not know this place."

"I'm sure the water has eroded the banks over time—"

"I do not mean the dimensions of the river; I mean the land, the people around it. They have been lost, stolen. They have disappeared like the dew before the sun."

"Amon"—I took his hand and gripped it in mine—"they . . . we . . . are still your people. We have new technology, we travel by different means, we have all kinds of jobs you've probably never even considered possible, but we are the same. We still have the same needs—we drink, eat, seek friendship and love. We worry over those we care for. We fight in battles. We are hurt. We become ill, and we die."

"Yes. But perhaps you no longer need a . . . relic . . . such as me. Maybe it is time for me to sleep under the glass like the others, never to rise again."

I wondered how it would feel to waken only once every thousand years, to see the world change and move on without me, to have no ties to anyone, no family. *He must be terribly lonely*. Though we were as different as two people could possibly be, I knew what being alone did to a person.

Turning my head, I stared at the blue river gleaming below. "The Nile has nurtured and fed countless generations, and it's still here serving and providing for the people of Egypt. Many may walk along its shore and take it for granted. They may not even think about the kings who rode its waves or the people who depended upon it for drinking water or for crops, but that doesn't lessen its impact. It doesn't lessen its importance. Your people may not know you. They may walk past you in the street and never feel your power, but that doesn't mean that they don't *need* you."

I didn't know what else to say. I knew how different this raising must have been for him when compared with the other times. Then he was celebrated and now he was forgotten.

Looking up, Amon said, "You are right, Lily."

"What? How?" I had just been thinking that I was very wrong.

"It does not matter if we acknowledge the sun; it continues to shine regardless of the heed we give it. If my efforts go without recognition, then so be it. I pledged my service to the people of Egypt, and I will continue to provide it until such time as Egypt no longer has need."

"When might that be?"

"When there is no longer a threat of darkness."

"That might never happen."

"Then I shall continue to serve."

Amon's hazel eyes looked haunted.

"How are you handling all of this? I mean, all the changes you see in the world must be staggering."

"You are how I . . . handle it, Lily."

"What do you mean?"

"It is difficult to explain."

"Can you try?"

"My mind can understand the world through your eyes. Take your phone, for example. If I concentrate, I can picture you using it. I see in my mind how you rely upon the device, and though I cannot understand it fully, I do not fear it."

"What about the planes and cars and skyscrapers?" He cocked his head and focused on me. "Wait, you're doing it right now, aren't you? Are you looking for the definition of skyscraper?"

"Yes."

"It means these large buildings."

"Ah. Though I can catch pictures and emotions from any person I choose, there is a special connection to you. It is more than the Eye. Our bond not only provides me with energy but also steadies me. Without you I would be a barque tossed upon a stormy sea without sail or anchor. I would be truly lost."

"So have you bonded like this with other people? When you rose before, I mean?"

"No. You are the first."

"Why didn't you bond with others? Didn't you need their help?"

"A bonding is a fusing of all five aspects of myself with another. Boundaries between the two people involved can easily become blurred. It is an . . . intimate thing."

"Is that why I have a hard time controlling what I say? I mean, it's like everything I think just spills out of me whether I want it to or not."

Amon nodded. "Your inner thoughts and feelings have been drawn to the surface. In the past, I have known where I was and the work I had to do. My jars of death were always near, so I did not need to rely upon another. My brothers woke the same day as I did, and together we accomplished our purpose without imposing our will upon a mortal. The bond was never enacted because it was never needed. I will always be sorry for the burden this connection places upon you."

I was quiet for a moment and then said, "I'm sensing there is more you're not telling me."

Amon looked away. "There is nothing that you need be concerned about. I will continue to tread very carefully so that you come to no harm. Speaking of that, you should rest now, Young Lily."

"You're tired, too," I said quietly. "Won't you sleep?"

Standing, Amon drew me to my feet and took a strand of my wet hair in his fingers. As he pulled it back from my face, he kissed my forehead—a gesture that surprised us both. "You need to sleep more than I, Nehabet," he said as he took a step back.

"What does that mean?"

"In my language, a *nehabet* is a precious water lily found in an oasis, and this water lily"—he tapped my shoulder—"needs to rest." When I started to protest, he shushed me with the tip of a finger on my upper lip. There is only one bed. My wish is for you to take it."

With a nudge, he sent me off to the bedroom. As I closed the door, I saw him turn back toward the window and run a shaky hand through his hair.

It was early afternoon when I fell asleep, and by the time I woke it was already evening. The bedroom window was open and night air wafted in, cool and carrying the scents of river, desert flowers, and exotic spices. Cracking open the door, I found Amon asleep. His long form was bent unnaturally on the couch, the food on the table still untouched.

Wheeling the cart of cold food into the hall, I got on the phone and quietly ordered more and then knelt in front of Amon as I waited for the food to be delivered. His new hair covered his eyes, and after a moment of self-denial, I shut off the part of my mind that was normally in charge of things and gently brushed the hair out of his eyes with my fingertips. The warmth of this skin drew me, and I wanted to just sit near him to feel the radiance of it.

His full lips were softened in sleep, and I realized that what I was seeing was the man, not the sun god. There were two sides to him, both engraved upon the same solid coin. Each version was powerful, handsome, and commanding, but Amon the man, who was vulnerable, who doubted himself, who yearned to feel a connection with other people, was the one I was more attracted to.

It was all too easy to imagine him, sleepy, sultry, and warm, opening his arms to me, and me kissing him, slipping my hands into his hair as we passionately embraced. When the idea floated through my mind that I could easily come to fall for someone like him, I removed my hand and chided myself for getting lost in girlish fantasies. I didn't know what had come over me and I wasn't prone to rationalization, but I decided to give myself a break. This was the one time in my life I was going to allow myself to indulge in breaking the rules; if I wanted to fawn over a gorgeous man, no one was around to notice or care.

Still, my old way of thinking crept back in. Even if I ended up liking Amon enough to want to do something about it, what did that mean? We could never have a future together.

But he was attentive—not only to me but to others. Sunny—there was something special that happened when Amon turned up the wattage; it was almost like I couldn't help being happy. Committed—how could a girl resist a guy who would give up his own desires and sacrifice himself to save others?

These traits along with many others cast a brilliant light upon the shadowy dream guy I'd first met. He disappeared and what was left was Amon. I could fall recklessly, dangerously, in love with a guy like him, but I couldn't create a scenario in my mind where that kind of relationship ended up being anything other than heartbreaking. Of course, my parents wouldn't approve of him unless he had a graduate degree or political aspirations.

The irony was that if I'd lived in Amon's time, my parents couldn't have hoped for a better match. He was a prince of Egypt, after all. Even without the power of the sun god, Amon had been going places. I wrinkled my nose, thinking that maybe he would have wed a sister, like the gods of old. Then again, perhaps he didn't have one.

Regardless, I'd been granted a temporary reprieve from planning an entire future for myself, and I'd always be grateful to him for that. I hadn't realized how heavy the weight of my structured life was until it was gone. Being with Amon made me feel like anything was possible. I no longer felt like the person called Miss Young, or Lilliana. With him, I was just Lily, or Young Lily. I liked being Lily much better.

There was a light knock at the door, so I set aside my reflections and opened it, allowing the server to bring in a new cart. He handed me a slip of paper to sign and then he was on his way. Amon woke as I was setting the food on the table.

"Are you coming?" I asked with a smile. "I have to confess, I think I'm ready for a feast."

Cocking his head, he studied me with wide green eyes. "And what are you celebrating, Young Lily?"

Lifting a glass full of orange juice toward him, I said, "Possibilities. Let's celebrate the unknown."

Amon came forward and took a glass, filling it from the carafe. "To the unknown, then," he said, clinking his glass against mine.

With relish, I filled my plate and didn't even allow myself to think about the fat, carbs, or calories. If something was delicious, I made sure Amon tasted it. As he exclaimed over the chocolate cake I'd asked him to try, he nudged a plateful of an Egyptian dish he loved toward me and encouraged me to eat it with my fingers. Another dish we scooped up with sections of a thin, flavorful bread. When we'd tried everything, feeding each other bite after bite, Amon got on the phone and ordered everything else on the menu we hadn't sampled yet.

We tried pizza together for the first time, and he loved the Margherita style the most. I introduced him to lobster and linguini, ice cream and Italian meatballs, steak tartare and spring rolls, and he had me taste a variety of local dishes. Some were similar to things he'd once eaten, while others were new creations.

Tasting every dish with Amon was an exhilarating experience. It felt decadent, adventurous, and, in a way, intimate. But above all else, it was fun. I realized then that I'd never actually feasted before in my life.

Amon's passion for food and for giving himself over to the simple plea-sures of taste and textures was a big departure for me. I found myself wishing I'd done it sooner.

By the time we were finished, I groaned, having never in my life eaten so much. It was just after midnight, and I wasn't sure if I should try to go back to sleep or watch a movie. I'd started to gather our dishes and place them back on the cart, when Amon gently wrapped his hand around my wrist.

Sliding his hand up my arm to my face, he pressed his palm against my cheek and said, "Hakenew, Lily."

"That means 'thank you,' right?"

"It means a bit more than a simple thank-you. It is a term imply-ing a deep sense of gratitude for another person. It is an expression of thankfulness for the enduring warmth and comfort one feels when in the presence of someone special. I do not thank you, Lily. I am thankful *for* you."

"Oh."

He continued "I have feasted many times, but I have never enjoyed it as much as this. My heart is lightened by being with you."

Blushing, I murmured, "I enjoyed it, too." Amon's green eyes stud-ied my face and then dropped to my lips as he came a step closer. I thought he was going to kiss me, but instead, he pressed his forehead against mine. Our noses touched, but unfortunately his extremely kiss-able lips were nowhere near mine.

Drawing back, I sensed his regret as he took a few steps away from me. "Please rest a bit longer, Lily. I will return soon."

With that, he was out the door and gone.

What did I do? I wondered. Maybe he wasn't attracted to me in the same way I was to him. Maybe he just needed me and when he was done, he'd have no problem setting me aside.

Feeling insecure, an emotion I despised, and about a boy, a situa-tion I'd never allowed myself to be in before, I berated myself for acting like a lovesick teen with an unrequited crush, reminded myself that I was above such things, and then headed to the bathroom to see if I had something stuck in my teeth. My teeth were fine, which left me vacillating between wondering why Amon wasn't attracted to me and telling myself that I was too confident in my own skin to care.

Picking up my hairbrush, I noticed that my hair was different. On each side of my face, there were two streaks that were no longer the same color as the rest of my hair. I inspected the strands. It looked like I'd gotten chunky blond highlights. Starting at the roots, I trailed my fingers down the highlighted locks and then gasped when I realized that Amon had touched my hair in the exact place where the highlights were.

The fact that my new highlights were most likely due to Amon's sun-god touch actually made me like them. My hair was now unique, very different from the Lilliana who lived in a penthouse suite in New York City.

This was a Lily with an adventurous streak, literally. This was a Lily who snuck out of the house. This was a Lily who ate things that tasted good instead of things that were good for her. I squared my shoulders and came to a realization. This was a Lily who deferred college for a year or two and traveled. And this was the kind of Lily who just might look like she deserved a hot Egyptian sun god for a boyfriend. I wet my hair again, applied some product, and scrunched it while I blew it out. With a curling iron, I twisted sections of my hair into loose curls, creating a bohemian style that reflected my mood. I was working on my makeup when I heard the room door open.

"Amon?" I called out.

"I am here, Lily."

He entered the room with a man in a business suit who was obviously under his thrall. They both carried a bunch of shopping bags on each arm. After depositing them all on the bed, Amon thanked the gentleman, murmured a few words, and he left, happy as could be despite the fact that I was sure he hadn't received payment for any of the items Amon was pulling from the bags. As he left, I spied the glint of gold on his name tag, and I jerked my thumb over my shoulder at his departing form. "You put a spell on the vice president of the hotel and made him schlep bags up here?"

Amon shrugged. "The store with women's clothing was closed and he was the only one who could open it."

Folding my arms across my chest, I gave him a look, but Amon ignored me and began plowing through the bags.

"I did not know which clothes would fit the best, so there are several different styles and sizes," he explained.

"You know, even if the security cameras didn't see you, he could get into a lot of trouble with his boss. He could even go to jail."

Amon waved a dismissive hand. "Since you explained the camera on your phone to me, I have discovered how to disable them wherever we go. They are quite simple machines."

"Okay, I'm just saying it might be best to lie low sometimes."

Twisting to look at me, Amon asked with a puzzled expression, "You wish for me to lie down on the floor?"

"No. Never mind," I said with a sigh.

Rifling through one of the bags, I found a button-down shirt and a pair of jeans much too large. Yanking the jeans from the bag, I held them up and raised my eyebrows with a smirk. "Wow, you really are a bad guesser."

Amon looked up. "Those are not for you. They are mine."

"Ah." I handed him the jeans. After gathering a few more items, he started to leave, but then stopped and turned around.

"Your hair is different."

"Yes, I noticed. Thanks for the highlights, by the way." I pulled a blond curl away from my face and let it go. Dropping the bags with a heavy thud, Amon came closer and tentatively reached out his hand, but then he paused as if asking for permission. "It's okay," I said. "You can touch it. I like the streaks."

Amon twisted a curl around his finger and gently pulled it straight. The tip of his finger brightened as he drew the curl out and I could actually see sunlit ripples travel down to the ends of my hair.

"It seems like where you touch my hair, it changes color."

"Yes." He watched the transformation with curiosity. "But I did not make it curl."

"No. I did that myself."

Amon let the newly blond strand go and then backed away a step. "I am sorry," he said.

"Don't be. Like I said, I like the color." He said nothing and just stared at me, so I asked, "Do you hate it? Is that the problem?"

"No. I find it . . . beautiful."

"Then what is it? What's wrong?"

"Nothing." Amon shook his head, turned, and said, "Dress in something comfortable. We will be journeying through what you call a sandstorm."

"Will we be coming back to the hotel?"

"Yes. We can return."

"Okay. I'll pack light, then."

Amon left, closing the door quietly behind him.

I couldn't get a sense of what was going on with Amon, and that bothered me. He was upset about something, but I couldn't tell what that something was.

Since I wasn't sure exactly what we'd be doing, I dressed in a pair of skinny jeans, boots, and a black tee. Just in case we ended up going someplace nicer, I threw a flowing black skirt with a handkerchief hem into my bag, along with my notebook, a few water bottles, a pair of sandals, and my wallet. Amon would likely take care of any fees, but I wanted to keep my wallet on me just in case.

Emerging from the bedroom, I found Amon dressed in a similar fashion. He'd slicked back and finger-combed his brown hair, which made it look almost black, and he wore a pair of dark jeans with a thick black belt and a gray shirt, unbuttoned so the white tee beneath it peeped through. His muscular physique was visible despite the double layer of shirts. *My goodness,* I thought. *Not bad, Lily. Not bad.*

Swallowing and clearing my throat noisily, I asked, "So, sandblast, huh?"

"Yes."

Amon had a falcon-like stare that made me feel vulnerable and powerful at the same time. My heart began hammering as I neared him, his eyes seeming to take in my every move at once. I got the impression that he could sense not only the rate of my heartbeat but also the pulse of blood through my veins, my sharp intake of breath as he slid his hands up my arms, and the way my skin tingled where he touched me. "Are you ready?" he whispered against the delicate skin beneath my ear, and when I answered, "Yes," my mind wasn't even on the place where we were going. I took a step closer and wrapped my arms around his waist. As the sand began to fly, I closed my eyes and buried my face against his chest. I sensed his surprise at the gesture but couldn't tell if it was a happy surprise or if he'd rather I kept my distance.

My ears filled with the buzz of the storm as sand licked my bare arms and wind lifted my hair. I experienced a moment of panic as the prickles of sensation numbed me, but Amon somehow spoke to me in my mind, soothing me with soft words in a language I couldn't comprehend. His hand slid up my back and cupped my neck and I had all of a few seconds to enjoy it before I could feel nothing and we sank into darkness.

The sand coalesced and we appeared in an alley between two buildings.

"Where are we?" I asked as I turned in circles.

"Itjtawy," he answered softly.

"Itjtawy as in . . ."

"My home."

"Oh." Amon's "home" was apparently now an industrial district on the outskirts of the vast city of Cairo. He began walking and I followed, not entirely sure it was safe to be walking there at that time of night. Within a few moments, Amon was able to find the Nile, and we walked along its banks as he studied the area. He stopped once and played with the top of a reed growing near the water.

"Papyrus," he explained, without me having asked.

I would never have guessed that the clump of tall green stems with dust-mop-style heads could have been used to make paper.

A bit farther down, Amon paused, backed up carefully, and counted off steps. "It should be right about here," he finally announced.

"What? Your home? How do you know?"

"No. My home would have been up on that crest. Can you see it?"

"That hill there? Yes, I see it. So what was here?"

"The temple. The one we would have prayed to Anubis in. I know where we are because this was the site of my first death, an experience I shall never forget. Even if I had, the Eye of Horus would show me what I was seeking."

"Oh, I see." I was itching to ask more questions, but I could see he was focused on the task at hand. "So what do we do?"

"Be still for a moment so that I may concentrate."

Amon sank to his knees, closed his eyes, and lifted his hands skyward, palms up. I wasn't sure what to do, but getting on my knees felt like the right thing, so I did. He began chanting, and after a moment, I felt the ground rumble.

Turning to me, Amon reached out a hand. "Lily!"

He pulled me up, crushing me tightly to his chest. Amon kept us both upright as the ground rolled beneath us. The dirt directly in front of where we stood rose as if something or—and I sincerely hoped not—someone was emerging from it. A horn pierced the surface and I worried that it was attached to an underground monster, but then the rumbling stopped and whatever it was that was sticking out of the ground remained motionless.

Cautiously, Amon stepped forward and reached out, pulling the object from the earth. It looked like a large ice cream cone, the sugar kind, but it was made of clay. Its sides were smooth except for the dirt that covered it, and on the top were Egyptian glyphs.

"What is it?" I asked as I moved closer.

"A funerary cone."

"What's a funerary cone? Is it used to nail the sarcophagus closed? Seems like it would break."

Amon shook his head. "No. They line the entrance of a tomb. These carvings here are a prayer meant for the deceased. And here, we find his name."

"So who is the deceased?"

Reverently, Amon dusted the surface and ran his finger over a portion, reading it out loud in Egyptian. He paused and looked at me before translating. "Me. This cone comes from the tomb of my last resting place. It is a message that I will find what I am seeking there."

"So your last resting place was—"

"Thebes. Not in Thebes exactly, but likely in the tombs near the Theban hills."

"Wait a second. On the box with all the artifacts in the museum there was a marker that said the mummy"—I shifted uncomfortably— "I mean, *you*, were discovered in the Valley of the Kings." I pulled out my smartphone and looked up the site.

"It's near where Thebes once was," I explained. "The city is now called Luxor. I hate to tell you this, Amon, but the Valley of the Kings is the archaeological capital of the world. Oh, uh, 'archaeological' means the digging up of buried relics."

Amon frowned. "Like me."

I winced, but said, "Yes. The point is that there are probably guards everywhere, and they haven't even discovered all the tombs in there yet. They find new stuff all the time. It's going to be like looking for a needle in a sand dune, not to mention you're going to have to do mind control on a lot of people for us to even get in there."

Amon was methodically dusting off the cone artifact as I spoke.

When I finished, he lifted his eyes and said, "I have to try, Lily. If I cannot succeed, then all will be lost. Will you still accompany me on this journey?"

Stepping closer, I placed my hand on his arm and said, "Of course. Now hand me the ice cream cone thing and I'll put it in my bag for safekeeping."

Once the relic was stowed, I expected to leave immediately for the Valley of the Kings, but Amon wanted to wait until tomorrow so he could renew himself in the sun before attempting the journey. He wanted to walk around the area that used to be his home. He held out a hand to me, and together we explored the land that was once supposed to belong to him.

As he talked, explaining to me what his home had looked like, the drab gray buildings disappeared and were replaced with a golden palace, fields of grain, and herds of cattle. I could envision Amon walking proudly among his people, riding a boat down the Nile, or feasting in celebration.

Soon we came upon a building that had been made over into a club. Techno music blasted and beautiful young people lined up, waiting their turn to get in.

"What is this?" Amon asked.

"It looks like a club. A place where people dance and celebrate," I added.

"My people dance?"

"Well, yes. People dance all over the world."

"Then, come, Lily. We will celebrate with them."

"I don't think I'm really in the mood."

"What do you mean? What is a mood?"

"Mood is a feeling . . . like when . . . Ugh, it's too hard to explain."

Amon peered at me in the darkness, his eyes flashing. He tilted his head, then said, "You do not enjoy dancing."

"As a rule, no."

He continued to focus on me, quickly discerning more than I was willing to show outwardly.

"You believe it is a poor use of your time and you are . . . embarrassed."

He'd pretty much hit the nail on the head. It was strange to have someone pick up on every little thing I was thinking. "Quit analyzing me, Sigmund Freud. I have my reasons, and you don't need to know every little thing."

Ignoring my statement, Amon continued to address the issue. "Lily, first, there is no possibility that your lovely, soft limbs could move in any way that would cause you shame. Second, there is enough work in the world, Nehabet. What good does it do to excel if you don't revel in your achievements? There must be a balance. Even a king celebrates. If he did not, how could he rule effectively?

"You must allow yourself to feel . . . joy, Young Lily. You must take pleasure"—Amon pressed his lips to one of my hands and then the other—"in just being alive."

The irony was that I'd never in my entire life felt more alive than I did the moment Amon kissed my hands. He'd kissed my forehead before, but when he touched his lips to my hands, electricity shot through me. Even though I knew his passion was more about enjoying life than about me, it was still powerful, and there was a part of me that wanted to latch on to that. "All right," I acquiesced softly. "We'll dance."

The inside of the club was dark and warm, but the music was fantastic—techno funk with a wicked beat and a slightly exotic sound. Immediately, I felt out of place since most of the women wore tight little dresses, high heels, and heavy makeup. Amon was leading us to the bar when I shouted above the din, "I'm going to the restroom! I'll be right back!"

The atmosphere was pulse-poundingly hot, but when I finally found the bathroom, it was an almost frigid contrast. Air-conditioning blew onto the women standing in front of the mirror primping, and I wondered if the men's room had the same feature or if it was specially arranged to keep the ladies happy.

After removing my clunky boots and swapping them out for sandals, I quickly changed into the skirt I'd brought and then plucked at my T-shirt, wondering what I could do to make it look more like I was going to a club than to a farmers' market. I was standing in front of the mirror frowning, when a girl applying lipstick asked me a question in another language. I just shrugged, lifted the hem of the tee, and made a thumbs-down sign.

The girl pursed her lips and raised her eyebrows, gesturing at herself, and when I nodded hesitantly, she pulled a pair of tiny scissors from her purse. I was even more hesitant then, but she didn't make a move until I nodded again.

With deft hands she cut the neck out of the T-shirt, making a wider neckline so the shirt slipped off one shoulder. She then took the bulk of the T-shirt hem and tied it in a knot at my back, revealing an inch or so of midriff. Finally, she turned me around to gather the hem of my skirt.

I was going to protest her cutting it, but she set down the scissors and wrapped the material around my body, tucking it in at the side so that I ended up with a sarong skirt that stopped just at the knee on one side and about halfway up my thigh on the other. I'd never in my life worn anything that left me feeling so exposed.

As a parting gift, the girl handed me her lipstick and rolled some of her perfume on my wrists and neck. The scent was exotic—a light floral and musk. I freshened my lipstick and fluffed my hair, said a quick thanks, then left the bathroom to seek out Amon.

After checking my bag and taking a claim ticket, I scanned the bar. Amon wasn't there or seated in any of the sections around the dance floor. Deciding he must have gone outside for air, I headed in the direction of the door, then stopped when I heard a ruckus coming from the dance floor that was even louder than the music.

Nudging aside enough women so I could see what was going on, I was shocked, not at seeing Amon in the middle of the crowd or his skin gleaming as if he were under a spotlight but at seeing him dance. I'd expected his style to be exotic and very different from modern dancing, but I hadn't expected that he would be doing a male version of belly dancing.

Amon had ditched his outer shirt, so the only thing covering his taut torso was the thin white T-shirt, which clung to him so tightly it looked like the seams would burst at any moment.

He turned in a slow circle, abs undulating and pelvis rotating in a way that was sensual enough to be illegal. Amon's dancing was like a mashup of Elvis and the Chippendales. The human sun god was a stomach-dropping, chest-popping, feet-sliding, shoulder-swaying, hip-rotating, flutter-inducing, liquid locomotive, and I was surrounded by women who couldn't wait to buy a ticket.

As Amon turned, his eyes took in his admirers and he paused. A huge smile lit his face as he shouted out to the crowd surrounding him, "Thank you, ladies, but my Lily has come. I wish to dance with her now."

Amon held out his hand and I stepped forward, ignoring the gasps from the women around me. One by one, they turned aside, some good-naturedly, some with jealousy obvious on their faces.

As Amon took my hands and began moving his body again, I jerked awkwardly back and forth in small movements and then leaned close to his ear. "If you think I'm doing what you did, you're crazy!" I said.

He drew me closer and then turned in a circle, matching each step with the beat. Then he slid his hand down my arm, took hold of my hand, and turned me, too. I was surprised I didn't miss the beat. By the time a few songs were over, I felt much more confident and was actually having fun. Amon spun me around until I collapsed against his chest, dizzy and laughing.

Eventually, the music changed to something slow. Amon seemed confused at first, and he watched with a curious expression as the other dancers paired off. A woman who'd been watching him before returned and asked him to dance. He shook his head and answered, "I am not meant for you. I am dancing with Lily."

As she left, I took a step forward, closing the distance between us, and ran my hands slowly up his muscular arms, over his shoulders, and around his neck. After standing stiffly for a few seconds, he relaxed and pulled me tightly against him. Slowly, we began moving together. His hands, splayed on my back, moved inch by tantalizing inch downward until they reached the bare skin at my waist. Wedging me even tighter against his body, he put his forehead to mine. The side of his mouth tickled my cheek.

If I shifted just a bit, I could be kissing him. But I was too much of a coward to make the first move. His hands slid to my hips and then back up to my waist. The tension and nervous energy I felt as his electric fingertips stroked my bare skin was driving me crazy. To distract myself, I stood on tiptoe and asked, "What did you read in her thoughts?"

"Whose thoughts?" he answered in a husky voice. His eyes, a darker shade than I'd ever seen them, glittered as they searched mine. "Ah, the woman who asked me to dance. She hunts for a companion to fill her lonely nights."

"I imagine most of the people here are looking for that."

"Yes. But she seeks for something empty. She holds out no hope for love."

Tilting my head at an angle to see his face better, I asked, "Do you?"

"Do I what, Nehabet?"

"Hold out hope for love."

Amon paused. His body froze in a way that anyone who'd seen him dance would have thought impossible. He didn't answer but instead took my hand and said, "Come, Lily. It is time to go."

He seemed impatient as he waited for me to retrieve my bag. When we stepped outside, I wanted to take a moment to allow the night air to cool my heated skin, but he tugged me along, not giving me a moment to think. We had barely rounded the corner of the club when Amon suddenly stopped and pulled me roughly against him. Before I could even form a question, he murmured some words in Egyptian and we were sucked into a whirlwind.

We had rematerialized in the bedroom of our hotel room. Amon abruptly said goodnight and left me alone, heading for the living-room couch and shutting the door firmly between us.

I listened at the door, but I couldn't hear him and I couldn't seem to muster the courage to open the door and confront him about his brusqueness. Amon hadn't hurt me physically, but he'd left me feeling vulnerable and rejected. I wondered what I'd said, what I'd done to make him desert me so abruptly, and whether he was feeling like I was feeling or if I'd been misreading him.

Sinking to the floor, I rested my head against the door and felt the hot sting of tears on my cheeks. I'd never cried over a boy before, but my emotions were all over the place since starting this journey. I was unstable, heated, and on edge. Amon had used a lot of energy today, and I was feeling it. Eventually, I crawled into bed, sinking into a fitful sleep, and dreamed that my tears were enough to fill the Nile.

Valley of the Kings

The next morning Amon knocked lightly on my door. When I opened it, attempting to wipe the sleep from my swollen eyes, he was not only dressed and ready for the day but looked as good as the night before. I drew my robe tightly over my new pajamas and tried to smooth my tangled hair.

After a cold, perfunctory glance he asked, "How soon can you be ready?"

I answered, "Fifteen minutes," and with raised eyebrows he nodded and closed the door behind him.

Ten minutes later, I was wiping the steam from the mirror and brushing the tangles from my heavily conditioned hair. This time seeing the blond streaks didn't make me feel impulsive or wild; instead I saw them as a symbol of what happens when you put yourself out there and it backfires. My limbs felt heavy and lethargic, which was most likely a combination of lack of sleep and the giant meal I'd scarfed down the day before.

I brushed my hair away from my face with harsh strokes and twisted it into a tight bun at the nape of my neck. As I jabbed some pins I'd found among the new purchases into the bun, I welcomed the little stings, considering them punishment for wandering too far outside my comfort zone. There was a reason that my mother constantly said "moderation in all things."

Eating too much rich food leads to feeling puffy and bloated. Not enough sleep, and energy wanes. Crushing on the wrong boy? Well, that is a recipe for heartache.

Unfortunately, I would spend the morning suffering a rich-food, sleepless-night, hot-guy-rejection hangover. But I had certainly learned my lesson, and I wouldn't be dabbling in *any* of that stuff again. I was getting right back on track to living my practical, boring, perfect life. My walk on the wild side had pretty much ended in disaster, but that didn't mean I couldn't hitch a ride back on the familiar wagon of level-headedness.

Exactly fifteen minutes later, I opened the door. "Will we be returning to the hotel?"

Amon looked me over, focusing his piercing gaze on my hair, and wrinkled his nose as if he found the severe style distasteful. "No. We have no need to return to Cairo," he replied.

"I see. Give me another minute, then." Turning my back on him, I stiffly gathered up the clothing I thought would fit me and stuffed extra things from the hotel room—soap, shampoo, a toothbrush and toothpaste, the small sewing kit and, of course, water bottles—into my bag.

Amon folded his arms across his chest and watched me. "You are angry. I feel it," he said.

"It's not your concern," I tossed back. Throwing my stuffed bag over my shoulder, I gave him a strained smile and said, "Shall we go?"

Amon took hold of my arm as I passed. "Lily, I am sorry if I hurt you. But I cannot give you what—"

I held up my hand. "*Please* don't finish that sentence. I don't want to hear any platitudes and I have no interest in listening to your interpretation of what I want. I'm over it. So let's not talk about it anymore. All right?"

Hazel eyes gauging my reaction, Amon nodded. "If that is your wish."

"It is. Now can we go?"

Moving to a more open space in the living area I held out my arms so we could disappear in a cloud of sand, but he ignored me, instead walking over to a tray and pulling off a domed lid. Steam poured from the dish. "Will you eat first, Lily?"

"No. I appreciate your asking nicely, though, instead of ordering me."

"Lily, whether you acknowledge it or not, your body is being taxed by supporting both of us. You are drained."

"It's nothing. I just didn't sleep well."

"It is more than that."

Amon came closer. Too close. My breathing hitched and I tried to back away, but he took hold of my upper arms. "Remain still," he directed in a quiet voice. With both hands, he cupped my cheeks, fingertips grazing the hair at my temples. Heat edged down my neck and trickled over my shoulders, spilling into my limbs, advancing like viscous lava. A hot flush remained as Amon slid his hands down to my neck, and I was fairly certain it was from more than just his magical doctoring.

As he stared into my eyes, tears began to fall from mine. "What have you done to me?" I asked, unsure of the exact nature of my question.

Amon wiped a tear away with his thumb and rubbed his fingers over it. He sighed heavily, and stepped away. "More than I should," he answered cryptically. He picked up several pieces of fruit and held an apple under my nose. "You *will* eat this later. Though I will refrain from 'forcing' you to eat it, consider my encouragement to do so of a strenuous nature."

"Yeah, whatever," I murmured noncommittally as I stuffed the fruit into my already overloaded bag. As I struggled with the zipper, Amon took the bag from me, draping it across his wide chest before he opened his arms. Keeping my head down, I stepped into his embrace. With the whisper of a few words in ancient Egyptian, sand began to twist around our bodies.

Soon sunshine encircled us, shining brightly through my closed eyelids. I waited for the sand to dissipate. It seemed to take longer than normal, but when I cracked open my eyes, I realized it was a natural breeze stirring the sand on the dune where we'd appeared.

"We are here, Young Lily," Amon announced.

I guess I had been expecting an Indiana Jones–type temple or something, but what we were looking at seemed more like a mine in the dust export business or a quarry of crumbling rocks. My ankle-high boots were already filled with grainy sand.

Amon led me down the hill, my feet sinking into the sand up to my calves in some places, and the valley came into view. Between the small cliffs was a well-cared-for excavation site. Piles of coarse stones and loose gravel had been built up big enough to look like rocky burial mounds.

The day was already stifling, and I pulled my shirt away from my skin, fanning myself with it to circulate some air. Already thirsty, I dug a water bottle from my bag, sucked down about half, and offered the remaining half to Amon. He refused it, saying I needed it more than he did, so I finished off the bottle about the same time we reached the valley floor.

We merged with a group of tourists heading for what looked like a small bazaar. Vendors had set up tables and tents to sell various souvenirs. Amon wandered off to take in our surroundings while I eavesdropped on a tour guide who was explaining how to buy tickets.

I took a map when he began passing them out, and I smiled and nodded at a middle-aged woman next to me, who said, "Isn't this so exciting? I've always wanted to go to Egypt. My husband finally got us tickets for our thirtieth anniversary."

"Congratulations," I mumbled as I studied her profile. She and her husband would be an interesting duo to draw. The woman had curly red hair that was graying at the roots. It was loosely gathered in a ponytail,

and a cheap plastic sun visor shielded her eyes. Her husband had a sunburned bald spot, cargo shorts hanging low beneath his potbelly, and a
vacation beard. But it wasn't their appearance that fascinated me; it was
more the way they interacted with one another.

As the woman talked easily with strangers, the man remained quietly by her side, chuckling at jokes despite the fact that I was sure he'd
heard them several times, and when he forgot where he had put his
glasses and began patting pockets, she told him without even looking,
"Check your head, dear."

The woman clucked her tongue. "What would you do without me?"

Smiling, the man answered, "I'd never want to find out. Shall
we go?"

With that, the couple headed off on their Egyptian tomb adventure
after paying what I considered to be way too much for a flashlight and
a stack of postcards.

Amon finally returned and pulled me away from the line. "I got us
a map," I declared as I held the document up.

"The map I require will be found within the tombs."

"Really? How does that work exactly?"

"The tombs are all connected, and each one will provide direction
to the next."

"Are you sure? Because they made it sound like there are only small
groupings of tombs. Nobody mentioned a tomb highway."

"I am sure. I have discovered an entrance that is not as frequented.
We will begin there."

"Okay, lead the way."

As Amon headed toward one of the entrances, I tagged along, trying to make sense of the map. "It says all of the discovered burial chambers are labeled with numbers according to the date of discovery. For
example, King Tut's tomb is called KV62, which means King's Valley
number 62. The most recent one, KV63, was rumored to be the possible
burial chamber of the woman believed to be King Tut's mother, Kiya,

but it ended up being a storage cave, full of mummification paraphernalia. Hey, did you know King Tut? I mean, personally?"

"I am not familiar with this name."

"Oh, his full name was Tutankhamun. He was a boy pharaoh."

"It is pronounced *toot-ahnk-ah-MOON*. *Tut* means 'the image or likeness of.' *Ankh* is 'living.' And *Amun* represents the sun god Amun. So 'Tutankhamun' translates as 'the living image of the sun god Amun,' and to answer your question, no. His reign must have occurred while I slept."

"I don't understand. Aren't *you* the living image of the sun god?"

"I have been imbued, gifted, with a portion of his power so that I may fulfill my duties, but I am not the sun god personified. It was common for the leaders of Egypt to align with one god or another. The pharaohs did this for two reasons. First, they believed that if they took the names of the gods for themselves they would receive divine aid, but perhaps more important, this also cemented the loyalty of their people. They made it so that to reject a pharaoh was to reject deity. This helped offset internal strife and rebellion."

"But didn't he know about you?"

"Who?"

"King Tut."

"As the centuries passed it was considered safer if the leaders of the time were unaware of our presence. We did not wish to be seen as a threat or as a means of inciting revolt if the people were unhappy with the current politics. Our purpose was merely to protect the land from darkness, not to rule."

"Then how is it you were welcomed with feasting and song?"

"There was always a group of priests who passed the knowledge of us from generation to generation. They made sure that we were well cared for when we woke, that our burial sites were protected, and that the rituals were fulfilled. The people who celebrated our return were the humble, the poor. They kept our secret, not those in power. Though each rising is different, they have always been our watchers."

"So since your sarcophagus was taken, what you're saying is that somebody stopped watching."

Amon shrugged as if it meant nothing, but I could tell my words hit the mark. "It is a different time now," he said after a moment. "Perhaps in this world they have forgotten."

We stopped at a cave opening that was almost completely boarded up. I consulted my map. "This one is called KV29. The guide says that it's likely just a shaft, that it hasn't been excavated yet, and that it's full of debris."

"This is exactly what I seek."

Amon began ripping the boards off the entrance with a godlike strength.

Nervously, I said, "Uh . . . I might be a little claustrophobic. Just saying. Also, I don't have a flashlight. Or a rope. Or mountain-climbing gear. Or a death wish!" I called out as Amon disappeared inside the dark hole.

Sticking his head back out, Amon held out his hand. "You will not die, Young Lily. I will be with you."

Gingerly, I stepped closer, avoiding the rotting wood that might hide rusty nails. I should've gotten a tetanus booster and probably a dozen other shots before I agreed to go on this crazy trip. If only the girls at my school could see me now. My classmates would be shaking in their designer shoes at the thought of trekking through the desert and entering an unexcavated tomb. I could tell my skin was getting sunburned, and there were grains of sand ground into my hair. If I ended the day with just those irritants I'd consider myself lucky.

We made it only fifteen feet or so into the tomb, the light from the opening still showing the way, before we were stopped by a wall of loose rocks. "How exactly did you expect to get through here?" I asked. "Tunnel?" Coughing from the thick dust we'd stirred up, I took a sip from a water bottle to clear my throat.

"I must use my power. Prepare yourself."

"Prepare myself? For what?"

Amon didn't answer, instead raising his hands in the air and closing his eyes. A rumble shook the cave, almost knocking me off my feet. "Hold on to me, Lily!" Amon shouted.

I didn't hesitate and quickly wrapped my arms around his waist, burying my face into his chest and yet unable to resist turning just enough so I could see the magic he'd caused.

Rocks and debris shifted, rising into the air. At first, it was just a light layer, but then loose gravel ascended and even the heavier rocks moved in their stony beds. Amon continued to murmur in ancient Egyptian and the rubble rose higher, shooting past us in a cloud of stinging dust. Pebbles came next, firing through the air like bullets. They blasted out of the cave opening, ripping off the remaining boards that covered the entrance and cascading down in a shower outside the tomb, where they quickly built up a large pile.

Amon strained a bit as he focused on the bigger rocks. They weren't moving as fast as the lighter debris, and he had to move them one by one. The last two were massive boulders and Amon brought us up against the gritty wall, pressing me tightly against his body as the rocks passed. I could feel him shaking as he guided them. With a heavy thump, they hit the entrance and blocked out all the sunlight.

"I guess we aren't getting out the way we came in," I murmured as Amon bent over, panting. His breaths echoed in the black space, and I felt his hand gripping mine.

"I am sorry, Lily, but I need you."

"It's okay, I'm here. What do you—" I cried out midsentence as Amon drew energy from me. This time it was very different. Before, it felt like a gradual draining, but now the pull was sharp and painful, like someone was vacuuming out my insides with a steel wool attachment.

After a moment of agony, Amon let go, though he was still panting. "Lily?" he called. "How do you fare?"

Little twinges of aftershocks rippled under my skin. Being pretty much blind didn't help, and I began experiencing extreme claustrophobia as well. "Not good," I gasped, feeling like I was going to throw up. "A little warning next time would be nice."

"But I did warn—"

"Never mind. Oh, boy, it hurts." I ached all over. "Is that normal?"

"The longer we are connected, the worse the pain will be for you when I borrow energy."

"Well, that's just fan-freaking-tastic." My head began to pound at the base of my neck.

"I will try to spare you as much as possible."

"Thanks," I murmured dryly. Fishing sightlessly in my bag, I found a small bottle of ibuprofen and popped a few, downing them with water. Amon groaned. "Are you in pain, too?" I asked.

He blew out a breath as he leaned back against the wall. "Yes. I experience pain when I expend a great amount of energy without having absorbed the power found in my canopic jars. Our connection is such that I experience your pain also."

"Talk about a double whammy. Here, hold out your hand." I stretched my hand out and bumped into his chest. Moving my palm up to his shoulder, I skimmed it down his arm and took his hand, opening it and holding it in place. I shook some tablets into his palm, counted, took back the three extra ones, and then handed him the bottle of water, placing it in his other hand.

"What is this?" Amon asked.

"Medicine from my world. It will help with the headache."

Grunting, Amon popped the pills and chewed. "The taste is abhorrent," he spat.

"You're not supposed to chew them. You swallow them whole. So," I asked as I put the ibuprofen back in my bag and felt for his arm, "what exactly are we going to do now with no light?"

"We will go down the shaft."

"How? I can't see a thing."

"I can see in the darkness." Amon turned toward me and two shimmery lights materialized in the pitch black just about where his eyes would be. It reminded me of the reflective eyes of animals at night.

"That's a little creepy. So you have night vision?"

"I call it eyeshine."

"Right, so I'm just supposed to follow you? Blindly?"

Amon's glowing eyes turned away from me and then returned. The effect was eerie. I felt like I was being haunted. "Perhaps it is not the most effective way," he admitted reluctantly.

"Will it be steep?" I asked.

"Possibly. It depends on what the intended use of the shaft was." Amon slowly turned, tucking my arm in his.

"I thought it was for air," I said as I walked beside him tentatively, testing out how to move in absolute darkness in a strange place. I clutched his muscular arm like a lifeline.

"Some of them are. Often there were secret shafts built for the priests who tended to our resting places. They kept funerary lamps lit and left behind food and other items they thought we might need should we awaken."

The heel of my boot rolled over a round stone and I staggered. Amon pulled me upright, placing one arm around my shoulders. His other arm was now in front of me so I could hold on to it like a safety bar on a roller coaster.

"Didn't the priests know that you rose just once every thousand years?" I asked as we started walking again.

"Sometimes records were kept and they knew exactly when we would rise, but other times they were wrong by a few hundred years." After progressing only about a dozen feet, Amon turned and rubbed his palms lightly up my arms. "How do you feel, Lily? Are you still in pain?"

"It's mostly gone now. I'm just tired."

"I do not feel we will make swift enough progress if you cannot see."

"Right, so what exactly are we going to do about it?"

Amon didn't answer but launched into a chant, his richly accented voice echoing off the walls. Gradually, I began to make out my surroundings. I gasped when I saw the light was coming not from a torch or a flashlight or a magic wand but directly from Amon's skin. His entire body glowed with a buttery light that illuminated the chamber around us, but wasn't so glaringly bright that I couldn't look at him.

"Oh, *wow*," I murmured in appreciation. Amon was beautiful. Glorious. He looked like a resplendent angel. His eyes gleamed like green embers burned within their depths. Amon said he was only the personification of Horus and Amun-Ra and had, at one time, been a mere mortal like me, but there could be nothing or no one as magnificent or as worthy of worship. Amon in his normal form was crush-worthy enough, but if he had appeared like he was now in ancient Egypt, civilization would have fallen at his feet.

Amon didn't seem to notice my speechlessness and just cocked his head at me as he offered his hand. I slid mine into his and thought that this must be what Lois Lane felt like when Superman offered to take her flying. At that moment, I felt all the pain, risk, and inconvenience was definitely worth it if it meant being on the arm of a man like Amon.

Even if he wasn't interested in me. Even if I was a lowly human girl trying to keep up with a man who had godlike powers. Even if the time spent with him was only because he needed me. I pledged to myself that I would enjoy every minute while it lasted. I was in a waking dream and having the experience of a lifetime. I'd never forget it as long as I lived.

Docilely, I let Amon take the lead, and we moved ahead quite a ways. The air was oppressive and hot, and despite the marvelous distraction that Amon provided, being in the middle of an Egyptian desert started to overwhelm me. Sweat pooled on my neck and lower back. With my free hand, I fanned my shirt to move air around my face. I asked Amon to stop so I could take another drink.

"Aren't you sweating at all?" I accused as I greedily sipped water.

"I am used to the heat of Egypt. Compared with the afterlife, the desert sun feels as comfortable as springtime."

"Your Egyptian afterlife sounds suspiciously like hell."

"It has its . . . challenges," he replied cryptically. He studied my face for a moment. "I can help"—he averted his eyes—"if you wish it."

"Will it hurt?"

"No. It may be slightly draining, but there will be no pain."

"Do it, then."

Amon slid an arm around my waist, pulling me close, and ducked his head up against my neck. "Wh-what are you doing there, exactly, Vlad?" I stammered nervously, ultra aware of the trickle of sweat making its way slowly down my neck right about where his lips were. "I thought you were a mummy, not a vampire."

Amon blew softly on my neck, the sensation causing goose bumps to rise pretty much everywhere on my body. "You must remain very still, Lily," Amon whispered, his breath tickling my ear.

"Um, okay."

Amon whispered and pressed his lips to my hot neck. Though I let out a little squeak, I remained stiff and unmoving, trying to remind myself that the very exquisite sensation of Amon's kissable lips grazing my neck had nothing to do with romance. I noticed that though the heat in the cave had begun to lift, the heat Amon was generating between us, however unintentional, was through the roof.

The sweat on my face and arms cooled, and the air around me felt moist and wet, like a forest in Oregon, a welcome change from the dry desert we were actually in. Amon murmured against my neck, "You taste like melted desert honey."

Unable to remain still any longer, I slid my hands up his arms to his shoulders, but Amon immediately straightened, raising his head. The urge to pull him close again was strong. Instead I asked, "What was that?"

"I sucked the excess warmth from your body and took it into my own. I have a great tolerance for heat."

"That's the understatement of the year," I mumbled as he moved farther away.

Without him near, I actually felt cold now, and wasn't sure if the sensation was due to Amon removing too much heat or if I simply craved his warmth.

"Thank you," I offered, and even though I was disappointed with his abrupt reaction to my touch, I couldn't help the contented smile I wore on my face. "I feel much better."

Amon took in my expression and replied stonily, "You are welcome. Come, Lily."

We came to a fork in the shaft and Amon stopped to consult some hieroglyphs. He pointed to the various pictures. "This is the map. To those who simply read it in a straightforward manner, it tells stories of pharaohs and of battles, but to those few who know of us, there is a hidden code. Do you see the crescent moon?"

"Yes."

"This is a sign of my brother. It means that his tomb has been hidden in an antechamber near the Egyptian leader mentioned here."

"What is his name?"

"My brother or the leader?"

"The leader."

"I do not know. He is recognized by his picture. I must seek the burial chamber of this man, and because the moon appears to the right of him, it means my brother's antechamber will be found off this man's right hand."

"But if that mummy has been discovered, then he has been removed. How will we know where he was positioned?"

"There will be a hidden door marked with the sign of my brother, the crescent moon. If we cannot discern which doorway is on the right-hand side, then we will seek the sign, but it is likely that there will be more directions found in the tomb of this leader."

"So do we go right or left? Anubis sent the funerary cone from your tomb, correct? So shouldn't we be looking for your tomb first?"

Amon bit his lip. "Let us begin by exploring the old tomb of my brother. If he is there, we can raise him quickly and he can help me find our remaining brother. Besides, nothing on this map indicates where I might have been discovered."

Amon led us toward the right, and it wasn't long before the shaft angled down steeply. "How are we supposed to get down there?" I asked "Skateboard? Slide? Mine cars?"

"What are those things?" Amon asked.

"A skateboard is like a wooden board with wheels. You ride on it. Mine cars are small chariots that run on tracks, and children play on a slide. It's made of smooth metal, and there's usually sand at the bottom so kids don't hurt themselves when they land."

"I will choose the slide."

"Wait a minute. There are all kinds of bumps and pits and rocks down there. It's not exactly going to be smooth sailing."

"May I have a bottle of water, Lily?"

I handed him one and, to my dismay, he poured the entire thing down the shaft instead of drinking it.

"That was a waste of perfectly good water," I mumbled.

"I must use some power again, Lily, but I am warning you now."

"Okay, fine. At least I know what to expect."

"Yes," Amon said, and then looked away. I sensed emotion rising in him. It tasted bitter, like regret mixed with a gritty determination. Standing in front of the angled shaft, he chanted, and I heard the hiss of sand shifting inside the tunnel. The hiss grew and became more agitated as small rocks and debris began to tumble. Curious, I stepped closer and peered down. It looked like a whirlwind was twisting inside the shaft. Everything, each loose grain of sand or rock, spun, gradually increasing in speed. Faster and faster the rocks and pebbles moved until I could see only streaks of black, gray, and brown.

What at first sounded clunky, like shoes thumping in a dryer, began to even out, and after several minutes, Amon took my arm and had me step behind him. With a thrust of his hand, what was left inside the tunnel whipped out past us and blasted against the far wall. As Amon braced his hand against the curved shaft, eyes closed, I approached and placed my palm against his cheek.

Amon's hand slid up my arm to cup my hand and he opened his brilliant eyes. "Take what you need," I offered.

"I will try not to hurt you," Amon pledged. The siphoning off of my energy was less invasive this time, but I still felt hollow. It left me with a deep emptiness, a hunger I wasn't sure could be filled. No wonder Amon liked feasting. If a feast had been set in front of me at that moment, I would have pounced on the food like a starving animal.

The once square shaft had now become almost circular, thanks to the wind funnel Amon had created. I wasn't sure what the water had done. It seemed too insignificant an amount to have aided the process and yet, he'd accomplished his purpose. Crouching at the edge, I ran my hand along the inside. It was smooth; the rocks lining it were even, flat, and polished.

Amon crouched down next to me. "I am unsure if the entire shaft is smooth like your slide, so you will ride on my legs."

I was suddenly uncomfortable. "I think I'll just take my chances behind you."

"I will not allow you to be further hurt, Lily."

"No, really. It's okay. I'll be fine."

"Lily, do not make me force you." Amon positioned himself at the top of the shaft and held out his hands. "Come," he beckoned.

"You know, for a god, you can be kind of a bully," I mumbled.

"I am not a god. I am a—"

"Yeah, yeah. I know. You're just imbued with powers, blah blah blah. Let's just get this over with."

Awkwardly, I sat on Amon's legs, and without any hesitation, he pulled my body back against him, nudging my legs up so they rested on top of his. He folded my arms across my chest and wrapped one arm over mine, leaving his other hand free to push off. "Are you ready?" he murmured in my ear.

"As I'll ever be," I grunted.

The awkward feeling turned into cold fear mixed with exhilaration. Amon whooped loudly, both arms now wrapped protectively around my body. Air whipped past us as we plummeted, and I had the sick sensation of being in free fall. Unable to stop myself, I screamed while Amon's laugh reverberated in my ears. The thought occurred to me that if we lived through this whole experience, it might be fun to take Amon to a theme park.

The shaft became steeper and the ceiling lowered, so Amon angled his body back and I could feel the tightening of his abs against my back. My cheek rested against his, so I had a good view as the ceiling dropped toward us. I worried that if it got too low we'd be wedged in a tunnel that would likely rip us apart at the speed we were going.

Just when I was sure the ceiling was going to rip off my nose, it widened again and the angle started to even out. Suddenly, the slide beneath us disappeared and my scream echoed in what must have been a much larger space.

Amon, no longer laughing, cradled me even tighter against his chest and we landed with a heavy thump on a pile of sand. Though Amon took the brunt of the fall, he kept me locked in his arms as we rolled down, finally sliding to a stop with Amon's body ending up on top of mine, pressing me into the stony floor.

Shabtis

Amon lifted his head. "Are you harmed, Lily?"

"I don't think so . . . ," I answered, my words trailing off as his concerned expression was replaced by something else.

I could feel a delicious sort of torment rise within him, tempting him.

His gaze dropped to my mouth, and my breath caught. I was in a dark, dusty tomb, spiderwebs in my hair, sand in my boots, with sunburned, sweaty skin, but none of these things affected me more than the drop-dead gorgeous sun god who was currently hovering over me.

I wasn't sure if what I felt was real or if it was a side effect of our connection, but I knew without a doubt that he wanted to kiss me. And Egyptian heaven help me, I wanted him to. But despite the fact that I was vividly imagining the press of his lips against mine, and the likelihood that he *knew* that I wanted to kiss him, he closed his eyes, murmured some soft words in his native language, and shifted, moving quickly off and away from me.

For some reason Amon was keeping me at a distance. I wasn't one of those girls who lacked self-confidence, but his behavior was disconcerting enough to make me second-guess my girlish charms. Maybe there was more to our connection than he was sharing.

I was determined not to allow any more self-doubt to color my emotional response, but Amon's repeated rejection left me feeling vulnerable and exposed.

As he turned his back to me and began studying the markings on the walls, I sighed, grabbed my bag, and murmured, "I was wrong. I think my ego was bruised in the fall."

Amon gave me a sidelong glance and frowned, turning back to the hieroglyphs without responding and effectively shutting me out. Sighing again, I chose a passage as far as the light from his body would allow. Finding more carvings, I called out to him, "I think I found something."

"What does it look like?" Amon replied. "Describe what you see."

Squinting in the light, I studied the form and answered, "The first part is the sun, moon, and stars, like you talked about. Then there's a guy with a weird-shaped head. I've never seen an animal that looked like that before. It may be a horse? Anyway, the guy looks like he's pushing a rock. Hold on. There are little symbols on the rock."

Tracing my finger over the carved grooves wasn't enough to help me make them out. Leaning closer, I gently blew on the stone and a light powdery dust rose in the air, leaving the symbols beneath more clear. "Wait a minute," I mumbled to myself as I backtracked a few paces. Sure enough, the large block I'd recently passed had the exact same carvings that the horse-faced god was pushing. Just to be sure, I dusted it off with my hand, took out a pen from my bag, and copied the markings onto my hand.

From around the corner, Amon asked, "What did you find, Lily?" his voice echoing in the large space.

"Just practice some patience for a few seconds and I'll tell you!" I hollered over my shoulder as I checked the symbols on my hand against the god's stone box. It was a match.

Pleased with my discovery, I headed back to the large stone and began pushing, wedging my boots into the grooves of the floor for leverage. As I struggled with the stubborn stone, I began describing what I'd found to Amon.

"It's in the shape of a stone roughly the size of your chest, and it's sticking out from the wall. The god on the picture is pushing, so I figure that's the thing to do."

"Yes, but what are the symbols you see?" Amon called from around the corner.

Gasping, I tried pushing the heavy stone to the right and then to the left, but the thing wouldn't budge. Turning around, I braced my back against it and pushed with my legs. As I panted, I explained, "There are four pictures. Top left is a full moon with horizontal lines through it. Bottom left is a rectangle. Top right is a sun half over the horizon, and bottom right"—I grunted and laughed in relief as I felt the stone shift slightly—"is a pair of walking legs."

"Walking legs?"

"You know, like a stick figure with two feet pointing in one direction."

The stone moved several inches, so I adjusted my feet, bit my lip, and pushed again just as Amon shouted, "Lily! Stop!"

"Amon? What's wrong?" I called out, but then the stone gave way and settled flush with the wall. Almost immediately the ground began to shake. A large section of it shifted and the side farthest from me gave way altogether, creating a slide that I was at the top of, with nothing to hold on to. My scream echoed as I slid down the rock. I scrambled frantically for purchase, vainly attempting to find a handhold to stop my descent.

Beneath me a gaping black pit waited hungrily to devour me, but right as I went over the edge there was a jerk on my arm that wrenched my shoulder painfully. My body banged against the side of the pit and I continued to look for something to grasp.

"Lily!" Amon cried out. "Hold on to me!"

"I'm slipping!" I knew that any second I was going to fall. As I swung wildly, I glanced down once again. Now that Amon's light was making things more visible, I cried out with desperation when I saw sharp spears and jagged rocks waiting below.

If I fell I would be impaled and would likely be joining the Valley of the Kings tomb as its newest resident. Morbidly, I wondered if I'd get my own chamber and number. I'd be KV64, or maybe KV65, unless, of course, they didn't discover me for a few thousand years. For all I knew I could end up as KV6565.

Amon's frantic murmuring didn't serve to make me feel any more confident in my chances, and then, to make matters worse, the dirt wall I was trying to cling to with my other hand started vibrating. Clouds of sand began to burst forth and swirl around me.

"Sandstorm not helping!" I cried out, choking and coughing, but a moment later the sand hardened, forming blocks that stuck out from the wall like steps.

"Climb on!" Amon hollered as he swung my body closer to the steps. Thankfully, I was able to clamber onto one of the narrow ledges he'd created, and I felt safe enough to tell him he could let go.

Amon scooted closer to the edge. "No," he pronounced. "I will hold on to you as you climb."

I carefully ascended the steps one by one, my back pressed against the crumbling dirt wall. Finally, I neared the top and Amon reached out, grabbed me under the arms, and yanked me up the rest of the way. He tugged me so hard that I lost my footing and collapsed against him. Immediately, I tried to back away, but Amon wasn't having it. His arms locked around me in a tight grip.

"I almost lost you," he said against my shoulder.

Twining my arms around his neck, I half smiled, half grimaced, the throbbing in my arm preventing me from truly enjoying the experience. "Thanks for saving me," I murmured.

Amon lifted his head. "Did you think I would not?"

"No. I was pretty sure you would. After all, it's not like there are a bunch of organ donors in these caverns."

Amon frowned. "I did not save you merely for your organs, Young Lily."

"No?" I teased, lifting my chin in a challenge. "Then is there perhaps another reason that you don't want me to die an untimely death?"

"There are multiple reasons."

"Such as?"

He shifted back, as he considered what to say. Finally, he offered, "You are . . ." He brushed his thumb against my cheek to remove a smear of dirt.

"Yes?" I pressed.

"You are . . . an excellent scribe," he finally said.

I dropped my hands. "Really? Is that all I'm going to get? It's nice to know my *penmanship*"—I spat the word—"is so important to you." I folded my arms across my chest, wincing at the movement, and stared him down.

Amon ran his hand up my arm to my hurt shoulder, and I hissed as he cupped it with his palm. After a quick chant he poured enough warmth into the muscle to rival a heating pad. Still, he avoided eye contact. "Lily, I do not wish to talk about this."

"I don't get it. You run so hot and cold. I don't understand what's wrong. Am I not beautiful enough?"

Amon gave me an astounded look. "Why would you believe this?"

"I don't know. You keep pushing me away. What else am I supposed to think?"

Amon's other hand moved up my arm to cup my uninjured shoulder. "Lily, I can honestly tell you that I have never in my long life come across a creature as beguiling as you. You are as fresh and as lovely as a budding flower kissed by the dew of a golden morning. I breathe you in and am filled with the taste of sunshine, life, and hope. You are much more than beautiful. You are . . . temptation personified."

An expression of shock instantly crossed his face as he muttered, "That is not what I meant to say. Please forget those words."

"Um, unlikely. Unless they were false."

Amon pursed his perfect lips and groaned. "The gifts I have received have made deception very . . . difficult for me. It was the truth."

"Then I *really* don't understand. If you like me that much, why won't you kiss me?"

Amon sighed, removing his hands when I indicated with a nod that my shoulder felt better, and turned away, placing his palms against the stone I'd moved. He let out a sad, sardonic laugh. "This is why," he said, nodding at the stone.

Taking a step closer, I peered at the offending rock. "What does it say?" I asked softly.

Ignoring my question, he moved around it carefully and held out his arm, beckoning me to hold on to him. When I'd crossed safely, he kept my hand in his, and after checking the hieroglyph map I'd found, continued down the passageway, leading me along. As we turned a corner, he said, without looking back, "Death. The symbols on the stone mean death."

"If someone really wanted to kill you, why would they advertise it?"

"The carving on the wall showing the sun, moon, and stars is very old, but the etching on the stone and the rock in the carving was recently created."

"So someone *was* watching for you."

"Someone was warning us of a trap. And someone else created it. I cannot discern how long ago that image was added. It could have been fairly recently, or it could have been created a hundred years ago."

Pondering his words, I followed him silently as we further explored the mysterious Egyptian tomb. Unfortunately, I wasn't able to fully process what was going on between Amon and me because we soon came upon a new section of the underground labyrinth that needed to be solved.

I asked Amon if we were likely to come across any more booby traps, and after I explained what they were, he told me that Egyptian tombs usually came with curses, not snares for the unsuspecting. Still, he seemed very uncomfortable with the idea of moving ahead, though he believed that the path we were peering down was indeed the correct one.

Tentatively, he led me forward, insisting on going first, but then suddenly, he froze. "Do not move, Lily," he whispered.

"What is it?" I asked quietly.

Reaching forward, Amon touched his finger to the air right in front of him and blood immediately pooled at his fingertip. "It is a deadly wire, created to sever the neck of the hapless person wandering the tombs. And this time, there was no warning."

We backed up slowly while Amon whispered some words. Sand rose from the tomb floor and swirled around his hands. The grains coalesced and solidified, forming a deadly-looking weapon—a knife. The blade burned with Amon's white light.

"Stand back," Amon warned.

Using the glowing knife, he slashed the wire. As he did so, it recoiled violently, like a whip, delivering a stinging slash to his cheek.

Amon cut another wire and another, his mood darkening with each discovery. After we finally made it to the end of the tunnel, consulted some hieroglyphs, and turned down another corridor, Amon finally began to relax.

Because he let his guard down, I did, too, and it came as quite a shock to both of us when I tripped over a slightly elevated stone and the walls began to shake.

"Amon?" I called out. "Is that you?"

"I am not causing this disturbance," he said as I stumbled against him. The walls shifted, and before we could get our bearings, we were trapped inside a stone box. It became deathly quiet. Amon attempted to use his knife to pry open the sealed edges, but he couldn't find a place to insert the blade. He stirred the sand around us and sent it scurrying into the corners searching for cracks. The sand just hovered in little clouds, not finding a way out.

I sat on the ground and dusted my hands off on my jeans. "So much for your Egyptians-don't-use-booby-traps theory."

Amon frowned. "It does not make sense. The tombs were never protected in this manner before."

"Maybe your so-called guardians who are missing in action set up the traps to protect you and your brothers so that you wouldn't be discovered."

"Maybe."

"In that case they should have set up a few more, since you were found anyway." I sighed. "Can you sandstorm our way out?"

Shaking his head, Amon explained, "If the sand cannot find a crack in this prison, then we cannot escape it in that manner, either."

Sitting down next to me, Amon dusted off his hands and held them up in the air, chanting different spells. When one didn't work, he tried another, and another. It was around the third or fourth spell that I noticed the light coming from his skin was waning. It actually flickered.

"What's wrong with your light?" I asked.

"I am not sure," he said as he lifted a hand to study it. "Let me try something."

A ball of flame materialized in Amon's palm, but it soon sputtered and went out. "I do not understand why this is happening," he said.

"Wait a minute. You can create fire with your hands?"

Amon nodded.

"You are full of surprises," I said in awe.

I took a few deep breaths and felt a niggling pain in the bottom of my lungs. "I . . . think we're running out of oxygen," I said, the pain in my chest now becoming a dull ache. "You need it to maintain your flame, and it's also affecting the light from your body."

Amon took my hand and switched off his light. Darkness deeper than that of a grave surrounded us. Desperate to figure a way out, I ran my free hand over the wall closest to me. "Try to see if there is an indentation or a trigger," I suggested to Amon. "In the mummy movies there is always a way out, we just have to find it." Amon worked on the wall opposite mine and then we moved on to the other two. When giving the same treatment to the floor, I came across a depression in the stone. "What do you think this is?" I asked.

Making his way over to me, Amon slid his hand on top of mine until he felt the stone I'd found. "I am not sure," he said.

It felt like a hollowed-out curve, similar to a mold for a sphere, but no matter how we pushed or beat on it, nothing happened. I sat down heavily with my back against a wall. Amon slid down next to me. "So this is it, then?" I said, more to the tomb than to Amon or myself. "We're just going to suffocate in here? What's next? The walls will crush us?"

Not a minute later, there was a terrible grinding noise. Amon stood to investigate.

"You've got to be kidding me!" I cried.

"The ceiling is lowering, Lily," Amon said. "Stay as low to the floor as possible."

"What are you going to do?" I asked, my voice trembling with the conviction that whatever he tried wouldn't be enough to save us.

"I will attempt to brace it," he panted.

"You'll be crushed," I wheezed.

"I do not know what else to do."

Little by little the ceiling dropped, and as strong as Amon was, there was no stopping its progress.

As I sat there cowering, hoping Amon would pull a secret sun-god power out of his bag of tricks to save us, I contemplated my impending death. At that moment, I realized my entire life had amounted to essentially being trapped inside a box. How fitting that I was now going to die in one.

Despite the fact that I liked to believe that I was a regular girl who longed for an adventure with a mysterious man, the truth was, I was about as far away from being a regular girl as I could be. I'd been conditioned like a pampered poodle to be utterly obedient and go only so far as my diamond-studded leash allowed. If the world got too crazy, I'd tremble at my parents' feet and let them make everything all better. I was a coward.

This little adventure with Amon was so far outside my comfort zone that I didn't even know who I was anymore. My outer shell had been ripped away and what was left was a raw, scared girl. My confidence, the marrow that made up who I was, and my grasp of what was real and what was imaginary had been ripped apart. The foundation at the core of Lilliana Young had crumbled and only broken rubble remained.

The irony was that as I waited for death, I realized that I was now finally living. I was experiencing the world. I'd run away from home, developed a serious crush on a guy who didn't feel the same, and traveled to the desert. I was in serious need of a shower, said whatever acerbic comments came to mind, and couldn't care less about the consequences of my actions.

And now, here I was, nearing death, and I felt . . . glad.

Being with Amon was the most invigorating thing that had ever happened to me and if I was to meet my end here, then at least I could say that I had truly experienced living in all its sweaty, uncomfortable, harsh, heartbroken, scary, sometimes deadly, but always thrilling glory.

If I was going to leave this earth, I would do it with a smile on my face and consider it a fitting end to the ultimate adventure. "All things considered, I think I'd rather suffocate than be crushed," I wheezed. "How about you?"

Amon panted. "Why do you speak like this?"

"I don't know. Just accepting the inevitable, I guess. Please stop straining yourself," I pleaded as Amon grunted and staggered beneath the ceiling.

The scrape of a shoe on the dusty floor told me Amon had heeded my words. Soon he was next to me, trying to catch his breath in a space almost devoid of oxygen.

"Are you going to die, too?" I asked.

"Perhaps not immediately, but losing you will weaken me to the point that my death will be inevitable. For the first time in millennia I will have failed in my duty."

"Yeah. Sorry about that."

Amon put his arms around me, pulling me close. "No. I am sorry for this, Young Lily. I did not wish to endanger your life."

"Yeah, well, I should have known that taking up with a mummy was not the safest bet." Stretching my hand above my head, I could easily press my palm against the ceiling now. Amon and I slid down a little, prolonging the inevitable. Turning my face in his direction, I decided to throw caution completely to the wind and asked, "So, does the weight of our situation inspire you to rethink the idea of kissing me? I mean, if I'm going to die, I'd really like to know what a kiss feels like first."

Amon murmured, "The weight of our situation . . . weight. Could it be that simple?"

Carefully, Amon moved around me and found the round groove again. He chanted, and I felt the sting of sand as it whipped past me with a hiss.

"What are you doing?" I whispered in the darkness.

Ignoring me, he kept on and then cried out in joy at the whir and click of the walls. The ceiling rose and the floor shifted. The momentum caused me to lose my balance and roll to the side. The cool rush of air filled the room as Amon took my hand and helped me stand.

Soft golden light filled my eyes as Amon's skin began to glow once more, and he pointed at the thing he'd created—a stone ball that fit exactly into the groove of the floor.

"What is it?" I asked.

"I once heard a story about weighted balls being used in the pyramids. A stone ball weighted just right was used to open secret passageways and doors. We were going in the right direction, but we did not have the weighted ball necessary to enter."

"So the depression we found was like a lock and the ball was the key?"

"Yes. Exactly."

The deadly box had opened up to a new passage. As we passed through the doorway, Amon leaned down and grabbed the ball he'd created, dropping the heavy item, which was about the size of a grapefruit but with the weight of a bowling ball, into my bag before placing the strap across his chest.

So I wasn't going to die after all. Gratitude filled me and I smiled, vowing to remember that even in the most dire of circumstances, it was better to live, explore, and face possible danger than to cower for the rest of my life inside a pretty box. From that point forward, daredevil would be my middle name.

"I think we should just assume that there are going to be more booby traps ahead," I said, still smiling.

"Yes. We should move cautiously," Amon said as he peered at me quizzically, probably trying to understand why I was in such a good mood.

During our careful advance, Amon didn't come across anything, and we passed through several corridors unharmed. After climbing a long series of stairs, we came upon another set of hieroglyphs. This time there was a clear indication that the secret tomb hiding the whereabouts of the sun god was close by. Amon decided that since we were so near to his last resting place, we should momentarily abandon the search for his brother and check out his tomb first to see if we could find his canopic jars.

We reached a stone wall with the symbol of the sun engraved upon it. Amon pushed a lever, causing a hiss, followed by an explosion of dust that blew over both of us.

A crack of light appeared. Undaunted, Amon shoved the wall, widening the gap, and we entered the tomb. The vacant room was filled with artificial light. We ducked into the next chamber and found it empty as well.

As Amon studied the hieroglyphs covering the walls, I stayed where I was and pulled out the map I'd been given earlier. "Amon, do you realize where we are?"

"We are near my burial chamber."

"Yes, but this is no ordinary tomb. This is KV63. As in, the tomb of King Tut!" Amon stared at me as if waiting for the punch line. I sputtered, "The point is, this is the most famous tomb here and we aren't likely to be alone for long, so we have to hurry."

Amon nodded and turned back to the carvings while I perused the map. Mumbling to myself, I said, "We came in through the treasury, so this must be the burial chamber. To the left is the antechamber, and just beyond that, the annex. The passageway out is over there." I pointed in the general direction of the exit.

Amon turned to me, ducked his head, and whispered, "If I was indeed buried here, I would not have been found near the pharaoh or in the annex or the antechamber. My tomb would have been near the treasury room. We were always hidden behind the great treasures so that marauders would stop and not search any farther."

"Well, apparently someone found you."

"Yes. But where? There is no indication that another mummy was discovered in this area."

"Maybe you were moved?" I suggested.

"Perhaps."

"Then maybe your canopic jars are still here."

"They may be." We searched all the walls and found nothing indicating a hidden chamber or canopic jars.

Starving, I pulled out an apple from my bag and felt grateful that Amon had forced me to bring some food along. As I searched for another water bottle, an orange fell out and bounced along the ground until it came to a stop in a corner.

When I picked it up, I found it had rolled right into a spherical depression, similar to the one we'd found before.

"Amon! Over here!"

He crouched down next to me and smiled. "You have found it." The hollowed-out sphere had a sun engraved in it. Taking the sand sphere from my bag, Amon whispered some words and the sand on the surface of the stone shifted, creating an exact impression of the sun to match the mold in the floor. Fitting the stone ball into the depression, he turned it slowly, and there was an audible hiss as the floor began to move.

A wall rose to block off the entrance to the treasury and, then the entire floor sank as if we were in a large elevator. When it came to a stop, we were several levels below King Tut's tomb. Stepping off, Amon removed the stone ball and the treasury room lifted, returning to its original position. It took the light with it, so Amon lit his skin. Before us was a vast chamber supported by stone columns.

Deeply etched engravings and paintings depicting fascinating events, very different from the ones in the other tombs, lined the walls. I saw the sun, the moon, and the stars, the great pyramids, images of the god with the giraffe head, and what I recognized as Anubis pointing to three men in the process of mummification.

"What does all this mean?" I asked.

"This is my story. My tomb," Amon responded quietly as he moved forward. He stopped at a large sarcophagus carved from wood. The detailing on it was exquisite, and I gasped when I realized it looked like Amon. Gingerly, I traced the curves of his face on the wooden image.

"It's you," I whispered.

"Yes."

"But there was a golden sarcophagus in the museum when you woke up. It looked like you, too."

"I do not know why or how I came to be in that sarcophagus. Perhaps a second one was created by those who watch over us, or perhaps I was relocated to protect my identity, but this is the one that was created for me by Anubis."

"Why isn't it golden, like King Tut's?"

"Neither I nor my brothers have a need to collect or display our power with great treasures. Our purpose is simply to serve. If there were rumors of gold or a treasure associated with us, then thieves and marauders would constantly seek us out."

"I like this better," I said as I ran my hand over the polished wood, which had been expertly carved and painted with great care. Amon's smile indicated that my remark had pleased him, but his thoughts and emotions were shadowed. "Amon?"

"Yes?"

"Why is your sarcophagus gleaming? It looks like someone just oiled it."

Amon walked around to the other side. "I do not know. Perhaps our caretakers have been here. I think we need to open it. Stand back, Lily."

Slowly raising his arms, Amon chanted softly. The top of the huge coffin shook and rose off its base. It was heavy, and Amon's arms trembled as the lid moved to the side. Lowering his arms, he gently set it on the floor, where it settled in the sand before falling against the side of the sarcophagus with a heavy thud. I went to him, offering to share my energy, but he waved me off and leaned against the coffin until he caught his breath.

I wasn't sure what he or I expected to find, but there was nothing. The huge casket was empty.

"I do not understand," Amon said, peering inside. "I should have awoken here. How was I brought to your city?"

"Someone must've moved you."

"But who? Why?"

"Maybe there was someone who didn't want you to wake up in Egypt. Do you have enemies?"

"Most people do not even know we exist."

"But some do. Who wouldn't want you to perform your ceremony?"

"The ceremony benefits all mankind. The only one it harms is the god of chaos, Seth, but he does not have a foothold strong enough in the modern world to cause us harm."

"Are you certain about that?"

"As certain as I can be about such things."

"Hmm . . . Well, first things first, do you see your canopic jars anywhere?"

We spent several minutes searching, but came up with nothing but dust. It wasn't until I was wandering back toward where we'd entered that I noticed the funerary cones lining the entrance to Amon's tomb. Sure enough, one of the cones was missing near the top of the arch. I called Amon over. He hoisted me up on his shoulders to get a closer look.

Though it was dark in the hole where the cone would be, there was unmistakably something inside. Overcoming my squeamishness, I reached in and touched what turned out to be a statue. There were, in fact, two statues nestled into the gap where the funerary cone belonged, each about the length of a pen. I pulled out one and then the other, handing them down to Amon.

Grabbing my hands, he helped me slide off his shoulders and then picked up the two statues and examined them.

"What are they?" I asked as I stared at them. One of the statues looked like an ancient pharaoh with little carvings across the torso and its arms folded across its chest. It was a beautiful jade color. Very striking, the piece was probably worth a fortune.

The other was shorter, almost half as tall as the first, and was made of dark stone. It held a large parchment that was torn down the middle. Its shape was similar to that of a heart, and there was an expression of delight on its ugly face.

"They are called *shabtis*. At one time, human servants were entombed with their leaders, with the understanding that they would journey to the afterlife with their masters and continue to act as servants for the dead kings or pharaohs."

"That's barbaric!" At Amon's confused expression, I clarified, "Cruel. Horrifying."

"Yes. Eventually this practice changed to entomb servants only symbolically. These statues represent those who would serve the one buried."

"So these guys are supposed to serve you?"

"In theory."

"Did they? Have you met them in the afterlife?"

"No. But I wonder . . ."

"Wonder what?"

Amon lifted his gaze from the statues to me. "There is a spell."

"I'm not sure I like the sound of this. Your spells don't work out so well for me."

Beginning to grow excited, Amon continued, "But if I raise them, they can use their power to help us. Do you see? Anubis must have placed them here. They can seek out my canopic jars, and then I will no longer need to borrow your energy. Our connection can be dissolved without risking—"

Amon stopped abruptly and I narrowed my eyes. "Risking what?"

He waved a hand. "It is unimportant. The benefits outweigh the risks. I will awaken them," he declared.

"Hold on there, Houdini. Don't you think we should talk about this? I mean, do we really need supernatural aid? I think we're doing pretty well on our own."

Amon took my arm and squeezed. A frosty fear that stretched like spiny fingers wove into his conscious mind, a dread that I realized he'd kept hidden from me. I caught only a glimpse of it before it was gone. Though I didn't know the cause, whatever was bothering him was terribly real. "You must trust me," he said as his eyes desperately searched mine.

His grip on my arm actually hurt. "Okay," I said softly. "We'll do it the sun god way."

Letting out a sigh, Amon released my arm and winced when he saw me rub it. Reaching out his hand, he cupped my cheek, then slid his fingers behind my neck, lowering his head to touch mine. "I am sorry I hurt you, Lily. It was not my intention."

"It's fine," I replied.

After a moment, he stepped back, placed the two statues on the ground, and launched into the weaving of his spell.

> Shabti servants, apportioned to me,
> You who molder in corruption,

I summon you from the realm of the dead.

No obstacle shall deter you as you make your way to my side.

Come! Come to the one who calls you forth.

Make arable the fields that sustain me.

Bank the raging floods that threaten me.

Convey the weighty stones that shelter me.

When death seeks me out,

Bear me away on swift wings.

You who were gifted to me by the great god Anubis,

Your duty is to me, and me alone.

Death is not your end for I am your beginning.

When I call you from the east, west, north, or south,

You shall say, "Here am I. Here is your servant."

Come, shabtis, and embrace your master!

When Amon finished, the little statues twitched, dancing in the dust like firecrackers. The violent movements became more and more pronounced and they rose in the air, rotating at blinding speeds.

Amon gestured that I should come to him, so I darted around the statues, giving them a wide berth, and grasped Amon's outstretched hand. The cavernous tomb shook, and I wondered if the trembling of the earth could be felt several levels above us by the visitors to King Tut's tomb.

A burst of dark smoke that sparkled with electric bursts of light wound around the statues, encircling them with thick black threads. Soon, I could no longer see the figurines. The clouds of smoke grew bigger and bigger and then seemed to draw into themselves and solidify into shapes resembling men.

Finally, the dark silhouettes completely formed and standing before us were two men dressed in a similar fashion to Amon when I first found him. The last place the smoke dissipated was around their eyes, and then they each took a breath. When they opened their eyes, smoke still rimmed their irises.

The taller of the two had a short cap of wavy gray hair. His face was kind and open, and he had expressive eyebrows. He immediately adopted a subservient attitude. The shorter one had curly black hair that blended into a full beard. Shifty eyes took in everything around him. It wasn't the fact that he looked like a pirate that made me mistrust him, but the cold, calculating way he stared at us.

Immediately, the two men threw themselves upon the ground and stretched out their arms.

Amon raised his hand and swished his fingers like he had when we first met and couldn't communicate.

He then addressed them. "Shabtis, are you ready to serve?"

"There is nothing else in this realm or any other that would deter us," they replied together.

"Then I have a task for you," Amon said with a satisfied smile.

Canopic Jars

The two shabtis rose from their prostrate positions. The taller one kept his eyes lowered, but the shorter raised his flinty eyes and fixed them upon me, his mouth slowly twisting into a leer that made me very uncomfortable. I took a step closer to Amon and wrapped my hand around his arm. This made the shorter man smile even wider.

"What is thy command, Master?" the taller of the two asked.

Addressing the inquirer, Amon instructed, "You, seek out the resting place of my brother, he who embodies the spirit of the moon god. And you"—Amon turned to the other servant, whose expression was now so full of humility that I doubted my original opinion of him—"find my canopic jars. Also, do not forget to leave a trail that I may follow."

The two men bowed before crossing their arms over their chests. "We live to serve you," they echoed before spinning into cyclones of dark smoke that rushed out of the catacombs in opposite directions.

When they were gone, Amon smiled. "You see? This is exactly the help we need."

"I don't trust the little one," I replied. "He seems devious, like he's planning an assault on us or something."

"Put your worries aside. Shabtis may not ignore the commands of

the one who gives them life. To go against the will of the one who summoned them is the most serious of crimes. If they do so, they condemn
themselves to wander the Mires of Despair alone. Without a guide, they
will be lost in the Caverns of the Dead, never again to experience a
moment of happiness, never again to have their ka reunite with their
body, never again to lay eyes on their loved ones. It is a punishment
worse than death."

"I still don't trust him."

A faint red light appeared, floating like an ethereal mist. It scattered when I ran my hand through it, but then the particles drew back
together to form a loose beam that drifted down one of the dark corridors.

Amon smiled. "There. I told you, he can be trusted. He has left us
a trail. Come, Lily."

I took Amon's outstretched hand and he led me through several
passageways. Very soon, it became obvious to both of us that we were
going in circles. Amon's mood darkened and he tried summoning the
errant shabti to return, with no luck. Despite the warning bells going
off in my mind, Amon attempted to trivialize the shabti's no-show and
reassure me that the servant must have been restrained from coming.
I, however, believed differently.

"Amon?"

"Yes, Lily?" he said as he took my hand to help me down a series of
stone steps.

"Why is it that the shabtis can zoom off in a cloud of smoke and find
your canopic jars and you can't?"

He gave me a sidelong glance. "It would drain my power and then
I would need to replenish it with your energy. I have used too much
already."

"Don't the shabtis draw on your energy?"

Amon shook his head. "They have stores in reserve, and when that
is used up, they will return to where they came from."

"So they're running on batteries?"

"I do not understand 'batteries.'"

"Never mind. It's just that it seems a little cruel to summon them, use them up, and then throw them away. Even if I don't like them very much."

"I do not throw them away. They simply return to the state they were in before. It is the way of things."

"Sometimes it's okay to question the way of things, you know."

Amon grunted noncommittally and then raised his head and inhaled a deep breath. "Something is wrong," he murmured, and his eyes snapped wide open. "Lily, run."

"What?"

"Run!" he shouted as he twisted to look at the top of the steps.

There was no visible end to the stairs, yet Amon rushed down them headlong, pushing me ahead faster than I thought possible. I heard nothing, but Amon seemed sure that something was coming, and I knew it would behoove me to trust him. I rushed down the steps as best I could but frequently lost my footing, sliding on the sand-covered stone.

Amon glanced behind us again, continuing to press me ahead. He followed close on my heels, and then I heard it, a soft gurgle, like running water.

Risking a glance back, I saw a viscous flood making its way down the stairs. Popping and hissing noises filled the cavern and I realized that the color of the fluid was not natural. Whatever it was, it wasn't water. It was much thicker, and its hue was suspiciously similar to that of the shorter shabti's trail of light. When the fluid got close enough to come into contact with Amon's heels, he howled and scooped me into his arms.

Instinctively, I wrapped my arms around his neck, pressing my body against his as he leapt from the steps toward a ledge that was entirely too far for a human to navigate. But just as I feared we'd fall to our deaths, he summoned a wind that blew us the rest of the way.

Amon landed, but the wind, still blowing powerfully, propelled us toward a rocky obstruction. Spinning his body at the last minute, Amon smacked into the cavern wall, taking the brunt of the collision on his side and back and protecting me from the impact.

Still cradling me in his arms, Amon slowly slid down the wall groaning in pain. I ran my hand over his bruised shoulder.

"Is it bad?" I asked.

Amon shook his head. "I will endure it."

Though I didn't ask if he needed energy to heal, he seemed to read my thoughts and touched his glowing fingers to a lock of hair on my cheek. In my peripheral vision I could see the change to my hair's color. For a moment, the lock glowed like Amon's skin. When he let go, it fell to my shoulder, a sparkling blond that faded to a sunshiny gold.

He asked if I was okay and I nodded, but he continued to fix his glowing hazel eyes on me, presumably to discern whether I was being truthful. The palpable heat that always existed between us was intensifying, and I became very aware that I was sitting in Amon's lap, hands wrapped around his neck, my body pressed against his. I had no intention of moving.

Nothing I was doing was even remotely Lilliana-like. *Lilliana* didn't fawn over boys, especially ones who seemed to only want to use her only for her parts, and not even in a normal-boy way. *Lilliana* was not a thrill seeker by any stretch of the imagination. And *Lilliana* definitely did not leap before she looked. It felt like another girl—let's call her Lily—had taken over my body, and her life was so much more exciting than mine. I liked seeing the world through her eyes, but it scared me at the same time. *Lily* survived ancient booby traps. *Lily* simply shrugged when impossible things happened. *Lily* aspired to be in a relationship with a boy who was not only unacceptable but who also came with his own mummy wrappings.

I mean, realistically, what was I expecting here? A sarcophagus built for two?

Still, there was one thing about this new version of myself that I really liked. *Lily* was brave—much, much braver than *Lilliana* had ever been. *Lily* would never let someone else decide her fate. *Lily* took her destiny into her own hands.

Amon held me loosely and cocked his head as he watched me, probably trying to figure out what was going on in my mind. It was confusing for me, which meant it would likely be next to impossible for him to sort through. The thought occurred to me then, that if I, Lilliana Young—no, scratch that, *Lily* Young—was brave enough to risk my life helping a sun god, then I was brave enough to make the first move, despite all the looming questions and unknown future possibilities that came along with it.

Sliding my hands into his gleaming hair, careful not to put pressure on any injuries, I stretched up to kiss Amon. But my lips never made it to his. Opening my eyes, I saw him leaning far away from me with a look of horror on his face.

"Lily, what are you doing?" he asked, though it should have been very obvious.

I stammered, "M-making the first move. I thought maybe you were afraid to."

Gripping my shoulders, Amon held me still as he scrambled away. He moved so quickly, I wouldn't be surprised if he used the wind to help him in his getaway.

Turning his back to me, Amon took a deep breath and said, "You must not continue to pursue this . . . this type of attachment."

"I don't understand. You wanted to kiss me, I could feel it."

Amon's frame stiffened. "You were mistaken," he said, and grimaced as if his shoulder was killing him.

"I don't think so."

"I have no interest in pursuing a relationship with you. The very idea is"—Amon had turned, fixing a steely gaze on me, but then he looked away—"odorous."

"Wait a minute. Are you saying I smell? As in stink?"

He sighed. "That is not what I mean. Can you smell that?"

I rose and took a step closer to the ledge, lifting my nose to sniff the air. I began to cough violently. "What is it?" I asked.

"A side effect, I believe, from the caustic substance on the steps."

We were soon encompassed by clouds of noxious fumes that made our eyes water. I was pretty sure that whatever gas was filling the cavern was eradicating the oxygen as well, since I was having trouble breathing. Either that, or I was allergic to the toxic rejection I'd just received. Maybe it was a combination of the two.

Thankfully, Amon was able to summon a wind to blow the vile vapors away from our little ledge. When we could breathe again, Amon noticed his shoes steaming. When he tried to remove one, he snatched his hand away. The residue had a soft reddish glow. I crouched down next to him and took his hand in mine, examining the burn on his finger.

Taking a water bottle, I poured a good amount over the burn and then used my T-shirt to dry it. An awkwardness had grown between us and I couldn't seem to look Amon in the eye.

He sighed. "Hakenew," he said, and stretched his other hand out to cup my chin. He lifted it and waited for my eyes to meet his. "For seeing to my injury."

"Welcome," I whispered.

"I am sorry to disappoint you, Nehabet," Amon continued. "It is not that I . . ." He paused, then tried again. "If I could explain . . ." Finally, he finished with, "You are not . . . undesirable."

The fact that he was admitting *something* pleased me more than I expected. Before he could do anything to stop me, I pressed my lips against the burn on his finger. "There. All better."

Amon's hazel eyes were fixed on my lips. I drew closer and this time he didn't move away.

I stopped a breath away from his lips. "So much for your not wanting to kiss me. Explanation," I murmured.

Amon blinked, turned his head, and uttered, *"Hehsy wehnsesh ef sah."*

"What does that mean?" I asked.

"'Son of a stunted jackal' would be the closest translation."

"Ah. Someday you'll have to give me a lesson on ancient Egyptian profanity. Hanging out with you, I can see where it might come in handy."

Twitching his fingers, Amon sandblasted whatever substance was coating his shoes until the steaming stopped and he could touch it without getting burned. "We will not talk of this now," he warned.

I stood and put my hands on my hips. "Fine. Just so long as you admit that you know what I know, that you feel."

Amon rolled easily to his feet. "Only a sorceress could speak volumes such as that and still say nothing."

"I'll ignore that for now, seeing as how you have an injury on your finger of such magnitude as to be of great distraction."

Amon narrowed his eyes. "You are indeed a witch."

I gave him a Cheshire-cat smile. "Speaking of magic, what are we going to do about you-know-who, our little stone tormentor?"

"I will send him back from whence he came," Amon declared.

"We're going to have to catch him first."

"Yes."

Amon stood on the edge of our little ledge looking out at the sea of red slime that coated pretty much everything below. He sighed, seeming to come to a decision. "Lily, it is too dangerous to continue our course when the path has been sabotaged."

"I agree."

"The only thing I can think to do is to take us directly to him."

Dusting my hands, I shouldered my bag. "Then let's go."

"But to do so, I must use your energy again. It will weaken you."

"Well, I'll recover, right?"

"Not completely. I have already borrowed your energy several times today. You do not notice the drain unless I use a great deal of power, but I have already depleted your stores significantly."

"By 'not completely,' I'm assuming you mean not today?"

Amon made a face. "The longer we are connected—"

"I know. I know. Risking my innards, blah blah blah," I interrupted.

"So let's do what we need to do to get me a good meal and let me sleep it off. I'll be right as rain tomorrow."

Amon frowned and didn't seem to appreciate my blasé approach to the whole thing, but both of us knew he pretty much didn't have a choice. Narrowing his eyes, Amon took my hand and pulled me close, then placed his hands on my cheeks. His gleaming eyes shone with conviction as he said, "I promise you, Lily, I will fix all of this."

"All of what?" I questioned, wrinkling my nose and enjoying the warmth of his hands as it seeped into my cheeks. Raising his head, Amon cried out in Egyptian, and I screamed in pain as the sand began to swirl around us.

A thousand needles pierced me. This time, as the sandstorm ripped my body apart, I was fairly certain that nothing could put me back together again.

But, as before, I was remade. Knit together with knives. I was sure there was not one part of me that wasn't throbbing. We'd materialized in a dark cave. Amon had doused his light, and I could make out nothing but his eerie glowing eyes.

He whispered, "Can you stand?"

Unable to trust myself to speak without whimpering, I nodded and took a step away from him. His arms trembled as he held me, and I remembered then that he was suffering alongside me. When he was satisfied that I could stand on my own, he said, "Rest here. The errant shabti is in the next cavern." He took my hand and pointed toward the right. "Can you see it?"

My eyes adjusted, and I saw a faint, unsteady light outlining the dark edges of the opening. "Yes."

"Stay hidden behind this boulder. I will return for you when I have completed the spell to send him back to the afterlife."

"Okay." Amon started to move away, but I caught his hand. "Amon?"

"Yes, Lily?"

Standing on tiptoes, I wrapped my arms around his neck. "Be careful."

He put his arms around my waist and squeezed. Some of his energy seeped back into me then, steadying me and keeping nausea at bay. Then he moved away. I could just make out his form as he disappeared through the antechamber opening. My body trembled, feeling the absence of his steadying arms.

Sweat trickled down my temples as I hid, and I wondered if Amon's cooling kiss on my throat had worn off. The idea that I'd soon need another wasn't an unpleasant notion, and I distracted myself from the pain by imagining just how I'd ask him. Just then I heard the sound of pottery breaking and Amon's cry.

I didn't know how to help him, but I knew I needed to try. On shaky legs, I quietly moved to the opening and peered inside. The sounds of a struggle were obvious, though the two men fought in utter darkness. Suddenly, the sound of clashing swords filled the air. I was able to make out a red streak of light circling a dark form, and when the green glow of the form's eyes confirmed it was Amon, I crept closer.

Spotting me with his night vision, Amon called out as he grappled with his enemy, "Save the jars, Lily!"

"Where?" I cried. "Where are they?"

"On the right wall!"

Blindly, I stuck out my hands and carefully made my way to my right until I came in contact with a gritty wall. A swirl of fresh air hit me, and I sensed that we were in a much larger space than I had originally thought. If this was where Amon's jars were, then it was likely that his body had been discovered here as well. Which meant there was an opening somewhere that led aboveground, although it was too dark to make anything out.

I felt my way along the wall. As I progressed, I heard Amon chanting spells, which seemed to be having no effect on the shabti servant. From the sound of things, the servant was stronger than Amon, which made no sense. Amon was powerfully built, even without his sun god attributes, while the shabti was small and round, surely no match for Amon.

Something was very wrong.

I progressed farther and was finally rewarded with a hollowed-out place in the wall, a partially unearthed rough rectangle about one foot wide and two feet high. Stumbling over a mound of dirt, I heard a crack as my boot crushed something tiny and fragile.

"Hope that wasn't a priceless artifact," I murmured as I fumbled in the darkness.

Desperately banishing the thought of hairy spiders and stinging scorpions, I gingerly reached my hand inside the hollow and scooped out handfuls of loose earth until my fingertips brushed against a smooth piece of pottery. Madly, I scooped dirt from around the object, unearthing it from its resting place like a sloppy paleontology student would a bone. Despite my frenzy, I was *trying* to be careful. Finally, it came free in my hands.

By tracing the shape, I was able to visualize the piece. The base was full and round like a bowling pin and tapered up to a neck small enough for me to wrap my hands around but big enough to accommodate something substantial, like—I wrinkled my nose—organs, for example. At the top, capping the object, was a rough-carved piece of wood, rounded with a sharp point.

"I found one!" I called out to Amon. "What should I do?"

I heard a grunt as Amon wrestled with the wiry shabti. "Open it!"

Cradling the jar in my arms, I gripped the top and pulled. It wouldn't budge. "Can't I just crack it against a rock?"

"No! You must not break it!" Amon called, the words rushing out along with his breath as he was slammed against a wall. The fighting stirred up the soft dust, and I sneezed several times. The final sneeze was so violent that as I twisted the top of the jar, it finally loosened.

With a triumphant cry, I wrenched the top from the jar. It made a popping noise, like a cork being pulled from a bottle. Light filled the container, and despite the fact that I definitely didn't want to see Amon's thousand-year-old organs, I peered inside.

Floating particles as tiny as grains of sand moved within and coalesced until they formed a light bright enough that I had to look away. Slowly, the golden light rose up and out of the container, where it stretched until two wings became visible.

The light began to look like some kind of bird, and when the head and beak solidified, it cried out, the same cry I'd heard in my dream. It was a falcon—a beautiful golden creature that gleamed as if it harnessed the rays of the sun.

The wings flapped, and the falcon made of light circled my head and flew higher and higher. Obviously, the room was much larger than I had imagined. As the falcon passed the two men in combat, Amon and the shabti became visible.

Amon had created a sand weapon—a sword—and he used it to cut the servant, but though the shabti staggered back with a wound on his forearm dripping blood, the injury glowed with a reddish hue and then disappeared.

It appeared that the shabti was using the red light to injure Amon, and I realized then that the servant had created two swords made of the red light, which clanged against Amon's smaller weapon again and again. Each volley seemed to weaken Amon, and I couldn't understand why.

The golden bird passed over me as Amon began to chant, weaving a spell that the falcon responded to. His ringing voice echoed off the walls of the cavern.

> I call upon the falcon, born in the golden fires of the sun.
> He who has slumbered is to be reborn this day.
> Lend your whole, living soul to the one rent in pieces.
> Offer your resilient wings, your piercing talons, and your discerning eye.
> Your home has stretched to the far edge of heaven,
> But today, you will find haven in my beating heart.
> Together we are reborn, renewed, and rejuvenated.

Your offering will be recorded in the annals of time and your service rewarded.

Come! Come to me and be remade!

The bird cried, flying toward Amon just as the shabti stripped him of his sword. Amon threw back his head and lifted his arms, and his whole body lit up from within. I could now see everything inside the antechamber and several things immediately became obvious.

First, there were three more rectangles in the wall, lined up in direct proportion to the one I'd found, and the other canopic jars were destroyed. They'd been smashed; their broken pieces littered the ground. Second, the fine powder that had caused me to sneeze repeatedly was not sand, but a shimmery red dust. Third, the shabti now had a clear view of Amon, who, without his sword, arms raised in the air, and head lifted, was defenseless.

As I cried out, the servant rushed forward and plunged both of his red swords into Amon—one in his stomach, the other in his chest. Amon staggered back.

At the exact same moment the golden falcon burst into a billion fragments of light. The glowing particles of the bird were sucked into its body through its eyes and then were gone. Amon slumped to the ground, the gleaming red swords protruding from his torso.

The shabti cried out in triumph as I cried out in horror. He turned to me then, the sickening leer pasted on his face. But he didn't see what I did going on just behind him.

Rising from the floor as if an invisible hand had lifted him, Amon yanked out the offending swords and tossed them aside. He opened his eyes, and in the dark cavern it looked like his hazel orbs were lit with a golden fire. As Amon took a deep breath, his body transformed. Where he had once stood, a large falcon now danced in the red sand. The giant golden creature flapped its wings and let out a screech that sent goose bumps shooting up and down my limbs.

The falcon was the most beautiful and the most deadly-looking creature I'd ever seen. I was mesmerized by it. Rising higher and higher into the air, it circled, keeping an eye on the shabti and me, and then, before I could understand what it was doing, it folded its wings and plummeted toward us.

The shabti shrieked and turned to run, but the falcon was upon him. Wings spread at the last second, its sharp golden talons grabbed the man, squeezing his torso mercilessly as the bird descended to the ground. Its beak snapped, ready to dismember the servant in an instant, but just before it could finish him off, the man screamed and disappeared with a puff of red smoke.

As I cowered in a corner of the catacomb, feeling nauseated, weak, and dizzy, the supersized falcon called out softly as it folded its wings and looked at me. I couldn't help but cry out and move back several paces, though I knew instinctively it meant no harm.

The bird lifted its head, and then its entire body burst into a golden light that coalesced, re-forming into the Egyptian prince I knew so well. Though his body was once again lighting the space, darkness crept in around the edges of my vision. I fell to my hands and knees, stirring up the red powder, which rose in soft puffs around my face. It tasted like a low-burning fire, but it didn't have a scent.

I managed to push myself upright and lifted my hands to examine them. They were coated up to the wrists in red dust. Though the back of my throat burned, I didn't have the energy to cough.

"Amon?" I whispered. "I don't feel so . . ." I pitched forward just as Amon caught me in his arms.

I could feel nothing.

I could hear nothing.

And a moment later, I could see nothing.

Chief Vizier

Images flickered at the edges of my consciousness, and though I tried to grasp them, they faded away before I could figure out what they meant. My body was floating between dream and reality. Gradually, I woke to the sound of voices. The fuzzy images took on focus and the bluish-whitish thing in my vision became an up-close-and-personal view of Amon's shirt.

It was dark. I was lying on a bed or a table of some kind, and as I gradually became more aware of my surroundings, I realized I was staring at canvas. It was the middle of the night, and I was in a tent.

To my horror, I found that I couldn't lift my limbs. I was paralyzed. It was like being buried alive. I started to panic, fear licking my mind and holding on with razor-like claws.

Before I began hyperventilating, assuming I was even able to do that, I focused on what I could do. Voices carried from outside, so I could hear, and my eyes seemed to work again. I attempted to blink, and after one or two tries it worked, though I still couldn't feel anything. It was like my entire body was asleep, so I spent minutes concentrating on making baby steps. First it was wiggling my nose, then my pinky on one hand, then the other.

After what seemed like hours, I was able to move my head to the left. It was a painstaking process of trying to force the inert muscles into obeying my mind, but eventually it worked. At least I had a nice new view. Amon was seated next to me sound asleep, his head resting on his arms, which were folded over the edge of what I now realized was a cot.

I couldn't speak, but at least I was able to look at his handsome face while I slowly regained the use of my limbs. He was wearing the same clothes he'd been wearing when we entered the tomb, and though he'd washed his face and arms, there were clumps of dirt in his hair.

Long lashes fanned out over his bronzed cheeks, and I realized that though there was no denying Amon was a beautiful sun god, I actually preferred him this way—a smear of dirt on his neck, exhausted from a hard day of work, and utterly . . . human.

I didn't even realize I'd been stretching my arm, until my fingers made contact with his hair. Immediately, Amon opened his eyes. "Lily?" he asked, wiping the sleep from them and scooting closer. "Can you hear me?"

As he took my hand, now cleaned of the red powder, I nodded, nearly imperceptibly. He caught the movement.

"Good. Dr. Hassan said you would awaken soon. I will retrieve him."

My throat closed off with my attempt to call him back. I wanted it to be just the two of us for now—I had so many questions—but I had to acknowledge that there would be time for questions later, and honestly, there wasn't much chance of me uttering a syllable, let alone a full question, any time soon.

There was a shuffling of tent flaps and two men came in with Amon. The older of the two set a lantern down on the table next to me and pulled a stool over to my cot, then took off his white fedora and set it on the table.

"There's my girl," he said with a clipped accent, lifting my eyelids to get a better look at my eyes. "I knew you'd be returning to us soon."

I liked his soothing voice. He seemed to be near retirement age, with a full head of white hair. His eyes were shiny brown, like melted chocolate, and his skin was darkly tanned from the sun. When he grinned I noticed he had not one but two dimples. Amon knelt next to him, peppering him with questions, worry obvious on his face. The man nodded sympathetically and answered patiently before turning in my direction.

"My name is Dr. Osahar Hassan, but most of my American friends call me Oscar," he said. Picking up my hand, he patted it and flashed the aforementioned dimples. "I am especially fond of the moniker when used by attractive young ladies such as yourself. Now, let's see how much progress we've made, shall we? Can you try to squeeze my hand?"

I tried, but could barely feel my hand in his, let alone give it a squeeze. Still, he smiled and said, "That's good! Excellent! She is much further along than I'd thought she'd be after the level of toxin she inhaled."

As my mind processed the word *toxin,* Amon nodded worriedly and asked, "How much longer until she is fully recovered?"

Dr. Hassan cupped his chin and stroked it as if he had a beard, a sign he'd probably had one at some time but now was rewarded with the rasping sound of a rough palm against skin that needed a shave. "I would say she should be recovered enough by morning to leave. The two of you are welcome to stay in the tent tonight."

Clasping the man's arm, Amon replied, "Your hospitality shall not be forgotten, Doctor."

With a sly but kind expression, Dr. Hassan hinted, "Perhaps while we wait, we can further discuss your insights on a few things."

"It would be my honor to oblige," Amon answered.

Little alarm bells clanged in my mind, but there was no way for me to warn Amon to zip it. From the small glimpses I'd gotten of the tent, when I wasn't distracted by Amon, I surmised that we were in an archaeologists' camp.

Dr. Hassan was likely not a medical doctor but a doctor of Egyptology. If Amon shared too much or said the wrong thing, Dr. Hassan might figure out that he hadn't been born in this century, and with me in a state of paralysis there wasn't much I could do to prevent them from carting him off for further study or, Egyptian heaven forbid, an autopsy.

Amon seemed attuned to my worried mind and turned to me. Touching my shoulder, he whispered, "We are still in the Valley of the Kings in a tent outside the temple of Hatshepsut." When I formed a mental protest, he added, "Hush, Nehabet, all will be well."

We are anything but well! Everything was wrong, horribly wrong, and now we were facing the enemy to all who were alien and different— scientists. We'd somehow gotten the attention of a person who could potentially be the most dangerous human on earth—a man who could figure out who and what Amon was.

My theory about the nature of the doctor's field of study was confirmed when Dr. Hassan introduced his assistant, Dr. Sebak Dagher. The younger man, who was clean-shaven and wore a colorful head-scarf instead of a hat, seemed friendly enough, but there was something hungry in his expression. Maybe it was just that he was young and had something to prove.

Seeing the two of them together made it official. They were definitely archaeologists. I should've guessed that when I saw the white fedora. Indiana Jones wore a brown one, and probably every archaeologist owned at least one.

The two men chatted amiably with Amon. They hadn't called the Egyptian-tourist version of the police to escort us off the premises, but that made me even more suspicious. Why hadn't they called a real doctor to examine me? Surely there was a first-aid station somewhere in the Valley of the Kings.

But even if there wasn't, they had to have access to a hospital, and yet here I was all decked out like a fallen Egyptian queen, hands placed gently over my chest as I "recovered." The men talked in English, but then switched to the language of the locals, which caused me to constantly strain to understand what they were saying from just the tone of their voices.

The two men seemed fascinated by Amon, but I couldn't sense any hesitation or fear in him, so I eventually stopped trying to understand and just focused on regaining the feeling in my limbs. From time to time Amon reached out and wrapped his fingers around my arm, sending little waves of energy pulsing through my body.

The men didn't notice except to exclaim over my quick progress. Dr. Dagher—which sounded too much like *dagger* for me to free him completely of suspicion—came to my side at one point and explained what had happened. He told me that I'd been the unfortunate victim of an ancient booby trap designed to prevent tomb raiders from taking artifacts.

I wanted to find out what kind of toxin I'd inhaled and why it hadn't been removed yet from a recently excavated tomb. And I really wanted to know, if Amon had been discovered there, why had he been transported to the U.S. so quickly? Why were the canopic jars still there? Why had Amon been moved from his original resting place, and who had done it? But I knew those questions couldn't be brought up to these strangers.

I could tell from Dr. Dagher's shifting eyes that he was keeping secrets. The way he kept looking toward Amon and his mentor, I got the sense that he'd much rather be listening in on their conversation than babysitting a mute American girl.

After leaving us for an hour or so, Drs. Hassan and Dagher returned to my side to check on me. Thankfully, they switched to English when they saw that I was alert.

"How did you come to be in the closed-off section of the temple?" Dr. Hassan asked Amon. "And where did you come in contact with the toxin?"

Amon lied smoothly, but his hand gripped mine so hard that even I could feel it; the muscles in his forearm were rigid. "We were inspecting the tombs closest to the temple when Lily ran her hand over a wall and it came away coated with the dust. Neither of us knew there was any danger. When she began to feel the effects, I carried her through several passages in my haste to escape the tombs, and then we emerged in the temple."

"I see." Dr. Hassan lifted his hat and ran his hand through his thick white hair before repositioning it on top of his head. "You must have emerged from the Anubis upper chapel, then."

"Your observation is likely accurate."

"Then you carried the young miss down to the first court. The one with the columns," he clarified.

"Yes," Amon replied easily.

Dr. Hassan's eyes glinted as he considered Amon, and I knew immediately that he knew Amon was lying.

"You do not believe what I have told you," Amon said.

"No," Dr. Hassan replied with an affable grin. "I was working in the upper terrace when I noticed the red dust footprints coming from the royal family chapel. Since that section is currently closed off and there are no outside passageways leading into it, I must admit that I am hoping you will tell me what really happened."

"I have told you what you need to know."

I flinched inwardly, waiting for the grin to disappear from Dr. Hassan's face. I imagined that in his anger at our uncooperativeness, he would summon the authorities and have us thrown in a dank cell reserved especially for those who disrespected important historical relics. Instead, the Egyptologist, his protégé at his side, sat back and changed the subject.

"The temple you wandered into is arguably one of the most famous monuments in Egypt. It was constructed by a female pharaoh named Hatshepsut. Do you know of her?"

Amon shook his head. "Not specifically. I do not know of any pharaohs who were women."

"There are a few, though it was very rare to have one rule as long as Hatshepsut. She reigned nearly twenty-two years, fostering the arts and erecting beautiful buildings, but after her death other pharaohs tried to erase the signs of her rule. Statues were destroyed and monuments were defaced.

"Many theorize that this was done to discourage people from remembering that Hatshepsut, a female, had led Egypt successfully, but I believe the cult of Seth was responsible for corrupting Hatshepsut's accomplishments."

I could tell that Amon was immediately curious. "Do you have evidence of this?" he asked.

"Yes and no. Most Egyptologists dismiss the idea that there is or was a cult that worshipped the god of chaos, Seth, but they do agree that Hatshepsut had a fascination with lionesses. In fact, the story of her birth has her born in the bed of a lioness."

"What does an affinity for lions have to do with the god of chaos?"

"Ah." The Egyptologist's eyes twinkled. "That is the question, isn't it?" he answered cryptically before continuing, effectively ignoring Amon's query.

"My research indicates that she might have joined a secret faction after a trip to northeast Africa to visit with the king of Punt. She returned bearing many gifts, including ivory, gold, myrrh and frankincense trees, and ebony. But I think there was another reason she visited, and it wasn't political. You see, when she prepared to go home, she was gifted with a pair of female lion cubs, which she raised as pets."

"She was a brave woman, then, but I am afraid I do not understand how this would lead you to conclude anything out of the ordinary," Amon said.

"Quite right. Normally, I would agree. Hatshepsut was certainly not the first or the last Egyptian royal to develop an affinity for a dangerous creature. But I say that there might be more to the story."

"How so?" Amon inquired coolly.

"It is disputed, but I have found signs indicating that Hatshepsut had special ties to the sphinx. We know, for example, that there was once an avenue of sphinxes that lined the path leading to her mortuary temple. Certain records discovered in Africa speak of the lionesses gifted to Hatshepsut, but one of them unmistakably said that 'The Lioness' came from Africa.

"This is in reference to the mysterious leader of a secret group called the Order of the Sphinx, a seldom-talked-about, highly controversial sect that many scholars dismiss as a fairy tale. I think not only that the order did exist, but that Hatshepsut might have been appointed their leader during that trip to visit the king."

Amon rubbed his cheek. "Interesting. Why do you think she was the leader and not simply a member?"

"Well, the sheer number of statues that graced the avenue of sphinxes was an indication of her respect for the creature. Then there's the fact that her temple was once surrounded by myrrh and frankincense trees, a sign that proves just how important that trip to Africa was." Dr. Hassan looked at me. "There is a statue of her as the sphinx in your Metropolitan Museum of Art in New York City."

I sucked in a quick breath. The need to kick Amon and tell him we had to hightail it out of the tent was urgent, but all I could get out was a little moan. Amon squeezed my hand and asked if I was in pain. I shook my head, mentally screaming at him that we were in danger, but if he got my message, he ignored it.

My rational mind told me it was highly unlikely that Dr. Hassan would know anything about where I came from. It was likely a simple coincidence that he'd brought up the Met, but my suspicions were hard to ignore. He seemed to know more about us than we knew about him, and that made me very uncomfortable.

"Please continue, Doctor," Amon encouraged him.

"The statue in the New York museum depicts Hatshepsut as the sphinx—her beautiful face is marked by the ceremonial false beard and headdress symbolizing her might; her body is that of a lioness. She was a powerful and handsome woman. One of the inscriptions in the temple says that 'to look upon her was more beautiful than anything; her splendor and her form were divine. She was a maiden, beautiful and blooming.'"

"Is she now"—Amon hesitated—"under the glass?"

"Ah, you are asking if it would be possible to see her?"

Amon nodded and swallowed. He probably wasn't even sure he wanted to know the answer.

"The answer is that it depends on whom you ask," Dr. Hassan replied. "Her final resting place should have been with her father, Thutmose I, but it is likely she was moved. Most Egyptologists believe that she was found in the tomb of her wet nurse, but I do not. The mummy discovered there is touted as being Hatshepsut, but I have found indications that her final resting place might be in another tomb altogether."

"What are these . . . indications?" Amon asked.

"Well"—Dr. Hassan leaned forward—"I have discovered a signet ring, a shabti figurine bearing her name, and a senet game with carved pieces that have the head of a lioness. The most important piece is one I call the lioness throne—a golden seat with armrests carved in the likeness of a lioness. These were not discovered in the tomb of the wet nurse, Sitre-Re, but elsewhere in the Valley of the Kings. Still, more than these trinkets, I know that her funerary temple was dedicated to Amun-Ra. Though she outwardly worshipped other gods, her temple was a strong sign of her true belief, for at its head—the one I believe you entered through, though you won't confirm that—is the most revered, and that was—"

"The Royal Family Chapel," Dr. Dagher interjected.

"Yes. But that is not its whole name. Its full name, its once secret name, is the Amun and Royal Family Chapel."

Amon sat back. "So the chapel was shared. It was dedicated to the royal family—"

"And Amun, the sun god."

As the Egyptologist continued to explain, I caught the rolling of his protégé's eyes. Clearly, whatever beliefs Dr. Hassan held were not shared by the younger man.

Osahar Hassan either didn't notice Dr. Dagher's expression or didn't care, so fervent was he regarding his theories. "I've already shared with you my belief that Hatshepsut was the leader of the Order of the Sphinx, but what I didn't tell you is that the order is an elite group of sun god worshippers that over the years split into two factions: the Order of the Sphinx, made up of females, and their male counterparts, the chief priests of Amun-Ra, led by a grand vizier." The impassioned man folded his arms across his chest. "So surely you must see that if she was the head of the order, then that would make her a very dangerous enemy—"

"To the cult of Seth," Amon finished.

"Yes. And it would explain why they attempted to wipe her very name from the pages of history." Dr. Hassan sighed. "If Hatshepsut was the head of her order when she ruled Egypt, then it would make sense for her order to move her elsewhere after death so that she might continue to fulfill her duty even in the afterlife."

"And what was her duty?" Amon asked.

Without blinking, the old Egyptologist said, "To be of service to the rising sun god. As head matriarch, Hatshepsut would have taught her order that the sun god would rise to fulfill a specific purpose and that he would require the help of one special woman who embraced the power of the sphinx. The placement of Hatshepsut's belongings was always near glyphs depicting the sign of the sun, the sign of Amun-Ra.

"It is my theory that she arranged her tomb to be in a special location, one that would guarantee that when the sun god rose, she would be the first to welcome him. I have spent my life studying the secret orders and the connection between Hatshepsut and Amun-Ra, and I believe they are more closely tied than we might imagine."

My feverish mind worked on the new information. *So does that mean that Hatshepsut's final resting place was near Amon's original tomb? Or would that have been the tomb where we found his canopic jars?* I hadn't seen any antechambers, but I hadn't been looking for any.

Perhaps the pharaoh queen had found Amon's tomb years ago, but then again, that would all depend on when she lived. I racked my brain, trying to remember the dates of various Egyptian pharaohs, but the best I could come up with was King Tut's approximate reign, the early thirteen hundreds.

I wasn't sure if Hatshepsut came before or after King Tut, but either way, she was probably not even close to being alive when Amon had last risen. His prior awakening would have occurred at the turn of the century, around AD 1000, which meant that he had likely been interred here during her reign, so it was entirely possible she had been aware of his resting place.

"Admittedly, there are not many who interpret the findings in the same way that I do, but then again, sometimes a new perspective can lead to exciting discoveries," Dr. Hassan said. "Would you agree, *Amun*?"

My heart froze. *He pronounced Amon's name perfectly. He knows!*

Somehow, Dr. Hassan knew about Amon! I recognized that it was probably my paranoia causing me to jump to conclusions, but the way my gut was twisting told me that something was very wrong. Even worse, the way Dr. Hassan was studying Amon made me think that he was trying to trap him into giving something away.

"It's Amon," the risen incarnation of the sun god corrected.

"My mistake," the wily archaeologist apologized, with the kind of smile that said he wasn't sorry at all.

Again I wished that Amon could understand why being here was dangerous. Of course, he probably considered himself invincible. Why were men so supremely self-confident, to the point where they lost common sense?

Amon played with my fingers. "That is an interesting theory."

"I believe it to be true. Hatshepsut was a beautiful woman. The Order of the Sphinx only accepted women of great beauty."

Dr. Hassan looked at me with a strange seeking expression, as if I could somehow corroborate his theory. The best I could do was give him a slight shrug and hope that he couldn't read the panic in my eyes.

He continued as if desperate to make us understand. "The mummy they discovered in the tomb of the wet nurse suffered from diabetes. She died of bone cancer, and had arthritis and bad teeth. That mummy is not Hatshepsut. I know it!" he cried fiercely.

Dr. Dagher stepped forward. "You must calm yourself, Osahar. It does no good to get worked up over this. This theory has put you on the outs with the archaeology community. If you want to have your full rights restored, you must at least attempt to accept that their conclusions might be accurate."

Dr. Hassan took a deep breath and gave his mentee a fleeting smile. "Yes, thank you, Sebak." He patted the young man's hand and sighed. "What would I do without your support? Eh?"

Sebak smiled. "I shudder to think what you would do without me." As the younger scientist retreated into the background, I noticed that there was no warmth in his smile.

"I am sorry to burden the two of you with my ideas," Dr. Hassan murmured.

"Without ideas, many discoveries would remain hidden," Amon volunteered. "I, for one, believe there may be some truth to your theory."

Dr. Hassan's melancholy expression suddenly lifted into a smile, and he nodded gratefully.

"Thank you. A woman such as Hatshepsut would have a tomb worthy of her. She would have been buried with her beloved lionesses, would have had a treasure room full of jewelry, furniture, linens, flowers, books. I will continue to look for her." He shrugged. "It is my life's mission. She calls to me across the centuries, and I will not abandon my search." Quiet fell over the tent as Dr. Hassan excused himself.

I desperately wanted to talk to Amon now that we were alone, but my body betrayed me. I was able to move a bit and groan, but Amon pressed his hand to my shoulder and whispered, "I do not believe that this man means us harm."

I wanted to shout that a man desperate for answers might do anything to get them. At the very least I wanted to talk to Amon about his jars of death and what the crushing of them meant, but Amon leaned toward me, bringing his lips to my forehead.

As with the cooling kiss he'd given me in the passageway, a kind of magic spread through my body when his lips came into contact with my skin. But instead of a chilling effect, my eyes and limbs grew heavy once more, and the worries plaguing my mind seemed less important. Before I was lost to Amon's sleeping touch, he said quietly, "Rest now. All will be right in the morning."

It felt like just a moment later when I woke to bright sunlight flashing across my eyelids. Slowly, I blinked my eyes open and noticed the tent opening flapping in the breeze, letting in a strip of sunlight that fell across my face, appearing and then disappearing.

I smelled the crisp air of desert morning mingled with the scent of frying meat, and my mouth watered. Hunger gnawed at my belly, and as I struggled to sit up, testing each joint and muscle as I did so, I wondered if my digestive tract was up to the challenge of a mystery-meat breakfast.

Amon, likely hearing my attempts to sit up, came in to help me. Leaning on his arm, I slowly made my way outside to the breakfast fire, where I accepted a heaping portion of what appeared to be Spam and eggs.

When the food was consumed and Amon seemed assured of my improved health, he began making excuses for us to leave. Dr. Hassan immediately asked his mentee, "Sebak, would you mind letting the group we are meeting at the temple know that we have been slightly delayed this morning?"

"Of course, Osahar."

Dr. Dagher headed over a dune and quickly disappeared. As Amon shouldered my bag and wrapped his arm around my waist to guide me away, I had the sneaking suspicion this would not end well.

I had noticed that my bag was awfully close to Dr. Dagher when we were sitting by the fire and I wondered now if he'd gone through it. I considered how far we'd have to go before Amon could whisk us away by sandstorm, if he even had enough energy to whisk us away at all.

I was lost in questions that I knew I'd have to wait to ask, so I mentally cataloged them, hoping I wouldn't forget anything important. We said our goodbyes, and had begun making our way down the path toward the tourist booths when Dr. Hassan asked his own question, one that caused us to freeze in our tracks.

"How many days has it been since you have risen, Great One?"

PART TWO

Alarmed and frightened murmurs ran through the crowd after King Heru finished his speech. There were shouts that the three princes must be saved, while others raised their voices to say that the sons must be sacrificed. One of the queens sitting on a nearby throne screamed and fell to her knees. The other two clung to her, their sobs spreading to people in the crowd.

The people strained forward against the line of soldiers. Waving their arms, they yelled to be heard over the din, but the three kings heard none of it. Full of sorrow, they stared at their wives and then turned to their sons, who were quietly conferring.

As one, the three young men approached the dais where their fathers stood. Heru's son addressed the crowd in a loud voice, "We three agree to be sacrificed to protect our homeland. With the blessing of our fathers, we will do what the formidable god Seth asks." The people responded with stunned silence for only a few seconds before once again filling the air with questions, cries of protest, and tears.

Heru spoke, putting his hand on his son's shoulder. "I do not ask this of you. Indeed, I would rather die a thousand deaths than live through the death of one I love as much as you. No." Heru turned to the crowd. "I ask you, my people, is it your will that we submit to these demands? Shall we allow the god Seth to strip us of our future?"

Though there were a few frightened people who advocated sacrifice, it was obvious that the majority wanted to save the princes, however steep the cost.

Heru addressed the crowd. "The people have spoken." His wife approached, and he gripped her hand, brushing her tears away while insisting, "We will find another way."

As the queens made their way toward their sons and the families began to confer, the priest Runihura stepped from the curtain's shadows and chanted in a low, menacing voice. Emerging from the curtain behind him was an impressive gathering of priests. Their eyes were black and they moved as one, heads turned toward Runihura. In their hands they clutched wicked daggers, which they raised as they advanced on the royal families.

Women in the crowd screamed as Runihura waved his hands slowly, conjuring a cloud of black smoke around him. His countenance darkened, and angry clouds formed in the brilliant blue sky, covering the sun.

"Fools!" Runihura bellowed with the sound of a thousand drums, leaving a frightening thrum in every heart. Lightning bolts struck the ground near him, and another face obscured the priest's features. "My wrath will be poured out upon you! I offered you a chance to pay homage, but you have turned against me. Be it known that I will take the lives of your young men. You will suffer for the insult you have paid me!"

Runihura thrust his fingers into his eyes and yanked the bloody orbs from their sockets. As the people watched, horrified, he squeezed each eyeball, then opened his hands, a puff of light rising from each palm. The light undulated in the air like a snake, and, with jaws gaping, one arc of light shot toward the son of Nassor, the other toward the son of Khalfani.

The light pierced their foreheads, and the boys cried out as the dark magic lifted them into the air and threw them across the temple. As the kings raced to the sides of their sons, the son of Heru drew his sword and barreled toward the evil priest. The once peaceful and pristine temple became a chaotic mash of clashing swords, screams, and slick blood.

Heru's son raised his sword, but before he struck, he asked, "Why? We worshipped Seth. We did what was asked. Why have you done this?"

Firestorms lit the empty eyes of the priest of Seth, who, with a crocodile smile, said simply, "Chaos. Egypt was once a wild, powerful nation, but I have captured it, domesticated it, and lulled it into complacency. For twenty years, I have tended it and spoiled it. And now I have led tame Egypt to the altar. It is time to throw the fat into the fire, a final sacrifice that will do in your once-great nation, utterly."

The son of Heru could stand to hear no more and plunged his sword into the traitor's chest, but the dying man just clutched the sword and laughed as he collapsed to his knees.

"Runihura was just a vessel," the possessed man uttered. "True, he was a devoted disciple, but"—he paused and gestured to Heru's son to come closer—"others will rise to take his place. Between you and me, young prince, the world as you know it will end. The three of you are the keys and one way or another you will submit and bow your heads beneath my heel." Delighted at the prince's horrified expression, a crazed Runihura began to laugh, but the sound quickly diminished as the man slumped weakly to the temple floor.

Having finished off the other possessed priests, soldiers surrounded Heru's son, who had gotten down on one knee to better hear Runihura. The prince grabbed the evil man's tunic. "What do you mean? How are my brothers and I involved?" he demanded.

Wheezing, Runihura answered, "You will find out for yourself soon enough, I should think." The disciple of Seth touched bloody fingers to his forehead. "I have turned my eye of vengeance upon you," he said in a rasping voice to King Heru, who had finally reached them. "Be warned that I demand the lives not only of your three royal children but of all the young men of Egypt."

The dying priest gathered his remaining strength and spat. Blood and saliva splattered across the king's cheek, spraying his white robes with red.

In a burst of anger, King Heru surged forward and plunged his own dagger in the neck of the priest, whose body finally slumped in death.

Heru's son let the body fall to the ground and was about to stand when he saw a gleaming light in the center of Runihura's forehead, where a third eye would be. Before the king could react, the light shot toward his son like a snake and pierced his forehead. With a brief shriek of agony, he collapsed in his father's arms.

The evil priest was dead, defeated, the cost being the lives of the three young princes, a price more than their families could bear. But Heru was king, which meant he needed to set his suffering aside and try to figure out a way to help his people. Though Runihura was dead, the king was not a fool. He would take the warning about the young men of Egypt seriously.

Everyone, king and soldier, queen and handmaiden, scribe and farmer, dropped to their knees and prayed. They did not, however, pray to the one who had caused the destruction of the young princes. Instead, the queens encouraged the people to seek the aid of the gods they'd long abandoned. And at the dawn of the next day, their prayers were answered.

Sandstorm

Amon stood very still. I'd linked my arm with his and was now digging my fingers into his forearm, deathly afraid for the two of us now that we'd been found out.

"You assume much . . . Grand Vizier," Amon quietly replied.

I sucked in a tremulous breath. I'd suspected there was more to Osahar Hassan than met the eye, and by the lack of response behind us, I knew that the pronouncement was right. Dr. Hassan had a much bigger role to play than that of simple archaeologist.

Glancing up at Amon, I noticed the tightening of his jaw. He still hadn't moved, and I wasn't sure what to do.

"Come, then," Amon demanded.

A desperate shuffling ensued, and a moment later the older man threw himself at Amon's feet. The archaeologist lifted his head, his face filled with wonder.

"I knew it!" Dr. Hassan called out, quickly dropping his gaze in a submissive gesture once again. "None of the others believed in the old stories. But I did not doubt. To have you rise in my generation is . . . it is a blessing beyond hoping for!"

"Is your man Sebak in the order as well?"

"He is, though he joined recently. He will be so happy; they will *all* be so thrilled!"

"Have you shared your knowledge of my identity with him?"

"No, Master. I did not want to say anything until I was sure."

Amon took Dr. Hassan's hand and bid him to stand. "I wish for you to keep this a secret for the time being," Amon said. "Can you do this?"

"Yes, Great One."

"First, you must not address me in such a manner. It is too obvious. Please continue to call me Amon."

"Yes, Mas . . . I mean, Amon."

"Very good." Amon graced the man with a smile, and I couldn't help but marvel at the hero worship Dr. Hassan was displaying. I glanced at Amon; though he seemed to handle his role of a god who walks among men like it was old hat, I could tell that he was uncomfortable. I wondered if he had always felt like that, or if it was somehow different now.

Sebak crested the dune before we could speak further, and Amon took the arm of Dr. Hassan. He whispered, "Where can we meet with you . . . alone?"

Dr. Hassan reached into one of his cargo vest pockets and withdrew a business card, flipping it over so he could write on the back.

"Here." He thrust the card and a set of keys into Amon's hands. "This is my address in the city. I will be there as soon as I can. But please, go and rest there as long as you like. I have no family, so you will not be bothered. Help yourself to anything you need."

Nodding, Amon slipped the card and keys in a pocket, waved at Sebak as if nothing was going on, and took my arm purposefully, quickly guiding me away. When we rounded a mountain of sand, I asked quietly, "How did you know?"

"That he was the grand vizier? I knew it from the moment he approached us in the temple."

"But how?"

"I was unable to control his mind."

"I wasn't aware you were trying."

"Yes. At first I was grateful for his help, but then when I knew you were recovering, I tried to make our escape. He would not hear of it, though I insisted as stridently as I was able."

"So you knew what he was talking about? You understood all that stuff about Hatshepsut?"

"Do you remember when I told you that we once were honored with feasting and song on the day we awoke?"

"Of course. Wait a minute, do you mean these are the guys who do that?" I jerked my thumb over my shoulder, indicating the men we'd left behind.

Amon nodded. "As far as I know, the Order of the Sphinx is new, but the chief priests, including the grand vizier, have been around for centuries. When I was a prince, our royal family had a vizier. His job was to serve the king. When Anubis took my brothers and me, my father charged the vizier with watching over us, or rather, over our tombs, and a vizier has always done so, no matter what century. The vizier has always been immune to mind control. It was a blessing given by Anubis. For what purpose, I know not."

"Then if you knew who *they* were, why didn't you want them to know who *you* are?"

We reached the tourist section as Amon was pondering my question. Not even using his hypno-power, Amon politely asked a man on the street, "Where can we find a taxi?" Not *golden chariot* but *taxi*. Amon was picking up life in the modern world very quickly.

The man pointed toward a small square.

"I have learned to be more careful from watching you," Amon finally answered. "No matter his title, it is not wise to simply trust that a person is honest and forthright. The devious shabti was a surprising example of the need to hide our identity. We must be exceedingly cautious. *Especially* where you are concerned."

"What's that supposed to mean? And while I'm thinking of it, why are we taking a taxi?"

"Though I care little for my own life, I will not risk yours. You say you are recovered, and yet I can sense the trauma I have caused. You need time to heal. Besides, manipulating a driver is far easier than traveling by sand. It was my fault that you were exposed to the toxin in the first place, and I will not test you further today."

"Your fault?"

"When I confronted the shabti, he blew the red dust hoping to disable me, but it did not work. My body cannot be poisoned."

"But mine can."

"Yes. I am sorry, Nehabet. I wrongly assumed your body would be resistant as well since we are tied together, but sadly this was not the case. To err in judgment once regarding the shabti could have been devastating, but to err twice in assuming you were safe shows a lack of clear thinking on my part. Being close to you has . . . distracted me. I assure you that I will make no such mistake again."

"They say to err is human, Amon. A mistake or two just means you're like us mortals."

Amon looked away. "The desire of my heart is for that to be true, but alas, it is not. I am not like a mortal man, Lily, however I wish it to be the case." Turning to me, he lifted his fingers and grazed my cheek. "Please believe I would not have put you in harm's way had I known."

"It's okay. I believe you."

Sighing deeply, Amon grasped my hand. Sensing the blame he was feeling, I tried to distract him. "Thank you, by the way, for saving me. I know it was you who kept me going. I fell asleep faster than Dorothy in the poppy fields."

"The toxin was not a simple sleeping potion," Amon corrected. "A little shuts down your body as if you are in a deep sleep, one that closely resembles death. If you breathe it in too deeply, are exposed to it for a lengthy time, or it seeps through a cut in your skin, it can kill you."

"Are you sure?"

"Yes. I had to suck the poison from your body and take it into my own. I suspect this is one reason Dr. Hassan assumed I was more than a mere mortal. He knew what the toxin was, and was very careful not to come into contact with it. He used gloves to wipe it away from your skin, and then he disposed of the gloves. When he wasn't looking I was able to remove the residual traces from your hair and clothing."

"He knew? But he said—"

"That you would awaken."

"Was he confident that I hadn't inhaled too much, or did his trust reside in you?"

"Perhaps it was a combination of both."

"So he risked not sending me to the hospital to test his theory that you were going to save my life?"

"It would seem so."

"He's a zealot, all right," I murmured as a taxi pulled up. "Lucky for me his theory panned out." Amon passed the driver Dr. Hassan's card and spoke to him briefly before finally settling back next to me.

"What was that about?"

"Just gleaning some useful information." He turned to look directly in my eyes. "My intention is for you to relax for the remainder of the day."

"Um, okay. And what exactly did you have in mind?" I asked.

Amon frowned. "I think it would be best to hire some women to tend to your bathing."

Shrugging, I picked up his hand and stroked the back of it. "Too bad. It would be fun to be waited on by my own personal sun god."

Amon's eyes narrowed as he gently pulled his hand from my grip. "I am not a sun god, I am a—"

"I know, I know. Would it kill you to humor me once in a while?" I sighed. "A bath does sound good but I assure you, I'm completely capable of bathing sans servants. Sorry you have to be in such close proximity to my odorous self."

He was quiet for a moment and I thought he'd drifted off, but then, in a soft voice, he said, "The truth is, if I could bottle your water-lily scent and carry it with me as I wandered the desert, even if I was sick from the sun and dying from thirst, only to be saved by a desert sheikh who wished to barter for it, and even should the trading of it save my life, I would not part with it for all the jewels, silks, and precious riches of Egypt and all the lands surrounding it. So to say your scent is pleasant to me is an understatement most villainous."

The emotions I sensed coming from him were confusing. Regret mixed with a deep-seated yearning was paired with frustration. I couldn't even form a response to a statement as touching as his. Men didn't talk like that. Not real, flesh-and-blood men, anyway.

What he'd just said to me was swashbuckling-guy-gets-the-girl, ride-off-into-the-sunset-together level of charm. I didn't think it was possible for him to actually mean what he said.

"Where'd you get that one? Off the inside of a sarcophagus?"

Amon shrugged but wouldn't look at me. "Those feelings are the truth," he finally admitted.

I studied his face, but there was not even a hint of humor in his expression.

"Oh," I said lamely. "Well, thank you."

Amon grunted, leaning back against the seat as he closed his eyes. Before too long the driver pulled over and pointed to a nice stucco house. We got out, and Amon's fingers clung to mine as he leaned in the window to talk with the taxi driver. Because Amon seemed to be taking his time conversing, I wriggled my fingers out of his and pried the keys from his other hand. He gave me a brief look that said *Don't wander too far* and turned back to his conversation.

I walked up the short drive to the house, grateful for the trees shading the path. The large sycamores provided a respite not only from the heat but also from the glare of the sun. Osahar Hassan's home was a small two-story, each floor with an overhang of interlocking red tiles.

Finding the right key, I unlocked the door and stepped inside. Despite the many large windows, the sun wasn't too intense, so the house wasn't too hot. Upon closer inspection, I saw that the windows were covered with a dark film that probably deflected the sun's rays.

Though the outside of the home appeared clean and pristine, all boxy lines and sun-swept tile, the interior was completely different. Every surface was cluttered with Egyptian treasures, from crackling parchment covered in colorful brushstrokes to large carvings. The knickknacks and collectibles were scattered haphazardly, with no design aesthetic whatsoever, and most of them needed a serious dusting. I wasn't able to tell if they were replicas or the real thing, but I suspected that a man given the responsibility of grand vizier over a centuries-old group of priests might have access to things others did not.

I was crouching, studying a gorgeous cat statue, when Amon came up behind me. He hadn't made any noise, but by now I was so attuned to him, I could feel his presence. I sensed his warmth as if the sun were at my back. Amon knelt next to me and ran a hand over the head of the cat. "Cats are revered in Egypt," he said. "Some were even trained to go on the hunt with their masters, capturing birds or fish. When a beloved feline died, the owners typically shaved their eyebrows in mourning."

"Interesting," I murmured, now more focused on the man beside me than on the statue.

"Yes. When the eyebrows grew back, the time of mourning was considered over."

"So seeing as how you are a bird now, are you a cat lover or a cat hater?" I asked, standing up at the same time as Amon.

"I am neither, I suppose."

Boldly, I reached up to trace one of his eyebrows. "Have you ever loved something enough to shave your brows in mourning?"

Amon captured my wrist and, gently lowering my arm, replied softly, "To come to love something that much would seem a cruel twist of fate for one who spends much of his existence in the Land of the Dead."

"I guess that would be true." Uncomfortable, I stood and walked the length of the shelf as if examining the artifacts, when instead I was contemplating Amon's very strange life. "Where do you go?" I asked quietly. "When you aren't here on Earth, I mean?"

Amon sighed. "It is best not to speak of it, Lily."

"But I need to understand. I need to know why you make all these sacrifices. I need to know if you're—"

"If I am what?"

"If you're *happy* there."

Rubbing his hand through his hair and cupping the back of his neck, Amon answered, "I am not . . . *unhappy*."

"That's pretty vague."

"The explanation is difficult."

"Please try."

After thinking for a moment, Amon began. "When my everlasting body becomes a . . . mummy, my ka, or soul, departs and must walk the path of the afterlife. My heart is not weighed on the scales of judgment like those who have gone before me because my stay in the afterlife is not permanent. Not yet. Though it is lonely, I drift through the centuries in relative comfort."

"What do you mean, 'relative'?"

"I am allowed to spend time with my brothers, but because we are bound to the service of Egypt, we are not given leave to retrieve our bodies and reunite with our loved ones. Instead, we pass the years acting as guardians to the gates of the afterlife."

"So there isn't an Egyptian version of heaven you go to?"

"I do not understand 'heaven.'"

"Like a paradise—a place where you can kick your feet up and relax and enjoy your death?"

"No. Not for my brothers and me. Perhaps, one day, when our work is completed, we might be able to rest from our labors."

"You sure got the short end of the stick when they were handing out pseudo-Egyptian-god duties. Isn't there any room for love in Egyptian heaven?"

"I love my brothers."

"That isn't the kind I'm talking about."

Amon remained quiet for a moment, and I wondered if he was even going to answer me, when he picked up a small carving and twisted it between his hands. "Do you know the story of Geb and Nut?" he asked.

"No."

"Geb was god of Earth and Nut was goddess of the sky. Rough and thick-muscled, Geb was immovable and steady, like Earth itself. Nut was lithe and beautiful. Stars and constellations adorned her skin, and her hair floated about her form.

"When they saw one another, they fell deeply in love, and Geb was determined that they be together. Nut whispered her vows and sent them to Geb on the tails of comets. In reply, Geb stretched out his arms as far as they would go and finally grasped her fingers. Using his powerful form, Geb called upon Earth's gravity, and slowly, the two came together, though they knew their love was forbidden."

"Why was it forbidden?"

"That part comes later. Though I know you have as many questions as the stars, try to content yourself to listen till the end."

I smirked. "You know me so well."

"Yes. I do."

"I'll try. But I make no promises."

Amon nodded, hazel eyes twinkling, and continued. "Once they were able to touch, they remained as close as any two things could be. Geb wrapped his arms around the willowy form of his secret wife and drew her to him. When he raised his knees, mountains formed, and Nut ringed them with the clouds of her dress.

"Geb lifted himself up on one elbow, and Nut rested her head against his chest, creating fog-shrouded hills and valleys. When they laughed, the land trembled and the sky thundered. They fit together so tightly, in fact, it soon became obvious that there was no room for mankind. To make a place for humans, Nut's father, Shu, god of the air, was sent to separate the couple."

"What happened?"

"Chaos. The two clung to one another, but Shu was powerful and drove them apart bit by bit. He sent cyclones and whirlwinds between them. The Earth shook and the heavens quaked and then, finally, it was done. Nut was wrenched from Geb's heavy arms. Geb could see his wife floating far above him, but he could no longer touch her.

"Nut cried bitterly, and her tears turned into storms and heavy rains that fell upon the flesh of her husband. Pooling in the recesses of his body, the salty tears became oceans, rivers, and lakes. The waves blanketed the man she loved, but he relished having even that little piece of her and willingly allowed a portion of himself to sink beneath them forever.

"This is why water in Egypt is considered the source of chaos as well as creation—chaos because it is a sign of a love destroyed, and creation because it was the symbol of the beginning of mankind's reign on Earth. Water unmakes and then creates anew."

"Were they never able to touch again?"

"Over the aeons, Shu's heart softened toward the couple, and they were allowed to touch at the four points of the compass. In the south and the west, their feet brush against one another, and in the north and the east, they thread their fingers together. But other than that, they are never to be together again. If they were, it would mean the destruction of life as we know it."

"I don't believe that."

Amon shrugged. "It is a story shared by my people."

"No, I don't mean that. I mean that I don't believe that doing your job, fulfilling your purpose in life, means there is no hope for happiness. No one, no god, could be that cruel."

Amon set down the little statue, which I now recognized as the god of Earth, Geb, beneath his wife, Nut, who rose above him. The space between their bodies was wide and cold. "Sacrifices must be made so that others may find happiness," Amon replied quietly.

Taking a step toward him, I reached up to brush my hand against his cheek. "But you deserve to have that kind of joy in your life, too."

Amon wrapped his fingers around my hand and drew it to his lips, pressing a warm kiss against my wrist. "There are many men who do not attain the things they want while in their mortal existence, many who do not get the things they deserve. Who am I to count myself as more worthy than they? If I reached out to grab the happiness you speak of, how many would suffer as a result? How many would die? How many would dwindle in pain and agony? I cannot be that selfish, Lily, no matter how much I might want to."

Amon's eyes, more tawny now than green, bored into mine as if begging me to understand. He wanted me to accept his ancient notions of duty and obligation and let it go, but I was a modern girl, which meant I wasn't going to sit like a princess who needed saving and pine for something I wanted. If there was one thing I knew about love, it was that it was worth fighting for, even if I had to pick up a sword to protect it. The miracle of finding love, real love, was a rare enough thing that it should give duty and obligation a run for their money.

Frustrated, I wrenched my hand from Amon's. "I don't get it. I mean, Geb and Nut, okay. Their being together physically crushes everybody, so I guess they can't be together, but you? What are they going to do? Fire you? Maybe that's a good thing. Maybe it's time someone else did the saving-mankind thing for a while. You served long enough. It's time to jump off the mummy train and live for a change, don't you think?"

"Lily, I—".

"Just . . . think about it. I'm going to take a quick shower, and then maybe we can get some food. We'll feast?"

"Of course, Lily," Amon replied.

As I climbed the stairs, I felt the stress of the past few days flood over me. I did need to relax. I was wiped out. The fact that I was getting so emotional again was a sign that I was not feeling like myself, which had been true from the moment I first met Amon, but right then, I felt even worse.

To my delight, I found perfumed oil in the bathroom. When I rubbed it into my skin, the smell of soft flowers and sweet musk surrounded me. The scent was exotic, with a hint of citrus, delicate and subtle, an aroma far preferable to the sweat and dust I'd gotten used to. While wiping steam from the mirror after my shower, I thought about Amon.

He had become important to me. At first, it had been a mixture of curiosity and fascination that led me to follow him on his adventure, but now that I'd spent more time with him, I realized it wasn't just fascination. I wasn't doing all of this for the adventure or the thrills anymore. I cared about him.

As crazy as it was, I was falling for a guy as old as the desert. One who could turn into a falcon at will. A man who could twist sand into any form he chose. A handsome stranger who had seemingly zero interest in love and who put his own needs after everyone else's.

I identified with that. How many times had I gone along with what my parents wanted even though I had no interest in whatever they were doing? How many empty relationships had I fostered with people who didn't care a whit about me? How much longer was I going to deny myself what I really wanted?

I found Amon sitting listlessly at the kitchen table, an empty plate before him. Surrounding him were mountains of takeout containers. The spicy fragrance of meat and vegetables wafted toward me, but I had eyes only for the man with his elbows on the table, hands holding up his head.

Walking up behind him, I touched his shoulder. "What is it?" I asked. "Not hungry?"

Amon covered my hand with his and pulled me around to sit next to him. "How do you feel?" he asked. "Are you refreshed?"

"Yes," I lied, giving him my best smile.

Cupping my chin, Amon studied my face. "Your skin is pallid and overly warm and you've lost flesh."

"All the girls will want to try the new Egyptian god diet when I get home. 'You can feast all you want as long as you're willing to be an organ donor.'" I laughed lamely at my own joke, but Amon didn't even crack a smile.

He let me go and pressed his head between his hands again.

"What's all this about?" I asked. "Was it the fight with the shabti? Are you still feeling weak?"

"The golden falcon strengthened me, Young Lily. It is not my health you should be concerned with."

"Then is this because of the other jars? They were all broken, weren't they?"

"Yes."

"Okay, so then what's the next step?"

"There is no next step."

"Well, we can still find your brothers, right? Everything will be okay, you'll see. Even without all your powers, I'm sure you can do what you need to."

"No, Lily, you do not understand. Without my jars, I will continue to drain your energy."

"So we'll move faster. You got one jar back, at least. That's something. We'll get your brothers as quickly as we can. You can't give up hope."

"Hope," Amon scoffed. "Hope for whom? For what?"

"Hope for a better tomorrow, for both of us. It's not over till it's over. Don't assume this can't be fixed. Let's just focus on one thing at a time. We now know that your jars are gone, so let's worry about your brothers next."

"My brothers. Perhaps," Amon murmured. "Perhaps my brothers *can* help. One of them *is* a healer."

"See? There you go. You're thinking of other possibilities already."

"The greatest possibility is that I will be the death of you, Young Lily. It would have been better for you had we never met."

"Hey." I scooted my chair a little closer to his. "It's hard to kill a scrappy New Yorker. Didn't anyone ever tell you that? Besides, if I'd never met you, my life would have been incredibly boring."

"Better boring than succumbing to everlasting sleep."

"You sure have a way with words. Everlasting sleep actually sounds pretty good right now."

"Yes. You should rest. Sleep, Lily. I will awaken you when Dr. Hassan returns."

"I'll make a deal with you. I will sleep as long as you feast. All this food and you haven't touched it, have you?"

"When you are ailing I find I have no appetite."

"Well, even demigods need sustenance, so eat up. I expect all this to be at least half gone when I return."

"Very well, Lily. I agree to your terms. I will eat if you will rest."

"Good. Unless, of course, there's a chance you want to rest together?" Amon raised an eyebrow, indicating such an idea wasn't even worth considering. "Ah, well, a girl can try." I sighed.

"Sleep well, Nehabet."

"And you eat well, Amon."

I woke to the feel of his fingers brushing hair from my face.

"Amon?"

"I am here, Lily. Dr. Hassan has come home."

The room was dark. "Did I really sleep that long?"

"Your body needed to rest."

Sitting up, I caught a whiff of soap. Amon's hair was wet and he wore new clothes. More than anything, I wanted to wrap my arms around him, press my lips against his neck, and let his wet hair tickle my cheek, but I knew he wanted to maintain his distance. And even though I fully understood his reasoning, I wasn't happy about it. I whipped the covers back and took his hand. "Let's go see him."

Amon led me to the roof, where we found Dr. Hassan sipping an icy-cold beverage by lantern light. Upon seeing me, he immediately set down his drink.

"There you are, my dear." Spreading his hands, he indicated the expansive rooftop. "What do you think? My own private temple."

"You're missing the pillars," I answered drily.

"On the contrary. I am charged with the care of the celestial embodiments of the gods. What better way to worship than by creating an outdoor sanctum without a roof so that I might perform my observances directly beneath the sun, moon, and stars? It's quite beautiful, is it not?"

I had to admit that the night sky was breathtaking. It was easy to see how ancient people could wish to find direction and inspiration from the constellations twinkling overhead.

Dr. Hassan interrupted my thoughts. "Are you quite recovered, young miss?"

"For the most part. But I hear that's pretty much no thanks to you," I added, still suspicious and wanting to put him in his place for allowing his zealousness to trump common sense.

Dr. Hassan had the decency to look chagrined. "Yes. Well. I was supremely confident."

"You risked my life on a theory."

"But my theory was correct."

"I could have died."

"You would have been dead already," Dr. Hassan professed bluntly.

"What? What do you mean?" I asked, shocked.

Leaning forward, Dr. Hassan clasped his hands and indicated to a chair. "Please. Sit."

Once Amon and I were settled and Dr. Hassan had set a tray of cold beverages before us, I gave myself a moment to assess him again. I was determined to proceed with caution in trusting him. Though Amon could do many things on his own, I knew that he was also relying on my modern-world smarts, and I didn't want to let him down.

The air was warm, but the slight breeze carrying the scent of desert rain and night-blooming flowers kept me cool enough that I wasn't uncomfortable, even with Amon's warm arm draped across my shoulders—I wasn't sure if his touch was meant in a romantic way or to comfort me or to just keep tabs on my health, but I'd take it, regardless of the reason. If Dr. Hassan hadn't been there and our situation hadn't been urgent, I would've enjoyed having a romantic dinner date on the roof. As it was, I needed to focus on other matters.

"Why don't you start by telling us how you found us," I suggested to Dr. Hassan.

"When Dr. Dagher and I came across you, to say we were shocked would be a bit of an understatement. The Great One"—Amon gave Dr. Hassan a look and he changed his word choice midsentence—"Amon," he said, and I could tell from his expression that saying the name sat wrong with him. "Amon was covered in the dust and yet remained unaffected. His lips were pressed against your neck, a death sentence, since the toxin covered your skin in multiple areas. I knew what it was immediately. The form of dust you came across hasn't been used for centuries, but there are records of it. That you happened upon it in the Valley of the Kings was incredible to say the least."

"It sounds like you were more interested in the discovery of the red dust than in getting us the care we needed," I said.

"Of course I was interested in it. I *am* an archaeologist. As far as the help you needed, I already knew you were beyond it. I determined that if you weren't dead already, you would be in mere moments. But then you kept breathing, and Amon finally acknowledged our presence. He was aware of us, though he was completely wrapped up in caring for you.

"I approached the two of you, and since I was no longer holding him back, Dr. Dagher rushed forward and accused Amon of defacing the temple and bringing the substance in with him. I believe Dr. Dagher thought you were drug-crazed. But I have had access to things, to stories, to information that he hasn't, and so I knew right away about the problem you were dealing with. I will admit that I selfishly kept you in my tent. I could not let Amon leave. Not when I knew, absolutely knew, what . . . *who* he was."

Dr. Hassan glanced at Amon. "The others never believed me, but I had a vision as a young man that I would one day witness your rising. I am the most fortunate of men!" he cried out, the fanatical gleam in his eyes relit.

"Yes. We get it," I said. "But let's get back to what happened next and save the worshipping for a more convenient time, shall we? Now, if I understand correctly, you next manipulated Amon into thinking that you were helping him. Is that right?"

"I *was*. I mean, I am," Dr. Hassan insisted, and then added, "I mean, I will be."

"I should think so." I narrowed my eyes.

"Of course. My entire existence, all of my work, all of my studies, have been focused on this one purpose."

I stared at the good doctor for a few uncomfortable minutes. He looked right back at me, his face open and innocent. "Fine," I finally announced. "I'm willing to forgive your duplicity as long as you help us."

"You may ask anything."

"Understand that we expect your complete honesty from this time forward. No more manipulation to further your own agenda. Amon's purpose must remain the priority."

"Yes, yes. Of course."

"Okay, so tell us all you know, starting with how Amon ended up in New York."

"Very well. But you must understand that I have made vows not to share this information with anyone outside of our order."

"Trust me, I'm in this one for the long haul."

It irritated me when Dr. Hassan looked to Amon for approval, but Amon smoothed things over by stroking my arm and assuring him, "Lily has given up more for me than any priest or devotee ever could.

Our connection is unbreakable. Palm to palm, we risk together, we live together, or we die together. Be satisfied that any knowledge or secrets you choose to share will be safe with her."

Turning, I looked up at Amon's face, but his gaze was trained on his servant, who, after removing his hat, immediately knelt at my feet. "Then I would follow every word that is uttered by your lips as well, my lady."

"Just Lily," I offered, embarrassed that this man would kneel before me. "Please, just . . ." I sighed. "Just help us."

"I will endeavor to do so, Lady Lily." Dr. Hassan settled back into his seat and adjusted the brim of his hat before he settled it on his head again. His tone was all business. "I do not know how Amon came to be in New York. That is to say, I knew that he had been moved, but I did not know *where* he had been moved."

"You're talking about his original tomb, under Tutankhamun's treasure room?"

Dr. Hassan blinked, obviously surprised. "You found this?"

"Yes, that's where Amon raised the shabtis."

"How fascinating! You must tell me of this."

"We will . . . later. First, you were saying he'd been moved?"

"Yes. I was aware of his location and had been caring for his tomb for quite some time. One day, I entered and felt the warmth of his presence missing."

"Interesting. So he's warm even when dead?"

"Not all people are sensitive to it. Apparently, you are one of the exceptions."

"As are you. Go on."

"So, I entered the tomb—this was approximately six months ago—and I sensed a change. The tomb had been disturbed. Though it was forbidden, I pried open the sarcophagus lid with a crowbar. Amon was gone."

Amon leaned forward. "Why didn't they take the sarcophagus?"

"Presumably, they wanted to remain undiscovered." Dr. Hassan

directed his next comment to me. "You must understand. Only someone using the darkest of magic could have even entered the tomb. It had
been protected, the sarcophagus sealed. I had done a sealing spell on
the entrance so that only I could access the tomb. If another archaeologist had stumbled across it, then I would have been instantly alerted.
The spell was designed to repel the curious and destroy those with evil
intent."

"So you cursed his tomb," I clarified.

"Essentially, yes."

"Then why could Amon and I get in without a problem?"

"The curse would no longer apply if the object being protected was
removed," Amon explained.

"I do not understand how anyone could get past it," Dr. Hassan said.
"I included all the standard spell variations: disease, death, the offend-
er's name being stricken from history, and, of course, that it would
affect seven times seven generations of his offspring."

"The thought occurs to me," Amon said, "that someone who was
not threatened by physical death might have bypassed your curse."

"That's true," I said. "And if he had no children . . ."

"And no body to get a disease . . . ," Amon added.

"Then he could enter the tomb with little risk," Dr. Hassan finished.

"And sending me to New York would make my accomplishing the
ceremony difficult, if not impossible, and yet no harm would come to
my body," Amon said. "Even should my remains be destroyed, it is possible for me to re-create my form, even if it had returned to the dust."

Dr. Hassan sat back. "But who has the power and the motive to try
to stop you?"

"I can only assume it would be him whom we were attempting to
thwart."

"You don't mean—"

"The god of chaos. Seth."

"You mean the one who caused all the trouble in the first place?"
I asked.

"Yes. It is possible he has gained a foothold in the world again," Amon said. "He used priests once before. Perhaps he has done so again."

"Priests?" Dr. Hassan echoed skeptically. "I doubt it. Our sect is above reproach. We choose our novices very carefully."

"As you said, there is more than one group now. Perhaps the Order of the Sphinx?"

Dr. Hassan shook his head. "No. That order is extinct. There hasn't been a matriarch since the time of Hatshepsut."

"I see." Amon rubbed his jaw. "Still, there is the matter of the shabti."

"Yes." I turned to Dr. Hassan to explain. "Amon raised two of them who had been placed above the entrance to the tomb. Neither of them has returned to us, and one of them definitely tried to kill us."

"Is this possible?" Dr. Hassan asked incredulously.

"That's how we got covered in the red toxin," I stated flatly.

"In theory, they must obey the one who raised them. They should have been subject to me," Amon said.

"This can mean only one thing," Dr. Hassan said.

"What's that?" I asked.

"You didn't raise them."

I stared. "Can the priests in your sect raise shabtis?"

"No. It is beyond our power."

"Then someone else, someone more powerful, is trying to stop Amon," I said.

"It would appear so," the Egyptologist answered.

"I do not understand why Anubis would lead us falsely in that manner," Amon said. "If the shabtis were impure, why, then, did they give us the funerary cone?" None of us had an answer for that.

As I sipped my drink, deep in thought, Amon turned to Dr. Hassan. "Doctor, did you hide my canopic jars?"

"I did. Forgive me, Amon, but when I discovered you were missing, I wanted to take no chances, so I hid them in an empty tomb. I will take you to them the instant you are ready."

"It is too late," Amon said sadly. "We were able to retrieve only one. The shabti crushed the others."

"But he would not be able to find them unless—"

"Unless his master ordered him to," Amon finished.

"Ah, I see. This is very unfortunate."

"That doesn't make sense. Why would they ship Amon off to the States and leave his jars behind?" I asked. "And if they left his sarcophagus here, why did the coffin in the museum look like Amon?"

"Ah, that I can speculate on," Dr. Hassan said. "Each time Amon sleeps, a new sarcophagus is made. Perhaps they hid him in the place I'd be least likely to look. I wouldn't think of looking in one of the old ones."

"They likely knew that without my jars, my powers would wane quickly," Amon explained. "And being an ocean away from Egypt would make completing the ceremony very difficult."

"Okay, but then they could still take the canopic jars and hide them somewhere else."

"It is unlikely since I hid them many years ago, prior to Amon being taken," Dr. Hassan said. "I always thought it was foresight on my part, but perhaps there were other forces at work lending me inspiration."

"Doctor? Where are my brothers?" Amon asked.

"Ah, yes. After you went missing, I had them both moved. The incarnation of the god of the stars is hidden in an underground cavern at the Oasis of the Sacred Stones. Do you know this place?"

Amon nodded.

"Very good. As for the embodiment of the god of the moon, he will be found in—"

A sudden wind whipped Dr. Hassan's hat from his head. After excusing himself to retrieve it, he turned back to us and stopped cold, staring over our heads into the distance. The whistle of the wind became sharper and stronger and Amon pulled me close, wrapping his arm protectively around me.

"What is it, Doctor?" he cried over the noise of the wind. We stood up and turned to look in the direction Dr. Hassan was staring. In the distance the stars disappeared one by one as something dark and sinister began to fill the horizon.

Amon gripped my arm tightly as the cushions whipped up and flew across the rooftop, a few of them fluttering over the railing and tumbling away far below.

"Amon?" I called out, worried.

"It's a sandstorm!" Dr. Hassan shouted. "We must get inside immediately!"

I turned to follow him, but Amon stood rigidly in place. "This is no sandstorm. The Dark One has found us."

Oasis of the Sacred Stones

Sharp bits of sand stung my skin as the storm grew closer.

"Go inside with Dr. Hassan!" Amon shouted. "I will attempt to draw the storm."

I shook my head vehemently. "It's too dangerous!"

"I will return for you. You will be safe here, Lily!"

Amon's eyes burned brightly. Pressing his hands together, he thrust out his arms, a burst of light emanating from his frame. The great golden falcon materialized where Amon had just been standing, and he lowered his head toward me. As he soared into the sky, I tried to see which direction he went, but the bird was soon swallowed by the dark swirling sand.

Despite Amon's warning, I stayed outside watching for him, hoping he would return quickly, or that, at the very least, our bond would assure me of his safety. But in a matter of moments, the entire house was swallowed in darkness, the sand even more brutal as it whipped across my skin. I shielded my eyes and had just decided to give up, since seeing even a few inches in front of me was no longer possible, when something clamped down on my arm.

I cried out in pain and glanced down. Tremendous force was crushing my forearm, bruising the muscles, grinding against my bone, ripping into me, but nothing was there. Suddenly, the pressure lifted and a crescent-shaped puncture appeared on both sides of my left arm. It looked as if a large creature had sunk its teeth into me.

Tears filled my eyes as blood welled in the wound and began running down my arm in little rivulets. The blood branched down to my elbow, dripping from there onto the roof. I stood still, shocked, my arm throbbing, when the invisible creature bit me again, this time on my leg.

The soft pants I'd dressed in ripped at the knee, flapping in the wind as jagged claw marks and scratches appeared on my calf. Dr. Hassan grabbed me as I staggered, and pulled me into the house. I sank into a chair as he doused all the lights, running from door to door and window to window, locking them and drawing the curtains, as if doing so would keep the storm, and whatever was attacking me, at bay.

He returned with ointment and several kitchen towels. Kneeling beside me, he dabbed at my wounds. Whatever elixir he used stung, and I clenched my teeth. "What was that? Did you see what bit me?" I asked.

"It is an omen," Dr. Hassan whispered gravely. "A very bad sign."

"An omen? An omen of what?"

"The Dark One rising."

"The bad guy? Seth?"

"No. If the god of chaos had risen, then the world would already be beneath his boot heel. This is merely a sign of his coming."

Sucking in a breath, I wrapped a clean towel carefully around my wounded arm. "This doesn't feel like 'merely.'"

"No, it doesn't."

I gasped as claws scrabbled and several large objects thumped heavily on the rooftop deck. Monstrous hissing and the sound of something trying to break down the door provoked me to peek through the curtains. Though I could hear the hefty creatures prowling on the deck, I could see nothing. Dr. Hassan's hands shook as he retrieved a first-aid kit and asked me to sit again.

"Does this kind of thing happen every time Amon rises?"

"No. This rising is . . . unique, in more ways than one."

A deck chair hit the door with a resounding boom and I cried out, but Dr. Hassan remained rooted in place.

"What if whatever it is gets in?" I demanded. "Aren't you frightened?"

"They cannot enter my home. It has been blessed," he stated, sounding like he was trying to convince himself as much as me.

"Blessed, cursed, it doesn't seem to make much difference to the bad guys. You grand vizier types rely a bit too much on your spells, don't you think? Common sense tells me we should vacate the premises. Preferably in a fast car."

"No!" Dr. Hassan paled. "You would be ripped to shreds should you venture outside at this time. We are safe in the house."

"Well, that's great for us, but what about innocent bystanders? Aren't you worried about your neighbors?"

"This storm is aimed at us. Those nearby might experience the strange weather, but the attack was meant to target you and Amon."

"Right." I shifted doubtfully in my seat as I listened to the splintering of wood. The creatures had apparently grown irritated with being denied another taste of my juicy self and were taking out their aggression on the patio furniture. Carefully, Dr. Hassan dressed my leg and then began tending to my arm. "So the Dark One likes to bite girls?" I asked as I peered at the wound. "I couldn't help but notice that you are pretty much bite-free."

"If the creatures were to bite me, then I would be able to see who is directing them. They avoid me on purpose."

"Someone's controlling them?" I asked in confusion.

"Yes."

"I thought it was the god of chaos, Seth."

"No. If it were, we would be facing much worse than these creatures. His powers are limited until the passing of the full moon. Until now I did not believe it was possible, though I must admit that I have sensed an increasing evil. I have shrugged off my niggling suspicions as the imaginings of an old man, but the creatures outside leave no room for doubt. The one directing them is his minion. His servant. My dark equal."

"Another priest?"

"I believe so. His power is . . . it's unprecedented."

"But you don't know who he is."

"I know *what* he is, but I remain unaware of his identity."

"So he's human?"

"He once was."

"What do you mean?" I asked hesitantly.

The white-haired Egyptologist sighed. "In a city called Shedyet there was a cult of priests devoted to Seth. The leader of that group was a necromancer named Apophis. Modern Egyptologists consider him the enemy of Amun-Ra and a god himself, but the records passed down through the viziers tell a different tale."

"So you believe he was not a god but human."

"Correct. Apophis was a vile, lecherous man who abused anything or anyone he considered weak and soft. He identified with the Nile crocodile and even kept several as pets, delighting in throwing them live creatures to consume. Believing himself to be a great seducer of women, he sought out the most beautiful, pure, and innocent girls from a variety of backgrounds, offering them riches, luxuries, or the illusion of power. Whatever it was he thought they might want—shelter, money—it was provided.

"It was all a part of his game. He'd lie in wait, much like the crocodile does when it seeks prey. When the girl took the bait . . . *snap!* She was caught between his teeth and there was no escape for her but death."

His story was interrupted when a fierce ripping sound by the window distracted us. Invisible claws hit the glass and then drew slowly down it, leaving large scratches. The glass didn't break. Dr. Hassan grunted. "The protection spell appears to be working."

"Let's hope it continues," I remarked. "You were telling me about Apophis?"

"He lured women, and when they were at their most vulnerable, he'd strike. In the temple he proudly displayed his conquests, and when he was ready to move on to the next victim, he would sacrifice the young maiden to a giant croc that he adorned with golden bracelets and a jewel-studded collar.

"All feared him. Many idolized him. Seth loved him.

"The city was renamed Crocodilopolis in honor of Apophis and his crocodile temple, and he was given a new power as a reward for his devotion to Seth."

"What was his new power?"

"A type of hypnotic control. Those subject to his gaze became spell-bound. They had no choice but to do his bidding. He was given a new nickname, the Eater of Souls, not only because he threw victims to crocodiles but also because of his ability to control the undead."

"Creepy."

"Yes. Apophis relished his new power but soon found he was not satisfied merely to lead mere mortals, so he made a pact with Seth, who promised him immortality if he could find a way to displace Amun-Ra and Horus, Seth's longtime enemies. Suffice it to say, Aphophis was defeated."

"What happened to him?"

"Seth never intended to keep his promise, so Apophis attempted to extend his life in other gruesome ways. However, in endeavoring to cheat death, he ended up turning himself into a monster."

"A monster like the ones roaming outside?"

Dr. Hassan raised his head, listening, while he considered his answer. "Let's just say that the creatures outside would be considered exuberant, yipping puppies compared with what he became."

"So you think that Apophis has returned," I stated, not really want-ing to hear the answer. The idea that there was a powerful magician even more monstrous than the things outside that wanted to devour me frightened me more than I liked to admit. I wrung my hands, wonder-ing where Amon was.

Dr. Hassan continued, "Not him exactly, but another like him who

has taken his place and who serves Seth in a similar manner—a dark necromancer with the ability to summon the creatures that attacked you."

"But how do you know?"

"That we have another necromancer on our hands?"

I nodded.

"The fact that he raised dark shabtis was the first clue. Only one
with the power of a god or the ability to summon the dead can give life
to a shabti."

"And the second clue?"

"The presence of the *biloko* outside."

"Biloko?"

"Invisible demons with crocodile snouts that, like Apophis, have a
taste for females, though, in their case, they prefer the sweetmeats of
the eyes, intestines, liver, and heart."

I shuddered. "Glad they didn't go for those first." My arm throbbed
and I fingered the bandage Dr. Hassan had wrapped around it. "I'm
not . . ." I gazed at him in the darkness. "I'm not going to turn into one
of those demon croc things, am I?"

"I shouldn't think so. According to the legends, there are no female
biloko. In the stories about them they do not replicate like a vampire or
a werewolf might. Their only desire—"

"Is to consume my flesh."

"Yes. I am sorry."

"Me too."

The crash of the patio table caused me to jump to my feet and duck
behind Dr. Hassan, clutching his arm. The wind pushed even harder at
the windows, gritty sand thumping against the house like small hailstones determined to rip it apart, and then, suddenly, the wind was
gone. Silence descended, and I found the lack of noise even creepier than
the heavy thuds of the creatures roaming the deck. The sound of our
breathing seemed louder than the rushing wind had been.

Cautiously, Dr. Hassan lifted the curtain and we peered into the
darkness. The rooftop deck was trashed. The furniture looked like it

had been spat out of a wood chipper. The cushions that remained had been ripped apart, and soft white fluff drifted across the deck like falling snow. But the storm was moving away from us, back in the direction it had come, and the stars were visible once more.

"Do you think it's safe?" I asked.

"It would appear to be. Please stay here while I check."

I watched through the window as Dr. Hassan walked across the deck. When he put his hands on the railing, it broke off. He stood watching the storm retreat, and after a moment or two, I joined him.

The door was bent from repeated impacts, with pieces of siding ripped away all around it. Deep gouges and claw marks covered every inch of the roof. I stooped to pick up a shredded pillow. Fluff stuck out prominently, and I couldn't help thinking that was what my intestines would look like spilling out from my slashed belly. I wondered what would happen if all my insides were consumed by demons. Would Amon still be able to benefit from my organs, or would he need a new donor?

"Do you think Amon is safe?" I asked.

"If he had been defeated, the world would be in chaos."

"It feels pretty chaotic to me already."

Dr. Hassan sighed. "I don't believe the Dark One has gained enough power to defeat Amon, at least not yet. But you need to know that even should Amon be safe, there is still the possibility that we will lose this fight."

"It's a little ironic that the grand vizier who serves the god of the sun is adopting the attitude of a gloomy rain cloud, don't you think? Personally, I'm not going to go there. We *will* find his brothers and we *will* complete the ceremony. I won't allow myself to think otherwise."

Dr. Hassan studied me briefly and then ran his hand over the edge of the broken railing. "I am sorry if this news depresses you, Lily, but I feel you and Amon must be made aware of all the possibilities. There are stories passed down that say a time would come when the ceremony to align the celestial bodies would no longer keep the Dark One at bay, and, from all appearances, that cycle has begun."

"Let me get this straight. Are you saying there's a chance that even if Amon sacrificed himself in this cosmic ceremony, it might not work?"

Dr. Hassan nodded. "It has been foretold."

"But we don't know for sure that it's this time."

"Nothing in this world is sure."

"Right. So this omen, these crocodile demons—"

"Are a sign that the Dark One has mustered sufficient power, recruited enough allies, and gained a significant enough earthly foothold—"

"To give Amon and his brothers a run for their money."

"I believe so."

Putting my hands on my hips, I said, "Well that's just fan-bloody-tastic."

I was helping Dr. Hassan move the broken pieces of his deck furniture into a pile when I noticed a bright comet in the night sky. It moved toward us quickly, then slowed, changing direction as it grew closer. Golden wings soon became distinct.

"Can the neighbors see him?" I asked.

Dr. Hassan shook his head. "The great bird is visible only to those who believe in him."

As the falcon hovered overhead, its body shimmered with magic and began to change into Amon's familiar form. The shadow of wings beat the air as his body slowly lowered to the deck. When his feet touched the wood, the golden glimmer of his feathered wings burst into a million pinpricks of light.

Instead of lowering his arms, he held them open to me. "Lily."

I ran into them.

Amon pressed a kiss to my temple, then addressed Dr. Hassan. "What has happened?"

"She was attacked by biloko demons."

Amon's grip at my waist and the back of my neck tightened.

"They came with the storm," Dr. Hassan explained.

"Then they know." Amon lightly massaged my neck, warmth from his fingertips soothing my tense muscles.

The Egyptologist let out a breath. "That is my fear."

"Who knows what?" I murmured.

"The Dark One knows that Amon is weakened and that he relies upon you," the doctor offered.

"Will they come back?" I asked against Amon's chest.

"I will make sure that they cannot harm you," Amon answered.

"That's not a no." I lifted my head and saw Amon's frown, the worry on his face unmistakable.

Closing his eyes, he cupped my neck. Warm pulses seeped into my veins and then melted away, the sensation lost just a few centimeters from the surface. "Lily," he whispered as his forehead touched mine, "what have I done to you?"

"I'm here. I'm fine," I said, patting his chest to get his attention.

"You are not *fine*." His eyes narrowed as he touched my bandaged arm lightly.

"It's just a little bite. No big deal."

"You are lying. There is severe damage to your tissues, and your bone is cracked in several places."

"Who gave you permission to do a sun god diagnostic X-ray of my body? Besides, Amon, it's not important. What's important is—"

He actually shook me. "*You* are important!" Ignoring my continued protests, Amon said to Dr. Hassan, "We must leave immediately to find my brothers."

Hassan placed his fedora on his head. "The god of the stars is closest. Follow me."

"She needs a healer. I would prefer to raise Ahmose first."

The Egyptologist shook his head and indicated we should accompany him. Inside, he reached under his bed and pulled out a bag, which he filled with strange items—archaeologists' tools, matches, strips of cloth, and various objects I couldn't imagine uses for.

"The personification of the moon sleeps too far away," Dr. Hassan said. "And to uncover his resting place will take time. If we go to him first, we'll have to backtrack to recover the personification of the stars, which would waste a day. If an attack happens here again, your brother can help defend Lily against the onslaught."

Amon considered this for a moment. It was clear that he didn't like the options. Finally, he said, "Very well. We shall awaken Asten first, but make haste, Doctor."

"Indeed."

Within a matter of moments we were out the door and speeding down the highway in Dr. Hassan's small car, which was about as dusty as the objects in his living room. We were headed toward the mysterious Oasis of the Sacred Stones, which Dr. Hassan said was only accessible to those brave enough to pass the sentinels and who understood how to access it.

I rolled down the car window and let the night air caress my cheeks, which had felt overheated since the demon attack. Though Dr. Hassan assured me there was no venom in the bite, the stinging throb hadn't let up, and despite the painkillers I'd taken, there was a definite achy feeling circulating my body.

Amon fluctuated between blaming himself and cursing the shabti and, finally, cursing the guy, whoever he was, who had summoned the demons. Frankly, his concern was starting to affect me. I constantly felt his eyes on me, and not in the way I would have preferred.

Finally, I said, "Stop looking at me like I'm at death's door."

"I cannot help my concern for you."

"You're freaking me out."

"I do not understand 'freaking.'"

"It's making me nervous. And can you turn down your internal thermometer? It's toasting me from the inside out."

"The heat that comes from my body increases as it nears time for the ceremony. I apologize if it causes you discomfort."

Amon removed his arm from my shoulders and clasped his hands in his lap, angling his body away from mine and as close to the door as possible. The space around me cooled quickly, though my head and shoulders still felt hot. I reached for his hand. "I'm sorry. Normally I like your arm around me, it's just—"

"Do not be concerned, Young Lily. When I am around you, I sometimes forget what I am, and because of that I have grown careless."

"You aren't careless. In fact, you're one of the most caring people I know."

Amon seemed appeased by my comment and squeezed my hand. He settled his head against the car seat and closed his eyes. I was glad, since he was likely exhausted.

We drove west for several hours, and as Amon passed the time sleeping, I quietly questioned Dr. Hassan, trying to discover what he knew about the ceremony and what would happen to Amon. He said he didn't know much more than I did, though I got the impression that he was holding back some information.

Sometime before dawn Dr. Hassan pulled the car off the road and drove behind some brush. "We must continue from here on foot," he announced.

"How far is it?" I asked.

"A few miles through the desert."

"I don't think she can walk a few miles," Amon countered.

"Perhaps she can wait in the car," the doctor suggested.

"No, she will remain at my side."

"Can we go by sandstorm?" I asked.

"No. To transport the three of us would require too much energy." Amon stared at a nearby dune for a moment and then said, "I have an idea."

Stretching out his hand, he murmured softly, and the dunes in front of us began to shift. Grains of sand twisted and writhed, and suddenly three horses burst from the dunes in a blast of shimmering powder. They approached us, nodding their heads and blowing steam from their nostrils.

"They're . . . they're gorgeous!" I exclaimed as Amon beckoned me

closer. The horses were the color of the sand, and they glittered as if little flecks of minerals were mixed into their coats. Their tails and manes
were flaxen cream-colored, several shades lighter than their coats. Their
large eyes sparkled like polished amber gemstones, and their hooves
looked like they had been dipped in gold glitter. "Where did they come
from?"

Amon stroked the neck of the mare and asked, "Do you remember
the story I told you about Nebu, the golden stallion of the desert?"

"Yes."

"These are from his herd."

"You mean Horus eventually found him?"

"Not exactly. It was more like Nebu found Horus. They formed a
bond, and whenever Horus, or in this case, a son of Egypt, has need,
Nebu will send his sons and daughters to help." Amon backed up. "You
will ride the mare. Let me give you a boost."

Grabbing hold of my waist, Amon lifted me high enough so that I
could throw my injured leg over the horse's back. Once seated, I started
to panic. "I've ridden only a couple of times before, and never bareback.
What if I fall off?"

"Hold tight to the mane," Amon admonished. "She will not let you
fall."

Threading my fingers through the silky strands, I leaned over to
whisper into the mare's ear, "I'll try not to rock the boat too much.
You're in charge. I'm just along for the ride."

The mare responded with a shake of her head and a musical neigh
as she took a few steps closer to Amon's horse, a handsome stallion a few
hands taller than my mare.

"Are you ready?" Amon asked.

When I nodded, he turned to the doctor. "Ready, Dr. Hassan?"

"Yes, yes." The Egyptologist waved his hand as he settled on the
back of his horse.

"Then please lead the way, Doctor," Amon encouraged.

At a hearty "Ha!" from Dr. Hassan, his horse leapt forward and ours followed. Though they walked, it was a fast walk that occasionally turned into a trot, which was a bit jarring on my backside but for the most part was comfortable.

I noticed that something jutted up from the dunes in the distance, making black shadows against the night sky. "Is that where we're headed?" I asked Dr. Hassan as my horse trotted closer to his.

"Yes. That is the oasis at the base of those mountains. We must get there before sunrise."

"What happens at sunrise?"

"The stones will show us the path, but only at a precise time."

Encouraged by Dr. Hassan, the horses moved a bit more quickly. The sky was lightening, and I could tell by the way Dr. Hassan kept glancing at the horizon that he was worried. Tall palm trees swayed in the predawn darkness, their heavy leaves rustling in the breeze. Suddenly, a larger animal cried out, its hooting echoed by others, and soon the desert was full of sound.

"What is it?" I cried.

"Baboons!" Amon shouted over the din. "They greet the dawn with howls."

I grimaced. "I think I prefer the morning song of birds. Are they dangerous?"

"To the wrongdoer, yes," Dr. Hassan answered.

"Uh, how would they know if I was a wrongdoer or not?"

"Normal baboons wouldn't," he said. "But these are guardians who serve Babi, the alpha male of all baboons. He is a sentinel in the afterlife. You see, all baboons are aggressive, omnivorous, and territorial, but these ones are doubly so. They have been summoned to protect the resting place where I hid Amon's brother. They will allow no one to pass who means him harm. I decided to take this precaution when Amon's body was stolen. It is said that Babi will eat the entrails of the wicked, and these baboons are just as dangerous. We will proceed with caution, but each of us must present ourselves for judging."

"And I thought college interviews were hard," I mumbled.

Our horses stopped at the edge of the oasis, and the cacophony coming from the baboons suddenly ceased. Tree limbs jolted and dark shapes moved over the ground and through the brush until mounds of living flesh settled before us. Teeth, shiny and sharp, were bared and glistening eyes winked like little flashlights in the darkness.

"We must hurry," Dr. Hassan said. "I will go first."

Amon helped me dismount and dismissed the horses with a bow of gratitude. With a mighty leap into the desert, they were enveloped by sand, the only proof that they'd ever been there the hoofprints they left behind.

Dr. Hassan had arrived at the border of the oasis, where the horde waited for him. A large male raised himself up and hooted softly. Others returned the call, and as Dr. Hassan stepped onto the grass beneath a palm tree, several of the creatures darted back and forth, circling him. They pushed against his shoes and his legs and tugged on his pants. A baby climbed his arm and picked through his hair, then leapt off and clambered onto its mother's back.

After this strange animal court was over, the noise died away and the doctor stepped through the mass to the other side. "Come, Lady Lily," he called over the backs of the baboons, which now stood observing me silently.

Amon clutched my arm and whispered, "I will allow nothing to happen to you. Do not be afraid."

I stepped into the horde feeling like a coward, and closed my eyes as the howling began. Heavy bodies shifted past me and I grimaced when one touched my injured leg, but gentle fingers brushed across the bandage, and when one reached out a hand, I took it. The sounds of the animals ceased abruptly, and a baboon pulled me with the lightest of tugs toward Dr. Hassan.

When Amon stepped into the oasis, the baboons stood transfixed and then, almost as one, they rushed forward and patted his legs and arms. After every primate had touched Amon, the big male gave a deep cry and all the creatures slinked back into the trees, disappearing as if they had never even existed.

Now that we'd been given clearance by the baboon guardians, we wandered deeper into the oasis, heading toward the sound of water. Dr. Hassan had begun running as soon as Amon had been let go by the troop. Amon helped me along so I wouldn't get too far behind, and just when I was about to protest that my leg needed a rest, Dr. Hassan slid to a stop at a deep pool fed by a waterfall.

Circling the pool were stones of every shape and size, which wouldn't have been that unusual except each stone had a hole bored through it. What perplexed me even more was when Dr. Hassan scooped up handfuls of the stones and began throwing them in the water.

"Quickly! Help me!" he shouted.

Amon bent down and gathered several stones, cupping them in his hands and then tossing them.

"What are we doing?" I asked as I tossed my own handful.

"Watch for one that floats," Dr. Hassan said as he worked. "A true adder stone will float in water."

"Adder stone?"

"An adder stone is used to protect a person from evil charms or nightmares. Since it is formed from the venom of adders, it can also prevent death from snakebite," Amon explained.

"There's one!" Dr. Hassan cried. "We need one for each of us, so keep searching," he added as Amon fished the floating rock from the pool.

Several handfuls later, we had a second stone, which Dr. Hassan told me to keep in my pocket. The sun would be up any moment, and the Egyptologist was throwing handfuls in a frenzy. Finally, a third rock rose from the depths, and Dr. Hassan leapt into the pool like a cat scooping up a fat fish for dinner.

Staggering out of the pool, he led us to a clearing, where he held his rock up to the rising sun. As dawn broke over the horizon, light shone through the hole in the stone and a pinprick of white light hit the water, angling up slowly as the sun rose higher in the sky. When the ray of light hit the mountain, I looked at Dr. Hassan.

All of his attention was focused on the mountain. "Come on now," he whispered. "We must find the opening." A few seconds later, he shouted triumphantly, "There! There it is!"

I saw a flash on the stony hill on the other side of the pool, as if a mirror were reflecting the light cast by the hole in Dr. Hassan's adder stone. The mountain rumbled, and I waited for something strange to happen—a skeleton army to appear, a mass of scurrying scarab beetles looking for someone to devour, some kind of sign of the Egyptian apocalypse—but the mountain settled and nothing happened. I peered across the water, but the shimmering light was gone. Pocketing his adder stone, the doctor stumbled down to the pool and started making his way around it.

"Why did we each need a stone if yours did the trick?" I asked him as we carefully made our way across the slick stones.

"You'll see," he answered cryptically.

Before long, we arrived at the foot of the mountain. A waterfall cascaded down the steep rocks, its spray wetting our skin. Dr Hassan came to a stop and lifted his stone to his eye. "Here we are, at last," he declared.

"Uh, where would that be?" I asked.

"Use your stone," he answered. "Look through it and you will see our path."

Pulling my stone from my pocket, I peered through the tiny hole and gasped when I saw an opening in the mountain. When I looked at the mountain without the stone, I saw nothing. Taking a step forward, I patted the mountain and found it as hard and impenetrable as it appeared, but then Dr. Hassan, stone still to his eye, stepped right through it and called out for us to follow.

I took a deep breath, positioning the adder stone so I could see through its hole, and murmured sarcastically, "What could possibly go wrong?" as I walked through a mountain.

God of the Stars

Absolute silence descended. Stone as thick and as solid as a tombstone pressed against me on all sides. Above was a rocky ceiling that seemed to lower with every step I took. The horror of being buried alive wasn't even the worst part. What really freaked me out was that I wasn't in a secret cave hidden within a mountain, I was passing through solid rock.

Mineral formations slowly moved over me as if my body was seeping into the rock itself, and there was a heaviness, like I was wading in a strong current. The only explanation I could come up with was that I had moved into a different phase or dimension from the one the rock existed in. My fingers pressing the stone to my eye shook, and I closed the other eye so I didn't have to see the mountain as I passed through it. My pulse felt thick as my heart beat in a noisy rhythm.

The taste of copper and salt hit the back of my throat, and though I tried to keep my mouth closed, I constantly gave in to the temptation to wet my lips. Unfortunately, there was no relief found in the process; my tongue only ended up coated with a thin layer of grit and minerals.

No matter which direction I looked, Amon and Dr. Hassan weren't visible, so I pressed forward, following the strange flash of light that appeared to be coming from the stone every so often and illuminating the area directly around me. Unlike a lighthouse, which helps guide boats and warns of hidden rocks, the illumination felt to me like it was drawing unwanted attention, and I fully expected a monstrous creature with a gaping maw to find me because of it.

Each time my surroundings lit up, I stopped breathing until I was sure there was no immediate danger. I began to sense little vibrations in the area that became more pronounced every time the beam turned off.

I pressed on until the blinking light vanished and I was left in the dark root of the mountain without a guide. Blindly, I took one step forward, then another. I began hyperventilating, wondering if the mountain would ever end, when suddenly I emerged from the rock.

Though it was still dark, there was an immediate, recognizable difference in the atmosphere. The weight that had been dragging on my limbs was gone; I felt a wisp of air brush my cheek and my ears popped. My hand came into contact with the solid rock behind me and I turned, touching nothing but empty space until my fingers found the wall again. Scuffling sounds echoed in the darkness. Then I heard Dr. Hassan. "Lily!" he cried. "Over here."

I stretched out my free hand and took a few cautious steps forward. "Where are you?" I called.

There was the sound of movement nearby, and I listened carefully, trying to make sense of the noises. Someone, or something, had emerged from the rock behind me. When I turned toward it, I saw its green orbs flashing in the darkness.

"Lily," Amon said as he closed the distance between us, "are you all right?"

"I'm . . . I'm fine. I think." Amon ran his hand over my arm and a light powdery dust as fine as talc slid and then settled on my skin, making me cough. I patted my clothing, trying to get rid of some of it. Apparently my brief hiatus into the world of being clean was over. Amon didn't seem to care that I was coated with grit. He took my hand in his and lit his body enough for me to see where we were—in a large cavern.

"Dr. Hassan?" I called as I spotted his form. He was on his hands and knees patting the dirt.

"Another foot and I would have had it," he announced as he got up.

"What were you looking for?" I asked as Amon and I made our way over to him.

"This." He lifted a thick, blackened stick and began fussing with one end.

"A torch?"

"Yes." He glanced at Amon and was momentarily awed by his natural light. "Unfortunately, those of us who are mortal are not born with inner flashlights." He raised the torch. "Shall I?" he asked Amon.

"If you would."

"Of course."

"Where are we?" I whispered nervously.

"We are still in the Oasis of the Sacred Stones, but we are deep within the mountain," Dr. Hassan said. "If you listen carefully, you can hear the waterfall. I hid Amon's brother behind it." He lit the end of the torch and Amon immediately turned off his light, which I assumed helped him conserve his energy.

"What was that strange light in the mountain?" I asked as Amon guided me around a large cluster of stalagmites.

"The light can be seen only with a true adder stone," Dr. Hassan said. "It allows passage into the mountain. The flash you saw was activated by the sun shining through the stone."

"A path forged by the sun god," Amon mused.

"Yes, in a way. It's a little trick passed down by grand viziers through the centuries. To direct the light we had to be in the right spot at the right time."

"Does it work like the Egyptian mirror trick in the movies?" I continued, curious to know if there was any science going on behind the magic.

"Not exactly. Creating a pathway was no mere reflection of light. You see, scientists believe the adder stone to be any rock that is naturally hollowed out by water. The superstitious believe it is created by a snake's saliva and that possessing one offers various protections. But I know its true nature. Do you know it, Great One?" At a look from Amon, the doctor stammered, "F-forgive me. I mean, Amon."

"I confess I do not."

"Ah, then perhaps you will indulge me as we make our way to your brother."

"Please continue, Vizier," Amon politely encouraged.

"Yes, well, the goddess Isis—"

"Who was married to Osiris," I added.

"That is correct. She missed her husband after he was assigned to the underworld."

"Wait a minute, I know this one. She tricked Amun-Ra into giving her his true name after she poisoned him."

"And do you remember how he was poisoned?" the white-haired Egyptologist asked.

After a moment of thought, I snapped my fingers. "A snakebite!" When the grand vizier raised his eyebrows, obviously impressed, I waved my hand and explained, "Amon's been teaching me."

"It would seem so."

"I remember that Isis got to visit her hubby, but what does that have to do with an adder stone?"

"Well, the snake that bit Amun-Ra escaped and inadvertently absorbed a bit of the god's power through its fangs. As a result, the progeny of that particular snake developed the ability to shine light in dark places. They hide themselves away in secret spots lest they provoke the wrath of the sun god once again. A true adder stone is the calcified remains of the head of one of those snakes, and when you look through its eye, you, too, can not only see in the darkness but also conceal your-self in a spot that even the sun god himself could not discover."

The stony object in my hand suddenly felt cold. I swallowed and let out a weak gasp as it slipped from my fingers. It lay there, pillowed in the sand, seeming to give me a snaky smile and a wink. Unable to resist,

I wiped my hand on my shirt, creeped out that my lifeline in the mountain passage was a snake's skull.

With the torch shining on it, the stone twitched like a small dinosaur skeleton coming to life. After a moment, I realized it was simply the light dancing on the ancient bone, but the effect was still unsettling.

Amon reached out to pick up my adder stone, but the sand shifted, spilling into a small crack in the ground that had been hidden. My stone sank along with the sand, and the crevice was too deep to fish the stone out with our fingers. Amon considered using his power to retrieve it but then decided against it and gave me a reassuring smile.

"If we do not find another way out, we will return for it. Do not worry," he said.

"Er, assuming we raise your brother, I did not think to find a fourth stone for him," Dr. Hassan said shamefacedly.

"All will be well," Amon said.

I hadn't actually been too worried, but Amon's reassuring smile disappeared quickly, which *did* cause me to worry. As we followed the grand vizier down the dark corridor, I hypothesized on what was causing my mummy-come-to-life's distress. He really didn't seem alarmed about the loss of my stone, and surely a snake's head didn't frighten a demigod. There was something more going on, but I couldn't put my finger on it.

Every few steps, Amon looked back at me with concern, and I realized he was more anxious about me than anything else. Puzzling out his mood, I wondered if things were really as bad as he believed them to be.

Sure, I felt exhausted, and my leg and arm throbbed where I'd been bitten, but I wasn't sick enough to be bedridden, at least not yet. I squeezed Amon's hand and was about to reassure him when we turned a corner and came upon a sarcophagus.

As the Egyptologist hurried forward, touching his torch to ones mounted on the wall, I took a few steps closer and got a good look at the depiction of Amon's brother. The wooden coffin was rounded and shaped similar to King Tut's, but where the boy pharaoh's had been decorated in gleaming gold, the final resting place of one who actually *was* a demigod was humble by comparison. The artistry of the coffin, however, was worth noting.

Like the walls of the tunnels, the side panels were decorated with symbols of the three brothers—the sun, the moon, and the stars—but the stars featured more prominently this time. I walked around the coffin and took in the images of three young men standing with a dog-faced man.

"Who is this?" I asked.

Amon crouched down next to me. "That is Anubis. This carving shows Anubis granting us the gifts of the gods as he breathes life into our bodies again. It is the time of our first rising."

"And this?" I circled around to the foot.

"This shows the defeat of our enemy, Seth."

"So Seth is the horse-faced god?"

"That is not a horse. It is a beast."

"Which beast?"

"All of them and none of them."

"I don't understand."

Dr. Hassan stepped to the other side of the sarcophagus. "Set, or Seth, as Amon calls him, is a shape-shifter."

"Seriously?"

Amon nodded. "He can take any form he chooses, which makes him all the more dangerous."

"He can become a hippopotamus or a crocodile," Dr. Hassan said. "A black pig or a cobra."

"Was Seth always bent on the destruction of Egypt?" I asked.

"He was the god of chaos from the time he was in the womb," Amon explained. "The goddess Nut was his mother; because he was impatient, he would not wait for his time to be born. Instead, he used his already sharpened teeth and ripped his way out, escaping through his mother's side."

"Power and fulfillment of his dark desires is his only purpose," Dr.

Hassan further explained. "Those who follow him care not for the lives of others. Their carnality, their bloodthirstiness, their insatiable cravings are all reminiscent of the beast they follow. Seth is a monster, and is depicted as such in drawings.

"Assigning him an animal token would be callous, for all creatures simply follow their natural instincts. Even the most feared animals—crocodiles, snakes, scorpions—do not harm for evil purposes. This is why the ancients created a nonanimal—a beast—to show to the world what Seth truly is and to serve as a warning should he ever rise to power again."

"Okay, so what's the next step?" I asked.

"I am afraid I didn't bring as much as I would have liked to in the way of preparation for Amon's brother's awakening," Dr. Hassan said. "I have but a little food and water to refresh him."

"He does not need those things to awaken," Amon replied kindly. "The spell I weave will be sufficient."

"But the traditional feasting, the music and festivities—"

"That you would have provided those things had you been able is token enough of your loyalty. The offerings you have brought will sustain him for the time being," Amon finished.

Dr. Hassan gripped his bag and fished through its contents, pulling out a bottle of water and a wrapped pastry. Reverently, he cleared a space at the base of the coffin, spreading out a red handkerchief and placing his meager offerings on top. Seeing his distress as he rearranged the items a few times, I unzipped my bag and offered to share the fruit that Amon had stuffed into it before we left the hotel. The fruit was sad and a little bruised, but the offering seemed to please the white-haired devotee.

Before he settled next to me, Dr. Hassan used the adder stone and ran his hand over the wall until the wall suddenly disappeared. He then dragged over a wooden crate and lifted a large jar from it.

"Those are his canopic jars, aren't they?" I marveled as I carefully touched one with a long-beaked bird on the top.

Dr. Hassan nodded. "I brought them here when Amon was taken and hid them using the stone," he explained.

He set each jar in front of us, and I couldn't help but be astonished that I was able to touch the ancient artifacts. In addition to the bird-topped jar, there were jars with a dog head, a human head, and the head of a ram. I wanted to ask Dr. Hassan what they symbolized, but Amon interrupted.

"Are you ready, Doctor?" Amon asked.

"Yes, I believe so."

"Uncap the jars as soon as you feel the breath of life upon your face," Amon instructed.

"Yes, Master."

Amon positioned himself a few feet from the coffin and I crouched next to Dr. Hassan, who was watching Amon with a zealous rapture.

The personification of the sun god raised his arms in the air and chanted. As he did so, the heavy top of the sarcophagus twitched on its base and rose several inches.

Amon began weaving his spell.

> The stars rise. The stars fall. The stars die.
> As do you, my brother.
> Asten—the embodiment of the stars.
> It is time for rebirth. For renewal. For remaking.
> Without you the sky is dark. The heavens quake with emptiness.
> The celestial realm needs your glittering glory.
> Come, Brother. Take up your quiver and your bow.
> Join me in our shared fate once again.
> The time is at hand to fulfill our purpose.
> My enemies will be your enemies.
> My allies will be your allies.
> Together we will bring order to chaos
> And strengthen the ties that bind the universe.
> When I live, you live, for I share my life with you.

When I breathe, you breathe, for I share my breath with you.
I am Amon, the guardian of the sun.
With the Eye of Horus I seek you out.
You wander in darkness, bereft and lost,
But I will light the path before you.

Amon's eyes glowed bright green, and an eerie verdant light illuminated the area in front of him. He moved his head as if searching for something, and the beams of light from his eyes shifted, too. Finding what he was looking for, though I could see nothing at the end of the light trail except darkness, he continued his spell.

Your body is dust, chaff before the wind,
But the wind obeys me, and the dust listens.
I beckon you forth from the land of the dead.
Come, Asten! Heed my summons.
Return to the form of the man you once were.
I call upon the four winds to lend me power,
And through them I give you the breath of life. . . .

Amon raised a hand and an eerie sound, like a monster inhaling, filled the cavern. Each puff of air traced a path back and forth on my skin. Goose bumps prickled along my arms and neck, and I nervously scanned the darkness, looking for the source of the sound. Dr. Hassan proceeded to open the canopic jars and streams of white light emerged from them, circling right above the sarcophagus. I couldn't help but compare them to scavenger birds seeking out the dead.

Suddenly, a fierce gust of hot wind blew my hair back. Amon raised his other hand and a second wind countered the first. Two more times he did this, and it felt as if we were encompassed in a whirlwind. It became so strong that Dr. Hassan and I had to cling to the foot of the sarcophagus to maintain our positions, but just as quickly the wind moved away from us and whirled around Amon.

Amon trembled, arms extended at chest level, palms facing up. His limbs shook as if he were attempting to lift a weighted barbell with just the tips of his fingers. Then, when I thought he could bear it no more, the wind shifted, dipping into the coffin, and a tightly wrapped form was lifted before us.

Yellowed bandages whipped back and forth, snapping in the air and partially unwinding from the body, revealing glimpses of decay and rot. Every mummy movie I'd ever watched played out in my mind, and I couldn't help but scoot back several feet, leaving Dr. Hassan in a worshipful state by himself.

Bit by bit, the wrappings peeled away and whirled around the decayed body in a maelstrom. Fragments of bandages seemed to be stuck to the skull. When an explosion of dusty particles finally freed the arms and legs, I gasped and fell back on my elbows. Coughing violently, and wondering if I was inhaling crumbling bits of Amon's brother, I cowered in place.

The power that Amon was channeling suddenly waned, the mummy dropping slowly back down toward the coffin as the high-velocity wind weakened. Turning my head, I saw Amon's eyes trained on me. He was concerned, that much I could easily read, but there was something more, something else in his expression—a kind of sadness. I realized then that his power must have diminished because I'd distracted him.

Facing forward again, I resolved to control my reactions. I needed to let the scary business of resurrecting a man who'd been dead for a thousand years play out as if I were simply watching a movie. There was nothing to be afraid of. It was all just a magic show—a trick done with mirrors and lights. Amon turned his head. His jaw tightened with renewed determination and the wind picked up again, more invigorated than before.

Sightless orbs and a gaping mouth rimmed with teeth peeked through the wrappings as they fell away. The body was withered, shrunken—a dried husk of a man. The remaining skin was stretched tight and looked like fragments of old leather. In some places it was ripped off completely, revealing grayish bones with hanging bits of flesh. I turned away and covered my mouth with my hand, desperately trying not to vomit.

Amon had once looked like this. *How could I have wanted to kiss him?* On the one hand, Amon was pretty much the hottest guy on the planet, both in the literal sense and in the good-looking-guy way. What girl didn't want a magically gifted, undead sort-of boyfriend who could give heated massages? But I wasn't a typical girl. I was realistic. And what was staring at me right now was a very realistic version of a decomposing, moldering dead guy whose expression was that of a man screaming as he was entombed.

How could I ignore the powdery clumps of flesh, the rotting wrappings, and the peekaboo yellow bones? Swallowing, I turned around and caught Amon watching me again. I realized he'd likely been using his special eye-power thing to read my mind. The idea that he knew what I was thinking made me feel ashamed and bristly at the same time. Ashamed because I should be made of stronger stuff. How could I imagine myself as the girlfriend of a real-life mummy/sun god if I couldn't handle a little rot and decay? And irritated that Amon could read me so easily. A girl had a right to her own private thoughts. I was handling everything pretty well, all things considered. I just needed a little time to wrap my head around the idea that the guy I liked looked like the body floating in the air during his off-season.

Amon was still trembling, which made me worry that he didn't have enough power to complete the process. Briefly, I envisioned what Amon's brother would look like if he ended up half-formed due to Amon's waning power, and shuddered. Thinking that I could help in some way, I rose and touched Amon's quaking arm.

Before I could say a word, he barked, "Get back, Lily!"

"But I just thought you might need—"

"You are mistaken," he hissed angrily. "I do *not* need you. Please stay by Dr. Hassan for your own protection."

"Amon . . ." I began, but then I saw the set of his jaw and felt the tightness in the muscles of his arm. He refused to look at me.

Resigned, I resumed my position by Dr. Hassan and wondered what I'd done to make Amon so angry. After I was settled, he began chanting again.

> Ibis—give flight to his spirit
> And ease his passage.

When Amon mentioned the ibis, a pinprick of white light formed in the darkness and traveled slowly around the room until it found the glowing green path created by Amon's eyes. Bathing itself in Amon's gaze, the light grew and spread until it became clear that the form was a bird, similar to Amon's falcon. This bird, however, had a down-curved bill that was a little bit longer than its tapered, thin neck. It beat its wings, hovering in the air near Amon, who nodded and said, "Welcome, Brother."

One by one, the four white lights that had come from the canopic jars merged with the flying creature. The bird cried out, circling over our heads, and then folded its wings and shot into the whirlwind. It burst into fragments of light that were sucked into the empty eye sockets of the mummy. The mummy's wrappings floated momentarily, as if seeking a way to remain airborne without the wind, and then sank slowly to the cavern floor like little kites with a broken string. For a moment, all was silent.

Then a white gleam lit up within the mummy, spilling out of its orifices and bones. The body shivered and moved. Bones aligned and twisted, cracking as they shifted. The skull turned to Amon and then faced me and Dr. Hassan. Its jaw clacked shut, and its arms unfolded and rose into the air. The mummy looked like a Vitruvian man made of starlight. I fought to suppress a scream. Amon resumed chanting.

> As you pass through this last portal of death,
> Cries of joy will greet you,
> Feasts will welcome you,

Your heart will beat again,
Your limbs will leap again,
Your voice will be heard again.
All that was lost will be returned.
Come, Asten, and fulfill your destiny!

The light emanating from the mummy intensified, radiating heat like a supernova as the discarded wrappings rose into the air, circling around it faster than before. The brightness coalesced, forming veins and a heart that beat forcefully. Then the light wrapped around the bones, thickening until it formed radiant muscles.

The light became so bright I had to cover my eyes, while my own heart pounded in answer to the audible beat of the mummy's. Pain lanced through me and I screamed and blacked out.

When I opened my eyes, the glare had finally faded. Head aching, I pressed my hands against my eyes and took deep breaths to clear the nausea. I heard Dr. Hassan move. He fell to the dirt floor and exclaimed, "I am honored to be in your presence, Great One!"

Hyperaware of the sounds around me, each one pounding in my brain, I heard the crunch of sand, some softly murmured exchanges in Egyptian that quickly morphed into English, and then footsteps coming my way. Through the gaps between my fingers, I saw a pair of bare feet stop in front of me. Amon had been wearing shoes, so unless he'd somehow lost them, there was no way those two feet belonged to him. Fleshy toes drummed in the sand, and I heard a laugh.

"There is no need to fear me, priestess. I promise that I will not bite. Unless, of course, you wish it."

My headache finally diminished to a dull throb and I allowed my eyes to lift from the incredibly tanned ankles attached to the feet in front of me to the man's muscular legs. Amon's brother wore a pleated white skirt almost exactly like Amon's when I'd first met him. Glancing around, I saw Amon down on one knee near the sarcophagus. He was breathing heavily, his arms trembling.

I gathered my legs under me to stand and the laughing man offered a hand, drawing me up close to him. When I tried to push away to go to Amon, he said, "Let him gather his strength. Raising us saps his energy and his was depleted to begin with." Over his shoulder, he added, "I was almost in danger of rising ugly."

He smiled at Amon and then leaned closer to me. My breath caught as he boldly wrapped an arm around me. I was too weak to push him away. "Between you and me, I am far too handsome for him to ruin my appearance *too* much," he said with a wink.

Because my nose was practically pressed against his bare chest, I couldn't help but agree. The creature I'd feared was now very nicely formed. Where a hollow rib cage had been, he sported a brawny chest. The spindly arms folded across the torso had become strong and powerful limbs that held me firmly yet gently. A clacking jaw was transformed into a roguish smile, and the sightless orbs had become chocolate-brown eyes glinting with teasing mirth.

Like Amon, he came into the world with a shaved head, wearing nothing but a white skirt, and he was every bit as handsome. Though it was obvious from their golden skin that they were from a sunny climate, the similarity stopped there.

They were both physically fit, so much so that if they'd arrived on Muscle Beach, they'd fit right in, but Amon was bigger, more solid than his brother. Their coloring was different and their bone structure, too. Where Amon's face was open, I could tell that this man hid things behind his eyes and affable demeanor.

I was standing there, frowning at the cleft in his chin, which was decidedly absent from Amon's, when the man addressed Dr. Hassan. "What a delightful gift you have laid before me, old one," he said, though he never took his eyes off me. "It almost makes up for the incredibly poor feast."

"Yes." Dr. Hassan rushed over to us. "I beg your forgiveness. You see, there were extenuating circumstances—"

Amon interrupted, though he wasn't fully recovered by any means. The deep hollows beneath his eyes and his paleness told me he needed my energy, but instead of replenishing himself, he took my hand and pulled me away from his brother. "Lily is not a priestess and she is not here as your plaything, Asten," he warned.

The god of the stars narrowed his eyes, the smile never leaving his face as he looked at his brother. He glanced down at our entwined hands. "Ah, I see. She is yours."

Amon frowned. "She is neither mine nor yours. Nor is she attached to anyone else. She belongs to herself."

"Does she?" Asten folded his arms across his chest. "Well then, a girl who belongs to herself has the freedom to choose whomever she wishes." He took my hand and kissed the back of it. "I look forward to the challenge of convincing you to spend your wishes on me," he said with a mischievous wink.

Sighing, Amon said, "Asten, this is Lily, and this is our vizier, Dr. Hassan."

"It is nice to meet you." Dr. Hassan strode forward and bowed his head.

"Yes, yes," Asten answered. "Perhaps you can worship me later. My brother tells me time is of the essence."

"It is," Amon said gravely.

"Very well." Asten crouched down near the offering Dr. Hassan had set up. "So"—the embodiment of the god of the stars reached down and plucked an apple from the small pile of food—"how much time do we have until the ceremony?"

After polishing the apple on his white skirt, which he lifted scandalously high, Asten bit into the crisp fruit, carefully wiping the dripping juice from his lip with his thumb while smiling at me. He held out the fruit and said, "I did promise to offer you a bite." The whole production was so over-the-top flirtatious that it made me giggle uncharacteristically.

The idea that I had been so frightened of him before seemed silly now.

"No thank you," I said with a grin.

"There is enough for two and not a worm to be seen. Will you reconsider?"

"No, I'm good. You go ahead."

"Very well. But the fruit would have been all the sweeter had your lips pressed against it."

"That is enough," Amon interrupted. "You will cease your insipid provocations."

Asten clapped his brother on the shoulder. "Come now. Surely, there is time for a *little* celebrating?"

Shifting uncomfortably, Amon said, "There is not, Brother. The Dark One has sent his minions and he grows strong."

Finishing the apple, Asten tossed the core toward Dr. Hassan, who scrambled to clean up after him. "What do you mean?" he asked as he took in Amon's clothes and then looked at me again. Shrewdly, he pressed, "When did you rise, Brother?"

Instead of answering him, Amon addressed Dr. Hassan. "Osahar, gather our things so that we may leave as soon as possible."

"Right away, Great One . . . I mean, Amon."

"Thank you."

Asten stared at his brother intently. "What has happened, Amon? Please tell me."

"I rose several days ago. I am sorry that the time of your rising is so short, but we have only a few days to locate Ahmose and subdue the Dark One before he gains enough power to stop us."

"Locate Ahmose? You do not know where he is? Then, where have you been?"

Amon raised his hand and Asten stopped asking questions. "There is much to tell you, but time is short. We will talk on the journey." Amon glanced at me and rubbed his thumb lightly against my cheekbone. "We must raise Ahmose, and quickly," he added.

Asten seemed to sober at his brother's obvious distress and gripped his arm. "I will do what I must, Brother. We will find him. We are in death, as we were in life."

"In death and in life, Asten."

I'd just bent over to pick up my bag when the cavern suddenly shook. I stumbled against Amon, who caught me easily. The shaking ceased abruptly, and I was about to ask Dr. Hassan if there were earthquakes in the area when the mountain rumbled again.

A hot wind blew through the cavern, creeping over my skin and then retreating. "Are you doing this?" I hissed at Amon. The sound of heavy breathing brought the fetid breeze again.

He shook his head, and with a searing inhale the air was sucked out of the cavern. My lungs tightened and I gripped Amon's arm as the torches wavered and then flickered out, casting us into complete darkness. Amon and Asten lit their bodies, and when they did, I felt the cool rush of oxygen enter my lungs. Asten's white light far outshone Amon's golden skin, and it became clear just how drained Amon was. His eyes gleamed green in the darkness, while Asten's were amber.

Dust rained down on us. Something moved just beneath the rock. Slowly, the hidden thing writhed and undulated, like a giant snake slithering beneath desert sand, circling to one side of the cave and then the other as the walls bulged.

"What is it?" I whispered.

"I do not know," Amon replied.

Just then, thousands of fissures broke open in the wall, releasing thin strands of light and setting the entire cavern aglow.

"It's beautiful!" I whispered.

"I do not think I would describe it the same way," Amon said as the glow intensified and began wriggling. Skinny, glowing shoestrings twisted through the holes and dropped by the hundreds onto the cavern floor.

"Those aren't—"

"They are," Amon answered me. "Worms."

"This is very creepy." I rubbed my hands up and down my arms. "Is this what normally happens when you wake him?" I jerked my thumb toward Asten.

The god of the stars spoke up. "Thousands of beautiful women? Yes. Thousands of insects whose only purpose is to lure fish? No."

"Guys?" I said, taking a few steps backward. "They're still coming." Long, luminous worms of all descriptions were writhing in ever-growing piles, and it wouldn't be long before we were buried beneath them. "Can we get out of here?" I asked. "You know, before our bones get picked as clean as Asten's?"

"You are not a very proper devotee to speak of me thus, are you?" Asten commented.

"I never said I was."

"I don't think these worms are what we should be worried about," Dr. Hassan interjected.

"No?" Amon said. "What is your worry, then, Doctor?"

Rumbling shook the mountain once again, and this time a giant crack appeared in the ceiling. Rocks and debris tumbled down, destroying Asten's sarcophagus and shattering the canopic jars. Out of the crack emerged a creature that belonged in a science-fiction movie—a worm the size of Godzilla.

Its gray skin oozed. The front half was all mouth with sharp, circular teeth that went back as far as I could see. As if sensing fresh meat, it angled its body toward us and squirmed farther into the cavern, its gaping mouth opening and closing, the sharp teeth clacking together like scissors.

Dr. Hassan gulped. "*That's* what I was worried about."

The Early Bird
Catches the Worm

"Run!" Amon cried as he grabbed my arm, pulling me toward the other end of the cavern. Dr. Hassan and Asten followed close on our heels.

Rocks fell all around us, and the creature emitted a frustrated screech before whipping in our direction, its razor teeth cutting through the space we'd recently vacated. The monster couldn't seem to wriggle out any farther from its hole, so it retreated, burrowing back into the mountain.

Even though rock separated us, the creature seemed to know exactly where we were. Amon said he thought it could hear us, and sure enough, when we stopped running, it stopped, too. Quietly, we made our way deeper into the cave, and for a brief time I thought we'd lost it, but Dr. Hassan accidentally brushed against a stalagmite, sending pieces of crumbling rock tumbling to the ground. With a loud cry that echoed from every direction, the giant worm chased after us and closed in fast.

Debris tumbled down as another crack appeared in the ceiling. It wasn't big enough for the worm's body to fit through, but a long purple tongue protruded, tasting the air directly around us. Catching our scent, the creature screamed and beat its body against the rock, trying desperately to break through.

"This way!" Amon cried as the top of the worm's head pushed through the crevice, tearing chunks of flesh. Its mouth snapped vainly as we ran past it to another section of the cavern and hid behind some rocks. I panted from our short run, still feeling the effects of Amon's power drain. The worm tunneled into the mountain, its body quaking the cave as it moved.

"We have reached a dead end," Asten said quietly.

"What do we do?" I hissed, panicked that I would shortly become worm food. "We only have two adder stones!"

"It is too late to escape," Asten murmured, almost gleefully. "Perhaps the time has come for us to fight." Amon's brother called upon the sand and it rose into the air, forming a bow and a quiver of arrows with diamond heads. "Will you join me?" Asten asked Amon. The god of the stars seemed completely unafraid and rather pleased at having the opportunity to test out his recently re-formed body. Amon, however, was hesitant.

"My powers are weak, Asten. I must get Lily to safety. She is my priority."

Asten stopped examining his newly made weapon and turned to his brother, studying him for a moment. "I see." With a brief glance at me, he added, "I believe she will be safe enough. You know the creature wants us, not a mortal."

"No. He will come after her. He has already sent his shadowy beasts once and they have a taste for her flesh now."

Asten raised his eyebrow and smiled brazenly. "I can hardly blame them," he said in an aside before giving me a puzzled glance. "But I confess that I do not understand why—"

"I will explain when our situation is not so dire," Amon interrupted, uttering the words quietly while watching the walls for signs of the creature.

Amon's light was barely visible in the darkness, and even if I weren't suffering its aftereffects, it would have been very obvious that raising Asten had used up most of Amon's reserved strength. I wasn't sure how he was going to survive raising another brother and finishing the ceremony, let alone fight a giant monster, when he had so little power remaining.

I was about to offer more of my energy, especially if he intended to go after the worm from hell, when Asten grasped Amon's shoulder and said, "If you cannot wage war as a god, then fight as a man, Brother. Just leave the rest up to me."

Amon looked my way, blowing out a shaky breath, and then clasped his brother's arm. He nodded and said in a hushed tone, "It is good to have you back, Asten."

Asten grinned as he placed the quiver across his back. "It is good to be back, and to have a back, now that I think about it. Of course, I am also grateful for my fully re-formed front, since I am partial to it," he said with a cheeky glance in my direction. "Shall we, Amon?"

In response, Amon twitched his fingers at the sand, millions and millions of little particles rose and became a pair of curved swords. There was an audible gasp from Dr. Hassan, who exclaimed excitedly, "The golden scimitars of Amun-Ra!" I tried to shush him before the worm heard us, but he continued, "To see them with my own mortal eyes is a blessing beyond anything I've ever dreamed of!"

Sure enough, the mountain rumbled as Dr. Hassan neared the end of his sentence. He clapped his hands to his mouth. "I am sorry," he whispered.

Farther down the corridor, great stones fell, releasing grit and debris. The four of us hunched, preparing for an attack. Amon raised his swords and Asten nocked a diamond-headed arrow. No one said anything as the creature quieted, unable to find a point of entry bigger than an apple.

With a flourish, Asten whipped his hands in circles. A sparkling black mist rose at his feet and soon enveloped us. Tiny lights winked on and off like fireflies. It looked like we were floating in space surrounded by thousands of miniature stars. I reached out to touch one and caught it between my fingers. As I rubbed my thumb over it, the star sparked, bursting on my fingertip with a tiny tingle of energy. "Ow!" I whispered.

"Did your mother not warn you to avoid reaching into the fire pit?" Asten remarked as he drove the mist around us in a circle.

"Something like that," I murmured. "Will it find us?"

"Not at the moment, but even I, as powerful and attractive as I may be, cannot keep this up forever."

"It is good to see you have not lost your magic touch, Asten," said Amon as he handed his swords to Dr. Hassan to hold. You would have thought he'd handed off a child, with all the care Oscar held them with.

The god of the stars merely gave Amon a how-could-you-even-doubt-it look in response, but the arrogant attitude disappeared as he watched his brother.

Amon clasped his brother's shoulder and continued, "I have an idea of how we can escape, but it will be dangerous."

"Danger will be invigorating after a thousand years of tedium," Asten replied as he carefully controlled the firefly smoke.

"It will require precise coordination."

"Tell me what you require," Asten said.

"First, we must separate. Draw the creature away from Lily and Dr. Hassan."

"I'm not sure that's such a—"

Asten interrupted me. "Very well. What next?"

"We will return to the original entry point where you were raised and lure the monster after us. There is a waterfall not too far from that area of the cavern, so the rock will be more porous."

"Ah, then it is your wish for the creature to break through."

"Guys, now I *know* that definitely isn't a good—"

Amon continued on as if I weren't speaking. "If we can cause it to break a big enough section of the rock, then we can make our escape through the opening."

Asten gripped his brother's shoulder. "Are you strong enough?"

"For that much, yes."

"Then let us proceed."

Amon finally turned to me. "When you hear the ceiling collapse, make your way to me as quickly as possible."

"But—"

"Take this." Asten handed me a pale rock. "You will need the light." He cupped his hands over the rock and whispered some words, lighting the stone from within. With a little squeeze of his hand, he took his bow from my shoulder and started making his way down the corridor, creating as much noise as possible.

With a small smile, Amon brushed his thumb lightly against my cheek and took his golden scimitars from Dr. Hassan. Following his brother, Amon ran, hollering and beating against the walls after he got a distance away from us. The mountain rumbled as the worm withdrew its probing feeler, screeched, and took off after Amon and Asten.

"They're going to get themselves killed," I mumbled as I folded my arms and tried to rub away the goose bumps that had risen when Amon and his warmth had left.

"Yes. Eventually," Dr. Hassan responded.

"You seem at ease with all this," I groused. "Aren't you worried about anything? Not even your own life?"

Dr. Hassan took the shining stone from me with a wave of dismissal. "My life is of no consequence," he said. "Every wonder I've seen, every magical moment is a gift I treasure and I count myself fortunate just to have lived long enough to see it. If I die today, I will journey to the afterlife as a happy and blessed man."

"Yeah, well, I have a few more things I'd like to do in life before I give up, so to speak."

"Yes, of course. You are young. You have not had time to even consider your dreams, let alone realize them."

Slowly, the glittering mist surrounding us dissipated, and the sounds of the brothers taunting the giant creature reached our ears.

"We're going to make it, right?" I asked, worried about Amon and Asten fighting the demon worm.

"I have no doubt. Light always overcomes the darkness." Dr. Hassan raised the glowing stone in his hand to prove his point.

"You've changed your tune. What happened to preparing myself for the worst?"

He raised his head, seeming to calculate my words. "You know, my dear, I feel I am of two minds on the subject. The scientist in me seems to be at war with the man of faith. But, for the time being, and in the face of these miraculous events, I have drifted across the line and into the faith camp. I always believed, you know, but when the secular world insists that gods are not real, you begin to doubt yourself. I think my faith has sustained me all these years, though I was unaware of it. And now I feel . . ." He laughed. "Well, a great sense of vindication is what I'm feeling at the moment."

"Hmm, I don't think I have the same degree of faith as you."

"Faith is merely a willingness to believe, and that belief becomes stronger and sharper over time until it can cut through your doubts as easily as Amon's scimitars."

I snorted.

Dr. Hassan pressed on. "My point is that Amon and his brother are not mere mortals aspiring to be gods such as our pharaohs of old. They are truly gods who walk among men. And what's more, they are warriors, divine protectors who aspire to fulfill their celestial calling. Surely seeing their power, experiencing it firsthand, can inspire you to have at least a little bit of faith."

"You're right. It's incredible what they can do and what they have accomplished, but as much as I'm impressed by Amon's power, I can see and feel what it's done to him. Having that much responsibility is not always a blessing. So, yes, I have doubts.

"I doubt that Amon has the strength to fulfill his role. I doubt he's happy being stuck in the sort of limbo afterlife he described, even should he succeed in his quest. And most of all, I doubt that this life, this sacrifice that has to be made over and over again, is worth it. Amon deserves more."

Dr. Hassan was quiet for a moment, his eyes seeming to bore into my soul. I stared right back, unshakable in my feelings. "Perhaps you are right," he finally acquiesced. "Perhaps Amon's consort is as sharp as his swords."

I was about to ask him what he meant by *consort* when the cavern shook so hard it could mean only one thing—the demon worm had broken through.

"That's our cue!" I shouted, and grabbed Dr. Hassan's arm to steady myself. Rocks fell all around us as we raced toward the far end of the cave. I lifted my free arm overhead in a lame attempt to protect myself from getting battered.

Making our way to the other side of the cavern was much harder this time. The entire structure seemed on the verge of collapse. We dodged fallen stalactites and broken stalagmites, and reached the other side with only a few minor scrapes and cuts. But the chaos and destruction we saw when we rounded the corner was overwhelming.

The giant worm hung from the ceiling, its soft body oozing bloody pus in several places. Water poured in from a fissure in the stone as Amon and Asten fought knee-deep in a pool of it. If the water had risen that quickly, then it would be above our heads soon. The diverted waterfall didn't seem to hinder the worm. It lowered its body into the stream and writhed back and forth like a grotesquely swollen water snake.

Amon slashed at its side, while Asten created magic dust that blew up in puffs of light bright enough to blind us. In retaliation, the worm opened its mouth, spewing neon-green slime and fat clumps of glistening saliva over everything within range. The rocks that its venom landed on hissed and popped. Thankfully, Amon and Asten darted out of the way quickly enough to avoid the toxic bile.

With a mighty heave, the worm pulled the rest of its body into the collapsing cave, twisting its tail toward Asten while keeping its gaping mouth of razor-sharp teeth aimed at Amon. I gasped in horror when I saw a snapping mouth housed in the tip of its tail.

"Asten!" I cried. "Watch out!"

Responding to my voice, the creature shook itself violently, knocking Amon aside in the process, and slithered toward me, leaving behind shining trails of gooey slime. Its probing sensor, which I now saw was one of several that darted out from holes in the sides of its head, wriggled like a long purple parasite, while its mouth moved in an anticipatory chomping motion. Amon attacked the beast vigorously, driving both of his scimitars deep into its fleshy body, but the worm ignored him and kept pressing on.

"Amon!" I cried as his body slammed into the ceiling.

"He will be just fine," a voice murmured in my ear. I whipped around, but could see nothing but darkness, and then a tiny spark burst on the tip of my nose.

"Asten?"

"At your service, my beautiful devotee. If you would be so kind as to follow me."

Enraged, the creature sped toward me, but a hand stretched out of the darkness and captured mine, dragging me into a whirling, dark fog full of sparkling fireflies. Asten suddenly became visible. The worm paused, its feeler testing the air just a few inches from our faces but failing to locate us.

As Amon hollered at the beast, causing the frustrated creature to turn toward him, Asten kept tight hold of my hand. He didn't allow me to get in a word of protest before guiding us out from behind the stalagmite and back toward the flooded section of cavern.

Once we reached it, I spied Dr. Hassan perched on a rock surrounded by water that would be waist-deep if he were standing in it. Even though Asten and I were on higher ground, the runoff from the waterfall kept rising and was over our ankles in seconds.

"If you would stand aside," Asten admonished.

"I don't understand. We have to go back and help Amon."

"Amon is perfectly capable of extricating himself."

"But—"

"Trust me." Asten gave me a look that wasn't flirtatious or cocky in any way. It was a pleading sort of expression, and one that he didn't seem too comfortable wearing.

"All right," I whispered.

Asten wove a spell and his body lit from within. A brilliant, starry-white light encompassed him and grew until it filled so much space, I had to back up and look away. The water was up to my knees now, and it lapped at Dr. Hassan's feet.

A deafening bird's cry drew my attention back to Asten. Instead of the handsome Egyptian prince, a sparkling white bird large enough to give the megaworm a run for its money danced back and forth in the water on long legs. It seemed at home as it dipped its head toward me, its tapered beak touching my shoulder gently.

Climb onto my back.

"Asten?"

Yes. Hurry. We must move quickly. Amon is tiring.

The great bird crouched down and I waded closer, taking hold of his neck, which was skinny compared with the rest of his body, but I could feel the powerful muscles beneath the downy feathers. "What if I fall, or get airsick?" I asked as I threw my leg over the bird's back and settled myself.

I won't let you fall, but if you get sick all over my beautiful feathers I will likely cast you off. His laughter echoed in my mind. After dipping his beak into a sodden pile of wriggling worms, the bird lifted his head and gobbled two giant mouthfuls before striding through the water.

Not the feast I was hoping for, but they will nourish me during the flight.

Grimacing, I stared at the gleaming worms and wondered if I would ever end up that desperate.

Asten extended his wings and flapped them before leaping dozens of feet in one powerful jump. I clung to his neck desperately as he hopped onto a rock protruding from the water. I glimpsed Dr. Hassan waving at us as Asten leapt into the air and spread his wings.

Surging wind whipped my hair back as the bird rose. The tips of his wings brushed the spilling waterfall and then we were out into the open sky, flying above the Oasis of the Sacred Stones. My stomach seemed to have been left in the cavern, and I wondered for a desperate minute if I was going to throw up. As Asten leveled off, circling over the mountain, I was finally able to get control over my stomach.

You are not sick, are you? he asked as if reading my thoughts. I wondered if, like Amon, he could.

I replied without speaking. *Can you hear me if I talk to you through my mind?*

Yes. Though it takes concentration.

"Then I'll just talk to you as long as you can hear me."

That is much easier. Thank you.

"You're welcome. Now let's go back and get Amon."

Do you remember that you agreed to trust me?

"Yes, but—"

Just then, Amon, in the form of the golden falcon, burst out of the hole in the mountain, a soaking-wet Dr. Hassan clinging to his neck. The falcon pounded his wings furiously and moved from side to side, which at first I assumed was an attempt to help Dr. Hassan safely onto his back, but then the giant worm burst from the mountain right behind them, mouth open, its body bruised and broken.

It clamped on to the falcon's tail feathers, and the bird cried out as it pulled away. The only prize for the monstrous worm was a single gleaming golden feather that spun in the air, dropping slowly until it met the wet rocks where the waterfall had once been. Almost mournfully, the worm screeched a final time before retreating back into the mountain.

The golden bird soon caught up to us and lifted his head to peer at me.

"Are you all right, Amon?" I called out, but as much as I concentrated I couldn't hear his reply.

If you have a message for him, I can relay it for you, Asten said. *I am connected to both Amon and Ahmose.*

"Really? What's that like? You can still hear Ahmose even though we haven't raised him yet?"

Wait a moment. Asten tilted his head as if listening to something far off. *Amon wishes for me to inquire as to your health,* he said finally.

"Tell him I'm fine." I glanced at Amon flying next to us and waved to reassure him. "Where exactly are we going, anyway?"

The grand vizier is providing directions to Ahmose. Amon warned me to prepare myself for an onslaught of questions due to your inquisitive nature. He also reminded me that you are not a devotee such as I am accustomed to and that you will not be falling easily into my arms.

"Both of Amon's statements are correct."

Then I would suggest that you commence with the questions, since I cannot fathom knowing a woman who does not desperately seek my attention.

A giggle erupted from me and I pressed my hand against my mouth. Girlish giggles were very unlike me, but there was a certain charm to Asten's firm conviction regarding his masculine appeal. It couldn't be said that the man lacked confidence.

What is your first question?

"What was Amon like as a boy?"

Ah. And I thought I would be delighting you with tales about myself. I am struck to the core to be brushed aside so, but I will indulge you since Amon and I were boys together and any story I tell you about him is sure to reflect a positive light on me as well.

Asten's wings settled into a gentle rhythm and I positioned myself in the most comfortable way I could as he began speaking.

Like Ahmose and myself, Amon was confident, brave, and strikingly handsome, though perhaps not as handsome as me. Where we differed is that Amon had great compassion for the downtrodden. He noticed things. Amon would see an old beggar sleeping by a field and hand off the basket of fish we'd just caught. In a crowd, he'd find the little girl who wanted to give him a weed and pass it off as a flower.

One time the three of us ran from our schoolmaster. We were boys and thought nothing of taking a day for some fun. Rather than be stuck indoors with our lessons, we decided to explore the countryside. We raced desert horses, played senet, watched the colorful boats sailing down the Nile, sought buried treasure, and stole delicacies from the market vendors when their backs were turned.

That afternoon we hunted—me with my bow, Amon with his swords, and Ahmose with his battle-ax and cudgel. We tracked our prey, an ibex, through some low hills only to find it surrounded by a pack of jackals. There were more than two dozen of the beasts, and, brimming with boyish overconfidence, we attacked. The jackals retreated, but by the time they did, the ibex had been ripped asunder. To celebrate the success of driving off the jackals, we camped in a fertile grove and roasted desert hares over the fire to sate the hunger in our bellies.

Returning to our home the next morning, we declared the previous day a resounding triumph. Though we knew our father would devise some sort of punishment for our desertion, we determined our freedom was worth whatever small price we had to pay.

But our teacher, who loved each of us, and Amon especially, did not want us to get into trouble with the king. We soon found out that after realizing we were spending the day elsewhere, our teacher attempted to track us down himself rather than disturb our father or mother.

In the course of following our trail, he came across the ibex's remains and stopped to investigate. Worried that we'd been injured, he pressed forward and was not too far from the grove when he was set upon by the remaining jackals. He did not survive. Our beloved instructor's gnawed-upon bones were laid before the three of us, and our father honored his sacrifice as a hero.

Amon changed after that day. He made a public vow that he would never again shirk responsibility. From that day onward, he trained dutifully and his behavior was above reproach.

"I see. That explains a lot, actually. So, what about you?"

What about *me?*

"Was your behavior also above reproach?"

Asten laughed. *Conformity and meeting the expectations of others does not suit me. I was saddened at the death of our teacher, but I did not blame myself like Amon did.*

"Then why do you still serve Egypt? You seem to love life and living too much to settle for thousands of years wandering the afterlife. Why don't you give it up?"

There was no response for a moment, and I was about to repeat the question when Asten answered.

I have considered it. In fact, it is the one thing that occupies my mind the most during my thousand-year sojourns. Well, that and imagining all the women prepared to give me a hero's welcome when I rise. But even though I can list hundreds of reasons to abandon my call, there is one very pressing reason why I keep doing it millennium after millennium.

"And what reason is that?"

The great bird tilted his head to gaze at the golden falcon trailing just behind us. His wings lifted and he soared slowly until the falcon caught up.

I love my brothers.

Asten's declaration was quiet but held undertones of a passionate dedication that gave me insight into the man he was.

It's as simple as that. I would not abandon them for all the nubile women in the world. Present company excluded, of course. If you agreed to fly off with me into the sunset, I'd abandon them in a heartbeat.

Patting his downy neck, I wondered, and not for the first time, what kind of a bird he was; I'd never seen one like him before. With a smile, I said, "No. You wouldn't."

For your information, I am a starlit ibis—a very rare and beautiful creature. As to your comment, give me the option, princess.

"You don't need one. Speaking of which, were there any? Princesses, I mean?"

Are you inquiring if I am available to woo?

I rolled my eyes. "I'm just curious to know what would have happened if you hadn't become demigods. I assume Amon is the eldest, so he would have married first, right?"

What makes you think he is the eldest?

"I don't know. I guess because he rose first."

He is not the eldest. Ahmose beat him by a few minutes, and I trailed behind by an hour or two.

"Wait. Are you saying you're triplets?"

What is a triplet?

"It's when three babies are born at the same time to the same mother."

Ah. I understand your confusion. We do not have the same mother.

"So . . . your father had mistresses? Concubines?" I added for clarity.

No. My father loved my mother and her alone.

"Then I really don't understand. How can you be brothers when you have different mothers?"

Our parents conceived us when they began worshipping Seth. We were born on the same day, each in our own kingdom. Because we were considered a gift of the gods, we were reared as brothers with the hope that we would unite all of Egypt under one ruler.

We took turns living in each kingdom. If blood had brought us together as true brothers, we could not have been any closer than we were. Since we were each, in essence, heir to our own kingdom, there was no jealousy or animosity among us.

"It sounds like a nice way to grow up."

There could not have been a childhood more delightful and happy than the one I had. Now then, I have told you somewhat of my upbringing, so perhaps you can distract me with some tales of your own.

"Oh, I don't think you'll find my childhood very interesting."

On the contrary, I find you very interesting.

"As a person or as a female?"

Can I not be interested in both?

"I suppose. What do you want to know?"

Why not start by telling me your greatest wish?

I laughed. "Why? Are you a genie who will grant me three wishes?"

You mock me, princess. I do have the ability to access the magic that flows between the stars, which is no trifling thing. Come. Tell me what your heart wishes for and I will fly to the farthest star to bring it back to you.

Even if I believed he could do what he said he could, what would I wish for? *Love.* The idea burst into my mind like a sunrise. Before Asten could grasp the thought, I tried to distract him by saying something else. "I'd like Amon to be well again. Can you do something like that?"

Asten was quiet for a few seconds, and then replied. *Ahmose is the healer among us. He will do what he can after he is awakened.*

"But will Amon even have the power to awaken him?"

If he does not, I will bolster him.

"Thank you."

You care for Amon.

"Yes."

Even though you are aware of his calling?

"Yes."

Then he is fortunate to have found one such as you.

I wet my wind-chapped lips and asked, "And what is it you would wish for, Asten? Surely you've thought of something in all those years stuck in the afterlife."

After a heartbeat, he spoke. *I dare not disclose the desire of my heart. To express it, even to one as understanding as you, is to cast my fate upon a cold universe. When I hold it within, I spill over with possibility, but once it escapes I am left bereft and empty.*

"I am sorry for the fate the three of you share. It seems very lonely. "

We three have each other. For that, at least, I am grateful.

He seemed melancholy, and for one as full of life as Asten, the mood was too sad. Changing the subject, I asked, "What is your favorite thing to do when you awaken? Other than the women, I mean. Amon says he enjoys the feast most of all."

Asten laughed. *Yes, food was always foremost in Amon's mind. The thing that I find most fascinating is to see how the world has changed while we slept in our tombs. I am the one who liked to head off to unknown places and find adventure.*

"Well, quite a bit has changed in the last thousand years."

Tell me.

"I don't even know where to begin."

Why don't you start with your own city? Where are you from? Your skin is pale, but you do not seem to be of Greek or Roman descent.

"No, I'm not from Greece or Italy. I live in New York, which is a part of the United States. That's where Amon rose."

Is that nearby?

"It's across the ocean."

Shifting, I burrowed into the soft feathers of Asten's back and started telling him all about New York and how I met Amon. The hours passed quickly as he listened, stopping me only to clarify terms he was unfamiliar with. So it came as a surprise when we began to descend, circling a small outcropping of hills.

Amon says we are here. Hold on to me tightly.

Asten tucked in his wings, and we plummeted toward the desert valley below.

Crocodile Temple

My stomach sank as I closed my eyes briefly and gripped Asten's long neck. In the middle of the barren desert valley there was a small brown dot, barely recognizable, and I wondered if it was an animal that had died in the sun, or a plant that had sprouted in the middle of nowhere. It turned out to be neither.

The supersized ibis banked, lifting his wings to slow his descent, then flapped them quickly as he bounced across the sand toward the object. Asten turned, lowering his body so I could slip off. When I hobbled away, he turned a brilliant white before bursting and coalescing into his human form. A moment later, the golden falcon landed nearby and shifted form as well.

"Lily," Amon said as he approached me. "Thank you for taking care of her," he added, gripping Asten's arm.

"It was indeed a privilege." Asten winked at me and then headed off across the sand with Dr. Hassan.

Amon slid his warm hands down my shoulders, gently passing his fingertips over my bound arm. "Does it still hurt?"

"Yes. But not as bad as a worm bite would have been."

"Do not jest about such things." Amon's expression was sober. "It could have killed you, and my power would have been insufficient to stop that from happening."

"But I'm okay. Your brother got me out in time. He used his star magic or whatever."

Amon said nothing as he touched my neck, and I could tell he was attempting to assess my injuries. I pushed his hand away softly but insistently. "Hey. I want you to stop worrying about me so much. I can promise you that if I really were that close to dying, I'd know it. We need you focusing more on this ceremony, don't you think? It's almost the full moon. We don't have much time left."

Clenching his jaw as if saying nothing required a monumental effort, Amon nodded. We started to make our way to where Asten and Dr. Hassan stood, but when I sucked in a breath from the sting of the bite wound radiating up my leg, Amon scooped me up in his arms and carried me, warming my body with his power. I knew he couldn't spare any of his remaining energy and was planning to protest, when he murmured in my ear, "Do not think to deny me in this, Nehabet. At the very least, allow me to do what I can for you."

Remembering Amon's tendency to blame himself and feel the need to help me, I settled back and enjoyed being close to him, figuring I'd return the favor later.

The intense sun directly overhead invigorated Amon, and his skin absorbed the light. As I stared at his handsome human face, I thought how silly it was that I had been so frightened before at the idea of falling in love with a mummy.

Amon couldn't help what he was. He didn't ask to be a hero of Egypt, let alone allow his body to rot for centuries. He was just a man caught in a celestial game—a powerful pawn the gods moved across the board and sacrificed for their own purposes.

I decided I would try to find a way to get Amon and his brothers out of this. But first, we needed to rescue the third brother. I was so wrapped up in my thoughts that I didn't even register everyone else standing in a silent circle, staring down at something.

"What is it?" I twisted to see what they were all gaping at. Amon accommodated me and turned so that I had a better view. What I saw made me suck in a shaky breath. Lying before us on the sand was a man. Burned, abused, and bleeding, with one eye ripped out, broken limbs, and bones protruding in several places, yet still he breathed.

"Master?" The man coughed drily, his spilt blood congealing in clumps of hot sand. Amon pressed me toward Asten, but I wriggled enough that he changed his mind and set me down instead. Amon crouched and touched the man's shoulder.

"I am here. Anubis sent you," Amon said. It wasn't a question but a statement. The man nodded. "What happened to you?" Amon asked, and in that moment, I recognized the broken form. It was the tall shabti who had been sent to find the god of the moon.

Apparently, he, at least, had been faithful. I sank down next to Amon, stretching my injured leg out alongside the man's.

"It"—he swallowed painfully, and my heart hurt as I saw that several of his teeth had also been broken—"it was the Dark One."

"He found you and injured you? Tortured you for information?"

The shabti shook his head and even that slight movement caused him to whimper. "He did not want infor . . ." He wheezed. "Information."

"Then what did he want?" Asten asked, sympathy coloring his expression.

"To stop the ceremony and to give you a mess . . . message." Tremors rippled through the man's body as he started seizing. Amon looked up at his brother, who nodded and lifted his hands, speaking in Egyptian and casting a spell over the shabti. Whatever Asten did seemed to help. The shaking stopped, and the shabti's one eye cleared somewhat.

"What is the message?" Amon asked kindly.

Fervor lit the face of the servant, and he gasped as an invisible power lifted his torso. His broken arms dangled at his sides, his eye rolling back until all that could be seen was a white gleaming orb positioned alongside the empty socket next to it.

In a sibilant voice, very different from the shabti's, words streamed from his mouth, and it took me a moment to make sense of them.

You come here seeking the power of the moon,
But he has been hidden in a dark cloud, his power vanquished.
You who weep will be cast into a devouring fire,
Where you will wail and gnaw upon your fingers,
For you will be unable to hold back the tide of darkness.
Already it swirls around you, snapping and ripping you asunder.
Flies fester and maggots tear the flesh from his bones.
But he can be liberated from his rotting prison.
The price? It is small. A trinket. A trifle.
All I seek is an eye.
But no ordinary eye will suffice to release one so great.
The Eye of Horus is the requisite payment.
It will be swallowed whole, devoured by chomping beasts.
Only then may you reunite with your lost brother
In the realms of the dead.
If you do not come for him,
Then I'll retort with a hellish deluge.
I will blacken the glory of the sun,
Squeeze bloody tears from the moon,
And shake the foundation of the cosmos
Until every last star in heaven shall fall,
And humankind will dwindle to utter nothingness.

The shabti's head swung back and hung loosely as he fell silent. Slowly, his body lowered onto the sand, which crept over him as if burying him alive. Soon only his head stuck out, and the sand on top of him solidified into a highly detailed structure that resembled an ancient Egyptian building.

I pressed my hands against my mouth, horrified. "Does that . . . ?

Did he mean that he has Ahmose and wants to trade him for Amon's . . .
eye?" I gasped, barely able to get the words out.

Staring at the empty socket where the shabti's eye had once been
made me sick, especially as I imagined the pain of losing it. It couldn't
happen to Amon. It just couldn't.

Amon and Asten didn't answer, and when I glanced up at Dr. Hassan, he removed his hat and hung his head. This was not good. I hoped
that maybe I had misunderstood, that something had been lost in translation. That Amon was not considering trading his eye for his brother.

Amon and Asten studied the structure atop the shabti for a moment
and then exchanged a long look. The sun god knelt at the head of the
dying servant and passed his hand over the man's face. "You have
assisted me well," Amon murmured. "You are released from your servitude. May your faithful service render you a blessed afterlife." With a
deep sigh, the man's life force escaped from his mouth and hovered in
the air for a moment before collapsing in on itself and disappearing with
a burst of light.

The body resting under the sand shivered. Thin beams of golden
light whipped around it in a whirlwind, and then the form shrank,
destroying the sand building in the process. Amon dug his hand into
the pile of sand and felt around until he found what he was looking for.
Slowly, he pulled out the shabti's stone carving and handed it to Dr. Hassan, who dusted it off soberly and placed it in his knapsack.

"We are headed to the temple, then?" Dr. Hassan asked after he'd
secured the bag.

Asten nodded. "The structure still stands?"

"Yes. Though it is slowly returning to dust."

"As are we all," Amon replied gravely. He and Asten drew Dr. Hassan aside, moving away several feet until I could no longer make out
what they were saying, especially because they were conferring in
Egyptian. I was irritated at being left out. When their conversation was
finished, Amon asked, "Dr. Hassan, if you would be kind enough to

escort Lily a bit farther down the valley? Asten and I must speak with one another alone."

"Of course."

Amon wrapped his hands around my waist and helped me to my feet. "And perhaps you could also see to her injuries?" he added as Dr. Hassan put an arm around my shoulder.

"Wait." I turned back to Amon. "I don't understand. What building was that in the sand? You're not planning to do something drastic, are you?"

Amon gave me a long, sad look before turning to his brother. Dr. Hassan dutifully guided me away and then crouched to take a look at my bandages.

"This will need to be re-dressed. Will you take a seat, my dear?"

Taking my hand he steadied me as I hopped to a large rock and sat down. While I handed him the roll of bandages he'd packed, I quizzed him on what was going on. He seemed reluctant to share and kept glancing back at the two men who stood far behind us.

"I believe we are going to the Kom Ombo temple, the crocodile temple."

"That's where Ahmose was taken?"

"If the messenger spoke the truth, which I believe he did."

"How do you know?"

"Because this area of the country was not always the wasteland you see today. When I hid Ahmose here, there was an oasis similar to the one where I hid Asten. He was buried in the hollow of the tallest tree and was also guarded by immortal creatures. The touch of the Dark One—"

"Brings death?" I swallowed.

"No." Dr. Hassan shook his head as he secured my new bandage. "He causes much worse than death."

"How can something be worse?"

Dr. Hassan stared unblinkingly over my shoulder for a moment. His eyes took on a glassy sheen as he seemed to be considering my question. "Ah," he said, as if someone were whispering the answer in his ear. Finally, he refocused on my face and smiled. "You see, even in death there is the memory of a life lived. The person or animal who passes on continues to nourish the earth, and generations are influenced by the lives of their ancestors. What Seth does is more than simple destruction. He unmakes."

"Unmakes?"

"Rewinds. Takes away every aspect of living until there is nothing left"—Dr. Hassan dug his fingers into the sand and let it trickle between them—"but barren ground. Even the footprints of those who have gone before are erased. This is what he wanted to do to Ahmose, Asten, and Amon centuries ago. He wanted more than a mere sacrifice; he wanted to unmake them.

"It would have been as if they'd never existed, and all the good that had happened because of them, all the lives they'd touched, would be erased. Their people would have suffered terribly, and the unmaking would have weakened the gods to the point of overpowering them."

"He can do that?"

"Oh, yes. You see, to defeat evil is to spread the light of goodness. This is what gives the gods their strength. In creating something good, as when Seth used his power to heal the land and bless the people of Egypt, he achieved a certain level of power."

"Because the people worshipped him?"

"In part, but it is not as simple as that. Their worship served to put Seth's fellow gods at ease. He fooled everyone, mortal and immortal, and seemed to be serving humanity when in fact he was setting it up for a terrible fall. The power he achieved in the making and serving of humankind was a fraction of the power he would have gotten from unmaking them. But to unmake requires time, and it's much easier to unmake someone who is already dead than someone who is living. This is why Seth asked his loyal priest to sacrifice the brothers."

"So when he tried to kill Osiris, he was attempting to unmake him?"

"Very good, Lily. You are correct. But before Seth could complete his work, Isis discovered the body of her husband, and she and Anubis remade him. Unfortunately, parts of him were missing and he could no longer live upon Earth."

"Which is why he now resides in the afterlife."

"Yes. Luckily, Seth's duplicity regarding Amon and his brothers was discovered in time and his plans were thwarted before he could finish what he'd started. Knowing that Seth would continue to attempt to unmake the three princes since he had invested so much energy in them, Anubis took them out of the equation by making them servants of Egypt and instilling in them the celestial powers of the gods. As long as they retain their power, Seth cannot destroy them and achieve what he seeks."

"In that case, why can't Seth just unmake other people? Like me or you or Amon's father, for example? Wouldn't he gain power from that?"

"In theory, yes, but the gods would be alerted and would intervene. In the case of Amon's, Asten's, and Ahmose's births, since Seth was the one who caused them to be born in the first place, the only god who would hear and respond to the danger would be himself. To destroy one's own creations results in an infusion of power so ultimate, nothing can be denied the immortal that achieves it. And yet, it comes with a terrible price."

"How did Anubis know to come and help if he wasn't alerted?"

"The people expressed such heartfelt prayers and concern for their beloved princes, especially the mothers of the princes, that the gods could not ignore their faithful pleas."

Our conversation was interrupted when Asten and Amon approached. Asten frowned at Dr. Hassan, giving him a meaningful glance. The doctor winced as if he'd been reprimanded, though no words had been exchanged, and nodded in obeisance. I wondered if they were angry with him for telling me too much.

In my mind, I had a right to know, so I took Dr. Hassan's hand and patted it reassuringly. "We have decided that we will seek out the temple," Asten declared. "It is imperative that we locate our brother."

Amon's head hung low, and he seemed to be having a hard time focusing. I closed my eyes and tried to sense what he was feeling, but it was like I was shut out by a wall made of stone, and no matter how high I climbed or how far along it I walked, there was no way around it.

"Amon?"

"All will be well, Young Lily," he whispered in a hollow voice. "You must trust in Asten's guidance."

"Forget that!" I spat as I stood, no longer holding back. The struggle to remain upright somewhat diminished my righteous indignation, but still I pressed on and jabbed Amon in the chest.

"I can't help but notice," I said as I poked, "that you are pretty much ignoring me and making drastic decisions without any regard for my feelings on the subject. As you are aware, I am as invested in the outcome of this adventure as you are, so I have a right to know what's. Going. On," I declared, punctuating each word with three final prods.

In all my life, I'd never voiced a demand to be involved, to be able to make a choice for myself. Doing so made me feel a bit proud. I doubted that I had the fortitude to assert myself in the same way with my parents, but doing so with Amon and his brother was a big step forward.

Amon wrapped his hands around mine, squeezing softly. "I am sorry, Lily. I did not mean to leave you by the wayside. I just want to protect you." He seemed so tired; his skin was cold. The sun radiating off his form wasn't warming him like it had before we encountered the dying shabti.

"I get that," I answered more gently. "I really do. But I'm made of stronger stuff than you think. You can tell me the truth. I promise I won't run away."

Asten watched us with open fascination, while Dr. Hassan looked embarrassed to be witnessing our exchange. For a moment I wondered if Amon was going to respond, but then he finally lifted his gaze and reached up to push some hair behind my ear.

"Very well," he said with a sigh. "But know that what must be done, must be done. I will leave it to Asten to explain everything."

With a final squeeze of my hand, he stepped aside and spoke briefly to Dr. Hassan in Egyptian. Then he chanted a spell to release the golden falcon. The great bird waited silently as Asten gave us some brief instructions.

"Both of you will be flying with me," Asten said. "Amon is too weak to carry someone right now. As to the matter of educating you regarding our plan, I will instruct you on the way."

I glanced at the golden bird. He stood, listless, and I wondered if Amon even had the energy to take off. He refused to draw on my energy and was slowly killing himself to save me, and I wouldn't have it, not if he was about to face down a powerful, necromancing evil priest, if not the god of chaos himself.

Asten changed into the starlit ibis, and Dr. Hassan and I mounted him, with me in front. With a jarring run and a mighty flap of his wings, the ibis took off and the golden falcon followed. *Okay, spill,* I thought.

Spill what?

"Talk. Tell me what's going on," I voiced out loud.

"Perhaps *I* might venture to explain?" Dr. Hassan politely inquired.

You may, the ibis replied. *But do remember your boundaries this time.*

"Yes, Great One."

"What boundaries?" I demanded.

"The brothers simply wish me to be mindful of the information I share. Some of the things that I . . . have discovered . . . are not my stories to tell," Dr. Hassan said simply. "What I can convey to you is this: on our way here, Amon shared his thoughts with me, and together we came to the conclusion that there is still time. Not all the signs are in place for the Dark One's rising."

"What do you mean?"

"I mean that we believe the chaos we've encountered comes from a different source than Seth himself. If we can raise Ahmose and the three can finish the ceremony, it will be too late for Seth to rise, and he and his power, no matter how great it seems to be at the moment, will remain dormant for another thousand years."

"So does that mean we are or aren't going to trade Amon's special eye for Ahmose?"

Dr. Hassan paused for the briefest of moments. "We are . . . not."

"That's better. So then, what's the plan?"

Dr. Hassan stuttered, "W-well . . . you see—"

Amon will distract the priest of Seth while we three locate Ahmose, Asten interjected.

"But what if he gets hurt?"

There was a long pause. *As long as Amon is in possession of the Eye of Horus, he cannot be overcome,* the starlit ibis stated matter-of-factly.

I waited a bit before replying. "Then you promise me that we will do everything in our power to get him out of there as soon as possible."

That is an easy promise to keep. I do not relish the idea of allowing my brother to remain in the hands of a demonic priest.

"Fine. As long as we're on the same page."

Dr. Hassan piped up. "She means—"

The ibis interrupted him. *I understand the general meaning. Amon is fortunate to have a devotee as loyal as you,* Asten said.

The rest of the flight was spent with Asten and Dr. Hassan talking about ancient Egypt. As I listened, the heat of the day thrummed in my body and I realized just how utterly exhausted I was. The fact that I hadn't eaten since the night before probably didn't help, but strangely, I didn't have an appetite.

My eyes felt sticky and dry, a condition that the wind made worse. Luckily, Dr. Hassan was with me, since I fell into a sleep so deep that I let go of Asten's neck. Hours must have passed as I slept, because when I opened my eyes, it was to a golden-orange sunset.

I woke with Dr. Hassan securely holding on to me. He must have seen that I was getting sunburned, because he'd placed his beloved hat on my head. Embarrassed, I thanked him for making sure I didn't fall.

Amon will be separating from us now, Asten said. *Is there a message you wish me to convey?*

I watched as the giant golden falcon shot past us, heading to an outcropping of hilly dunes on the other side of the Nile, while we continued southward.

"Tell him I . . ." Again I refrained from expressing what I really wanted to say. "Tell Amon I expect to see him again. And soon."

After a moment, Asten gave me Amon's reply. *He says it is his utmost desire to look upon you again as well and that he will make every attempt to ensure that happens.*

Asten's feathers, gleaming with starlight, winked out as we passed over a city. "Do you think the city's radar can see us?" I asked Dr. Hassan. "I suppose if they *were* aware of us, they would have launched a missile by now."

What is a missile? Asten asked as Dr. Hassan cleared his throat.

"A missile is a large weapon made of metal that bursts upon impact, destroying everything in its range, which varies depending on the yield. In this case, our modern technologies would not apply."

"Why not?" I asked.

"Because Amon and Asten cannot be seen by technology," Dr. Hassan said. "And we are too small to be of any interest to those who would be watching the skies."

Asten cloaked the three of us in firefly smoke, so the fact that he chose a main street with an apartment building on one side and various businesses on the other as a landing strip wasn't too much of a concern.

As Asten changed from his ibis form into his human one, Dr. Hassan took measure of our surroundings. "The temple is approximately one mile northward. Do you see the light coming from it?"

"Yes," Asten replied. "We will approach covertly and Amon will communicate with me the instant he learns of our brother's whereabouts. Come, Lily. Dr. Hassan will lead us and you will stay close to me." When I gave him a dubious look, he hurried to add, "Amon insisted."

The three of us began walking, with me quickly falling behind. Finally, Asten stopped and placed his hands on my shoulders. "There is not much I can do to ease your pain. I cannot heal injuries like Ahmose. Perhaps you will allow me to carry you?"

"It's all right. I can make it," I said stubbornly as I hobbled, each step shooting biting pains through my leg up to my hip joint. I wondered if Dr. Hassan was wrong about the biloko not having venom, because my limbs felt like they'd been hollowed out. My blood coursed heavy and thick, pounding against my temples, as if it was no longer circulating but coagulating in my veins. On top of that, I was dizzy, but I attributed it more to the flight than to the itching bites on my leg and arm.

Asten frowned as he watched me take a few more steps and then admonished, "Time is of the essence, Lily. I must insist upon carrying you."

"Fine, but I'd rather have a piggyback ride."

Asten frowned. "I believe you misunderstand. I can become the ibis, which is a bird. I do not shift into an animal of a porcine nature."

With a mutual chuckle and a little help from Dr. Hassan, I was soon settled on Asten's very warm and very bare back, my legs wrapped around his waist and my arms draped over his shoulders. "This will be much faster. Come, Hassan," Asten urged as he trotted forward.

Even barefoot, Asten crossed rock and sand, pavement and gravel without so much as a flinch. He moved quickly, pausing only to reassess our direction, and then pressing forward. Dr. Hassan followed silently. When we stopped behind some trees, Dr. Hassan, panting from his exertions, helped me climb off Asten's back.

"What do we do now?" I whispered.

"We wait," Asten said, staring intently into the darkness as he listened for Amon's voice.

Feeling anxious about Amon, I took my notebook from my bag and sketched the temple to try to kill time.

The Kom Ombo temple was not as well preserved as other archaeological sites in Egypt. It rested on a high dune, and the Nile stretched to the east. Kom Ombo looked more like a Greek temple than the Egyptian ones I'd seen so far.

Several wide columns supported a crumbling upper segment that appeared to be a roof terrace with only a piece of the pylon gateway surviving. Each column was lit with a soft yellow gleam that gave the whole building a haunted air, especially when the wind picked up and whistled between its cracks and crevices. It was almost as if the ghosts of priests and pharaohs from the past were whispering in the dark shadows of the columns.

Dr. Hassan pointed to my drawing. "The right side is called the House of the Crocodile, and this half is the Castle of the Falcon."

"I thought this was the temple of Apophis, the crocodile god."

"It is. But do you see the dividing line, right there?" He pointed to the building. "If you cut the temple in two, there would be equal parts on both sides. There are mirror entrances, two courts with a central altar in each, double hypostyle halls, an identical pair of colonnades, and one chapel for each side. Each section of the temple was managed by a different head priest.

"In ancient times the Nile ran much closer to the temple. Crocodiles, revered as sacred creatures, lounged in the hot sun on the riverbank next to the entrance. Later, when the Nile shifted, the crocodiles left. Regardless, there were and perhaps still are hundreds of mummified crocodiles in and around the temple grounds."

"Interesting. But who was the second half of the temple dedicated to?" I asked. "Did it have something to do with Amon? I'm assuming it did because of the falcon."

"Not Amon per se, but Horus—one of the gods who lent him his power."

"But what are—?"

I was distracted when I heard Asten gasp, and whipped around. "What is it?" I hissed. "What's happening?"

Asten took a deep breath and then schooled his expression. "It is no less than we expected. Gather your things. We must seek Ahmose." Under his breath, he murmured, "Let us hope that the sacrifices were not in vain and that we will find him."

Quietly, we made our way into the temple, searching in the dark shadows of the columns and looking behind any slab of stone big enough to conceal Amon's brother.

"Amon and the dark minion of Seth are engaged on the other side of the temple. Ahmose is hidden here. At least, that is what he told Amon."

"Will you be able to sense him?" I asked.

"I cannot hear his voice until he has been called from the realms of the dead. His body is no different from these ancient corpses'." Asten pointed to a walled-in section covered with clear glass. Behind the glass, there were dusty dead crocodiles of various lengths.

"Ah, those are some of the crocodile mummies I mentioned," Dr. Hassan pointed out.

"Thanks. I figured," I whispered.

Asten had cloaked us, but there was no sign of Ahmose or a sarcophagus anywhere in the crocodile section of the temple. We checked every room, doorway, and standing stone, but encountered nothing except the sting of windblown sand.

"We are deceived," Asten murmured.

"Well, yeah. The bad guy never shows his hand. Come on, let's go rescue Amon," I said, and took a step back toward the center of the temple, but Asten darted his arm out to stop me.

"It is too late," he whispered.

"What do you . . ." I paused as the wind became more forceful. A dark cloud of sand swept the length of the open court in a whirlwind. ". . . mean?" I cheeped as Asten scooped me up in his arms and began to run.

Dr. Hassan darted around a large column and through a doorway. "Here, Great One! We can hide!"

Inside the dark room, we plastered ourselves against a wall, hoping to remain undetected. When the sandstorm passed by, we waited for several minutes. I looked up at Asten, who gave me a relieved smile. Just when we thought it might be safe, a tremor rocked the temple. The dirt floor beneath us sank several inches and I staggered against Asten, who caught me easily.

There was a small opening at the top of the wall opposite us, but it looked much higher than it had just moments before. Lifting my finger, I pointed to it and started to mouth *Something's wrong* to Dr. Hassan when I felt a heavy pull on my ankles. It was a squeezing sort of weight, like being caught in a boa constrictor's clutches. I looked down and was puzzled to see my feet were buried beneath the sand. *How did that happen?*

I distinctly remembered the floor being hard-packed when we'd come in. Suddenly, my eyes flew to several objects. A heavy stone across the room was now one-third sunk into sand. Crumbling rock at the base of the wall was completely gone. And my bag, which I had thrown to the ground when we'd come in, was half buried.

It didn't make any sense. I tried to pull my legs free but only sank deeper. The sand was now halfway up my shins. "Asten?" I cried in a panic, squeezing his arm.

"I know, Lily. It was a trap."

"Dr. Hassan?" I called out, twisting to see him.

"I am here," he replied weakly. He had sunk up to midthigh.

Turning toward the wall, I scrabbled for purchase, trying to reach something that would halt my descent, but my actions served only to speed up the process.

"Stop, Lily," Asten demanded quietly.

"Isn't there something you can do? Some sort of magic to get us out?"

"I have tried. From the time I first noticed the quicksand, when the room shook, I have tried weaving spell after spell. It makes no difference. The Dark One has cursed this sand. Once you are captured by it, it does not let you go."

"But we'll suffocate! We'll die!"

"Yes. *You* will. As for me, I will spend eternity buried alive."

"This can't be the end! Why are you giving up? Surely Amon can save us!" I thrashed back and forth wildly and sank up to my chest.

"Lily!" Asten cried. "Moving makes it worse! You must remain still!"

Stretching my arms up, I desperately clutched his fingers, the pressure of the sand like a vise on my chest. But instead of Asten pulling me out, I dragged him down with me. I could no longer turn my head enough to see Dr. Hassan. Tears ran down my face as I hyperventilated. The sand crept up to my neck, my arms so heavy I finally dropped them. This was it. I was going to die a horrible death, one of the worst I could imagine.

All things considered, I would have preferred being crushed in the stone cube in the Valley of the Kings. At least then, I would have been with Amon. A slight tug on my hair tilted my head back. I had a few more seconds of breathing.

The sand stretched gritty fingers over my scalp, filling my ears. I managed to suck in a huge breath, and then it was over my mouth, creeping over my forehead. I closed my eyes, and sank into the viscous abyss.

God of the Moon

Drowning in quicksand is a little better than drowning in water. There is no thrashing, kicking, or head shaking. No desperate struggle for the surface. No glint of sun above to beckon you not to give up. Just a quiet shrouding. An inevitable sinking, as if your body has been bound in a warm cocoon.

I would imagine that the sensation is not unlike birth. The sand slides upward, over your skin, which is disorienting since it feels like it's flowing in opposition to gravity. Intense pressure squeezes your limbs and torso. Your lungs burn with fiery pain, but you wait, and wait, and wait, hoping, praying, and pleading for the travails to be over, wishing for that moment of delivery when the cold rush of air finally allows you to scream.

But then you realize that you aren't dreaming. That this isn't a birth, a becoming. No. Instead, this is an ending. There is no light at the end of the tunnel. The shifting sands lead nowhere. Waiting and holding your breath is pointless. You will be swallowed whole.

The mind settles at last, finally resigning itself to fate as you prepare yourself for death. You wonder what the sand will feel like when you breathe it in. Will it hurt? Will you cough? Will you feel the grit filling your lungs? How long will it take for you to suffocate? And what will happen to your body after you're dead? Will you sink to the bottom, eventually hitting solid ground, or will you

just fall forever, sliding through slippery nothingness until the sand rips the
flesh from your bones and little pieces of you are messily strewn around in the
quagmire?

These were my thoughts as my body sank. Every object that
touched my skin, sand and other, was a new sensation. The pressure on
my lungs, the tugging on my body hurt in a way I'd never experienced
before.

I became hyperaware of my surroundings, which was why, when
my legs suddenly became cold and the sand creeping up my pants began
to slide back down in wet clumps, I knew something had changed. That
there was at least a pocket of air directly beneath me.

Even though my lungs were ready to explode, I held my breath for a
few more heartbeats, then shifted. My lower half dangled freely, but my
upper half, the half that needed to breathe, was still stuck. The quicksand seemed to clutch at my shoulders and hair, unwilling to give up its
victim.

Desperately, I dug down, scooping handfuls of sand until my fingertips broke through and a dry wisp of air tickled the pads of my fingers.
I kicked and thrashed, wriggling my exhausted body until, with a wet
sucking noise, the sand gave way and I was expelled into a dark cavity.

Choking, I sucked in a quick breath as I fell, not knowing if I was
going to hit solid ground and die or be sucked back into the quicksand
and have to go through it all over again. My ears were full of sand, but
I thought I heard a ghostly voice calling my name. Gasping and wheezing, I flailed at the air, my body twisting and somersaulting as I dropped.

I developed a sudden sympathy for Alice, slipping down the rabbit
hole. I didn't know what I wanted the most—to stop falling, to throw up
and get it over with, or to be able to see. Any one of those seemed like an
incredibly precious gift at that moment.

As I plummeted, the minutes stretched long and torturous, and I
came to accept my fate. I was no longer hoping for deliverance. *If I were*
going to get out of this, it would have happened already, I told myself. No,
I was in some kind of never-ending limbo. A terrible purgatory that

reminded me of all my weaknesses, faults, and regrets, and there was no way out. Perhaps I was already dead. My eyes stung with tears and I whispered a name. It wasn't the name of my parents or my grandmother; it wasn't even God.

"Amon?" I whispered in a tremulous voice. "I'm sorry."

With my death, his time on Earth would be short, but there might still be enough time for him to bond with someone else. I was imagining my happy reunion with Amon as disembodied spirits and wondering whether the Egyptian version of the afterlife overlapped with the Anglo-Saxon version of heaven, when I hit something. The impact knocked whatever little bits of sand I'd breathed in right out of my lungs with the force of a gunshot blast. Coughing violently, I tried to figure out why I wasn't dead. The gritty object that broke my fall was now wrapped around me, smothering me. Then it spoke.

"Cease your wriggling, Lily. You are safe."

Stilling, I stretched out my hands and touched a sand-covered chest. "Asten?" I whispered.

Two gleaming golden-bronze orbs twinkled in the darkness. "Were you expecting someone else?"

"No. Not at all. I was expecting to die, actually," I choked out.

Asten grunted. "Not today, it seems. Are you injured?"

"Injured?" I echoed, as if not understanding the word.

"Can you stand?" he clarified slowly.

I blinked. "Oh. Yes. I think so."

"Good." Asten set me on my feet. "Now that you are here, you can help me with Hassan."

"Dr. Hassan is here?" I gasped.

"He is. His body is heavier than yours, so he emerged more quickly than you did."

Asten moved away and I stumbled after him, stretching my arms out in front of me.

"Ah, I forget you cannot see in dark places." Asten lit his body and surrounded us in a soft white bubble of light. Other than the hard-packed dirt floor under our feet and a few small pebbles, there was nothing else.

"Where are we?" I asked.

"I do not know."

We came upon the crumpled form of Dr. Hassan and I knelt at his side, pressing my fingers against his neck. His chest rose and fell under my other hand. "His pulse is strong," I said. "It doesn't look like anything's broken."

"His limbs should be intact. I caught him, as I did you."

Looking up at Asten over my shoulder, I asked, "Weren't you hurt by the fall?"

"I am not bound to the earth in the same way as you. The power of the starlit ibis grants me the ability to control the speed at which I rise and fall."

"Hold on. Are you saying you can fly?"

"Yes. You have seen this."

"No. Not as a bird. I mean, can you fly as a man?"

In answer, Asten raised his arms slightly away from his sides and his body lifted into the air. Motionless, he hovered several feet off the ground and then slowly lowered.

Shaking my head in wonder, I turned back to Dr. Hassan. "So if you caught him, then what's wrong?"

"I do not know. Perhaps he is simply unconscious."

I slapped the doctor's face lightly. "Osahar? Can you hear me? Wake up!" I shook his shoulder, but he remained unconscious. "Can you carry him?" I asked as I picked up his beloved fedora and shoved it into my bag.

"Yes."

"How long?"

"As long as is necessary."

"Okay, good. Let's try to find a way out of here, then."

Asten crouched down and scooped up Dr. Hassan, throwing him

over one shoulder like a suit coat. "I will follow you, Lily. Where would you like to go?"

"I guess . . . we should try to go that way." I pointed ahead.

We wandered for what felt like hours, though I had no real sense of time. The only excitement was finding my backpack. Asten turned his nose up at the bruised banana I offered to share, so I shrugged and gagged down the mealy fruit, happy to find anything to fill my empty belly. As we walked, I scratched and rubbed at the itchy grime coating my body and attempted to wring it from my hair.

I began to despair. Every pebble we came across looked the same, and when I made a little pile of them to resemble an arrow pointing in the direction we went, it had completely disappeared when we doubled back not a few moments later.

Dr. Hassan finally stirred. He moaned, and Asten set him down. I trickled some bottled water into his mouth and wiped away as much of the crusted sand from his face as possible.

"What? What happened?" he asked. "Where are we?"

"We don't know." I wet a strip of fabric Asten had torn from his already too-short skirt and bathed Dr. Hassan's face. "We fell through the quicksand into this place. There's nothing here but us."

I pulled Dr. Hassan's once white, now filthy and crumpled fedora from my bag, brushed away some sand stuck to its brim, and handed it to him. He gave me a kind smile and took the hat.

"Ah, this was given to me in honor of my first real archaeological find—an exceedingly rare stone carving of Bast." The band on the fedora broke as he tried to reshape the hat. "Well, perhaps it is time to set the past behind me and focus on the future."

"I'm sorry, Osahar," I said.

"Think nothing of it. We were lucky to escape with our lives."

"Yes, but we haven't exactly found a way out."

"Lily is correct. There does not appear to be an end to this dungeon," Asten said. "But it might be possible for *you* to be able to see something I cannot. Would you agree, Hassan?"

A meaningful glance passed between the two men, but I couldn't figure out what they might have meant, and honestly, I was too tired to care. Dr. Hassan struggled to his feet with Asten's help.

"I'll see what I can do," he said cryptically.

Slowly turning in a circle as he perused the darkness, Dr. Hassan muttered absently to himself. After a few moments, I had begun wondering if he'd hit his head on a rock and was having a mental lapse, when he turned to us and said, "I am afraid we are trapped in an oubliette."

"An ooblewhat?"

"An oubliette—a dungeon with no exit other than the way through which one entered. It is a French term meaning 'a place of forgetting.'"

"Do you mean it's a place people throw you so you are forgotten, or it's a place so dark and empty you go crazy and forget who you are?"

"A bit of both, I would imagine."

"So if there is only one entrance and we came through quicksand, then the only way out—"

"Would be back through it."

"Is that possible?" I turned to Asten.

"I can fly us up to the sand, but it was infused with magic and even I cannot pass through the barrier."

"So we're trapped."

"For the moment," Dr. Hassan said quietly.

"Are you saying you know a way out?"

"Just because there is no perceivable alternate exit does not mean another exit does not exist. I believe there may indeed be a way to escape."

"Then let's go!" I'm sure excitement was visible on my face even in the dim light. I'd been trapped in way too many claustrophobic places on my adventures with Amon and didn't relish the idea of being stuck in an oubliette any longer than I had to be. The only thing that kept me from panicking and hyperventilating was worrying about Amon.

I grabbed Dr. Hassan's arm and pulled him forward a few steps before he stopped me. He patted my hand and said, "It might be best to free Ahmose before we leave."

"F-free Ahmose?" I stammered.

"My brother is here?" Asten demanded.

"He is. Or, I should clarify, his sarcophagus is here."

"But where?" I asked. "We didn't see it. How do you know this?"

Dr. Hassan hemmed and hawed before saying, "It is not far. Come."

We followed him for a few moments and then he seemed to disappear into thin air. I froze. "Dr. Hassan?" I called out nervously.

"I am here, Lily."

"Where?"

"Here. Take my hand. It might help."

He was suddenly before me again and held out his hand. After two strides he stepped up onto nothing, turned around, and smiled. "Just trust me."

Asten gripped my other hand and we slowly clambered after the doctor. The place we entered was different from the one we'd left. We were still surrounded by darkness, but large boulders now littered the ground. The oubliette played tricks with my mind, and the shadows at the edge of Asten's light lent sinister shapes to the rocks surrounding us. I often turned abruptly thinking the boulders were actually giant skulls that cackled at us as they ground their pebbly teeth.

Dr. Hassan walked right up to his bag. "Ah, there it is."

As he dusted it off, I asked, "Where are we? How did we get in here?"

"We are still in the oubliette, but this is a different section. The two of you were trapped in an optical illusion."

"I don't understand," I said.

"Are you familiar with the impossible staircase?"

"Yes, I studied it at school in art class. Wait, are you saying we were trapped in one?"

"Something like it. If we had stayed there, we would have wandered in circles forever."

"Do they have a lot of those in ancient Egypt?" I asked. "Is that how you knew about it?"

"Not exactly." Dr. Hassan seemed uncomfortable. "Ah!" he exclaimed. "There it is. I can sense the warmth of Ahmose's body. He is right over there."

"But what about his canopic jars?"

Dr. Hassan smiled. "If they did not open the lids, then all should be well."

"But—"

"Stand aside." Asten gently nudged me away from Dr. Hassan before I could finish my question. He lifted his arms, and the top of the sarcophagus rose in the air.

Like us, the casket was filthy, coated with grit and mud. Still, little spots of polished wood shone through. After the lid crashed to the floor and Asten confirmed that the body inside was indeed that of his beloved brother, he began chanting.

Dr. Hassan knelt at the foot of the coffin, took out a half-empty bottle of water and a crumbled pack of crackers from his bag, and placed them on a flat rock. He gave me a sheepish grin. "I know it's not necessary, but I am a man of tradition."

"I'm sure he'll appreciate it," I whispered, and offered him a small smile.

We sat quietly and watched Asten as he wove his spell. Now that I knew what to expect, the idea of bringing a mummy back from the dead didn't frighten me as much as it had the first time. Asten murmured,

THE MOON CANNOT WAX OR WANE. THE MOON IS
    DEATHLY COLD.
AS ARE YOU, MY BROTHER.
AHMOSE—THE EMBODIMENT OF THE MOON.
IT IS TIME FOR REBIRTH. FOR RENEWAL. FOR REMAKING.
WITHOUT YOU, THE MOON IS ECLIPSED. THE RAYS OF THE
    SUN HAVE NO MIRROR.

THE CELESTIAL REALM NEEDS YOUR GLITTERING GLORY.
COME, BROTHER, TAKE UP YOUR AX AND YOUR CUDGEL.
JOIN ME IN OUR SHARED FATE ONCE AGAIN.
THE TIME IS AT HAND TO FULFILL OUR PURPOSE.
MY ENEMIES WILL BE YOUR ENEMIES.
MY ALLIES WILL BE YOUR ALLIES.
TOGETHER WE WILL BRING ORDER TO CHAOS
AND STRENGTHEN THE TIES THAT BIND THE UNIVERSE.
WHEN I LIVE, YOU LIVE, FOR I SHARE MY LIFE WITH YOU.
WHEN I BREATHE, YOU BREATHE, FOR I SHARE MY
    BREATH WITH YOU.
I AM ASTEN, THE GUARDIAN OF THE STARS.

Asten paused briefly and turned to look at me and Dr. Hassan.

WITH THE EYE OF HORUS WE SEEK YOU OUT.
YOU WANDER IN DARKNESS, BEREFT AND LOST
BUT WE WILL LIGHT THE PATH BEFORE YOU.

I expected Asten's eyes to light a path similar to the way Amon's had, but instead a fog with little crackles of electricity surrounded us. It snapped and buzzed like a fluorescent bulb on the fritz, the light burning brightly one moment, then going dark the next. Dr. Hassan groaned.

"What's wrong?" I asked, turning to him. He waved me off, but his hands shook as he lowered his head into them and began rocking back and forth. "Asten?" I cried. "Something's not right."

"I must concentrate, Lily. Hassan will be fine."

YOUR BODY IS DUST, CHAFF BEFORE THE WIND,
BUT THE WIND OBEYS ME, AND THE DUST LISTENS.
I BECKON YOU FORTH FROM THE LAND OF THE DEAD.
COME, AHMOSE! HEED MY SUMMONS.
RETURN TO THE FORM OF THE MAN YOU ONCE WERE.

I CALL UPON THE FOUR WINDS TO LEND ME POWER
AND THROUGH THEM I GIVE YOU THE BREATH OF LIFE....

Once again the sounds of heavy breathing surrounded us. Dr. Hassan lifted his head. "You must open the canopic jars, Lily," he said. "There is one hidden in each corner of the casket. Find the small button located at the bottom of each corner and push it. That will open the padded box and reveal the jar within. Hurry!"

The first wind hit me right in the face. Standing up, I pushed forward against it and peered inside the sarcophagus, getting an up-close-and-personal view of Ahmose's scattered remains. Like Asten, bits of tattered wrappings appeared to be stuck to the dried husks of his limbs, but unlike Asten, Ahmose's body was much more decayed and damaged.

The second wind came, smacking me hard against the sarcophagus. The body inside did not rest in the repose that had surely been intended for it. Broken bones lay strewn everywhere, a likely result of the coffin's fall through the quicksand. The sarcophagus had seen better days. Thick mud and debris coated both the inside as well as the outside.

I prayed that the jars had not broken. It would be a miracle if they hadn't, and we sorely needed one. It was hard enough for me to have Amon bound to my organs. That level of intimacy was too much to share with one Egyptian demigod, let alone two.

Swallowing, I felt the push from the third wind. It was like standing in a hurricane. I clung to the coffin to maintain my balance, my hair whipping across my face and neck and leaving little stinging bites.

Expecting the bones to rise up at any moment, I hurried about my task and quickly found the button. I pressed it and a panel popped out. Hidden behind it in a thickly padded cubby was the first jar. Thankfully, it was whole and made of stone, which made me optimistic about the possibility of finding the others intact. "It has the pharaoh's face on it! Does it matter which one I open first?" I shouted.

"Just get them open. Quickly!" Dr. Hassan yelled, then gritted his teeth in pain and squeezed his shaking hands into fists. Something was definitely wrong, and I knew it must be more than just the pressure of the wind. He looked like he was having a seizure, but when I headed toward him, he shook his head vehemently.

Being a little less careful with the jar than I probably should have, I wrenched off its lid and didn't even stop to watch the white light that emerged from it before seeking the next jar.

The second corner was blocked by the bound feet of the mummy, whose legs were no longer attached to its hips. My fingers trembled as I nudged one exposed foot aside, found the button, and pulled the canopic jar out. The white light that rose joined the first, both of them circling in the air right above me.

Finding the third jar was difficult. It wasn't tucked away in its proper corner. I searched the hidden space, stretching my hand as far as I could reach, but found nothing. Desperately, I looked up and noticed something gray beneath the bandages covering the mummy's torso.

Swallowing, I steeled myself and peeled back some of the bandages. The jar lay nestled in the empty space where part of the mummy's rib cage used to be.

The fourth canopic jar was the most difficult to obtain. A pile of bones filled the final corner of the sarcophagus, the skull sitting prominently in the middle of them.

My hands shook as I thrust them into the clumps of mud, clothing, and bone lining the coffin. Repositioning the mess, I moved the pieces as respectfully and as quickly as I could, saving the skull for last.

Ahmose's empty eye sockets seemed to be staring at me as I worked. Lifting his skull and placing it next to his femur with a quick apology, I found the last button and yanked out the final jar. My hands were slick with mud and whatever fossilized bits of Ahmose remained, so it took several tries, but finally I wrenched off the lid, and the white light inside rose and began circling overhead.

After wiping my hands on the rim of the sarcophagus and wishing, not for the first time, that I had a suitcase full of wet wipes, I rejoined Dr. Hassan and nodded to Asten.

Slowly, as if battling a tremendous force, small fragments of Ahmose's body, including the tiniest bones, rose from the grit inside the coffin and churned in a circular path. They were soon followed by larger bones. Most of the pieces were bare and easily shook off whatever bandages remained. It looked like his entire body was caught in a blender.

CRANE—GIVE FLIGHT TO HIS SPIRIT
AND EASE HIS PASSAGE.

The electricity-filled fog swelled in size, becoming gray and stormy. Tiny lightning strikes flashed through the cloud until there was a violent storm and the cloud burst, leaving behind only a pinprick of white light. The light moved, wandering aimlessly in the dark spaces that Asten's light could not reach. "No, Brother. You must return to me," Asten cried out.

The embodiment of the stars lifted his hands and beckoned the light. Dr. Hassan trembled nearby, and I nudged my body closer to his to offer support, but he didn't seem to be aware of my presence. After a few moments, a concerned Asten breathed a sigh of relief as the tiny seed of light finally returned, growing until it took on the shape of a silver bird.

It looked more like Asten's starlit ibis than Amon's golden falcon. The creature made of silver light began to circle Asten. "Come, Brother. It is time."

With a trumpeting cry, the bird soared toward the sarcophagus, where the four lights from the jars merged with it. It was quickly encompassed by the whirlwind and exploded in a burst of silvery light that was absorbed into the skull's eye sockets.

The frame came together like a puzzle. Arms linked to shoulders. Legs to hips. The vertebrae snapped into their proper places. The right hand shook repeatedly and then I heard the sudden crack of wood as two finger bones that had been wedged tightly in the fragmented side of the coffin shot up into the air and clicked into position.

Shiny beams ran down the limbs of the floating skeleton, and the creature that would easily fit in as a Halloween decoration or hanging in a medical office began to writhe. Newly made veins filled with quicksilver blood, and shining muscle formed over gleaming bone as a heart began pumping. Light shone through the eye sockets in two beams that fell upon me and then Dr. Hassan, and I wondered if Asten's brother could see already, even before his eyes had returned.

Asten finished the spell.

> AS YOU PASS THROUGH THIS LAST PORTAL OF DEATH,
> CRIES OF JOY WILL GREET YOU,
> FEASTS WILL WELCOME YOU,
> YOUR HEART WILL BEAT AGAIN,
> YOUR LIMBS WILL LEAP AGAIN,
> YOUR VOICE WILL BE HEARD AGAIN,
> ALL THAT WAS LOST WILL BE RETURNED.
> COME, AHMOSE, AND FULFILL YOUR DESTINY!

I shielded my eyes until the light faded, pleased that I hadn't passed out this time. Asten's brother hovered above us, resplendent and shining. The skirt he wore was as pristine as if it had just been made, and his body, clean and radiant as a newborn's, put all of us standing in our filth to shame.

Slowly, he lowered his arms and descended to the ground next to his coffin. He spoke quietly to Asten and then approached me and Dr. Hassan. At first, I assumed Dr. Hassan had fallen to the floor again in a sign of deference to the moon god, but upon closer inspection, I realized he was unconscious.

Concerned, Ahmose knelt and rolled Dr. Hassan onto his back. He asked me a question, but it was in Egyptian. I tried to explain that I didn't understand, but he smiled kindly and moved closer to Dr. Hassan. Like Asten and Amon, Ahmose had risen naked except for his white skirt. Like them, he was very handsome, but he was larger, with thick muscles on his shoulders and arms.

Ahmose began weaving a spell over Dr. Hassan. As I moved to the other side of the doctor and held his hand, I couldn't help but study this third brother.

It was easy to see why this demigod preferred an ax to a bow and arrow. At the same time, he treated Dr. Hassan with the utmost care; his thick fingers squeezed the Egyptologist's shoulders with the lightest pressure. Not something I'd expect in a man of such stature.

When he was finished with his spell, Ahmose lifted his gaze to mine once more, and I felt captured in his silvery-gray eyes. Dr. Hassan recovered and stood up to speak with the men for a few moments before accepting the bottled water I offered. I'd planned to offer a welcoming handshake to Ahmose as I rose from the floor, but seeing how grimy I was, I changed my mind.

"Well, welcome to the world," I said. "I'm Lily."

Ahmose quirked his head at me and narrowed his gray eyes, then looked at his brother, who spoke to him in Egyptian. Ahmose nodded and said something that sounded like "Ah" before murmuring a short spell.

"I am Ahmose, the personification of the moon," he said with a warm smile.

"Nice to meet you, Ahmose. The man you helped is your vizier, Dr. Hassan."

"I am pleased to know you. Both of you." He indicated politely.

"Yes . . . so, Asten, is there anything else, or can we get a move on? I'm worried about Amon," I explained while Ahmose gave me a considering look.

"Yes." Ahmose looked around. "Where is Amon?"

"We must find him quickly. The minion of the Dark One has him in his clutches at this very moment. I fear there is little time," Asten explained.

"Then we will rescue him, Brother." Ahmose patted Asten's shoulder.

The three of us had just turned to Dr. Hassan, who was explaining his idea for escaping the oubliette, when suddenly Ahmose and Asten screamed, falling to their knees. The last thing I saw before Asten's light went out was the two of them cupping their hands over their eyes, blood streaming between their fingers.

PART THREE

As rays of sunlight burst over the horizon, the god Anubis appeared. He did not come in the form they expected—a deity with the head of a jackal and the body of a man—but as a human. Anubis was beautiful by any standard. He seemed a benevolent god, reserved in manner but kind all the same. At his side was a faithful companion, a large dog, black, with brown markings. The dog was muscular and noble in appearance in a way that echoed the god. Sitting obediently at his master's side, his pointed ears tilted up, he whined quietly, echoing the mood of the people surrounding him.

Anubis motioned for the kings to stand and, though speaking primarily to them, addressed the crowd. "People of Egypt, your great loss is ours. Seth has done much damage this day, and though we cannot undo what has been done, we can offer you this." He paused as his eyes swept the crowd.

"We will protect the young men of Egypt by keeping the Dark One at bay through a ceremony that must be enacted once every thousand years. Because your young sons of royal blood were willing to sacrifice themselves for their people, we will honor them. Instead of spending eternity in servitude to Seth, they will devote themselves to protecting those they love—a noble enough cause to gladden the hearts of any mortal, I should think.

"Though they are dead, they will be called back each millennium and will be granted a short reprieve from death so that they may continue to do the work of the gods until such time comes that the gods"—he gave a faint flourish of his hand—"and Egypt, of course, need their services no more."

The kings and queens fell to the feet of Anubis and wept in gratitude. The bodies of the three young men were brought to him. When he came to the first, he said, "Prince of Asyut, son of Khalfani, I, Anubis, god of the stars, have answered the cry of your people, and to protect them, I grant unto you a portion of my power. You are now scribe, mediator, celestial magician, cosmic dreamer, and speaker of words. Henceforth, you will be called Asten, which means 'a star newly lit.'"

Anubis cupped his hands, and when he opened them, tiny stars swirled between them. The god blew on his hands, and the stars sped toward the fallen prince, settling on him like delicate dandelion snow before sinking beneath his skin, leaving in their wake little pulsing lights that eventually faded.

Then the Egyptian god moved to the second brother. "Prince of Waset, son of King Nassor, Khonsu, god of the moon, has granted unto you a portion of his power. You are now healer, master of animals, pathfinder, and bringer of storms. Henceforth, you will be called Ahmose, which means 'a waxing moon.'"

After he spoke, Anubis put his wrists together, and in the space between his palms and fingers, a soft silver light grew until it formed a crescent. Once it had solidified to his satisfaction, he took the object between his fingers and flicked it. The tiny moon circled in the air like a discus until it struck the forehead of Nassor's son. There it grew brighter upon his skin until, like the stars, it, too, sank, and the light diminished and disappeared.

Finally, Anubis stood before Heru's son. At a worried look from the king, the god paused and put a hand on his shoulder. "Both the great god Amun-Ra and his son, Horus, wish to bestow gifts upon your son." Anubis addressed the queen. "Your special prayer for your son will be answered, but this will happen in our own time, and in a different place. Is this agreeable to you?"

Fresh tears fell upon the woman's cheeks as she nodded. "It is, Great One."

"Very well. Prince of Itjtawy, son of Heru, Amun-Ra, god of the sun, has granted you a portion of his power. You are now revealer of secrets, champion of the troubled, bringer of light, seeker of truth, and protector of the Eye of Horus.

You will take upon yourself the very name of the sun god. Henceforth, you will be known as Amon."

Lifting his hands, palms up, to the morning sun, Anubis collected its golden rays, and when the light spilled from his hands, he thrust them toward the body of the third royal son. The light arced off his palms and fell upon the chest of the young man, who breathed in and opened his eyes.

Sunlight bounced from his chest to the other two fallen princes, and as their chests expanded with breath, they sat up. When the last of the sunlight was absorbed, each prince stood and embraced his parents.

"Tonight you will feast," Anubis said. "Spend this precious time with your loved ones, for this evening we must complete the ceremony to align the sun, the moon, and the stars so that the sons of Egypt will be protected from the chaos of the Dark One."

The people feasted in celebration, but their happiness was short-lived. Though Anubis had indeed returned life to the fallen princes, their time in mortality was short. That evening, he returned to complete the ceremony, and when it was time, he took the three royal princes with him, leaving behind three families in mourning, a legend that would be passed down from generation to generation, and three mummies with a special purpose to fulfill—a destiny that would cause them to rise again.

In the Eye of the Beholder

"What's happening?" I shouted. "Did something go wrong when we raised Ahmose?" Reaching out blindly, I caught the sleeve of Dr. Hassan's shirt. The labored breathing and pain-filled gasps of Amon's brothers was agonizing. Making my way over to them, I crouched down and ran my hands up a powerful pair of arms until I cupped a man's face. It was Ahmose.

Sticky blood caked his cheeks and I tried to wipe the wetness away with my thumb. "Tell me," I said. "How bad is it?"

"It . . . it is not us."

"I don't understand. What do you mean, it isn't you?"

Asten reached out to touch my shoulder. "He means we are fine. It is an attack against us, but we will heal from—"

Ahmose cut off Asten. "That is not what I meant to say. The thing that injured us—"

"Is not something we need to discuss at this time," Asten pressed on. "It will only cause unnecessary worry. Trust me on this, Brother, and leave well enough alone."

Pausing, Ahmose said, "Very well. I will trust your judgment."

"Is one of you well enough to give us some light to work with?" I asked.

"Perhaps, if you can heal me, Brother?"

Ahmose grunted. "Yes, of course. Give me your hand."

I scooted back so Asten could take my place, and Ahmose's deep voice wove a spell over his brother. Whatever he'd done was finished quickly, because Asten's body lit from within once more. The light started off at a very low wattage, sort of like an energy-saving bulb, but then it grew in intensity.

Without turning to me, Asten asked, "Do you have enough water to create a damp cloth?"

"Sure. Just a minute," I said. Dr. Hassan offered a handkerchief and I used the little water remaining to wet it. "Here," I said, handing it to Asten.

He took it from me, keeping his back turned. I heard a ripping noise, and both men began cleaning their faces. The bloody trails were not obvious on Asten's cheeks since his face was still coated with grime and muck, but Ahmose now had unmistakable marks on his otherwise pristine new skin. His gray eyes were bright with tears, but they didn't appear to be injured.

"So? Does one of you want to explain what just happened?"

Ahmose looked to Asten, who calmly replied, as if bleeding eyes happened every day, "It was merely one of the signs that we are getting close to the time of the full moon."

I gave him an I-don't-believe-a-word-you're-saying look and turned to see what Dr. Hassan thought of this, but he wouldn't make eye contact—a sign that he was also keeping something from me. "I don't buy that for a second," I finally said. "Do you think I'm just a docile female from your century who will believe anything a man tells her?"

Ahmose cocked his head and smiled. "I have never met a woman in any century who takes a man at his word. My experience has always been that women are generally more discerning and harder to deceive than men."

I wagged my finger at Ahmose. "See? You're quickly becoming my favorite brother. And as such, you will surely be willing to tell me the truth."

Shrugging, Ahmose said, "I must defer to Asten's understanding of the situation. He has been awake longer than I have."

"Yeah, for less than a day!"

Turning to Asten, whose mouth was set in a stubborn line, Ahmose entreated, "Perhaps she needs to know."

Asten folded his arms across his chest and sighed. "She will find out soon enough. I fear the blow may weaken her further."

"I'm not weak."

"You are weaker than you know."

"Dr. Hassan, please tell them that I'm fine."

Dr. Hassan stepped forward and took my hand. "There, there. All will be well. Perhaps we could continue this discussion after we find Amon?"

Amon was pretty much the only thing that would distract me. "Yes," I acquiesced, remembering we'd left him in the hands of an evil priest. "Let's get out of here and rescue Amon, and then the three of you have some explaining to do."

Spinning, I scooped up my bag and threaded my arm through Dr. Hassan's, waiting for him to guide us out. As he began to lead, I heard Ahmose whisper to Asten, "Oh, I like her."

"I do as well," Asten replied. Then he said more loudly, "Though she makes a poor devotee, and she has a bad habit of decidedly not swooning at my feet, as any female in her right mind should."

"Then I like her even more." The two brothers followed us.

"Stop," he commanded.

"What? Did you see something?" I asked.

"You are injured."

"Yeah. Some biloko demons got ahold of me."

"Biloko?" Ahmose traded glances with his brother and then knelt down to inspect my leg. "I can heal this, but the other must wait until the three of us are united. Even then . . ."

"The other?"

Asten interjected. "Ahmose, just do what you can for her leg and arm."

"Very well." Ahmose nodded. "Please, take my hand, Lily."

He had a very nice voice, deep and comforting. I placed my hand in his and he wrapped his big fingers around it, cupping the top of it with his other hand. Warmth trickled into my veins as little pulses of silver light lit his skin.

The soothing sensation traveled to the injury on my arm and flowed down to my leg, an itching, tickling tenderness washing over my damaged limbs. I gasped as the burning feel of the bite disappeared, leaving a warm, relaxed tingle, as if the two limbs had just been given a shiatsu massage.

Ahmose opened his eyes. "There. How does that feel?"

"It feels amazing! Thank you!"

"It was a small kindness to thank you for the sacrifice you are making in helping us."

"Yes, she has done much." Asten rushed in and took my arm, guiding me away from his brother, who tagged along behind us good-naturedly.

Winding our way through the ghoulish boulders, I glanced back, wondering why Asten was trying to keep his brother and me apart. His diversions would be obvious even if I weren't an astute observer of people.

Dr. Hassan strode ahead, then suddenly stopped, staring hard at the nothingness in front of us. He held out his hands and patted the air, running his fingers along invisible lines until I heard a click.

"Found it!" he exclaimed with a smile. Grabbing on to a piece of something imperceptible to my eyes, he pulled, and then thrust his hands away. A large section of the space in front of us slid aside, revealing a long tunnel with steps at the far end. "That portal is our way out." Dr. Hassan pointed to the hole he'd made.

"How? How did you do that?" I asked.

"Oh." He blew out a breath and scratched his head. "Well, it's difficult to explain."

"There is no time, Doctor. Amon awaits," Asten reminded him.

"Yes, yes. After you, my dear."

Carefully, I stepped through the hidden door and into the tunnel. Again we needed to rely on the light created by Asten and Ahmose. Black chains with cuffs hung from metal hooks. High overhead I saw broken stonework that had once been crisscrossed arches. Sunken alcoves held carved statues of Egyptian gods that wore tortured expressions.

"What is this place?" I said, and cringed as my voice echoed through the empty halls.

"I believe this is a secret gathering place for the minions of Seth," Dr. Hassan whispered.

We passed a large room that contained a floor-to-ceiling statue of the horse-faced god. Great puddles of dark liquid pooled in the cracks and crevices of the stone floor. "Is . . . is that blood?" I asked hesitantly.

Dr. Hassan kept his eyes forward and draped an arm across my shoulder, effectively blocking my view. "It is best not to think on such things," he said after we passed. "But suffice it to say, I am very certain that the god of chaos has been worshipped here."

We climbed the stairs of the long passageway and were met with a series of doors and tunnels. "Which way?" I asked.

"Follow me," Dr. Hassan said.

Neither Asten nor Ahmose protested Osahar's leadership, so I made a mental note of it, adding to my list of strange things regarding the relationship between the brothers and their grand vizier. I continued along without asking more questions, despite the fact that I was bursting with them, as usual. Something was definitely going on between Dr. Hassan and Asten, and I wouldn't be surprised to find out that Ahmose, newly risen though he might have been, was caught up in it, too. Why they would feel the need to keep secrets was driving me crazy.

When Dr. Hassan found the door he wanted, his face brightened as if he'd just discovered the secret of the universe. At last we came to a final set of stairs and he announced, "We are freed."

At the top was a heavy wooden door locked from the outside. The four of us pushed against it, but thick chains rattling on the other side made it seemingly immovable.

"Vizier, if you would watch over Amon's young lady, I will attempt to open this door," Ahmose said.

"Wait a minute, who told you I was . . . ?"

I glanced over at Asten, who gave me a charming smile and shrugged his shoulders.

"Well, you're wrong. Both of you. Amon is just my friend."

Ahmose had placed both of his big hands against the door. Bracing them there, he turned to look at me with his steel-gray eyes. "You are bound to one another. As his brother, I can feel this, even without Asten's girlish whisperings."

Frowning now, Asten countered, "Nothing is certain at this point. Besides which, why is it that I must put up with your insufferable mockery century after century? Just because I am more handsome than you and my body is not covered with enough hair to rival a jackal's is no reason to call me girlish. Your jealousy is unbecoming."

"Yes, you are very pretty, Asten. Normally. You are not now, of course, since you are covered in filth. It is too bad this dungeon does not have a mirror so you could check your appearance. I know how proud you are of it. I am sure you would be devastated to see your current state."

"Bah! Perhaps we should have left you to your eternal sleep a bit longer. You are as moody as a wrinkled fishwife. Is this about what happened with those devotees at our last rising? It was not entirely my fault, you know."

"Ah, Asten. You cannot help but draw all the attention to yourself." Ahmose felt along the cracks in the door with his fingertips. I wasn't sure what he was looking for, but he seemed to lend only half of his attention to arguing with his brother.

"All it takes to gain a woman's notice is to listen to her," Asten said.

"I listen. I was just not blessed with the skill to beguile women with my words like you were. Couple that with your handsome face and no woman even notices my presence."

"I'd notice you," I said offhandedly. "And I think you're both very handsome. Any girl would be lucky to gain the interest of either one of you."

Asten grinned. "Your beauty is eclipsed only by your rare level of wisdom."

Shaking his head, Ahmose said, "Do you see how he uses his tongue to shamelessly flatter women? Please reassure me by saying you would not fall for his common tricks."

"Um . . ." Ahmose had moved to the other side of the door and was investigating every knobby bump in the wood as I spoke. "If you don't mind, I'd rather not talk about how Asten uses his tongue."

Asten winked at me and Ahmose froze, his face turning bright red as he said, "I apologize. I did not think how my meaning could be misconstrued."

"No problem." I found Ahmose's discomfiture charming. It was refreshing, especially in such a big, self-assured man. When he glanced at me shamefacedly, I offered him a wide smile, which seemed to make him relax a bit. He turned back to the door.

"Ah, I have found the path," Ahmose said. "Now, if you would kindly stand back, I will see if I can make a way for us to escape. I would ask you to help, Asten, but I would not want you to muss your hair."

Asten folded his arms. "I do not have any hair. And neither do you. Your skull is as bare as a goose egg, which is just as well since your hair never looked as good as mine anyway," he said, obviously not wanting the playful exchange to cease.

Ahmose sighed, but there was a smile on his face as he said to me, "It is true. He is the most handsome of us, which is miraculous considering how often I have punched the smug snake charmer in the face." Over his shoulder he said, "I'll give you your millennial welcome-back-to-the-world-of-the-living beating after we rescue Amon."

"I look forward to it," Asten said, openly grinning. "Now get the door open."

"Yes, Brother."

Ahmose whispered a spell in Egyptian, touching the pad of his thumb to a circular knot on the wooden door. Silvery light moved from his thumb into the wood, leaving gleaming trails of different sizes over the surface like roads on a map.

The light grew brighter and brighter as the door shook. Ahmose stepped back and wrapped an arm around me, turning my face halfway to his chest. "Cover your eyes," he said. I did, but peeked through the cracks in my fingers.

The shaking grew fiercer and then the door exploded, sending fragmented chunks, like broken puzzle pieces, ripping through the air. When it was over, I asked, "How did you do that?"

Ahmose tilted his head. "I am the pathfinder," he said simply.

"But that's not a path. It's a door."

"Yes. I found the path of weakness in the door."

"Amazing!" Dr. Hassan said.

We stepped through the doorway and emerged from an abandoned building a few blocks from the temple. Suddenly, I became light-headed, from lack of sleep, almost dying, not eating anything substantial for a few days, or a combination of the three. I stumbled over a piece of door and Asten caught me. "Ahmose," he said, "is there anything that can be done to sustain her?"

The brothers exchanged a meaningful glance. "Not until we find Amon," Ahmose replied.

"It's okay. I'm sure it's just low blood sugar," I said. "We'll get something to eat as soon as we save Amon." I couldn't help but notice that both brothers kept glancing my way as we walked and they held out their arms to support me even when it wasn't necessary.

Soon we came to the temple, this time entering through a back door on the Horus side of the building. It was still dark, but dawn was coming.

I wasn't as aware of my surroundings as I should have been, and at first I didn't even realize it was me making noise when there was a loud crunch from glass littering the floor. Everyone had stepped around the glass but me.

"Sorry," I whispered as I froze in place.

"What a shame," Dr. Hassan murmured. "Someone has stolen the ancient medical instruments that have been on display here and they've broken the tablet depicting evidence of my Egyptian ancestors performing intricate surgery."

"Ew . . . that—"

Screaming distracted me from finishing my sentence about the grotesque scene I had just imagined thanks to Dr. Hassan's description. "Amon!" I cried as Ahmose lifted me quickly over the broken glass and we darted toward the sound. Before I took two steps into the next room, Ahmose cut me off.

Placing his big hands on my arms, he looked me in the eyes and said, "We will go together."

I nodded, desperate to do something, and shifted on my feet restlessly while Ahmose and Asten created weapons. They held out their hands, murmuring softly as tiny grains of sand rose in the air from every corner of the room. When the sand gathered wasn't enough to make weapons, it was joined by a steady stream from outside until a big enough ball had formed in front of each of them.

Asten's sand elongated, shaping itself into his bow and a quiver of diamond-headed arrows, but Ahmose's dusty particles separated into two equal-sized orbs. One solidified, becoming a gleaming silver ax. Its double edges were sparkling and sharp, and its surface was covered in engraved hieroglyphs.

The second weapon looked like a hammer, except it was several inches longer. Instead of a claw to remove nails, one end was a thick spike, and the other held a wide plate as big as my hand with dozens of painful-looking darts embedded in it. A pointed barb at the top completed the deadly weapon that Dr. Hassan told me was a cudgel.

"Stay well behind us," Ahmose said as he gave his weapon a twirl to test its balance. "If it is safe enough, your task will be to free Amon. Do you understand?"

"Yes," I whispered.

Dr. Hassan took a few digging tools from his bag and handed me a trowel caked with dirt, keeping two pointed files for himself. We adjusted our bags over our shoulders and nodded at the Egyptian warriors standing at the ready before us.

Adrenaline was pumping through my veins as I danced on my feet and gave my weak-looking trowel the once-over. Asten offered a small smile and said, "Let us proceed."

Stealthily, the two brothers moved forward, following the sounds of the screams, and when they signaled each other that the coast was clear, we moved ahead. We had passed three rooms before we finally came upon guards.

There was something . . . unnatural about them. During the brief glance I managed to get, I noted that their bodies were not correctly proportioned and their eyes gleamed ghostly white. Dr. Hassan pressed his back against the wall next to me. He looked nervous, which scared me more than the ghouls standing between us and Amon.

"They are Masaw Haput—those born of death," he whispered. "You would call them zombies."

"Zombies? Are you serious?"

"This is further proof that we are dealing with a gifted necromancer."

"So how do we fight them, then? If they are already dead, how do we kill them?"

"You do not . . . kill them," Ahmose interrupted. "*You* will remain hidden. And they will return to the state from which they were raised when we dispose of the evil one who called them forth."

"What are we supposed to do now?" I asked Dr. Hassan.

"Remain here, I would assume."

I peeked at the zombie warriors, who stood as still as statues. Their gray, sunken skin and bones were covered with strips of black leather. The bones that were exposed and no longer able to bend using ligaments were wired together somehow, their joints connected by long staples. Some rotten limbs must have remained attached by the armor strapped onto their bodies, otherwise, zombie armor seemed a bit superfluous, if you asked me.

Amon screamed again, the sound louder this time. "We've got to save him!" I hissed, trying to keep my voice low. A powerful blast of energy from behind the closed door shook the walls and a chunk of rock tumbled down near us, releasing a cascade of dust.

Dr. Hassan's raised brows indicated its size. "Lily!" he cried. "Get down!"

I ducked as Dr. Hassan sank his two files deep into the zombie warrior's chest. It just stared at the two of us, breathing raggedly. Then, raising its sword overhead, it let out a supernatural scream, its jaw unhinging, a metal staple the only thing holding the jaw to its skull.

Just as the sword was about to come crashing down upon us, it was met with Ahmose's silvery ax. The god of the moon thrust back the creature's weapon as he lifted his and took its head off in a mighty swing. "Come, Lily," said Ahmose, holding out his hand.

Asten stood on the other side of the hall, bow lifted. As he let loose a gleaming diamond-headed arrow, a dozen more guards rounded the corner, like feral beasts scenting fresh meat. The arrow hit the remaining guard at the door right between the eyes and the creature exploded. Immediately, Asten pulled another arrow from his quiver. "Lily! To me!" he cried.

Dr. Hassan followed closely on my heels as I made my way to Asten. When all the zombies were incapacitated, Ahmose joined us. We were about to break through the door when it opened, more undead warriors pouring out.

As Asten and Ahmose fought the new horde, I glanced behind me. The fallen were rising again. In fact, the warrior whose head Ahmose had chopped off had located it and set it back on his shoulders, albeit at the wrong angle. He would be upon us in moments.

"We cannot weave the spell until Amon is freed!" Asten exclaimed.

Through the mass of bodies in the doorway, I saw a mist of red with a man standing in the middle of it. I knew this had to be the necromancer.

I grabbed Dr. Hassan's hand. "We must break through and free Amon!"

"But they said to wait for an opportunity."

"We'll have to make our own opportunity!"

We darted between fallen bodies and avoided being caught except for one headless zombie's arm latching on to my leg. I kicked hard enough that it released me; then I crouched down and continued on. Ahmose's arm hung limply, and Asten had a deep wound on his thigh. Both had several bite marks, which didn't bode well, considering they were fighting the undead.

I wasn't sure if Dr. Hassan was still behind me or not, but I rushed to Amon. He was tied to a chair facing the red mist that obscured the features of the man behind it. I ignored the mist and began sawing on the ropes that bound Amon's arms. My wimpy trowel wasn't making much headway.

"Ah, Lily," the ghostly shadow said. "We've been waiting for you."

The voice sounded familiar, but I couldn't place where I'd heard it before.

"Well, I'm glad I didn't disappoint you, then," I said, not allowing anything to distract me from freeing Amon.

Amon's head had been lowered onto his chest, but at the sound of my voice, he raised it, his words filled with pain. "Young Lily?" he gasped.

"Yes, it's me. Just hold on. We're here to rescue you."

"I'm afraid your rescue attempt is fruitless. You see, I wanted you to come," the smooth, sinister voice answered from within the mist.

"Really? Is that why you threw us into the sandpit?" I asked.

"Not at all. You stumbled upon that on your own. How did you get out, by the way? I am curious."

"Uh-uh. Not sharing information with the bad guy, thank you very much." One of the ropes binding Amon finally broke. I started working on the second. "Now, if you'd like to share some information with *us*, I wouldn't be opposed," I said to the shadow. "Like why don't you come out here and introduce yourself properly? That is, unless you prefer the title Dark Minion Necromancer of Seth, like I've been calling you."

Laughter echoed through the room. "I am going to so enjoy getting to know you better, Lilliana Young."

I broke through the second rope. "Okay, that's creepy. Didn't know the dark minion knew my name."

I risked a glance back at the door to see how Asten and Ahmose were doing. But just as soon as there were only a few zombie guards left, the shadow lord shot a stream of red mist toward them. "Lily? Where are you?" they shouted.

"I'm here!" I called out, but their eyes were gleaming in the cloud like Hollywood spotlights on a cloudy evening.

"They cannot see or hear you now, which will make our exchange much more intimate. Of course, Amon is incapacitated enough that I will allow him to listen. I take such delight in that, you know." The shadow stepped closer, and though its visage was still dark, it became obvious that he was a man and very unlike the monster zombies he'd created.

I heard a deep chanting resonate from within the red cloud, and a cloaked man stepped forward and seized my arm. His mouth was the only visible facial feature, and it was currently turned up in a suggestive leer.

The last rope hung by just a few threads. If Amon had been at full strength he could have broken it, but he just sat there, his back to me, slumped in the chair.

The necromancer priest yanked me toward him and stretched out his long fingers to caress my cheek. "Ever since my biloko demons got a taste of your flesh, I must confess that I've been distracted by the idea of savoring you myself."

Narrowing my eyes, I gave him my most lethal hands-off socialite stare and channeled my best rich-girl snark. "I think I would prefer the biloko demons, if I had to choose."

He shook me when I flashed a mocking smile. "You would not say that if you knew who I am. What I have become."

"Really? I'm a New Yorker. Nothing surprises me."

"Perhaps consorting with Egypt's sons has left you . . . jaded. Despite that, I intend to impress you"—he smiled—"one way or another. You see, I have been remade into much more than the man I was. The power

of one long dead has filled me. I am"—he paused for dramatic effect—
"Apophis." He dragged out the ending of the name with a sibilant hiss.

Wrinkling my nose as if I smelled something distasteful, I replied,
"I figured as much. It explains the smell. All things considered, I'm more
impressed with Egypt's sons. You're just a cheap imitation of a lecherous
wannabe god with a crocodile fetish. Consider me unimpressed."

"I am much more than that!" he screamed, throwing me across the
room. When I landed, I rolled until I stopped with a thud against the
wall. My already exhausted body didn't want to get back up. Slowly, I
rolled over in time to see the cloaked minion of Seth stalking toward
me, but he was stopped by the sounds of chanting filling the air.

"No!" he screamed as he whirled around. A trembling Dr. Hassan
stood behind Amon, holding the final broken rope in one hand and a small
silver object in the other. "Foolish man! Do you know what you've done?"

Pinpricks of light filled the room, reminding me of Asten's firefly
smoke. Swirling golden, silver, and white sparkles collided, becoming
larger. Then they surrounded the cloaked minion, circling his body
faster and faster. He screamed, and when he arched his back, the hood
covering his head fell away.

I gasped, and Dr. Hassan stepped forward, unbelieving. "Sebak?" he
exclaimed. "You betrayed me! Why?" Dr. Hassan's face grew red. "You
swore to uphold the order!"

Trapped, Dr. Sebak Dagher, now the incarnation of Apophis, spat
back venomously, "You are an ancient relic, unworthy and unwilling to
seize the power at your disposal. I would have killed you long ago if you
had trusted me enough to reveal the location of Amon's canopic jars."

The lights squeezed tighter. "The Dark One is rising, and there's
nothing you can do to stop it!" Desperate now, Dagher continued fanatically, "His hand will not be stayed. He will make his throne from the
bones of those who oppose him. Make no mistake; the powers of the
Dark One *will* prevail."

"Sebak, there is still time!" Dr. Hassan shouted. "You must stop
this! You cannot possibly win."

Ignoring Osahar and turning to me, Sebak said, "I look forward to the opportunity to gaze into your lovely *eyes* once more." He thrust his arms forward and red light poured from his fingertips and out the door. Striking his hands together, he disappeared with the sound of a thunderclap.

The red mist surrounding Asten and Ahmose dissipated and the two brothers quickly used their power to thrust aside the bodies of the zombies littering the floor, along with those still barreling toward the door.

Ahmose rushed to my side while Asten went to his brother. Injured again, I limped over to Dr. Hassan, who looked completely stricken at the betrayal of his assistant. After squeezing his hand, I went to Amon. On the floor at his feet was a tray of ancient tools, likely the ones stolen from the display.

A pool of sticky blood surrounded the tray. Kicking it aside violently, I knelt at Amon's feet and took his hand. Rivulets of blood had dried on his arms; crusty dark stains flaked from between his fingers. Deep slashes marked several places on his thigh, and ugly stab wounds peeked out from between the fragments of what was left of his shirt.

I ran my hand carefully up his arm. "Amon? Can you hear me? We're here," I said. "It's over now."

He started, his hair hanging limply over his lowered head.

"Lily?" he said, his voice breaking.

"Yes. It's me. Your brothers are here. You're freed now."

Amon's hands clutched the sides of the chair, the tendons in his arms standing out as he trembled. Finally, sucking in a breath, he lifted his head.

The sight of him filled me with horror.

A loud sob followed by desperate gasps echoed in the room, and it took a moment for me to register that the sound was coming from me.

The beautiful golden god of the sun, the one I now accepted I was falling in love with, looked up and reached out blindly.

His once-beautiful hazel eyes—now dark, bloody, very empty eye sockets, the stuff of nightmares—turned toward me.

Crocodile Tears

"Amon?" I pushed the hair from his forehead, flinching at the feel of his cold skin and the sight of the horrible things done to him. Amon's sparkling hazel eyes were gone, and my heart was as broken and empty as the man who sat before me.

His lips were cracked and dry, and his breath rattled in his chest as if he were an old man beaten down by pneumonia. Bitter tears stung my eyes and slipped down my face. I couldn't look at him any longer, so I laid my cheek against his knee instead.

The irony was that even gravely wounded, Amon felt the need to console me. His hand gently smoothed my hair. "Hush, Nehabet. All will be well," his voice rasped. He began coughing so violently that I raised my head and cupped his neck, murmuring to him until the coughing subsided. When he took his hands away from his mouth, they were wet with fresh blood.

I sucked in a determined breath and stood, but too quickly, and I staggered. Steadying myself, I shook off the supporting hands of Amon's brothers and turned to Ahmose. "Will my energy help heal him?"

"No!" The surprising outburst seemed to be all that Amon could bear. Something broke inside him and he slumped against the chair, unconscious.

"Your bond does enable the transfer of energy," Ahmose said quietly, "but I doubt that your remaining strength will be enough to heal him."

"Regardless, he wouldn't want to put you at risk," Asten added. "The fact that he absorbed all the pain he experienced without sharing even a little shows the depth of his concern for you."

"What do you mean? Are you saying he deliberately avoided taking my energy? That he blocked our connection?"

"The times you stumbled or felt weakened were moments when he lost control, but he has been depriving himself of your strength for some time."

"It was foolish of him to allow himself to become so enfeebled," Ahmose said.

"Would you not have done the same if you felt as he does?" Asten countered.

Ahmose grunted and folded his arms across his chest. "He is closing off his future paths by choosing this course."

"Perhaps the path that remains is the one fate has determined for him."

Ignoring Asten's comment, Ahmose explained, "Without his three other canopic jars, Amon's powers have waned significantly. At this time he is nearly as mortal as you are. If he didn't have the strength of the falcon, it is likely that the incarnation of Apophis would have destroyed him. I cannot journey to the past to ensure his well-being, but I will lend whatever energies I can to him now in the hope that it will be enough. As a mortal, your life essence is already dangerously sapped, Lily. I dare not take any more."

"Well, I don't care. Between your healing ability and what remains of my energy, how much of this can we fix?"

Ahmose sighed, rubbing his jaw as he peered at my determined face. "I may be able to heal what is broken inside his body enough so that he can function, but his eyes are a different matter."

"May I contribute something?" Dr. Hassan asked.

Ahmose shook his head. "Only the one bonded to him can transfer energy. Even if Asten joined with me and we drained you dry, Lily, it would not be sufficient to restore his eyes *and* invigorate him enough to perform the ceremony. Restoring that which has been torn from our bodies is extremely complicated."

"The ceremony is the most important thing," Asten stated. "Amon still has his third eye. That will sustain him until Seth is bound once again."

"His third eye? Do you mean the Eye of Horus?"

"Yes," Asten answered. After a brief glance at Dr. Hassan, he continued. "The Eye of Horus is likely the reason Sebak focused on Amon's eyes."

"He wanted the power for himself," I speculated.

"That is correct, but Amon took precautions before he gave himself up," the god of the stars said. "Unfortunately, it seems to have backfired."

"What precautions? What do you mean?"

Sighing, Asten ran a hand over his bare scalp. "We knew that the dark priest would try to take the Eye, so we transferred it."

"How? Do you have it, then?"

"No. I am afraid I am the one currently in possession of the Eye." Dr. Hassan stepped forward. "Amon made me a temporary vessel to hold it for him. It was how I could discern hidden places within the oubliette and found a way out."

"Yes," Ahmose said. "But a mortal can sustain the Eye for only a short time. If we cannot transfer it back to Amon soon, your doctor will begin to have irrational thoughts, which will lead to hallucinations and, eventually, madness. My soul was almost lost because the Eye was not focused."

"Do you mean when we raised you?" I asked.

"Yes. The Eye guides us when we are called forth from the afterlife, and without Hassan guiding me properly, I could have ended up lost in the dark places between."

Filing that information away, I said, "So as long as we give the Eye back quickly enough, we should be fine, right? What part of that plan backfired?"

"Hiding the Eye accomplished our purpose in that Sebak could not steal it and harness its power, but now he knows it is in someone else," Asten explained.

"So, he'll come after Dr. Hassan?"

"No. He believes *you* are in possession of the Eye," Ahmose said.

Dr. Hassan fiddled with his hands. "Sebak *is* slightly obsessive."

I folded my arms. "That is a bit of an understatement."

"Yes. I fear he made you his target from the beginning," Dr. Hassan said, "knowing that you were Amon's greatest weakness, and now that he believes you have the Eye—"

"He'll come after me with even more resources."

"And now that he has channeled the incarnation of Apophis," Ahmose said, "his previous obsession will become an undeniable hunger."

"He will not rest until you are in his grasp, Lily." Asten's normally jovial expression was grave, giving me a good indication of just how serious my situation was.

"Oh."

Finding out that I was the target of a dark, reincarnated crocodile god in not one but two ways was not exactly how I wanted my Egyptian adventure to turn out.

"At least we know now how the dark priest obtained his power," Ahmose said.

"We do? Did I miss something?" I asked.

"He has stolen the power stored in Amon's three other canopic jars," Asten explained.

"But that power was not meant for a mortal, even one sustained by Seth. It has damaged him, fractured his mind," Ahmose said.

"You see, we were each granted four gifts of the gods," Asten said. "The exception was Amon, who received a fifth gift, the Eye of Horus. The other four are stored in the canopic jars, and we take them into ourselves upon rising."

"So what are the four gifts that Sebak stole?"

Ahmose said, "Amon was given the names Revealer of Secrets, Champion of the Troubled, Bringer of Light, and Seeker of Truth."

"How exactly are those considered powers?" I asked.

"Being the Bringer of Light enables Amon to call forth the golden falcon."

"Okay, so he got that one. What can the other three do?"

Amon's brothers looked at each other and then at me. "Even *we* do not know the full extent of our power," Asten said. "It is rare that we need to use our powers other than to complete the ceremony."

"But to use them is instinctual, and we can sense when one of us is drawing upon this power," Ahmose said. "Sebak was using Amon's power, but it was warped, distorted, almost as if the power was being used in the opposite way in which it was intended."

"So . . . instead of being the champion of the troubled, Sebak is the champion of the one who *causes* trouble?"

"Exactly."

"And you can sense this power?"

"Yes," Asten continued. "Sebak has used Amon's power to discover lost spells and distort others, such as the spell used to raise us. He has perverted it to summon the dead, warriors with no minds of their own who suffer endless torment in broken forms. It would be a kindness to return them to the afterlife."

I cleared my throat. "Then here's a crazy question. Can we get Amon's powers back?"

"Perhaps," Ahmose said. "But we must convince Sebak to relinquish them."

"It is not likely," Asten interjected. "To give up the powers he must voluntarily set them aside. Most men cannot or will not make that sacrifice."

Dr. Hassan, quiet for the last few moments, spoke up. "Perhaps I can reason with him."

Asten and Ahmose gave each other a doubtful look. "Sebak's purpose will be to challenge the ceremony," Asten said. "If he can disrupt the ritual, then he might garner enough power to raise the god of chaos. Seth will be at his strongest right before the full moon."

"When is that?" I asked.

"Tomorrow evening," Ahmose said. "The stars will be aligned and the gateway that bars the Dark One from returning to Earth will be open for a short window of time. Our job is to build a barrier powerful enough that he cannot cross during this interim."

Dr. Hassan said, "It is early morning now. That gives us approximately forty hours. But is it even possible to stop him?"

"With Amon, yes," Asten said.

During this conversation, I'd never left Amon's side. He remained unconscious, but I kept my hand wrapped around his arm, hoping to feel a little trickle of my energy leave me to fortify him. But there was nothing, no sign of life other than his shallow breathing. "Let's heal him, then," I said, ready to make the necessary sacrifice.

"Not here." Ahmose stepped forward and picked up Amon, slinging him over his shoulder. "We need a place we can rest, and we will all need to feast so we can be at our strongest tomorrow night."

"We can go back to my home," Osahar suggested.

Asten shook his head. "I would assume that your assistant knows where you live."

"Yes," Oscar replied sadly.

"Then we need another place," Asten said.

I rubbed my sticky arms. The idea of a feast, a shower, and a long nap was so very appealing. "Didn't we pass a hotel on the way to—?"

My comment was interrupted by the sound of a deep rattle and a hiss. Something had riled up the zombies even more than they already were, and I suddenly remembered the arc of power that Sebak had sent out just before he disappeared. The unmistakable scrape of claws on stone and the clank of armored limbs resounded in the air.

"Sounds like the biloko are back. Can we sandblast our way out? Or maybe use Asten's firefly-cloud thing?" I asked after surveying the room and finding there wasn't another door.

"We need to conserve our strength for the ceremony and healing Amon," Asten said. "Seeing the state he is in, I would like to avoid any unnecessary expenditures of power. If we have no other choice, we will do what we must, but for now I suggest that we fight our way through.

"Lily," he continued, "stay behind Ahmose. I will take the lead. Dr. Hassan, you will flank me, and then Ahmose and Lily will follow. Do you understand?"

Nodding, I reached out and picked up the only weapon I could find—one of the scalpels that had likely taken Amon's eye—and tried to ignore the bloodstains on it.

Asten still had his weapon, so he raised his bow and aimed a sparkling diamond-headed arrow at the door, which was buckling under the weight of the many creatures trying to get in. With Dr. Hassan gripping the silver handle of Ahmose's battle-ax and Ahmose with the cudgel in one hand and supporting Amon with the other, we prepared to make a run for it.

The door banged open and a heap of undead fell into the room looking for us.

Asten took out three in quick succession, while Ahmose beat another two so hard they twirled in a mass of limbs and fell to the side. Grabbing Dr. Hassan, Asten shoved him ahead. Eager to vacate the zombie-filled room myself, I pressed close to Ahmose, Amon's hair tickling my cheek, and followed.

Ahmose slammed the door shut and, risking a small use of his power, ran his thumb along the seal. "They will not escape now," he said.

When he finally shifted, giving me a view of what lay ahead of us, I froze.

I had been expecting invisible biloko demons. Their bites were painful, but not being able to see them kind of helped. What waited for us were definitely *not* biloko demons and not zombie soldiers, either.

Moving stealthily closer was a horde of snapping crocodiles. What's more, it looked like half of them were missing pieces. Some even had wrappings. "Seriously? Croc mummies?" I called out.

"I don't believe all of them are mummies," Dr. Hassan said as he waved the silver ax back and forth in the face of one, getting ready to give him the croc version of a pedicure.

He was right. Some of the beasts looked alive, while others were obviously undead. "There's too many of them!" I exclaimed. "How do we get out of here?"

When one of Asten's arrows glanced off the scaly head of a giant crocodile, Asten cried, "Hassan! Jump on my back." Scrabbling onto Asten as best he could, Dr. Hassan wrapped his arm around Asten's neck and held out the ax with the other. "Now, Lily! Take my hand. Ahmose, grab her other hand."

I was flanked by the brothers, who closed their eyes and rose into the air. An aggressive croc lurched upward in an attempt to snag a limb, but Ahmose saw I was in danger and yanked me higher.

His actions pulled me away from Asten, and with Ahmose carrying the combined weight of me and Amon, I dangled and fell, landing on the back of a croc mummy that did not like the fact that its remaining back leg broke off upon impact. It spun quickly and snapped at me, grabbing my shirt in its teeth. Violently, it tugged, wrenching me over the side of its back.

Unfortunately, another crocodile mummy was waiting for me on the other side. The second croc scrambled closer and swung its heavy head into me, pinning me and clacking its toothless jaws, while a third latched on to my backpack. Claws ripped easily through my jeans. Desperate, I tried to scrabble away from the creatures, but the first croc had clamped too tightly on to my shirt for me to escape.

"Lily! Grab on to me!"

Ahmose had sunk down to jaw-snapping level and wrapped his arm around my waist. I held him tightly, one arm wrapped around his muscular back and the other grabbing on to Amon. Ahmose rose in the air, lifting the stubborn mummy croc with us.

Asten drifted closer and raised his arm. With a quick jerk, he thrust an arrow into the eye of the croc and its whole body shook and then exploded into a shower of sparkling dust particles.

Without the extra weight, Ahmose seemed to recover somewhat, though I could tell carrying two people strained him. We floated over the river of crocodiles and out into the dawn sky.

Ahmose and Asten headed for a small cluster of trees on the other side of a dune, and once again I was thankful that cameras could not detect them. After setting Dr. Hassan, Amon, and me down, both men panted. We weren't too far from the road, so I said, "Why don't I take it from here? I'll be right back."

Like any self-respecting New York City girl, I was well versed in putting on my best face in even the most challenging disasters, and this qualified as a doozy. After tying my ripped shirt at my waist and rolling my torn jeans, I twisted my mud-caked hair into what I hoped would pass for dreadlocks and headed down the street to a main intersection, channeling the idea that I was simply a backpacking bohemian teen who'd fallen on a bit of hard luck.

Within fifteen minutes I'd located a cab large enough to hold all five of us and managed to convince the driver to wait by promising him a very generous tip.

Though the driver raised his eyebrows at Asten's and Ahmose's lack of clothing, what really concerned him was Amon. Dr. Hassan had tied a handkerchief around Amon's head to cover his empty eye sockets, but the blood was not as easy to conceal.

When the driver protested, I said, "It's okay, the blood is fake. It was a college assignment, to do a reenactment of a temple sacrifice for film class. He was up all night." I wasn't sure if there was a college in Kom Ombo, and even if there was, I was pretty certain that they wouldn't allow filming or reenactments of any type in historic temple sites.

The driver gave us a dubious look and kept glancing at us in the rearview mirror all the way to the hotel. As I prepared to exit, he asked about the giant tip I had promised.

"Just a minute," I said, and stuck my head out of the car to speak with Asten.

"Can you hypnotize him?"

"What? What is 'hypnotize'?"

"You know, convince him he's been compensated."

The driver, who knew enough English to get the drift of what we were saying, began to make a scene about us taking advantage of him, but Asten quickly raised his hand and put the man in a trance. After a few murmured words, the driver happily left us to our own devices.

After a little more hypnosis, we found ourselves in a lovely balcony room. "Okay, let's heal Amon," I said, and knelt next to him on the floor where Ahmose had set him down. I was extremely worried because I couldn't feel a wisp of a connection between us. When I touched him there was no warmth. I couldn't taste his emotions, and mine had been relatively stable of late.

Ahmose was leaning over his brother, hands pressed against Amon's chest. "Not yet, Lily. I have healed him enough to ensure his survival, but to transfer your energy will be a delicate process. If I make a mistake, it will likely kill you, so I need you to be as strong as possible before we make the exchange."

I blew out a breath. "Okay. So what do you want me to do?"

"Eat," he said frankly. "Rest. Bathe. Whatever you must do to relax your mind, nourish your body, and prepare your soul."

"You make it sound like this is going to be my last meal."

"I will do my best to ensure it is not."

Biting my lip, I reached out to stroke Amon's hair. "You're sure he'll be okay while I reenergize?"

"You may leave him in our hands," Asten said. "We have watched out for each other all our lives and we will continue to do so."

"Okay." As I pressed a kiss on Amon's forehead, I caught a whiff of myself, and said, "I'll be in the shower. Dr. Hassan, can you order a room service feast?"

"Of course."

We had two connecting rooms, so I left the men in one bedroom, crossed the connecting section, and headed into the second. It took the better part of a half hour before the water cascading over my scalp and down my body ran clean. By the time I was done, I was so tired that I felt like a zombie myself. Still, I efficiently wiped the steam from the mirror, applied lotion liberally to every exposed bit of skin, examined my various new scratches and scars, and brushed my hair.

With no clean clothes to change into, I wrapped myself in a robe and sought out the men to tell them the shower was open. When I entered the room, I found only Ahmose and Amon. Ahmose was sitting on the floor next to his brother's body, elbows resting on his knees, hands covering his head.

"Catching a quick nap?" I asked.

"No, I—"

Ahmose lifted his head and sucked in an almost indiscernible breath. There was the tiniest flash of something in his gray eyes, but he closed them quickly and turned his head. "Asten and the doctor are seeking some clothing for you."

"Oh. That's nice. I just wanted to let you know the shower is free."

"I will bathe after Asten returns."

Ahmose still wouldn't look at me. "I'm making you uncomfortable, aren't I?" I said. "You probably aren't used to seeing a woman in just a robe."

"I am respecting the boundary that exists between us."

"Boundary? What do you mean?"

"It is not right to look upon my brother's woman when he cannot. Especially if that woman is as beautiful as you are."

I smiled. "And I thought Asten was the flatterer." Putting my hands on my hips, I said, "I'm not sure Amon feels as strongly about me as you believe, but regardless, I'll leave you in peace."

"Lily," Ahmose called out just as I was about to close the door. "If Amon does not feel that way, then he is a fool."

The sincerity in Ahmose's voice sent a slight shiver down my spine. "Thank you, Ahmose," I answered over my shoulder as I left.

Unable to sleep while Amon was uncomfortable, I sat in a chair with my robe wrapped around me and allowed the quietness to sedate me. Not running for my life, or being distracted by a dark priest, allowed me time to really focus on how I felt. And it was worse than I'd ever felt in my life. Ahmose had called me beautiful, but when I looked in the mirror all I saw was haggard ugliness.

My usually soft skin was dry and bruised, the purple, green, and yellow spots still sore when I pressed my fingertips to them. Though I'd washed and conditioned my hair several times, clumps of it had fallen out in the shower, and my brush, which I'd meticulously cleaned, had so much hair caught in the bristles I could have used it to stuff a pillow.

No amount of lip balm could heal my cracked lips. I'd definitely lost several pounds, enough that my ribs stuck out. Overall, I looked like I needed to be hospitalized. Attempting to rehydrate myself, I gulped down glass after glass of water, even though it tasted like it had come directly from the Nile.

Finally, there was a soft knock on the door. Dr. Hassan stood on the other side, bag in hand, which he thrust into my arms. "We did the best we could. I hope you can find something there you'll feel comfortable in."

"Thank you," I said, clutching the bag to my chest.

"The food will be here momentarily. I believe I will take this opportunity to avail myself of a shower as well."

"Do you want to use this one?" I asked.

He shook his head. "I'll share the second room with the others."

With a brief smile and a nod, he closed the door behind him. He'd done a good job shopping with Asten and I realized it was likely that Asten had way more experience with women's clothing than Amon did. The idea made me smile, but the smile soon disappeared when I thought of Amon.

I dressed in a drawstring pair of khakis. They were a little too big, but cinching them at the waist did the trick. Then I pulled a loose tunic over my head and found a pair of sandals that fit perfectly. After tying back my newly thin hair with a scarf, I headed out of the room to see what the others were doing.

Asten was picking through the food that had recently arrived. When he saw me, he said, "Now, this"—he held up a plate full of roasted meat—"is what I call a feast." He took the plate into the room where Ahmose waited with Amon and then returned, frowning. "Why are you still standing there? Fill your belly, Lily. You do not need to wait for permission."

By habit, I put a few bits of green salad on a plate and spooned on a few roasted vegetables. Asten watched with an incredulous expression as I took a seat at the table. "Is that all you are going to eat? You need more. Meat will fortify you. Here." He shoved a giant piece of fragrant lamb onto my plate and brought over several more items.

Sighing, I looked at my overflowing plate and wondered if all Egyptian men fed their women like this, or if it was just the former princes. As Asten ate, sitting across from me, he watched every bite I took. Pushing the food around on the plate, I finally looked up at his scowling face. "It doesn't feel right to eat without Amon," I said. "He was the one who taught me all about feasting."

Asten's severe expression eased. "I understand, but consider the fact that you must sustain your body so that you can sustain Amon."

"Are you trying to say I'm eating for two?" I teased.

"I do not comprehend your meaning."

"Never mind. I promise I will try to eat more."

A freshly showered Dr. Hassan entered the room. He'd managed to find cargo pants and a vest and even a new fedora, but brown instead of white.

"Good," Asten said. "Now I am going to bathe, and when I return, I expect at least half of this food to be gone."

I ate until I couldn't take another bite and then went to relieve Ahmose so he could shower. With a soapy hot towel, I bathed Amon's face and carefully cleaned the wounds on his chest and arms. The water quickly became red with his blood. I'd been through six bowlfuls of it by the time Ahmose came back.

At first I didn't recognize Ahmose and Asten. They looked completely different in modern clothing, and, like Amon, they had grown out their hair. Ahmose had a short cap of dark hair, while Asten's was a bit longer than Amon's and was slicked back. Both of them looked like they belonged on a fashion runway.

"Not that you both don't look good," I began, "but doesn't growing your hair use up some of your power?"

"The power necessary was tiny compared with what we need," Ahmose said.

"Besides," Asten countered, "we are hoping we can save up the energy and travel as mortals to the site of the ceremony."

"The pyramids, you mean." When they looked surprised, I waved my hand and explained, "Amon told me."

"Ah," they said. Both men shifted back and forth uneasily until Dr. Hassan entered the room. "Are you ready, Lily?" Amhose asked.

"Yes."

"I wish you had rested more," he admonished as he knelt down beside me. When I shrugged unhappily, Asten approached and gave me a small smile. "Do not worry overmuch. Ahmose is a very skilled healer. If anyone can guide Amon on the path to return to us, it is he." I nodded, placing my hand in Ahmose's large one.

"Channel as much energy as you dare, Brother," Ahmose instructed Asten. Then he closed his eyes and placed his hand on Amon's forehead.

He began chanting in Egyptian, and I gasped as silver pulses of light appeared beneath my skin. The light coalesced, traveling down my arm into my hand, and then jumped from me to Ahmose.

The silver energy lit Ahmose's hand and then briefly pooled on Amon's forehead before sinking into his skin. Amon's chest rose as he breathed deeply. My arms trembled and I suddenly realized I couldn't swallow. I slumped against Ahmose's arm, utterly exhausted. Asten stood on the other side of Amon. His eyes were closed and his arms stretched forward, palms up in a meditative manner.

A white fog trickled from Asten's fingertips and a stream of it shot toward me while another stream hit Ahmose directly in the chest. I breathed in, becoming increasingly attuned to Amon's brothers. I tasted a sort of icy salt and realized it was a flavor belonging solely to Asten. It was the tang of the stars. When I exhaled, I could see my breath and my lips felt frosty. The white fog I'd exhaled drifted down and became a third stream between me and Ahmose.

The triangle connecting the three of us allowed me to sense the innermost desires of both Asten and Ahmose. Asten longed to explore everything he had missed out on while he lingered for centuries in the afterlife. Ahmose wanted to work with his hands and secretly wished for a family. Then I sensed another presence in our circle—one I immediately recognized—Amon.

I felt him acknowledge his brothers and rejoice at having them near him, but then he noticed I was there. *Lily?* I heard him speak in my mind. *No! Lily! Why is she here? She cannot do this! This will cement the bond!*

Ahmose answered his brother. *The bond is essential, Brother.*

No! I will not allow it.

Amon struggled with Asten and Ahmose, not wanting their help but desperately needing it. His anger and hopelessness made me shrink away. I felt like an intruder. It was very clear that Amon had no desire to be with me, even if it meant his survival.

Distantly, I heard Ahmose's spoken words, "He is rejecting the transfer."

"He will not have the strength to complete the ceremony," Asten warned.

My ethereal self was forcibly pushed back into my body and I blinked my eyes open. The fog connecting me, Asten, and Ahmose dissipated, and both men jerked back before righting themselves.

"What was that? What happened?" I demanded.

"He will not allow me to channel your energy."

"Why?" Tears filled my eyes. I knew I was drained and overemotional once more, but I was too tired to control myself. I hollered, "Why is he being so stubborn? Does he despise me so much that he will risk allowing darkness to fill the world?"

"He does not . . . despise you, Lily," Asten said.

"Look," I said as I angrily wiped my tears away, "you don't have to defend him. He's a big-boy-slash-Egyptian-god who makes his own choices."

I attempted to get to my feet only to find that my legs wouldn't move.

"You are weakened from the energy transfer," Ahmose explained.

"But I thought—"

"I was still able to channel some of your energy, but I do not know if that will be enough. In the meantime"—Ahmose stood up and scooped me easily into his arms—"you need to sleep."

Hurt by Amon's rejection, I didn't protest, saying nothing when Ahmose tucked me into the bed in the next room. When he closed the door, I wasn't sure if I'd be able to rest, but sleep found me immediately. I didn't stir for sixteen hours. When I woke, two things instantly made me alert. First, the light of a nearly full moon spilled over the bed, meaning we had less than twenty-four hours to save the world. Second, there was someone watching me. Seated in a chair in the corner of the room, wearing fresh clothes and a pair of sunglasses, his long legs stretched out and crossed at the ankles, was Amon.

Pyramids

"Amon?" I whispered in the moonlit room. "How are you feeling?"

"Not bad, all things considered," he replied.

"Your brothers—"

"Are resting. As is Dr. Hassan."

"Oh." I wasn't sure what to say. The trauma of what we'd been through and the thought of what we still needed to overcome was too much, the sting of uncertainty too real for me to feel completely comfortable with him.

Lamely, I asked, "How are your eyes?"

He half smirked, half grimaced. "I wouldn't know, as they are not with me at present."

"Sorry," I murmured. "That was an insensitive question."

"Do not feel sorry. I am the one who needs to apologize. My brothers have expressed their concern over you."

"They have?"

"Yes. There seems to be some confusion regarding our bond."

I wet my lips and felt my heart thudding against my chest. What he said next would either break my heart or heal it. "What did you tell them?"

"The truth. That I have no desire to seal this bond with you and that I will take no more of your life essence. In fact, I would like to express my regret for what has been done to you thus far."

"I see."

"My brothers are of the opinion that I will not be able to complete the ceremony without you."

"Are they right?"

Amon worked the muscles in his jaw before answering. "No. Dr. Hassan has an idea that should keep Sebak at bay long enough for the three of us to complete the ceremony. My brothers have agreed to this plan believing that you will remain at my side until I return to the afterlife."

"I can do that."

Amon sat forward, pressing his hands together. "Young Lily." He sighed. "It is *my* wish that you go home. Now. *Before* all of this happens."

"But your brothers seem to think you'll need me."

After a brief dark laugh, Amon said, "Not in the way they think." He paused and rubbed his hand over his jaw. "I believe I still have sufficient energy to do what I was called to do."

"And if you don't?"

"Then so be it."

Amon sat back in the chair as if utterly exhausted by our conversation. The wounded young man in my room was a shadow of the man I'd come to know. He didn't speak of love, or say that he would miss me, or even that he appreciated the time, let alone the energy, that I'd given to him. What was even more disturbing was that he seemed to now lack faith in his purpose.

The god of the sun was damaged. Betrayed by his body. An eternal being without hope. The despair and the loss he radiated was evident, even with him blocking our connection. Gone were his sunshine smile, his delight at discovering the world around him, and his belief that he could overcome any odds by fulfilling his duty. He was definitely not the person I'd come to know and had fallen in love with.

"Amon? There's still a way out of this. There has to be."

"No, Lily. There is not."

"Tell me. It's more than just your eyes, I can feel it. You don't have to hold back. I can help."

Amon let out a long, slow breath. Then he lifted his head, his expression unreadable. "You are weak, Lilliana. Mortal. I could crush you into powder with just my mind if I wanted to. There is no place for you at my side. It is time you came to terms with that."

I momentarily lost my breath. What he'd said hurt, though I acknowledged the truth of his words. I *was* weak and mortal. And, like Asten said, a poor excuse for a devotee. The worst thing wasn't the mention of my weakness or that he didn't want me with him—I might be able to get over that. I harbored no illusions about my strengths and weaknesses.

No, the hardest thing to hear was my full name—Lilliana—cross his lips. He'd never called me that before, and the formal way he said it reminded me of just who I really was. Lilliana. The name my father used in his tolerant-yet-stern voice. It was what my mother called me when she wanted to make sure I heard her instructions or when she introduced me at parties.

Until now, it wasn't a name that Amon had ever called me.

Lily was the name of a girl who headed off on fantastic adventures. But at my core, I was the prim and proper, going-places-whether-I-wanted-to-or-not Lilliana. I felt as if Amon himself had slammed the door on the golden birdcage I had dared to look out of.

With Amon I'd thrown caution to the wind. I should have known better. *Lilliana* should have known better.

Stiffly, I jerked the blanket back, not caring that Amon was there. I'd stripped down to my underwear sometime in the night, draping my new clothing over the nightstand. It wasn't like Amon could see me anyway, which was good considering the hot, angry tears that had begun rolling down my face.

I was jerking the tunic over my head when Amon cleared his throat. "You should be aware that I can see you."

"What?" I said, spinning, the slacks clutched in front of me. "How is that possible?"

"Hassan returned the Eye of Horus."

"But I thought that was a mind-reading kind of thing—a way to see pathways."

"The Eye is many things, and it would seem it can do even more than we supposed."

"Well, turn it off so I can finish getting dressed."

"The image is gone. You may clothe yourself now."

Though he assured me he wasn't peeking, the corners of his mouth were turned up in a small smile. Deciding that modesty was the least of my worries, I quickly slipped my pants on and rummaged under the bed for my sandals.

"How did you configure it to see, anyway?"

"You misunderstand. I cannot see. The Eye merely showed me an image like the one you demonstrated to me on your . . . phone."

"Well, congratulations on your little going-away peepshow. If you'll excuse me, I'm going to see if there's any food left."

"*Lily.*" The way he said my name stopped me in my tracks. Amon rose, reaching out his hand until he touched the wall. Then, feeling along it, he made his way to my side. His nostrils flared when he was within a foot of me, and he paused.

Tentatively, he reached his fingers out until they made contact with my hair. "I did not intend to embarrass you or cause you discomfort," he murmured. "The Eye responds to the wishes of the person in possession of it. This is why Dr. Hassan suddenly knew the answers to the many questions he had in his mind."

"So you were wishing—"

Amon ran his fingers down my hair, golden light spreading across the strands, adding more highlights to my dark brown tresses.

Stepping back, Amon let out a sigh. "To see you again before I departed this world."

I waited a heartbeat or two, giving him time to add to that comment, but he didn't. Lily and Lilliana fought a war inside my mind. In the end I didn't know who won. Was it the weak side of me that wanted to repair and forgive, or the strong side? Did Lily have unresolved business with Amon, or was Lilliana desperately clinging to the hope that she could be something more, mean something more to someone like him?

Either way, I decided to let him off the hook. He *was* saving the world, after all. The least I could do was not obsess over him like a typical teenager.

"Can I see? Your eyes, I mean?"

He considered for a moment and then shook his head. "It is not the image of me I'd like you to remember."

"You don't think I can handle it?"

"You balked at Asten's raising."

"Well, yeah. It was my first mummy revivification, you know. You should have seen me at Ahmose's. I handled it much better."

Amon smiled, and I sensed that he, too, did not wish to part on a bad note. "Perhaps you should tell me about it."

"Have you eaten?"

"I was hoping to feast with you a final time," he said.

"I suppose that's the least I can do. We'll call room service and order up a farewell feast. I wonder if they serve breakfast at this time of day."

"Do you think they will have some of those circular breads filled with sugared fruits?"

"Danishes? I'll check."

We fell back into our familiar companionship, yet there was an unspoken tension that lingered between us. I overanalyzed every word for hidden double meaning. Each touch burned my skin as if I had pressed a hot poker to it. My emotions were all there just beneath the surface, bared, raw, and prickly.

Once our food arrived, Amon's spirits seemed to lift. We ate together, him pushing plate after plate toward me, often cocking his head to listen for the sounds of me eating, while I told him about the quicksand and finding Ahmose's sarcophagus. When I couldn't eat another bite, I moved my plate away and sipped a glass of sparkling water.

I groaned. "I feel like I ate a rhinoceros."

"Impossible," Amon said as he took the last date-filled Danish and cut it in half, offering a piece to me. "If you had, there would be a horn protruding from your body."

Laughing less easily than I once had now that I knew our separation was imminent, I said, "How do you know there isn't one?" I immediately felt sorry that I'd said something like that to a person who'd just lost his eyes.

Amon took my comment in good stride. "I may not know, but I know a way to find out."

"Oh, really. How?" I eyed him suspiciously.

Reaching out, Amon took hold of my arm, pulling me to my feet, and ran his hand slowly up my arm. Pausing at my elbow, he rubbed it with his fingers. "Hmm, this piece feels as scaly as a rhinoceros, but a horn would be much sharper."

I smiled, making a mental note to pack a bottle of very expensive lotion the next time I went on an Egyptian holiday. Amon ran his hands over my shoulders and up my neck. He spent a moment prodding at my cheeks and tweaking my nose, and we both laughed. Sobering, he swept his warm hands down my back.

When he got to my waist, his fingers found the side slit on my tunic and caressed my bare skin. His thumbs drew little circles before his fingertips trailed over my quivering stomach to my belly button.

Tiny warm pulses shot into my belly and I sucked in a breath.

"So soft," Amon whispered, his hands moving to my back again as he drew me closer. My hands slid up his chest and my arms wrapped around his neck.

I relished the feel of his arms and looked up at his face. It was startling to see the dark sunglasses, with my own reflection staring back at me, rather than his lovely hazel eyes. Though I lifted my head, waiting, hoping for the kiss I'd long imagined, he pressed his lips against my forehead instead.

"I will miss you, Lily."

Something broke inside me. His soft words carried more power than all of the amazing things I'd seen him do. The gracious gift of those six syllables was a kindness I'd sorely needed. But until that moment, I didn't know how much.

"I'll miss you, too," I said, my eyes filling with tears. I had been more inclined to weep this past week than in my entire life. No wonder there were so many songs about love. What I'd been through with Amon would make an epic one.

He must've heard me sniffle, because he cupped my cheeks, wiping the tears away with his thumbs and replacing the wet trails with his golden warmth.

"Lily?"

"Yes?" I answered, blinking to clear my vision.

"I am reluctant to inform you that there is absolutely no evidence that you have consumed a rhinoceros."

I laughed and then cried harder. Amon smiled. "It is time to wake my brothers. Dr. Hassan will take you to the airport and then meet us at the pyramids after securing our transportation. I am sorry I cannot send you back via sandstorm as I promised. If I had more power at my disposal, I would draw the weeks together so your parents would not know you were missing."

Nodding, I answered, "It's okay. I understand."

"Dr. Hassan said you would need paperwork?"

"Don't worry about it. I'll call my parents. They'll take care of everything."

"Will they be angry with you?"

"Let's just say this situation is pretty much as epic a rebellion as any teen could accomplish." When he tilted his head in confusion, I added, "Yes. But I'll survive."

"Good. It will ease my mind to know that you are safe. I am sorry, for everything, Young Lily. I did not mean to draw you into our cause so completely."

"Don't apologize." Daring a final touch, I cupped his cheek, slowly moving my hand down to his shoulder and squeezing. "Despite my ragged emotional state, it's been the time of my life." Amon took my hand and brought it to his lips. After he pressed a warm kiss on my wrist, I cleared my throat. "Now let's go wake up your brothers."

Lacing my fingers through his, I guided him to the other side of the suite. Asten was already awake and having a serious conversation with Dr. Hassan. I left Amon with them while I sought out Ahmose.

The incarnation of the moon slept with his cheek pressed against his hand. The other bedroom was parallel to mine, so the rays of the nearly full moon fell upon his face, giving his skin a silvery sheen.

"Ahmose?" I said quietly. "It's time to wake up."

Blinking, the big man shifted as glowing silver orbs met mine. He smiled. "You look better, Lily."

Twisting the ends of my tunic, I answered, "It was thanks to your healing and many, many hours of sleep." He leaned up on one elbow and the sheet slipped down to his waist. Though I'd been around him when he was bare-chested before, it somehow seemed a bit more intimate now. Ducking my head, I said, "We'll wait for you outside."

Quickly, I vacated the room and took a seat next to Asten. He gave me a long look and then glanced at Amon. "How are you feeling?" he asked.

"I'm all right. I'm actually more worried about the three of you."

"Oh? Why is that?"

"Well, the fact that Amon is sending me packing means I won't know if the three of you are going to make it through the final ceremony. I suppose I would know if you failed because then the world would end, darkness would reign, et cetera. Still, it would be nice to know that you, you know, survived to return another day, so to speak."

Asten frowned as if trying to fully understand my speech, and then he looked at Amon, who sat with his sunglasses aimed at nothing. Amon's expression was unyielding, his jaw tight.

"I see," Asten answered slowly. "I thought we talked about this."

"Lily is under my care," Amon said. "I will decide the level of risk that is acceptable. She is returning to her life in New York and that is the end of the conversation."

"The end of what conversation?" Ahmose said as he entered the room, tugging a too-tight shirt that said I ♥ EGYPT over his head.

After stifling a giggle that made all three brothers turn in my direction, I sat quietly, curious to hear what Amon would say.

"I was telling Asten that my wish is to send Lily home," Amon said.

Ahmose sighed. "You know that the odds are not in our favor."

"It does not matter. I will not risk her life."

"Should she not be able to weigh the risk on her own terms?" Ahmose continued.

"It is not fair to use her for our gain. Lily goes."

Asten joined in. "Brother, we are not saying we wish her harm. On the contrary, we, too, would wish to protect her from the perils of our world, but should the need arise—"

Furious, Amon spat, "Should the need arise? We have served the gods for millennia, acted as their sacrifices time and time again! Perhaps, in seeing our failure, they could deign to manage their own affairs for once. I, for one, refuse to compromise this innocent mortal girl simply to grant more leisure to those who have long been silent."

"The gods have blessed us," Ahmose started.

"They have *cursed* us!" Amon countered. "Abused us. Bled us dry. And for what? To stop a problem they allowed to fester in the first place. Why is it that we must continue to act as their cosmic gatekeepers?"

I bit my lip. Apparently, the information Dr. Hassan had shared with me about the gods protecting the brothers from Seth was not common knowledge. The Eye had shown him much. I felt a twinge of jealousy that I hadn't been able to access it as well.

How nice it would be to have instant answers to any question. I glanced at Dr. Hassan, who gave a slight shake of his head. Evidently, he didn't want to share that information with them just then. I decided to wait and question him about it later before I brought it up to the brothers.

"Brothers," Amon went on, "we agreed to this bargain to serve our ancestors, but they have long since entered the afterlife. We protect the world, but the world fears us, or worse, does not care. We exist, but have no life. We do our duty, but there is no joy in it, at least not for me. I will not steal the precious opportunity to live, to be mortal, and to be free, from Lily. She deserves more. I will not take from her what was taken from us."

Quiet descended, and finally Ahmose reached out and placed a hand on Amon's shoulder. "Very well. We will respect your decision."

"But—" Asten began, then stopped when Amon raised his head. Asten muttered unhappily, "We will respect your decision."

"Good," Amon answered as he rose. "Now, let's get this over with. Dr. Hassan?" Osahar stood quickly and moved next to Amon, who placed his hand on the vizier's shoulder. "Take us to the airport."

"Yes, Master." This time Amon didn't protest the title.

In a matter of moments, Dr. Hassan and I had gathered our meager belongings and we were in a taxi before dawn, headed to the airport. After we arrived, Dr. Hassan purchased tickets for the three brothers on a tour bus headed to the pyramids of Giza. He told them he would join as soon as possible.

Ahmose and Asten held me close as they hugged me goodbye, wishing me well in life. Amon merely took hold of my shoulders and planted a brotherly kiss on my cheek. "Farewell, Lily," he said stiffly.

"Is that the best you can do?" I teased, though the pain of knowing I'd never see him again had risen to the surface.

He misunderstood my comment, or maybe he didn't. "I will do my best not to need you," he replied.

Wordlessly, I nodded, and before I could formulate another reason for him to stay with me a moment longer, he was stepping up onto the bus. Ahmose and Asten waved from a lowered window, but Amon, who sat just behind them, stared straight ahead, an undecipherable expression on his face. I sensed nothing from him and realized he must have completely cut off our connection as easily as he had dismissed me from his life.

Taking a shaky breath, I turned to Dr. Hassan as the bus rounded the corner and disappeared into traffic. "Okay, so I guess we should call my parents first."

"That will not be necessary."

"No?" I asked, confused. "They'll need to know that I'm okay and send me the papers I need to get out of here."

"Yes, yes. We will call them, but not today."

"Why not?"

His eyes sparkled as he spoke. "Because you aren't going home yet, Lilliana Young. You are coming with me." Darting a glance around, he read an overhead sign. "Yes. It's this way."

Quickly, he wound through the many people around us, heading toward a ticket agent.

"Where are we going?" I asked after he finished his conversation with the agent in his native language.

"The pyramids."

"What?"

Stopping momentarily, Osahar explained, "Despite Amon's insistence that your presence is not necessary, both Asten and I believe that the fate of Egypt, nay, of the world, might rest in your hands. The question I must now ask you is, what would you sacrifice to ensure Amon's survival?"

There weren't too many people in the world I would give up anything for.

Those I sketched who were truly in love saw only each other. It was clear in their eyes. These were the people who would die for one another. Who would rather put themselves through suffering instead of watching a loved one be in pain.

That depth of emotion was missing in my life. Except for my grandmother, I wasn't sure there was anyone who'd be willing to die for me, who loved me that much. More than anything I craved a deep connection with another person.

When I met Amon I thought I'd finally found it. Here was a person who understood what it meant to sacrifice something for someone else. Now I knew exactly what my type was. It didn't have to do with eye color, or height, or how muscular his frame was. It was that elusive quality, so difficult to capture. I wanted someone who loved me so much he'd be willing to die for me.

I believed Amon was that person. He was willing to die for the world, anyway. And even though he'd turned me away, I was still pretty sure he'd sacrifice anything for my safety. Perhaps it was his sense of duty that kept him at a distance. Perhaps he wanted to die and be finished with his celestial calling. Or perhaps he just wasn't as interested in me as I was in him.

Regardless, I decided that even if the feelings I had for Amon weren't mutual, he deserved my support. He was a man worthy of love, and if I was ever going to be the kind of person who might be worthy of someone's attention in return—not that I really believed I'd find someone else like him—then I needed to be willing to sacrifice myself for something outside of my own wants and desires.

I had to take a leap of faith and see where it led me.

"Anything," I replied after letting out a deep breath. "I'd sacrifice anything to help him."

"Excellent. That is all I need to know. We must hurry to beat them there. It shouldn't be too difficult. The bus will get them there in time, but the two of us will get there faster."

"How?"

He smiled as the agent handed him a set of keys. "We're driving."

It was normally at least a ten-hour drive to Giza from Kom Ombo, but Dr. Hassan made it in eight, stopping only after I insisted it was absolutely necessary. When we entered Cairo, instead of continuing on

to the pyramids, he asked me to wait in the car while he entered an outdoor market. He returned twenty minutes later, arms loaded with bags,
which he threw carelessly into the backseat.

"What's all that for?" I asked.

"You'll see."

He'd been cryptic about this top-secret vizier plan for the entire
drive, skillfully evading my many questions. I only knew that I was
an important part of his plan and that he'd arranged everything with
Asten.

When I reiterated Amon's desire for me to leave Egypt, Osahar said
that if all went according to plan, Amon would never even know I was
there, which suited me fine. Maybe my rejected heart would heal just a
tiny bit if I knew I'd helped save the world, and if it also meant I could
avoid being spurned by Amon once again, then all the better.

It wasn't long before the pyramids came into view. Dr. Hassan
wound through the busy crowded streets until he arrived at the edge
of the pyramid complex. Tour buses were lined up on the hard-packed
sand. A few white-shirted men wearing hats policed the area on camels.
I was surprised to see tourists climbing up the sides of the pyramids.

"Aren't the sites under protection?" I asked.

Dr. Hassan waved his hand in the air. "Don't get an archaeologist
talking about site preservation. It would take weeks for me to come
down from my soapbox, and frankly, I don't have the time right now."

"Okay, but with all these tourists, how are we going to accomplish
anything?"

"Ah, the tourists and merchants will leave the moment the brothers
arrive."

"How?" When he grinned, I said, "Wait. Don't tell me. I'll see,
right?"

"Right."

He parked the car and we grabbed the many bags before heading
toward the Great Sphinx. At least the monument we reached was roped
off so no one could touch it. Flashing his credentials to the one guard

fending off dozens of tourists, Dr. Hassan opened a gate and bade me to follow him.

I stepped in the footprints he made in the sand, looking up when we reached the front of the Sphinx. It was hard to believe I was actually standing there. I was so absorbed in my surroundings that I jumped when Dr. Hassan nudged my arm.

"This way," he said.

After leading me into an ancient stone structure that looked like a series of empty chambers, he reached behind a brick that jutted out a bit at the end of the room and pushed on something. A mechanical rumbling shook the area we were in, causing a cascade of sand to drop over the entrance. The back wall moved aside, revealing a series of steps that led down into darkness.

"Archaeologist hideaway or grand vizier secret?" I asked as I pointed to the opening.

"Grand vizier," he mumbled as he gathered his things. "Come."

I stumbled along, descending steadily until the door closed and we were surrounded by complete darkness.

"Dr. Hassan?" I whispered worriedly.

"Wait a moment."

My eyes began to adjust and I noticed a series of large stones placed in alcoves. They glowed like the rock Asten had given me in the Oasis of the Sacred Stones.

"Did Asten make those?" I asked.

Osahar shook his head and started down the steps again. "Perhaps he did at one time. All I know is that they are regenerated each time the ceremony is complete. The light has faded over the last thousand years, but when our task is done, it will be so bright down here you would think it was our own personal sun. My theory is that the pyramids generate the power somehow."

"Interesting." The heavy bag bumped against my leg. "So are you going to tell me what all this stuff is for now?"

"I am creating an effigy."

"You mean like a voodoo doll?"

"On a much larger scale."

"Why?"

"There is a spell that will weaken if not destroy Apophis."

"And you hope it will work on Sebak?"

"Yes. I will need your help to construct it."

We arrived at the bottom of the stairs and stopped in front of a heavy door. Osahar took a key that hung from a chain around his neck and fit it into the ancient lock. I was almost afraid it wouldn't turn because the lock was so old, but the key worked and the door opened without even a squeak. Inside the large room were a worktable and a giant dresser-sized glowing rock.

Pressing my hands against the rock, I found it warm, but it didn't burn me. I could feel a hum of energy coming from it. Old parchments and books lined handmade shelves, and various tools, both modern and ancient, hung from a pegged wall.

"Did you make this space?"

Dr. Hassan shook his head. "I have added to it over the years, but this has been here since the time of Amon's birth." He pointed to one tunnel and then another, in a different corner. "These underground passageways connect to the pyramids and even run beneath the Sphinx. It is how we viziers recover the bodies of the brothers when their time on Earth has elapsed," he finished quietly.

"Oh." Though I knew that Amon had to die so that he could rise again, the idea that his body would be recovered and painstakingly preserved was disturbing. I had a sudden urge to rush out to his tour bus and beg him not to go through with it. But instead of giving into my emotions, I reminded myself that I was just a mortal girl who had journeyed for a time, however brief, with gods come to life. Who was I to judge whether their task was a worthy one and whether the sacrifices made were justifiable?

I didn't know yet what Osahar had in mind for me, but if there was something I could do to make what Amon had to endure easier, then I was willing to see it through. "What do you need me to do?" I asked.

"Take these bags and form a body."

"Like a scarecrow?"

"Exactly."

Reaching into the bags, I found a pair of pants, rope, a knife, and several pillows of different sizes. As I stuffed smaller pillows down the pant legs, Dr. Hassan cut into the large pillow and placed a tool and a comb inside. "These belonged to Sebak," he said.

After we'd dressed the makeshift scarecrow, Dr. Hassan handed me a very gaudy crocodile-skin jacket. "Is this real?" I asked.

"He is part crocodile now. To minimize his power we must destroy every part of him."

"So what's the spell?" I asked as Dr. Hassan finished preparing a potion.

"It is more of a ritual than a spell. Is the effigy ready?"

"I think so. It's just that you have more clothes and a fedora in the bag. Did you need more layers?"

"No. Those are for later. Please bring the remaining bag. I will carry the effigy."

Dr. Hassan picked up a mallet and a weighty-looking metal rod, then hefted up the effigy. He led me through one long tunnel after the next. Finally, we climbed another set of stairs, which seemed to go on forever. When we emerged we were on top of an ancient structure. The sun had just set and the orange sky was slowly turning purple.

"Where did everyone go?" I asked, surprised to see the previously crowded valley as deserted as a church on Monday.

"They are here," Dr. Hassan said. "Like I said, when the sons of Egypt set foot on the soil surrounding the pyramids, the people in the vicinity immediately depart. They are suddenly distracted or they remember they have to be somewhere. I have a theory that it has something to do with the energy the brothers give off." He sighed. "There are so many questions I wish to ask. If only there were time. The scientist in me mourns the limited amount of time I have to be among them, but the vizier in me is grateful to have had even that."

I could identify with his mixed feelings.

Squinting in the fading light, I made out three black dots standing by the Sphinx. "I see them!"

One of the brothers strode forward, just passing the Sphinx, when a hissing sound, like sand falling through an hourglass, filled the air. The noise grew louder and became unbearable.

"What is it?" I yelled as I pressed my hands against my ears.

"It is the dark priest of Seth," Dr. Hassan replied.

Quickly he took the rod and pounded it with the mallet until it was embedded in the roof. I jumped to help him secure the effigy to the rod. Just as we finished, the hissing noise stopped and an eerie quiet descended on the landscape.

A breeze lifted my hair from my neck and I slowly turned. Amon, Asten, and Ahmose stood in a spot where a quivering mass of blackness now erupted between them and the pyramids.

"What's that?" I gasped.

"That, my dear, is an army of the dead."

An Eye for an Eye

I couldn't help the shiver that ran down my spine. There were literally thousands of zombies standing between the brothers and the pyramids. The black mass was like a shuddering scourge of desolation, just waiting to sink its teeth into three juicy demigods. Ahmose and Asten had given up so much of their strength to sustain Amon that they were almost as drained now as he was. Even if they did decide to fight, Amon would literally be fighting blind.

"We have to help them!" I cried.

"We will. But we must wait for all the players to enter the arena."

As soon as Dr. Hassan said that, a rumbling shook the ground and a fissure opened in the middle of the zombie mass. Brilliant light shone from the opening as mist flowed from it. Even far away, I could clearly see the giant crocodile claw rising out of a crack in the earth. The claw stretched out, digging deeply into the soil before a giant body heaved out after it. It was a horrendous monster: half man, half Godzilla, with a long crocodile tail.

"Is that . . . Sebak?" I called out incredulously.

"I am afraid it is," Dr. Hassan replied.

The edge of the moon broke over the horizon, bathing the landscape in its brilliant silvery light. Bravely, the three brothers stood before the creature, which was larger in scale and in height than the Sphinx. As one, they raised their hands in the air. The spell they chanted grew so loud I could easily hear it, though I didn't understand the words.

Light bubbled around them—a swirling mass of silver, gold, and white. The shimmering bubble grew and then burst in a supernova, spreading light in all directions before settling on the ground and encircling the pyramids. Then, slowly, the light rose upward, forming a wall that grew until it arched over our heads in a transparent iridescent dome.

Dr. Hassan gave a satisfied grunt. "There. Now we cannot be observed from the outside. For all intents and purposes, the citizens of Cairo will see only a massive storm cloud covering the pyramids. They will not be able to see or hear anything occurring within the circle of light. All outsiders with an interest in viewing the pyramids tonight will turn aside, completely forgetting that they even attempted to visit."

I wasn't sure if that was a good thing or a bad thing. Surely if the people of Egypt knew their gods were fighting to keep dark energy at bay and to prevent the rising of the god of chaos, they would, at the very least, be concerned.

In comic books, regular citizens often rose up in defense of their heroes. Granted, they also got in the way and frequently had to be saved from death, but in this case, the distraction of mortals might help stave off the zombies. Of course, with our luck, they'd probably get bitten and join the zombie ranks.

Turning to Dr. Hassan, I asked, "Now?"

"Yes. It is time."

Dr. Hassan pulled out an ancient book and ran his finger down a page until he found what he was looking for.

Asten's voice rose from the cloud, as clearly as if he stood next to us.

THE STARS WHISPER THE WILL OF THE COSMOS.

A hiss, like ocean foam washing across the sand, echoed around us and some movement overhead caught my eye. Through the flickering dome, the stars burned brighter than I'd ever seen them, which shouldn't have been possible since we were so close to a major city.

They pulsed brilliantly, the familiar constellations seeming close enough to touch. The more-distant stars appeared closer as well, and as I gazed overhead, I felt weightless, like I could float upward into the night sky and become lost in the universe.

I was able to see the colors of the stars with my naked eye, which I knew was impossible. I could make out the rings of Saturn, a binary star, and a distant galaxy. Then, all of a sudden, the world shifted.

The stars fell.

Or rather, they were moving, the night sky spinning like a top, with each star leaving a streak of light behind it. Dizzy, I reached for Dr. Hassan's hand and the spinning heavens slowed to a stop. The patterns of the stars overhead were no longer familiar. It was almost as if I were looking at the sky from the perspective of a different point in the galaxy.

Ahmose spoke next, his deep voice echoing in my mind.

"The moon fills the air with thrumming power."

The luminous full moon, which was only halfway over the horizon, shone brighter and brighter. Its silvery light spilled over the land in almost liquid form, bathing everything in the pyramid zone with a mercurial glow. The speed of the moonrise accelerated until it was almost directly over the top of the temples before it stopped.

I froze as Amon's rich voice swept over me. Despite the power that emanated from it, I could still hear a slight quaver, a resigned tinge of sadness, and I wondered if it was possible that he regretted sending me away. That he might miss me as much as I missed him.

The sun uncovers all hidden pathways
And exposes all that is secret and shadow.

When he uttered the last word, a bright light burst forth and emanated from the three servants of the gods, who stood facing the darkness. The light rose, encompassing everything in the dome, burning so vibrantly that the visible world became white. It took several moments before I could even recognize shapes. A shadow nearby spoke to me.

"Can you see me, Lily? I should have warned you not to look."

The blur in front of me went in and out of focus. "No. It's all hazy."

I heard Amon's voice once again and his words gave me courage.

Stand firm, my brothers.
Steady your hearts.
We will charge them as the falcon, the ibis, and the crane.
We will slaughter and destroy them,
Returning them to the dust from whence they came.

Dr. Hassan patted my hand. "The battle has begun. I need to weave my spell. When the time comes you must hand me the correct object."

He passed me a box. Inside it, he'd put several objects. I nicked my finger on one as I was feeling around, and realized it was a small knife. There was also a lighter, a metal rod about the size of a kid's baseball bat, a length of heavy chains, a stoppered bottle of liquid, and a weighty object with a plastic cover. It was a tool of some kind, but I couldn't really tell what it was from feeling it. Dr. Hassan asked another question, but I was distracted by the sounds of battle. I worried about Amon fighting blind. Now that I was affected in a similar way, the idea of being surrounded by undead that I couldn't see, and facing a giant crocodile demon ready to gobble me up, was terrifying. Dr. Hassan cleared his throat. "Lily, I will begin."

I turned my face in his direction, ready to help.

In a booming voice, he shouted,

I, the grand vizier, guardian of the three points
Of the triangle of impossibility,
Call upon the afterlife to lend its strength.

He'd never spoken of a triangle of impossibility. I wondered what that was. Taking some quick mental notes, I added the phrase to a long list of unanswered questions. *Was there some magical triangular object that he held? Why was he guarding three points and what were they? Was the afterlife the same thing as the netherworld?*

Dr. Hassan went on.

We defend the path between
The earth, the sky, and the places beyond,
But our enemy has come among us.

Osahar turned toward the sounds of fighting and raised his arms in the air. He'd started to come into focus a little bit more, but everything was still blurry.

Treacherous one, we warn you to retreat!
Do not seek to come against us.
You cling to darkness and abhor the light.
You seek camaraderie with evil, and so,
You will receive the recompense of the one you embrace.
You have chained yourself to chaos.

Assuming that was my cue, I wrapped the chain around my arm, pressing my fingers against the other items in the box so I could grab them quickly.

Your venom is as strong as a thousand vipers'.

I heard a hiss and realized the sound was coming from the scarecrow we had made. Goose bumps broke out over my flesh, and I staggered away. I wasn't sure if the snakes I heard were real, representations of Sebak, or if it was a mental trick—nothing in this crazy world seemed impossible—but in any case, I moved as far back as I dared, still unable to see exactly where the roof ended.

You have made your teeth as knives.

I heard another monstrous sound, and this time I knew what it was—crocodiles. Gasping in fear, I shifted nervously, but there were no long bodies or dark shapes coming after me. The effigy bucked and snapped against the tape we'd used to bind it to the rod.

We who are your enemies revile you.

Dr. Hassan approached the effigy representing Sebak and spat upon it. The bound figure swung its head back and forth wildly, the shape of it now very different from the figure we'd created.

We who would diminish your power smite you.

"Lily, now!" Dr. Hassan sputtered, and I desperately fingered through the objects, finally selecting the metal rod.

With a cry, Dr. Hassan hit the figure three times and I heard a sharp snap like bones breaking. A scream full of rage blossomed, not from the doll-figure, but from the giant creature by the pyramids. I squinted, focusing on the chaos of color below.

As I peered down, the first thing I could make out was the crocodile beast that Sebak had become. He'd climbed the great pyramid and was about halfway up, but his left front leg hung limply at his side and one of his back legs seemed to have given way. He clung to the pyramid with a massive claw as he struggled to right himself. Broken bits of stone cracked away from the edifice, shattering as they hit the lower levels.

Ahmose, his body silver and shimmering, lifted his cudgel in the air and brought it down upon the monster's other leg, shattering the bone. Then he transformed into a silver crane. It was the first time I'd seen him in bird form. The crane leapt from the pyramid and circled the sky, seeking his brothers. Below him the zombie horde had clustered in two places, and I was just able to make out flashes of gold and white at the center of each. We needed to hurry.

We who would strike fear into your heart pierce you.

I quickly handed Dr. Hassan a pocketknife, my eyes finally adjusting from the light. The effigy writhing in front of us was nearly as monstrous as the creature below. The face looked eerily similar to Sebak's human one, but its skin was reptilian. It had fangs, and the tongue that darted out from between its lips was forked like a snake's.

Leaping forward, Dr. Hassan thrust the small knife into the heart of the creature and left it there. It screamed—a horrible, bloodcurdling sound. Heaving, it wrenched from one side to the other, tearing away the tape on its upper torso. The Sebak effigy lunged forward, almost catching me, but Dr. Hassan pulled me out of its reach at the last possible second.

The only thing holding the creature on the post now was the tape securing its ankles.

"Lilliana," the creature said, "you've returned. Come and let me peer into your beautiful eyes," it hissed, dragging out the *s* with a flick of its tongue.

"It's no use," I replied as bravely as I could. "I don't have what you're looking for."

"Yes, you do," the monster affirmed.

"I don't. Amon didn't give me the Eye. I never had it."

It laughed, the sound making every nerve in my body stand on edge. "I am not a fool. I know you do not have the Eye. But it matters not. The incarnation of the sun god will do anything for you. Including giving me the power I seek."

"You're mistaken," I answered, mustering all the bravery I could. "He left me behind. He doesn't even know I'm here."

A clicking noise came from the creature's throat in a mocking sort of sympathy. "Then perhaps he should," it said, with a dangerous leer.

As it spoke, its eyes rolled to the back of its head and a red mist circled its body.

"No!" Dr. Hassan yelled. "No!"

The body shook in great convulsions like it was being electrocuted, before it slumped lifeless and empty. When the red mist cleared, the form had returned to its original state, except that the clothing and pillows were now ripped apart.

"What is it? What just happened?" I cried.

"Quickly, Lily, the chain!"

Approaching the effigy, Dr. Hassan passed the chain to me around the form and then I handed it back. We went back and forth until we had wrapped the chain around the effigy several times. Then Dr. Hassan said:

We who would see you bound fetter you.

Nothing happened. He looked out over the edge of the building toward the distant pyramid where the creature that was Sebak had rallied.

Again, he cried out:

We who would see you bound fetter you!

"Why isn't it working?" I asked.

"I thought as much. It is too late. He has called forth his essence."

"But can't we, you know, call it back?"

Dr. Hassan shook his head. "The ceremony must be completed. We will have to go to the creature itself."

"Are you serious? There's no time! They're barely holding back the zombies as it is."

"We must go! Quickly, put on these clothes!"

Dr. Hassan yanked open the remaining bag, which contained clothes that I at first thought were meant for the effigy. There wasn't time to ask why he wanted me to dress in a cargo vest and pants, and the items were big enough that I could easily slip them on over my other clothes. As Dr. Hassan approached me, with the chain wrapped around his wrist, he took the box, placed a lighter and what I now recognized as a small ax into one of his vest pockets, and jammed the fedora I'd scooped out of the bag onto my head.

Placing his hands on my shoulder, Dr. Haasan looked me square in the eyes and said, "When the time comes, you must pretend that you are me and lead Amon to the top of the great pyramid. Do not speak to him. Wear these gloves so he does not feel the smallness of your hands. Here, take my jacket, too."

He thrust my arms into the sleeves of his jacket, yanking it up and over my shoulders as I fussed with the drawstring cargo pants.

"This is important, Lily!" he went on. "If he knows it is you, he will not complete the ceremony. The god of chaos must not be allowed to return. I know it is a hard thing to ask, but when you feel the pull on your energy, you need to open yourself to it. Allow Amon to take what he needs. Do you understand? Tell me you understand!"

Numbly, I nodded. A million questions flew through my mind, but I couldn't seem to focus on a single one. Standing on the edge of the building, Dr. Hassan cried out in Egyptian, and far below, a tremor shook a group of zombies, throwing them away from the thing they focused on as if a bomb had gone off. The starlit ibis rose in the air with a powerful flap of his wings and zoomed toward us.

He landed and changed to human form.

"Asten?" I took a step closer. He was bleeding heavily and bruised. Cuts and deep slashes leaked red rivulets over his chest and arms; his shirt hung in tatters. The dark hair he'd seemed so proud of was drenched with sweat, and locks of it hung over his eyes.

Asten took a deep shuddering breath, glanced at me, and then turned toward Dr. Hassan. "Does she know what to do?" he asked, exhaustion emanating from his entire body.

"She does. She is ready."

"Then climb upon my back." He added, "The battle is a sore one, Hassan."

Dr. Hassan patted his shoulder. "The ritual is nearly complete. There is just a minor complication."

I was about to make a comment about the complication not actually being minor, but then I looked at Asten and couldn't bring myself to say it. Instead, I said, "Take care of yourself, Asten."

He gave me a weak smile. "My initial assessment of you was entirely inaccurate," he said.

"Oh?"

"Yes." Reaching out his fingertips, he grazed my cheek and my skin tingled. "I have never met a more dedicated devotee," he said quietly, "Goodbye, Lily." Dropping his hand, Asten burst into his starlit ibis form.

After Dr. Hassan and I climbed on, Asten rose into the air. I felt a rush of wind as he headed directly toward the largest pyramid, where the great crocodile god who was Sebak hovered, watching in monstrous delight as his zombie army held back the sons of Egypt from completing their work.

The moon was so large and close that I felt as if we were flying directly into it. I couldn't be sure, but it seemed to me as if it hung directly over the pyramid. It was possible that I'd miscalculated a bit, but I knew that if the three brothers didn't complete the ceremony before the moon passed over the pyramid, it would be too late.

The ibis cried out and Sebak turned his head toward us. With a scream he surged upward, tearing Asten's white wing with a scaly claw. The wing broke with a snap and we plummeted. Asten broke our fall with his body. We landed on the far side of the pyramid and Asten changed back to human form, panting as he cradled his arm.

"Go! Go!" Asten said. He gave me a small smile as Dr. Hassan grabbed my arm and led me around the side of the pyramid. Before we turned the corner, I saw Asten take a running leap off the pyramid, somersaulting in the air before landing in the horde, an arrow in each hand despite the break. He thrust the arrows into the eyes of two zombies, who both exploded in a cloud of dust.

Dr. Hassan led me down the length of the pyramid. My feet constantly slipped as I tripped on loose rocks. Before we got to the end, a horrible claw sank into the side of the pyramid directly in front of us. Sebak's transformed body rounded the corner. The sight of his ghastly grin was enough to stop me in my tracks and make me run in the other direction, but Dr. Hassan paused for only a moment and then kept running, leaving me behind.

"Dr. Hassan, wait!" I called as I scrambled after him.

"Ah, Lilliana," the creature said, working a giant tongue over sharp teeth the size of stalactites. "I thought I'd have to seek you out. How appropriate it is that you should come to me of your own volition."

Dr. Hassan had disappeared and I was halfway up a pyramid, facing down a crocodile demon all on my own. I had no weapon. No plan. No powers. Then I realized that Sebak's obsession with me had allowed Dr. Hassan to escape. If I could distract Sebak enough, then perhaps the brothers could complete the ceremony.

"It must have been very hard for you to submit to being someone's assistant," I said. "A man of your ability having to grovel to another with less talent is a shame."

His eyelids blinking sideways, the creature lowered his big head and snapped his jaws shut not a foot from where I stood. "So easily frightened," he said, laughing.

"I'm not frightened," I lied. "In fact, the biggest emotion I feel for you is pity."

"Pity?" he spat. "You pity *me*? I am the most powerful creature the world has ever known! Even your pathetic sun god cannot best me."

"Yes." I nodded my head. "That is true. But don't you see? You've traded one overseer for another. You cannot deny that your yearnings and your gifts were given to you by Apophis."

"Speaking of yearnings"—Sebak's new head drifted closer, his tongue darting out and tasting the air around my body—"I've long denied myself the opportunity to sample you for myself. The biloko demons left me . . . hungry." The fleshy probe made contact with my arm, which, thankfully, was covered with too many layers for me to feel it, but then it touched my face.

The sensation was not unlike being licked by a dog—that is, if the dog were actually an anaconda with saliva that stung like little knives. My cheek felt like it had been scrubbed with a razor blade. I wiped it with my gloved hand and it came away smeared with blood.

"Ah, you are delicious, my dear. I will enjoy having you all to myself once I dispose of the others."

"See, that's not really you talking. That is Apophis. Even now he influences you. He is the one giving you these feelings."

The monster shifted closer. "Apophis gave me nothing. I stole his power for myself."

"Even if that were true, when you allow the gateway to open, Seth will come."

"So?"

"So you'll just be under the thumb again of someone who holds more power than you. I guess I just don't get why you'd want that to happen. Do you want the world to view you as inferior? As a lesser god?"

"Seth will reward me. I will be as great as he. Together we will darken the force of the sun, cause the stars to recede in the heavens, and make the moon as blood. Once we have defeated the other gods, I will steal his power as well. I will rule all."

"Frankly, I doubt it. How often does a man in power give it up? They have to be forcibly removed from the position."

"Then I will remove him."

"Wouldn't it just be easier to let the brothers do their job? Prevent Seth from coming at all? Then they'll go away and you would be all that remains."

He blinked as if considering my words, and then dismissed them. "It won't even matter once I have the all-powerful Eye. Speaking of which . . ."

Wrenching his large body closer to me, Sebak slammed a limb past me, the claw digging into the side of the pyramid, effectively trapping me.

"Incarnation of the sun!" the creature called out, his voice carrying through the desert night. "If you want to see your young woman again, I suggest you bring me the item I seek!"

After a tense moment, I heard Amon's voice cry back from far below. "You cannot deceive me, vile creature! Lily is safely on her way home. Come to me and fight so that I may return the favor you recently offered me!"

I finally saw Osahar. While I'd been keeping Sebak occupied, he'd managed to hook the chain around Sebak's hind claw. With a cry, Dr. Hassan leapt off the pyramid holding on to the chain, his body flying over the dangling limb. The croc monster roared and twisted to see what was going on. Dr. Hassan hung from the bottom of the chain and chanted:

We who would see you bound fetter you!

Sebak screamed, crashing into the side of the pyramid, and then froze, pinning me in place. At the same time the zombie army froze. With a burst of silver light, bodies flew in every direction. The silver crane rose in the air and headed toward the top of the second pyramid. I spied Asten's human form running toward the smallest pyramid. Dr. Hassan let go of the chain and dropped, rolling to a stop several levels down from me. Wincing, he got to his feet and started climbing up to where I stood.

Sebak's eyes followed us, but his body remained immobile. When Dr. Hassan reached me, he tried in vain to free me from the monster's grip. When he was thwarted, he climbed farther, until he could reach the demon's head.

"Sebak," Dr. Hassan said, "do not throw away your life in this way. You are the most talented archaeologist I've ever worked with. Give up the power you have stolen and we will spare your life."

"If you truly understood power, you would know that I would rather die a thousand deaths than give it up," the beast replied. "No. The sun god is weak. He will not be able to complete the ceremony. The god of chaos will come, and when he does, he will raise me up and reconstruct the body you have damaged, and I will return to take my revenge upon you"—he paused and gave me a crocodile smile—"and on her."

"I am truly sorry, my colleague. Sorry that you were deceived so utterly and that your lust for power has resulted in such devastation and the loss of a brilliant mind. Goodbye, Sebak."

Dr. Hassan took a deep breath and cried:

We who will defeat you defile your body!

He pulled the ax out from his jacket and lifted it over his head, ready to swing it into Sebak's giant demon eye, when I heard an achingly familiar voice.

"Stop!"

Amon blindly made his way up the side of the pyramid toward us. I sucked in a breath and pressed my free hand to my lips to contain a sob. His skin, where it wasn't bleeding, was gray-tinged, and the sunglasses covering his eyes were gone. The empty sockets where his eyes should have been made my heart hurt. He was missing some fingers on one hand, and bites covered his shoulders, face, and neck.

"Hassan?" he called.

"I am here, Master," Dr. Hassan cried out. "What is it? Why do you want me to stop?"

"Was he . . . ? Is he speaking the truth? Is Lily here? Was she captured?"

"Of course she is here," Sebak taunted. "She is not even damaged . . . much."

There was a pause, and then Dr. Hassan addressed Amon. "You must believe me when I say that Lily is safe. Sebak has lost his mind."

Amon's head lowered for a moment, but then the muscles of his arms tightened. "Very well." He reached out a hand and Osahar grabbed it, pulling him up the last few steps. Gripping the doctor's shoulder, Amon asked, "Will you allow me to slay the vile beast?"

Dr. Hassan searched Amon's face. "Of course," he said, understanding Amon's nonverbal communication, and placed the ax in his hand. "Do you need me to guide you there?"

Amon shook his head. "No. I will use the Eye."

Seeing Amon approach, Sebak panted, "She *is* here! I am telling you the truth!"

"I cannot measure the truth of your words since you stole the power contained in my jars of death. As it is, I trust that my grand vizier would not deceive me," Amon said quietly.

Dr. Hassan lowered his head regretfully while Sebak laughed. "Ah, I see you intend to turn a blind eye to the situation. How appropriate." Amon's grip on the ax tightened. "I suppose it doesn't matter if you believe me or not. You *will* fail and I will rise again. I have served my master well and will be rewarded generously for my efforts."

Angling his head toward the giant monster as if looking directly at him, Amon leaned closer to the frozen creature and said grimly, "Speaking of turning a blind eye, I believe I must return the favor." With a dangerous smile, Amon raised the ax, leapt onto the crocodile head, and

sank the blade into its blinking eye. When he had done the same thing
to the other yellow eye, Amon dropped the bloody ax. "I wish for this
rising to be finished."

"Yes," Dr. Hassan said. "I will be with you momentarily."

Amon carefully moved to the side and sat down on a pyramid step
a few feet from where I was pinned. Propping his elbows on his knees,
he lowered his head into his hands, his body shaking.

How horrible this whole experience must have been for him. All I
wanted to do was comfort him. Put his head in my lap and stroke his
hair. Try to make him forget the pain and the suffering that he had
known. If I could have stolen him away from this horrible duty, the terrible responsibility that he insisted upon fulfilling, I would have. But I
couldn't even let him know I was there.

Dr. Hassan lit the body of the inert Sebak on fire and then finished
the rite.

We who would see you burn scorch you.

The scream of a thousand deaths filled the air as the giant body of
Sebak, the incarnation of Apophis, burned alive.

The sons of Egypt are noble.
The gods of the sun, the moon, and the stars are braced.
The points of the Impossible Triangle are imbued with power.
You cannot defeat us,
For we will not be moved.
Depart Apophis,
Ye cursed crocodile!

After the last phrase, Sebak's body shook, causing the area surrounding the pyramids to rumble. Rank vapors of black smoke rose
from the body and the fire burned brighter and hotter until Sebak's
entire being was consumed in a flash of red.

When his body disappeared, the ashes blowing away in a soft breeze, I stood, testing my limbs, and then heaved a sigh of relief that I was still in one piece. I stepped forward, looking down at the valley, and saw a dissipating red mist, the only sign that there had ever been a tremendous battle between zombies and mummies.

Tiredly, Amon rose from his seated position and said, "Come, Hassan. It is time to end this work."

"Yes, Master. I will now take you to the top of the temple, and when the ceremony is complete I will recover your bodies."

Amon said nothing, his face angled away from the pyramid as if he was looking for something in the distance. "Do as you will," he said quietly.

Dr. Hassan beckoned me to Amon, putting a finger over his lips to make sure I knew to be quiet. When I was standing in front of Amon, Dr. Hassan said, "If you would put your hand on my shoulder, I will lead you."

Amon stretched out his arm and brushed his hand against the fedora before finding my shoulder. He nodded. "I am ready."

With a shooing motion, Dr. Hassan waved me forward. I wasn't sure how long I could keep up the ruse, and I was fairly certain that Amon would notice I wasn't Dr. Hassan, but he didn't say a word. He just placidly followed me until we reached the top of the pyramid. I went slowly, careful lest he should fall.

Blood from his torn hand dripped down the front of my jacket. When I saw it, an echoing tear trickled down my cheek. When I stopped, I took his hand, saddened that the thick glove prevented me from feeling his touch one last time, and placed it on the flat stone above.

"Wait here," Amon said, and took his position, planting both feet solidly on top of the temple.

Raising his arms in the air, Amon began chanting, his skin brightening a little, though it was very clear that his power was sorely diminished and his arms were shaking. The full moon was right above us, and from my perspective it looked like Amon was cupping it with his hands.

The bodies of Asten and Ahmose shone like gleaming bonfires on their respective temples, but Amon's body remained dim. As the three men chanted, I saw silvery light gather from the moon and shoot down to Ahmose. The twinkling stars loosed some of their light and a beam of it swirled around Asten.

Asten's and Ahmose's pyramids shone in the night, glowing white and silver, but the pyramid where I stood with Amon was still dark. Power swirled in the night sky, lighting up the heavens like an aurora borealis. Trickles of the silver and white light shot toward us. Amon's arms stopped trembling, his body glowing brighter.

The brothers recited their spell and a mist of starlight headed straight for me. To my surprise, it enveloped me, and I gasped as the pinpricks of light tingled over my skin and then sank into me. I felt a pull. I knew then that this was Asten's way of channeling my energy to Amon. I naturally resisted, but then I saw a golden light encircle Amon and remembered to willingly offer myself, and my energy, for it to work.

Closing my eyes, I imagined that I was offering Amon everything—my heart, my mind, my soul, and my body. The pull became stronger, and I sucked in a breath through my teeth at the pain. I fell back as something broke away inside me, and I drifted—painless, dreamy, and fulfilled in a way I'd never been before.

Lying on my back, I gazed up at the cosmos. Pulses of energy lapped like waves across my body, starting at my head and then moving all the way down to my toes over and over again. A humming filled my mind as golden light erupted all around me.

Sunshine mist angled above me, floating up and away from me, into Amon's skin. The effect was invigorating him, and his body grew brighter. The thought occurred to me that if I had to die, this was the very best way to go. I couldn't feel the stones pressing into my back or the emotional loss of leaving life behind. All I could sense was the wonder of the universe and how small a piece of it I was.

Above me the eruption of lights broke apart and became three points. With my eyes, I traced them in the sky—one white, one silver, and one gold. The three had formed a constellation. It was beautiful. But then, something opened in the sky above it—a dark rift—with a terrible evil coming through. It looked like an iridescent storm, but I could tell it was much more than that.

As the sky roiled and churned, fear flooded through me and I whimpered, unable to prevent the sound from coming out. A sinister, malevolent, and ominous face grew, and I knew it was just a matter of time until we were all consumed by it.

Thick hailstones rained down, pummeling my weakened body, but I could barely feel them. When the hailstones came close to Amon's golden aura, they disintegrated, but I was outside of that circle of protection. An icy ball hit me on my temple and I felt the wetness of blood. It was cold. No. *I* was cold. Trembling, I tried to move, eager to hide myself from the thing that seemed to be watching me, but I found I could not so much as lift a limb.

Desperate to escape and unable to do so, I felt my eyes fill with tears. Gone was the peace of a few moments ago. I knew then that we were too late. Seth was here and he was coming for us. I wasn't just going to die; I was going to be unmade, erased. My family wouldn't even remember I'd existed. What was worse, Amon would forget me entirely. Somehow, that idea seemed the more tragic of the two.

Then the three points of light shot in arcs like falling stars, twisting as they angled toward their brother lights. Next, they angled downward, zooming toward the pyramids. The beams shot down the pyramid shafts and emerged on the other side. The trails they left formed a series of triangles that connected everything. *It's the Impossible Triangle,* I thought, as I gazed in awe.

The center filled with swirls of white, gold, and silver, and the inside grew brighter and brighter until it merged into a powerful pillar aimed directly at the crevice that had been made in the universe. A stream of light hit the storm cloud and consumed it, and with a final burst of energy, the crack sealed, disappearing in a brilliant storm of white, gold, and silver light.

Slowly, the light dimmed, and the tails creating the Impossible Triangle were reabsorbed. The white ball of light shot toward Asten, the silver floated lazily past the moon and settled upon Ahmose's shoulders, and the gold ball zoomed back to Amon, who caught it in his hand. It sank into his body and he staggered back a step.

"It is done," he said. "Come, Hassan. I will take you with me."

I couldn't move. Couldn't speak.

"Hassan? What is wrong with you? Where are you?" Amon descended a step or two until his foot made contact with my shoulder. "Hassan?" Squatting next to me, Amon lifted my arm and tried to get me to talk. He removed my hat and slapped my face lightly, then suddenly stopped as his fingers touched my hair. He ran his hands over my face and neck. "Lily?" he gasped. "No." He wrenched the heavy jacket off me, scooped me up in his arms, and pressed his face in my neck. "No!" he screamed.

I realized he thought I was dead. I wasn't. At least, I didn't think so. But there was no way for him to know that. Even I couldn't tell if I was breathing. Maybe I *was* dead and was now having an out-of-body experience. Amon pressed his lips against my cheeks and forehead; his arms trembled and his breathing was ragged. If he still had his eyes, he might have been weeping. *How sad not to be able to weep,* I thought.

Clutching me close to his body, Amon uttered a spell, his voice breaking. The top of the pyramid became liquid and we sank into a darkness that closed over our heads.

Heart Scarab

We passed through layers of stone as if it were water, coming to a stop deep inside the pyramid. Large rocks, like the ones in Osahar's underground tunnels, sat in the corners providing light. Amon's feet touched the gritty soil and he staggered, but he held me close, cradling my body as gently as he could. My head hung across his arm while he stretched out a hand to feel where he was. After bumping into a raised stone slab that looked suspiciously like an altar, he carefully lowered me onto it.

Amon smoothed my hair from my forehead and folded my arms across my chest as if I were Cleopatra on her deathbed. I wanted to scream, to shout that I was alive, but I was trapped inside my own body. He knelt at my side, tremors racking his body as he pressed his forehead against my stomach, I wished more than anything to comfort him.

"I am so, so sorry, Lily," he murmured. "I did not wish this for you. How oblivious I was in thinking I had generated enough power on my own.

"I should have known that my brothers would deceive me. They did not understand why I chose to send you home, why I would risk allowing chaos to reign, why I challenged the very reason for our existence.

Now the thing I feared the most has come to pass. How could I not have sensed that the sweet energy seeping into my soul was yours?"

Lifting my hand, Amon clutched it, rubbing my knuckles with his thumb. Little pulses of sunshine ran through me—surely that was a good sign, or at least a sign that I wasn't really dead.

Amon continued. "The only consolation I had in leaving you behind was believing that you had a chance to live, to exercise the right every person born on this earth takes for granted—finding happiness. Now you have gone, left this world in search of the next. My greatest and only wish is to follow you, but my path is not the same as yours. My destiny calls me elsewhere."

Dropping his forehead to my hand, he added, "Forgive me, Lily. Forgive me for taking you away from your home, for the burdens I placed upon you, for causing this tragedy, and, most of all, forgive me for the things I would not allow myself to say."

Light coalesced a few feet behind Amon, and a handsome man appeared with a black dog at his side. If I hadn't been almost dead, I would have loved to draw him. His thickly muscled torso was bare and he wore a pleated skirt, but his was black instead of white. He had a head of shiny black hair.

He looked like he was around my father's age, but he had that kind of ageless beauty any woman would be attracted to.

"Amon? What is this?" the man asked.

Amon lifted his head. "Anubis," he said. "This is Lily. A mortal. I was forced to rely upon her energy during this rising and it has resulted in her death."

"How . . . interesting." Anubis took a step closer. Leaning over to get a good look at me, he noticed that my eyes were open and I was watching him. He winked as he straightened up, and I concluded that I liked him but didn't entirely trust him. "Tell me how this happened," he requested of Amon.

The incarnation of the sun got to his feet, keeping my hand wrapped in his as he turned toward the nearby god but looked at a spot just beyond him. "Apophis and Seth lent a portion of their might to a mortal, the same mortal who took my eyes and stole three of my canopic jars, absorbing my powers into himself. This is why I needed Lily."

"I see. Has this mortal been overcome?"

"He has. And Seth has been locked away for another millennium."

"Then you have done your duty admirably. Are you prepared to relinquish your powers so that they may be stored for future use?"

"I am. Though there is now only one remaining."

"I would not be too sure about that."

Amon cocked his head. "I do not understand. Sebak's dark shabti opened my three jars and his master absorbed their energy."

"Yes, but as is often the case, there are certain . . . substitutions that can be made."

"What substitutions?"

"You must never underestimate a willing sacrifice. Do you remember when Seth asked your fathers to sacrifice you long ago? You told your people that you were willing to go through with it."

"Yes, I remember."

"There is great power to be had when a person gives of himself to protect those he loves. This is why the gods imbued you with their energies in the first place."

"What does that have to do with my situation?"

"In giving of herself so freely, this young woman restored that which had been taken."

"You mean Lily's death returned all of my powers?"

"No, not her death. Her love. Lily's sacrifice for you was in every way as powerful as the sacrifice you made for your people. The gods cannot deny such a forfeit and have bestowed a great gift in exchange for it. Her love for you has returned that which was stolen. You will still need to give it back, of course, until the time of your next rising, but at that time you will be fully restored."

Amon turned his back to the god and took a few steps away.

Anubis gave him a sharp look. "Are you not grateful for this gift?" he asked.

"I am . . . sorrowful that it was necessary."

"Ah. I understand."

"Would you . . . ," Amon began, "I know she is not one of us, but might you consider easing her journey to the afterlife as you do for me and my brothers?"

Rubbing his jaw, Anubis glanced quickly at me and smiled. "I might. If she were actually dead."

"What?" Amon spun around and felt his way back to the altar. He picked up my limp hand and stroked it. "She is still alive? Then why can she not speak or move? Why can I not sense her?"

"Her energy has been depleted to the point of near death."

"Is there anything I can do for her? Can I bring her back?"

"Yes, and I think deep down you know what must happen."

I could see the moment when Amon realized what was necessary. "Is there not another way?"

"Not one that I know of. You will have to nullify it, of course, when it is done. Otherwise—"

"I am aware of the ramifications." Amon squeezed my hand and I could barely feel the pressure. "What if she cannot do it?"

"I will be here to aid her in any way I can." Seeing Amon's hesitation, Anubis added, "If you would rather leave her here and allow the natural order of things to determine the outcome, that is also an option."

Amon sighed deeply before squaring his shoulders. "No. I will do it."

"You should know that this is merely a formality," said Anubis. "As much as you tried to prevent it from happening, it did. Now it is only a matter of you saying the words."

"I was hoping that would not be the case."

"Really?" Anubis said, smiling as he folded his arms across his chest. "If it were me, I would be hesitant to cast such a thing aside . . . until it became necessary, that is."

"I hoped to spare her the pain."

"Mortal pain is short-lived."

I frowned at the god's words and thought, *Says you.*

Anubis continued, "Whereas *your* suffering lasts a very long time. A good memory could make your internment seem bearable."

"Perhaps, in truth, I wanted to spare us both," Amon said.

"Ah, well, this is a good lesson to reflect upon until the next rising."

"Yes, Anubis," Amon answered quietly.

I wasn't sure I understood much of their conversation, but whatever it was about, Amon wasn't happy about it, and I couldn't help going back over their words and counting the number of times *pain* was mentioned. Whatever was going to happen could not be good.

Anubis moved back, his faithful dog at his side, as Amon began chanting a spell, one that I recognized. It was the incantation he'd used to bind the two of us, but this time the words were slightly changed. Wind ruffled my hair, though we were entombed inside the pyramid.

> With the power of my mouth,
> The power in my heart,
> I utter a spell.
> As our forms are bound this day,
> So are our lives.
> Tirelessly, she has served me,
> As I have served Egypt.
> Make light our feathers.
> Make swift our wings.
> Make steady our hearts.
> We combine the strength of our bodies,
> And, in doing so,
> Pledge to renew one another.
> Where she is unknown, I will attend.
> Where she is alone, there will I be.
> When she is weak, I will sustain,

Even unto death.
Our hearts are firm.
Our souls are triumphant.
Our bond is unbreakable.

By the time Amon finished the spell, he was leaning over me, holding me in place as a strong wind threatened to blow me off the stone slab. Our prior bond had drained me, made me feel ill, but the bond he formed now was exactly the opposite.

I sucked in a deep breath as a burning sensation ran through my veins. It was hot, but it didn't hurt. My whole body glowed with a golden light. I suddenly felt aware of Amon. The strength of his body was my own. The pain where his eyes had once been caused my eyes to sting and blur with tears. The heaviness in his heart almost made me weep.

"Amon?" I said weakly, and he reached out for me, pulling me to his chest as he buried his face in my neck.

"Lily," he sighed.

"What . . . what just happened?"

He leaned back, lowering his head so I wouldn't have to look at his empty eyes. "I have sealed the bond between us," he answered softly.

"I don't understand. What does that mean? Weren't you already bound to me?"

"It was a temporary thing. I had hoped to avoid this. What is between us now is virtually unchangeable."

"Why? Why would you want to avoid it?" I wiped the tears from my cheeks, irritated that they were falling.

"*Lily.*" Amon ran a hand over my shoulder and cupped my neck. "It is not for the reason you are thinking. Open your mind to me and understand."

Blinking rapidly, I sniffed and tried to do what he said, but I was too wrapped up in the idea that he was once again rejecting me. Amon gripped my shoulder and shook it slightly. "Close your eyes and try to feel what I feel."

I closed my eyes and focused on Amon. I felt the thrum of his pulse, heard the softness of his breathing. The thump of his heart distracted me for a moment, and then I saw through his eyes. Not his real eyes, but I was able to see what he had seen. I was swept up in a vision through what I now realized was the Eye of Horus.

All at once, I understood . . . everything.

"Amon?" I cupped his cheek. "I didn't realize how you felt. I thought you didn't want to be with me."

"I could not allow myself to even consider it. But I wanted it. More than I ever wanted anything."

Anubis cleared his throat and Amon let me go and turned toward him, his back stiff. "Perhaps I am becoming soft in my old age," the god said, "but I will give the two of you a few moments. Oh, and Amon? You owe me one."

The handsome god gave me a final wink before whirling both of his hands in the air. With a thrust of his fingertips, the gray clouds of smoke gathering around them were pushed toward Amon's head, obscuring his expression. Amon screamed and shoved his palms into his eye sockets.

The smoke sizzled and then danced away, forming new fingers on his damaged hand, healing the bites, cuts, and bruises on his skin and his leg. When the smoke disappeared, he lowered his hands and blinked. Amon's eyes were back. With a grunt of satisfaction and a quiet woof from his dog, Anubis disappeared in a flash of light.

Immediately Amon's hazel eyes brimmed with tears and he reached out to touch my face. His sunlight warmth trailed down my jaw.

"Can you . . . see me?" I asked.

"Yes."

"Does it hurt?"

He smiled softly. "Almost more than I can bear."

I took his hand in mine. "You're still planning to leave me, aren't you?" I asked quietly, not really wanting an answer.

"I do not have a choice."

"Are you sure?"

"Lily, if there were a way for us to be together, I would do anything to make it happen. Do you not know this?"

"I do now." I ran my hand up his face and through his hair. He closed his eyes and I could actually feel how much he longed to be close to me. "How much time do we have?" I whispered.

"Anubis will give us only a few moments," said Amon, reluctantly leaving me to pace toward the end of the chamber. I followed him but stopped when I noticed an open shaft.

"Will I have to climb out through there?" I asked.

"No. The heat channeled through the pyramids during the ceremony has melted the rock along the shaft. You would suffer terribly if you tried to enter it."

"Oh." I wasn't sure what to do or say. I'd never lost anyone before. Not even a pet. I could sense his determination to do the right thing and yet the right thing felt wrong.

Amon ran a hand through his hair and seemed to come to a decision. Circling the altar, he approached me. "You do not need to worry about going home now. I have enough power to bend time and return you to the moment you left in New York City."

"So . . . it will be as if all this had never happened?" I said weakly.

Amon took a step closer and cupped my neck, my back now pressed against the pyramid wall. "You will forget all about me, in time," he said, looking deeply into my eyes.

"No." I shook my head. "I could never forget you."

"Perhaps not." Amon smiled forlornly, playing with the loose hair on my shoulder. "You know, Anubis was right about one thing."

"What's that?"

Pressing his hands against the stone wall on either side of my head, he murmured, "Eternity is a long time to exist without something to remember."

Then his lips were on mine.

I'd waited so long for his kiss, and it was so much more, so much better than I had dared imagine. Golden sunshine burst behind my closed eyelids as I became a being entwined with the sun.

His hands pulled me against his body and I melted into him, my limbs tingling and warm. Amon's mouth moved over mine, slowly, like he could make the kiss last forever.

Heat filled my body and I flourished like a rare flower that could blossom only for a day before being consumed by the fire of the sun. A rosy flush unfurled on my cheeks as his lips grazed slow trails over each of them. Warm pulses of energy lapped my spine as he ran his fingertips down the length of it, finally stopping at my lower back.

Amon.

I wasn't sure if I spoke his name or merely thought it, but the idea of using my mouth for more than kissing him suddenly seemed impossible. My entire body was all at once both sun-drowsed and sun-scorched.

An inferno ran through my veins and my world was molten, combustible, burning. The passionate heat smoldering between us could energize a dozen cities. I wanted to drown in his light. Amon was like the quicksand that had nearly consumed me—liquid, hot, powerful quicksand—and I was lost.

When he finally pulled away, we were both winded. My lips were swollen and hot, my limbs trembled. My skin was luminous in the aftermath. Amon found a loose strand of hair and ran his fingers down its length, smiling as the golden light made it even brighter. "Beautiful," he said. "You are perfectly, magnificently beautiful. The suffering of every bitter trial I will face for millennia will mellow as long as I can remember the taste of your sweet lips."

Wrapping my arms around his waist, I buried my face in his chest and asked, "Do you have to go?"

As he cradled me against him, I felt him kiss my hair. Instead of answering, he said, "I want to give you something."

He stepped away and twirled his fingers. Sand rose and formed a mound in his palm. He cupped his other hand over it, whispering a short incantation as light gleamed from between his fingers. When it diminished, he beckoned me closer.

Lying on his palm was a jeweled scarab. Its carapace was made of green emeralds the same shade as Amon's eyes when they glowed in the dark. Small flecks of gold and tiny diamonds outlined the wings and head.

He pressed it into my hand. "It's heavy," I said.

"It is . . . *Amset*," he whispered. "It is my heart."

"What do you mean it's your heart?"

"What do you know about mummification?"

"Um, not too much. I know your body is preserved and wrapped and your organs are placed in canopic jars."

"That is true, in most cases. But not all organs are taken from the body. The heart is left behind."

"Really? Why?"

Amon murmured, "'The heart is the seat of intellect and the tongue speaks to make it real.' When we enter the afterlife, our hearts are weighed on the scales of judgment, and if we are deemed worthy we are wrapped in robes of glory. If our hearts fail, we are fed to a demon."

"Well, won't you need it?"

"I have never seen the scales of judgment in all the time I have spent in the afterlife. I do not think I ever will. Not unless I truly die." Amon brushed his thumbs across my eyebrows and kissed me softly on the side of my mouth. "Anyway, how can I keep it? It no longer belongs to me." He paused for a moment, and then added, "Perhaps it is wrong for me to ask, but in giving you this token, I hoped that you might look upon it once in a while and think of me."

"How could you begin to imagine that your request is a presumption? Of course I will. I'll hold your memory close to my heart forever." My eyes brimmed with tears, but I would not allow them to fall. I didn't want to waste our last precious minutes with him trying to comfort me. If he had to leave, then I wanted to put on as brave a face as possible.

He smiled. "When our bond is broken, you might feel differently.

You might wish to forget. Even so, I am grateful to have had this time together."

"Wait." I drew back. "You said when our bond is *broken*?"

"Yes. It must be dissolved before I depart this life."

"What do you mean dissolved? I don't want to break our bond. You know how I feel about you."

"If we do not end our connection you will never find a moment of happiness. As long as you live you will not love another. Your mind will journey with me in the afterlife as you dream. It will lead to madness, Lily. It would destroy you."

I folded my arms. "Is this what Anubis was talking about? The pain he mentioned?"

"Yes. It is the reason I kept my distance from you."

"It's why you wouldn't kiss me before, isn't it?"

Amon nodded. "If I had kissed you, it would have sealed the bond. The longer the connection is allowed to continue, the harder it is to break. Even now, having been formally bonded with you only this short time, there will still be echoes, times when we will call to one another across dimensions, but the sooner we break it, the better it will be for you."

"So, assuming I agreed to this, how would we go about breaking it?"

"You must kill me."

He stood there, arms at his sides, fists clenched, his beautiful eyes staring at me, willing me to look at him. I turned away and crumpled to the ground.

"This is a sick joke, right? You're not seriously asking me to sacrifice you?" I gasped.

"It is the only way to break the bond," he said softly. "Once a connection between one of us and a mortal is sealed, the only way to sever it—"

"Is to literally cut you out of my life."

Crouching down next to me, Amon squeezed my shoulder. "You must slay the one who cast the spell. I wanted to spare you this, but it was the only way to heal your body."

What he'd said made me look up. "Anubis said something about the spell just being a formality. What did he mean by that?"

"He meant . . ." Amon paused. "He meant that my heart had made the choice long before I was willing to acknowledge it."

"Well, I can't. I can't do this. I won't kill you, Amon. If Anubis wants it done, he's going to have to do it himself. I can't be here for it, and I certainly can't do it myself."

"You *must*, Lily. The consequences, should we fail, would be disastrous for you."

"No." I shook my head, tears finally spilling over and blinding me. "No!" I said, more loudly.

Sighing and running a hand through his hair, Amon sat down next to me, pulling me onto his lap. I sobbed, wetting his neck with my tears. "Hush, Nehabet," he soothed as he stroked my back, filling my frame with warmth that I wanted to reject but instead lapped up like I'd never feel it again. In the pit of my stomach, coldness stayed with me no matter how much liquid sunshine he shared.

Quietly, he murmured, "You know that my death is inevitable, regardless."

I nodded against his chest.

"Even though our bond will be broken, I will think of you," he promised gently. "My love for you will not diminish. During each night that passes I will bring your image to mind. You are mine—my Nehabet—a rare desert flower that blooms in the waters of the oasis.

"As the days and the years of your life go by, I will keep watch over you, and when your blossom closes its petals, finally surrendering to the night, I will meet you at the dawn of your new existence and I will be your guide in the afterlife."

Sniffling, I said, "I'm not sure your afterlife and mine are the same."

Gritting his teeth, he said, "It does not matter. I will find you. Do you believe this?"

"I believe you," I said quietly.

He kissed me again, softly, his lips lingering on mine, and I tasted the salt of my tears. We were interrupted by the whine of a dog.

Amon lifted his head. "Anubis."

"I apologize for not making my entrance more timely, but I have already seen to your brothers and I cannot delay any longer." He glanced at us and furrowed his brow. "Have you explained to her what must be done?"

"I have," Amon answered. "But it is a hard thing to ask."

Anubis waved his hand. "I will be here to assist her."

"When it is complete she must be returned to the time and place she first met me."

"Yes, yes. I will arrange it. Now come, Amon, it is time."

Amon helped me to my feet, giving me a final hug as he slid the jeweled scarab into the pocket of my cargo pants. When he pulled back, he shook his head briefly, indicating it was a secret between us, then he took my hand, guiding me to the stone altar.

After giving me an unashamedly electrifying last kiss despite our audience, Amon stroked my cheek, obviously reluctant to let go. Finally, he lay down upon the altar. My breath stopped and my heart started racing. *I just can't do this.*

Anubis waved his hands and four canopic jars appeared on a nearby dais. "Amon," he asked authoritatively, "do you willingly cede the powers gifted to you by the great god Amun-Ra?"

"I do," Amon answered.

I bit my lip and wrung my hands, expecting Anubis to now bring out the rusty tools and scoop out Amon's organs. Instead, Anubis opened his hands and a ball of golden light lifted from Amon's chest and shot toward the handsome god. Quickly, Anubis thrust the light away from him and it flew into an open jar. A lid materialized from the sand in the shape of the Sphinx's head, then slammed onto the opening and sealed it with a beam of light.

This was done three more times. One lid became the head of a baboon. Another formed into the face of a jackal. The final light did not emerge from Amon's body as a ball but as an ethereal winged creature. It was his golden falcon. The bird circled above us, gazing at me with a golden eye, the tips of his wings grazing my cheek as he flew past. He glided toward the row of canopic jars and then hovered over the last one. In a stream of light he flew into it, and the final lid—a falcon-headed one—sealed the jar shut.

"What about the Eye power?" I asked. "Will you take that, too?"

"The Eye of Horus will stay with him during his sojourn," Anubis answered patiently. "Now"—he produced a beautiful jeweled knife out of thin air, its wickedly curved blade gleaming sharp and deadly— "the rest is up to you."

He pressed the hateful weapon into my hand and I reluctantly took it, gripping it numbly in my fist. "I can't," I sobbed. "Please don't make me do this."

Anubis sighed. "This was a mistake. She does not have the fortitude to see beyond herself."

"She will do it," Amon replied. "She is stronger than you think." Amon took the hand that didn't hold the knife and pulled me closer. His skin no longer gleamed now that his powers had been taken. "Lily," he began, "do not think about what will be lost. Think instead on what has been won."

"Nothing's been won," I said, leaning over him. Fat tears dripped off my cheeks and onto his chest.

"We defeated Sebak. We kept Seth at bay. Is that not a triumph?"

"It doesn't feel like one."

"Then know that you have won my heart." Gently, he brought my hand to his chest, spreading my fingers over it. He took the hand holding the knife and brought it next to my other hand, the tip of the blade touching the skin directly over his heart. When my shaking hands were in place, he reached up and ran his fingertips down my jaw. He smiled—a beautiful, heartbreaking sunshine smile. "I love you."

A whimper of protest came from my throat as he rose to kiss me, but the kiss was brief. Amon lay back down, eyes wide, as a trickle of blood leaked from the corner of his mouth. Panicked, I backed away a few inches and, to my horror, saw that the sharp blade was embedded in Amon's chest up to the hilt.

"No," I whispered. "Amon? No!" I screamed, pulling the knife from his chest. Blood pooled up from the deep gash and flowed down the side of his body. "What just happened?" I cried.

Anubis came over to check Amon. "I gave you a little nudge to get things moving."

"You did . . . *what?*"

Anubis glanced at Amon and then turned and looked right at me. "*I* helped. I told him I would. Hmm . . . better say your goodbyes now. He has only a few seconds."

"Amon?" I leaned over him. "I'm so sorry." I couldn't see him through my tears. I angrily brushed them away, pressing kisses on his brow, his cheeks, his lips. Vainly, I tried to staunch the blood that seemed to be pumping in an endless supply from his chest. "This isn't what I wanted," I whispered.

Amon sucked in a breath, fluid gurgling in his lungs, and then his body convulsed and his beautiful hazel eyes, which had been looking at me, froze, unblinking. Slowly, the air he'd just drawn in leaked from his mouth and then he was gone.

I cupped his face in my hands, stroking the hair from his brow. With my eyes full of tears, hands trembling, I whispered in a quavering voice, "I love you, too."

I said a silent prayer that wherever he was, he would hear me and know the depth of my feelings.

Anubis grunted in satisfaction. Angrily, I whipped around and jabbed my finger at him, absolutely not caring that he was a powerful god. "We weren't ready!" I accused.

He smiled. "I am pleased to see you have more fire in your heart than I previously believed, but let us be honest. You never would have been."

"You don't know that."

"I would have you know, young woman, that I am an excellent judge of character. In fact, judging characters is my forte, if you will."

"I don't care *what* you do in your day job. You could have been more patient. More sympathetic."

"What difference does it make? You will have a broken heart. He will have a broken heart, though in his case, both literally and figuratively. Prolonging your time together would not diminish the pain. It only serves to make the separation more difficult to bear."

Gritting my teeth, fiery indignation filling me, I spat, "You know what? You don't deserve him as your servant. You . . . you're *unworthy* of his sacrifice."

Anubis lost his smile, his eyes narrowing as he took a step closer. "Because I am a very forgiving all-powerful deity, and because I know that your emotions are not in control right now, I will attempt to forget your disrespect. I will warn you, however, to give your words a bit more regard in the future before you choose to utter them.

"Now, if you will remain quiet, I will allow you to watch as I prepare your beloved incarnation of the sun god for the afterlife."

Anubis generated a thick pad of wrappings with a flick of his wrist and wiped the blood from Amon's chest. As he did so, he spoke to me. "Do you know the true purpose of a pyramid?"

My eyes darted up to the god, knowing he was trying to distract me from what was happening. Anubis's dog nudged my hand and looked at me with mournful eyes as his master repeated the question. "What? No. I guess not," I said.

"It is a place of ascension. It is also called a house of nature, a house of energy, and a house of the soul." Anubis raised his hands and Amon's body lifted off the stone slab. He had crossed Amon's hands over his chest, in the style most common for mummies. As I watched, Anubis rotated his wrist in a circle and sand rose from the floor, creating long strips of cloth that wound around Amon's feet and started enveloping his entire body.

Anubis continued, "You see, a body is much like a pyramid. It can channel vast amounts of energy. It can house a soul, and yet it is made of natural materials that eventually return to the dust from whence it came. But, to fashion a mummy is to create an everlasting body—one that will be fit enough so that the ka, or the soul, that leaves it, may take it up once again.

"To accomplish this, there are certain things that must be done when a person dies. The first is to preserve the body, as I am doing now." The wrappings had now reached Amon's neck and I could no longer hold back my tears as the linen cloths completed the process and covered his head. Anubis peered at me underneath Amon's floating body, and said, "I am attempting to comfort you. Please pay attention."

I glared at the god, but he ignored me and went happily back to his macabre duties. He fashioned a beautiful sarcophagus out of the sand—a polished wooden casket, richly ornate with carvings depicting Amon's recent battle with Sebak and his army of the undead. I gasped when I noticed a likeness of myself standing with Amon at the top of the pyramid.

"It . . . it's lovely," I said in awe as I reached out to run my hand over it. With my fingertips, I traced a depiction of a girl with sun-streaked hair, wrapping her arms around a man gleaming with the sparkling rays of the sun.

"Do you like it? Sarcophagus art is one of my specialties." Anubis cleared his throat and I stepped back as Amon's wrapped form floated toward the coffin and then settled into it. "As I was saying, to create a mummy three things must happen."

"Preserve the body," I whispered as I stood to see what Anubis was doing. He was stooped over Amon. He created beautiful jeweled brooches from the sand and then placed them one by one in the sarcophagus next to Amon.

"Very good," the god of mummification said. "You have been listening."

"What are those?" I asked.

"Protective amulets. They will ward off those who seek to do evil as Amon's body sleeps. Even though the current grand vizier is approaching through the tunnels and will be here soon enough to remove the brothers to a hidden location, I feel it is now imperative to take every precaution. I did not think the amulets were necessary before, but the fact that Amon's body had been removed from the vizier's care this millennium proves that no safeguard should be ignored. Now—" Anubis lifted his hand to draw up more sand, but nothing appeared. "That is odd," he murmured.

"What's wrong?"

"The last piece is the one that goes over the heart. It is in the shape of a scarab."

"A heart scarab?" I asked.

"Yes." Anubis peered at me. "Do you know where his is?"

My throat tightened, and instead of answering, I asked a question. "What happens if you don't have it?"

Anubis scratched his ear. "Nothing, I suppose. The heart scarab only helps the wandering ka find its body, but Amon should not have a problem with that."

"Good." I decided then to keep the heart scarab a secret. If there wasn't anything detrimental about me keeping it, then I wanted it. It was the only piece of Amon I'd have after all this was over.

"There. The body is finished."

"So what's the third thing?"

"The third? We haven't even performed the second."

"Oh. I thought the amulets were the second thing."

"No. The second part is invigorating the body by providing sustenance."

"Won't food, you know, rot after a few days?"

"Yes, but I did not say I would provide food. The word I used was 'sustenance.'"

I frowned and folded my arms. "I believe I do have some familiarity with the word."

"Many people misunderstand it," he said, ignoring my statement. "By sustenance, I mean that I provide energy, enough that the body will be sustained for at least a millennium, and perhaps a bit longer. The strength necessary to maintain Amon's body when he wakens is contained in his canopic jars."

"Which is why he needed me when he couldn't find them."

"Yes."

"But won't sharing your energy drain you?"

"Since I am a god, my stores are vast enough to sustain the three sons of Egypt in the interim without detriment to myself."

He leaned over Amon's form and touched his shoulders. I could actually see the energy in the form of light begin at Anubis's shoulders and roll down his arms and into Amon's body in waves. When he was finished, he stepped back.

"There. And now the last thing." He walked to the head of the sarcophagus and impatiently waved his arm, gesturing me over. "Come. You may join me in this final act."

"What do I do?" I whispered.

"We must recite a spell from the Book of the Dead and commemorate his name as we do so. In naming him, we connect his body, his ka, or soul, his ba, which is his character, and his shuwt, or shadow. The name is the fifth piece that binds the other four together."

Wardens of the sky, the earth, and beyond,
The sacred barque has begun its journey,
Taking with it this cherished son of Egypt.
His name was given by the great god Amun-Ra.
It will be reclaimed. It will be recovered.
Bestow a wreath of vindication upon his neck,
For he has overcome his earthly travails.
Give his soul peace, and when the time comes,
Let him find his way back to his body.
The Eye of Horus will be his guide.

We are they who remember his name after death.
We are they who carved his name on this sarcophagus.
We are they who engraved his name upon our hearts.
He is, AMON, henceforth and forever.
We call his power, his soul, his body, and his shadow, and give this name
  to each.
May this body be protected,
So that he can rise in glory once more.
Go forth now, Amon, to a place of rest,
Until such time as we shall meet again.

When his spell was complete, Anubis raised his hands, palms up, and a swirling cloud of sand solidified until it fashioned into an ornately carved lid. It lowered with a definitive thump, settling in place, and I felt as if my heart was locked in the sarcophagus with Amon.

A grave heaviness settled over me and I couldn't breathe. I was suffocating. I placed a trembling hand on the polished wooden face as darkness crept in at the edges of my vision and the last thing I remembered was collapsing.

When I regained my senses, the heat of the pyramids was gone. I found myself surrounded by Egyptian relics, but something was different. I placed my hand on a cold white tile floor and pushed myself up to a sitting position.

A noise nearby made me turn. In the shadows stood a large, handsome man leaning against the wall, a statue of a pointy-eared dog sat at his heels.

"Anubis?" I gasped. He was dressed like a businessman in a suit and tie.

He stepped forward. "I will leave you where you first discovered Amon. Goodbye, Lilliana."

With a wink, Anubis and the dog statue disappeared. "Wait!" I called, but there was no answer.

Scrambling to my feet, I noted irritably that I was once again wearing my designer shirt, cropped trousers, and Italian leather sandals. My bag, notebook peeking out, was propped against a wall, and the college brochures were arranged in an efficient semicircle. "Amon?" I cried, and dashed toward the sealed-off section in the Egyptian exhibit.

Beyond the plastic I found the same copper mirror, the same tools, the same boxes and sawdust, but there were no telltale footprints. No sarcophagus. No large box with a sign that said UNKNOWN MUMMY FROM THE VALLEY OF THE KINGS. Amon was gone. It was as if he had never been a part of my life. Never existed.

A golden gleam caught my eye and, hopeful, I made my way over to it, only to find the golden statue of a falcon—*Horus the Gold*. I pressed my hands against the glass, tears sliding down my face. I tricked my mind for a brief, indulgent moment into thinking he was here, with me. But he wasn't. Amon was gone.

Sucking in a shaky breath, I wiped my face and, bag in hand, exited the exhibit. Numbly, I walked toward the museum entrance and was surprised when a hand touched my arm. "Miss Lilliana? Are you all right?"

I let out a shaky breath and attempted to smile, though I wasn't sure my lips were able to form much more than a grimace. "Hi, Tony," I said. "I'm fine. It's just been a really, really long day."

"Ah, then have a good evening, Miss Young."

"I will. Oh, and, Tony?" He turned. "Please call me Lily."

He gave me a warm smile. "Of course, Miss Lily."

As I exited the museum, the scents, sights, and sounds of New York City overwhelmed me. They were familiar but no longer what I loved.

How could I forget the sand-swept vistas, the desert oases, the ancient pyramids, and the mummies brought to life, and go back to the life I knew before? I was utterly changed from my time with Amon. It wasn't right that we had to be separated. I couldn't even put flowers on his grave.

Still, I was grateful to know that he existed somewhere and would continue to exist long after I was gone. I took some comfort in his promise to watch over me wherever he was, and deep in my heart I knew he would always be with me.

Amon had said that a bond like ours meant we might see each other in our dreams. I knew that killing him was supposed to have broken our bond and yet he didn't feel so very far away. Closing my eyes, I lifted my face to the sun and felt its warmth on my skin, imagining it was Amon caressing my cheek. The heat traveled down my shoulders and torso before it focused on my heart.

It burned, and I smiled as I felt my heart beating. Then I looked down, puzzled as I felt something shift in my shirt pocket. I reached inside to find Amon's heart scarab. It wasn't my heartbeat after all. It was the stone drumming a slow rhythm, its soothing beat warm and alive in my palm. Though the odds seemed insurmountable, Amon's heart was a small miracle that gave me hope.

With a small secret smile, I folded my fingertips over the heart scarab and raised my other hand to hail a cab.

EPILOGUE
Scales of Judgment

"Bring him forth," the goddess Ma'at proclaimed.

"I do not understand why this is necessary. It never has been before," the young man protested.

"What is going on here?" Anubis asked as he entered.

"This young man must place his heart on the scales of justice," the goddess explained patiently.

Anubis ran a hand through his hair, relieved to have changed out of his modern-day clothing. "But he is not really dead. His judgment is suspended until he is released from his duty."

"In this case, he must be evaluated. He bound himself to a mortal and was slain by a mortal. If the death of their union is to be final, then there must be an assessment."

"But his death is not final."

"That is immaterial. All things must be balanced." She indicated the golden scales set before her. "His heart must be weighed to determine if his actions on Earth are worthy."

"They were," Anubis vouched.

Ma'at chastised, "Above all things we are charged with following the laws of the cosmos."

Anubis grunted. "Fine. Then get it over with."

The beautiful goddess took an ostrich feather from her headdress and placed it on the scale closest to her, then smiled benevolently at the young man standing by Anubis. The gods stared expectantly as he stood quietly, head lowered, and fists clenched.

After a silent moment passed, Ma'at spoke. "You are aware of what you must do, are you not? Anubis, perhaps you had better explain things."

The young man answered with a determined gleam in his eyes. "I know what I must do."

"Then you may proceed," the goddess denoted, with a small gesture toward the scales.

And with a secretive gleam in his eye, the young man flicked his wrist and disappeared.

ACKNOWLEDGMENTS

As I do in all my books, I first have to thank my always-willing-to-eat-sandwiches husband, Brad, who is my tireless supporter in everything I do, and my mom, who moved in with us as I was writing this book. She's both a constant help and a constant distraction, which keeps my life constantly interesting.

I also would like to express my deep appreciation for my sisters, Shara, Tonnie, and Linda, and my sis-in-law, Suki, whom I jokingly label Assistant #1, Assistant #2, etc. They cart around bags, books, laptops, posters, luggage, and ever-increasing amounts of stuff that I need at events and conferences. They smile while taking pictures, arranging my hair, powdering my nose, ordering me to drink water, and entertaining my fans while I take bathroom breaks. They're always excited about my work and full of advice that I only listen to half the time even though it's always good.

I'm also thankful for my brothers, Mel, Andrew, and Jared, who all actually attended book signing events this year and managed not to roll their eyes as I talked about kissing. Whenever I need to write about what makes a good guy, I never have to think too hard.

My early-reading group is mostly made up of my siblings, but it also includes a few very special people: Linda, who has championed my books since the beginning; her husband, Neal, who creates all my fun posters, stickers, and promo stuff; and Fred, a good friend who checked up on all my Egypt references and his wife, Liz, who reads him all my chapters since he doesn't really like to read. Imagine!

My agent, Alex Glass, has always been willing to yoke himself to the same wagon and help me pull it along. His insight is immeasurable. The team at Trident Media Group work with him seamlessly, and I wish I could name them all but I fear I would leave several of them out. Suffice it to say they are all amazing and a credit to their profession.

This time I have a new publishing team to express gratitude to, and that includes Tamar Schwartz, Angela Carlino, Heather Lockwood Hughes, and especially Beverly Horowitz and Krista Vitola, who were both willing to take a chance on me and welcomed me and my mummies with open arms into the Delacorte Press family. I'm so blessed to have such a supportive team at my back.

To my fans: I don't even have words. You guys are all so dedicated to me and my tigers, and even though you've had to wait for the last tiger book, you have all generously made room in your hearts for my mummies. I appreciate you all so much!

Lastly, I wanted to thank my dad. He passed away while I was writing this book; it is the first novel I've finished that he didn't get to read. It's been a hard road without him, but I know that he would be immensely proud of it and would brag about it to everyone he knew while pressing freshly published copies into their hands if he could. He was a great man who is sorely missed by all who knew him.

Continue reading for a preview of the second book
in Colleen Houck's Reawakened series,

RECREATED

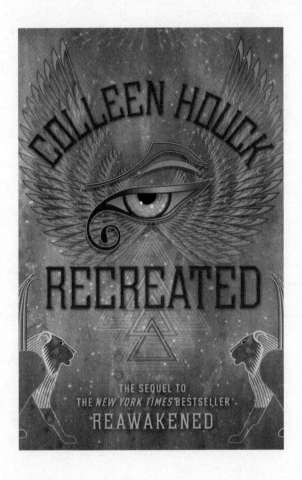

PROLOGUE
Lost

How could I have done something so foolish? Amon thought. Leaving the safety of the afterlife for the uncertainty of the netherworld had been a bad decision, a dangerous one. But Amon had felt as if there were no other option. Besides, death was what he sought, though admittedly he would have preferred a gentler one.

As he wandered the stone path leading to, he hoped, a temporary refuge, Amon wondered what form death would take. Would he be swallowed up by a monster that would slowly digest him over centuries? Would he be flayed alive by a creature whose expertise was in making a man suffer? The best case he could think of would be death by venom. The netherworld was full of venomous creatures bent on the destruction of those who wandered into their nests.

Even though Amon courted death, he didn't wish to succumb to it just yet. Lily had only recently returned to her mortal life, and it would be years before there was even a remote chance that he could be with her again. Amon had promised to meet her in the afterlife. Exactly how he would accomplish that now he didn't know, but he had decades to figure something out. The truth was, even if he hadn't met Lily and fallen in love with her, he still would have given up his calling. It had been so many years. Too many. And death wasn't the worst thing he could imagine.

His brief sojourns into the realm of mortals were no longer enough. If he had reunited with his brothers before the judging, they would have known what he was up to, would have talked him out of it. That was why he leapt before he saw them again. He wanted more. He needed more than just a pale shadow of a life.

So he had forsaken his duty. Forsaken his brothers. And now he'd forsaken the gods themselves. There would be a reckoning, but he didn't care. Lily was the only remaining tether linking him to the path he walked. The only reason he didn't give himself over to the next plane of existence. Wherever that might be. So, he fought to bide his time as he waited.

As the days passed, he tore asunder every gnarled and frightening beast of the netherworld that challenged him. Some came at him because he was reckless. Some, he suspected, were sent as punishment from the gods. Others were drawn to his melancholy state. The brief moments of respite he earned were too short. No matter where he went or how evasive he was, the demons always found him.

Though he'd left his mortal body behind, his wandering soul still felt the pangs of the flesh. Fortunately his needs were markedly less than they were in the human world. When Amon thirsted, he begged the spirits who lived in the trees for gifts. When Amon hungered, he stole provisions from the stores of the creatures he slaughtered, and, occasionally, if nothing could be found and the pains of his empty stomach became overwhelming, he roasted the bodies of the beasts he'd slain.

When he was utterly exhausted from the terrors he'd brought upon himself, and he was relatively safe, Amon slept. It was always brief. Always fitful. Dreaming was the only happiness he felt in his otherwise horrifying existence.

The worst part about wandering the netherworld wasn't the endless barrage of monsters or dangers that threatened a second and permanent death. It wasn't the separation from his brothers, his constant companions for thousands of years. It wasn't even the loss of purpose he felt, the absence of self-assurance he'd always possessed, or the knowledge that he had a place in the cosmos, one he was if not satisfied with, then one he accepted.

No. The worst part was also the best part.

He could feel her.

Lily was in another place, another world, and yet, he could allow himself to be with her. When he was certain that no attack was imminent, and he let his tired body rest, he'd close his eyes and see her. That was the part Amon loved. He could hover near her like a ghost. He couldn't speak to her or touch her, and she didn't know that he was there, at least not consciously. Her subconscious mind, though, could sense he was near, that he was watching over her, much like a guardian angel. This was a tremendous blessing. But it was also a curse.

Amon knew a connection as powerful as theirs went two ways. He had hoped that they might simply meet in their dreams. That their bond had been brief enough that their minds would brush gently against each other as they slept. But the link between them proved stronger than that. As Amon walked with Lily through New York, he knew she also journeyed with him through his land of nightmares.

His decision to leave paradise had caused terrible consequences for the girl he loved, and now that he was in the netherworld, there was no getting out. The gods would not help; he'd abandoned their cause. Death would be his only reprieve, and yet every time he thought he'd hurt her enough and would give up, give in to whatever dark creature was currently seeking his demise, he'd feel her, an unconscious appeal to keep trying. To hold on a little longer.

Amon sought answers to his dilemma by peering through the Eye of Horus, but the things he saw confused him. Sometimes it teased him with glimpses of a possible future. A way out. If he could just last long enough, survive in the form in which he currently existed until Lily's natural, mortal death, there was a chance he could find her. That their bond would draw them together once more.

Other times, he saw Lily as a different person, a different creature altogether from the girl he knew. He envisaged himself tortured and abused. His brothers jealous and angry. The gods at war with Chaos. These visions made no sense. Chaos was being held at bay for another millennium. The gods getting together for a meal wasn't even likely, let alone a war.

The uncertainty Amon felt was normal. He was used to the strange shadows of the future and past mingling together. The Eye saw all, and yet nothing it revealed ever made sense. Events were never in the proper order. It took a tremendous amount of focus and energy to direct the Eye to show him any one particular thing. To prevent himself from going crazy, Amon spent much of his time trying to ignore the visions that rattled his brain. Since he'd entered the netherworld, though, the Eye had gone into overdrive.

Still, the Eye's energy drain was worth it when he asked to see Lily's future. The things he saw gave him hope. Hope that they might be together again, that there was a possible future where he could again hold her in his arms.

There were moments when he saw himself cupping her face in his hands, tenderly kissing each of her closed eyelids, tasting the salt from the tears that slowly trickled down her cheeks. These blissful flashes were all he needed to know. The rest he'd let the universe worry about. Perhaps it was selfish of him to maintain their connection, but he just couldn't let Lily go. Not yet. Not when there was a chance.

Though Amon knew that she likely walked the netherworld with him in her dreams, there were times, however brief, when they both slept. During those occasions, it was possible to communicate with her, but Lily's mind always blocked him out, her body so exhausted from the trials of their connection that her consciousness shut down and she slept deeply.

When this happened, he didn't push. She needed to rest, and as badly as he wanted to talk to her, there was no point. He'd doomed the both of them to this fate because he was weak. If he had only loved her enough in the beginning to leave her alone or had sent her away earlier, maybe none of this would have happened.

Of course, without Lily, it was quite possible that he and his brothers would be dead and the world overrun by Chaos. Still, if he'd been a little more vigilant regarding his emotions, then she wouldn't be suffering now. She'd be just another human girl, one of billions in the world. No one of any importance, and certainly no one the gods would be paying any attention to. No one except him.

Amon sighed. The truth was that as long as Lily held his heart, Amon would fight. He was beholden to her; if she wanted him to press on, he would find a way.

Reprieve

"Amon!" I jerked awake, my pulse racing as the nightmare slowly ebbed. I'd taken to keeping a night-light on near my bed ever since the horrors that took over my dreams still haunted my dark room when I woke. Some terrible creature had cornered him. It had screeched in a satisfied way, its putrid breath stinging my nose as its tongue darted out to lick the blood from a gash on Amon's shoulder. It all felt so real.

Shivering, I wrapped my arms around my body and slid from the bed as I headed to my favorite spot on the balcony overlooking Central Park. Once there, I rubbed my hand over the head of the falcon statue perched on the railing.

The bird reminded me of Amon's golden falcon form, and when the sun warmed it, the heat stored in the metal carving seemed to linger, even in the late hours of the evening when I paced my room unable to sleep. It soothed me when I touched it and I could picture Amon as I'd last left him and not as the bruised and pain-filled man he was in my dreams.

He was lost to me. I knew that. I acknowledged that I should try to move on, maybe try to date someone else, but the memory of my Egyptian sun prince come to life was a hard one to beat. Amon wasn't perfect, but he was pretty darn close. Even now I could easily picture him standing near me—his golden skin warmed by the sun, the glint in his hazel eyes, and that secretive smile hiding behind his defined and very kissable lips.

Sighing, I leaned on the railing and looked out at the park. I was in love with a guy who was centuries old and currently moldering away in an elaborately decorated sarcophagus fashioned by Anubis himself. His spirit half, the half that was supposed to be in paradise while he waited for the next time he was needed, haunted my dreams.

Either he was in grave trouble or something was seriously wrong with me since I'd returned from Egypt. Still, the creatures I saw in my dreams were much more horrifying than any I could have made up. I wasn't that creative. Even worse than my suspicions that Amon was in danger was the problem that I couldn't tell anyone about it. Nobody even knew he'd existed.

Well, that wasn't exactly true. Dr. Hassan knew, but he lived on the other side of the world. I'd written to him when I got home, and his elated response made me smile even though I'm sure he'd figured it out when he couldn't find my body on the pyramid after Amon and his brothers had saved the world. I was more than a little proud to be a part of the whole thing, even though fooling Amon into siphoning off my energy had nearly killed me.

It took a month to get a reply from Dr. Hassan, though I'd fanatically checked the PO box I'd leased for our secret correspondence every day. He'd told me not to worry, that Amon had the protection of the gods, that he'd hidden the brothers well, and that I should be proud of the sacrifices I'd made to keep the world safe.

That was pretty much the extent of his letters. They got progressively shorter as time went on. It was as if he, too, wanted me to just forget everything that had happened and move on with my life. But how could I? Amon haunted my dreams. Not that I wasn't happy to see him. I was. But the horrors he faced were enough to send any girl, even one who had seen the things I'd seen, running for the nearest mental institution.

My parents were worried. My lack of sleep was starting to show, though I tried to act as though my life was simply business as usual. They had no idea that I'd nearly died, fallen in love with a drop-dead (no pun intended) gorgeous mummy come to life, and spent an extended spring break in Egypt. The fact that I'd actually made it through to the end of the school year without my grades falling was a major accomplishment.

They didn't know about my experience with Amon in Egypt and how much it had transformed me. I myself didn't know how much I'd changed until I got home. I thought it would show on my face, all the emotion, all the trauma, all the . . . death, but my parents only noticed my hair. My brown, no-nonsense straight hair was now riddled with random sun-kissed highlights of different shades. They didn't like it.

The first thing my mother said was, "What were you thinking?" Immediately she picked up the phone and lectured our hairstylist, who didn't have anything to do with it but who cleared his schedule instantly to repair the "damage." I told her quietly but sternly that I was rather fond of it and that my intention was to keep it. To say they were shocked at my little act of rebellion was an understatement.

As much as they protested my decision to keep my new highlights, they outright refused my request that they call me Lily instead of Lilliana. As a result, I began to feel like a stranger in my own home. To keep the peace, I told them I'd go to the college they wanted as long as I was allowed to spend the summer at my nana's farm in Spring Lake, Iowa. I figured it didn't matter anymore where I went, and the compromise went a long way toward assuaging the fears my new hairdo ignited.

Once I got the acceptance letter, they backed off and left me to my own devices, which meant I could mourn the loss of Amon without anyone taking notice. One month after another went by, and then graduation was upon me.

As I gazed in the mirror the morning of graduation, I was dismayed to see that my golden highlights, the last tangible proof I had of Amon's touch, were fading. At this rate, they'd be gone by Christmas. I indulged

in a good cry before showering and dressing for my graduation ceremony.

If my mother noticed my too-bright eyes, she probably chalked it
up to my being emotional about leaving high school. The truth was, I
didn't care about high school. I didn't care about college or boys. I didn't
care about much of anything anymore.

The time soon came for me to depart for the summer, and I was
surprised that my parents wanted to drop me off at the airport. Maybe
they noticed more than I thought they did, or perhaps they were just
feeling nostalgic about me growing up and leaving the nest. Either way,
the drive felt a bit awkward.

I stared at my reflection in the window.

My eyes were large and dull; my hair was wound in a perfect,
tight bun at the nape of my neck; and my lips were stretched in a thin,
unforgiving line, as rigid as a ruler. In fact, that was what I looked like:
a schoolmarm. A smirk lifted the corner of my mouth as I imagined
how much Amon would hate my hair like this. He preferred it wild and
unbound.

After a few quiet goodbyes and some stiff hugs, my parents relinquished me to the chaos of the airport. Inside, a range of emotions hit
me all at once. I remembered being there with Amon a few short months
earlier, and how with the wave of his hand and a charming smile, he
could wrap anyone around his finger.

I boarded the plane and strapped in, remembering how even the
most mundane actions like buckling a seat belt were completely new
and foreign for Amon. Though I actually did try not to think of him, it
seemed that was all I could do, and when I shut my eyes, rocked to sleep
by the plane, I found myself in Amon's world once again.

*He wasn't fighting a monster, which was a relief, but he had a wicked
wound on his thigh that was seeping blood onto his leggings. Sucking in a
breath, he tore away the fabric around it and wrapped it in the bandages he'd
created from the sand. Some kind of armor lay discarded next to him, and Amon
shrugged out of a tunic before dipping it in a small, natural basin of water and*

scrubbing his arms and neck. I hoped the precious drops trickling down the side of a boulder were enough to both quench his thirst and clean his wound. The area was very desolate and dry.

Though the sight of his bare chest was distracting, I was more absorbed by the expression on his face. He was exhausted and hurting, and not just physically. I wondered if he missed me as much as I did him.

"Amon?" I whispered involuntarily.

In my dream he froze and looked around, eyes shining with an iridescent green light in the darkness. Though he'd never been able to hear me before, I still tried. One day he might. After a moment, the tenseness in Amon's shoulders relaxed, and he settled down with his back against a rock and closed his eyes. His bare chest rose and fell in a rhythm that slowed as the minutes passed and then something changed.

As his body continued to sleep, a gentle pressure wrapped around me.

"Lily?" I heard his familiar voice and squelched a sob.

"Amon? Can you hear me?" I asked the ethereal darkness.

"Yes. I can hear you, Nehabet."

"Is this real?"

He didn't answer right away but then eventually said, "I wish it were not."

"What's happening to you?" I asked desperately. "Why are you suffering? I thought you were in the afterlife. I thought you were at peace. Why are you tormented night after night?"

"I am no longer under the protection of the gods. I have relinquished my station."

"I don't understand. What does that mean?"

"It means that I would rather suffer than continue to do their bidding."

"But if you don't save the world, who will?"

"They will find another to replace me."

"I still don't understand. Are they punishing you?"

I felt his sigh as much as I heard it. "They did not choose this for me. I am the one who decided to walk this path."

"It's a pretty difficult path, Amon. Can't your brothers help you?"

"We are separated. There is nothing they can do for me now."

"I hate seeing you like this."

"I know. I am sorry for causing you pain. I didn't think our connection would be this strong." He paused for a moment before adding, "You are in pain, too, Young Lily."

Bitterly, I said in a shaky voice, "Not like you."

"No. Not like me. But you are hurting nonetheless. It is my fault. My loneliness has caused this."

"Your desire for human connection didn't cause this. The gods did. They don't understand. Everyone needs to be loved. It's completely natural."

He laughed sardonically. "I was human, Lily, once. But I am something altogether different now. I gave my humanity up for the greater good."

Thunder boomed in the sky above Amon's still form, roiling clouds shifting like a churning ocean. Lightning struck and his body jerked awake. I felt the loss of his presence, as if a warm blanket had been ripped away from me. As the ground shook, he staggered tiredly to his feet and summoned his armor made of sand to strap onto his form. Amon lifted his face to the wind as he closed his eyes and said, "I love you, Lily. But it is time for you to wake up."

He raced into the darkness to face whatever beast awaited him as his words echoed in my mind. "I love you, too," I whispered, even though I knew he could no longer hear me.

I felt a nudge on my shoulder as someone said, "Wake up, miss. We've landed."